MASOUD

British Library Cataloguing-in-Publication Data
A catalogue for this book is available from the
British Library

ISBN 0 86356 374 0

This edition first published 2004

Saqi Books
26 Westbourne Grove
London W2 5RH
www.saqibooks.com

Masoud Banisadr

# MASOUD
## Memoirs of an Iranian Rebel

**SAQI**

# Dedication

*For all those who wish to know what I – like many before and after me – went through and will go through.*

*For love, not hate, as I do not hate anything but hate itself.*

*For my mother, from whom I learned the meaning of the word 'love'.*

*For Sarvy and Hanif, my children, for when they want to know why and how, and to many more children who lost their parents and their normal lives, and couldn't understand why.*

*For everyone I cannot name, for obvious reasons: my sister, friends, family and everyone who encouraged me and helped me to accomplish the writing of this book.*

# Contents

# 1

# Happy Thursdays, Black Fridays

I was running, not knowing what I was running from, knowing only I had to run as fast as I could. My heart pounded as though it wanted to burst from my mouth. Under my feet I felt something slimy, moving. It felt alive – I was not certain but hoping to be wrong. The slimy things were everywhere; I couldn't keep my balance. Suddenly I felt something curling around my foot. I saw nothing, but could not deceive myself any more. The sticky things were alive and moving around me. I don't know if it was my fear or the sliminess that made me fall. Then they curled around my body, and I saw them: they were snakes.

With a cry, I jumped from my bed in a cold sweat. I was about six years old, and sleeping with my mother as I had done since my parents' divorce. My cry awoke her too; she took me in her arms and tried to comfort me. When I told her my dream she laughed and said, 'Well, I can't say that was a bad dream. After all, they say: "*Har keh binad khab morgh 'o mar'o mahei namirad ta babinad padeshahie* [He who dreams of birds, snakes and fish will not die until he sees himself a king].'"

I had the same dream many times after that, but always with

snakes, never fish or birds, and they were always frightening. But my mother taught me to pray before sleeping, to kill any bad dreams.

My parents divorced in 1958, when I was five years old. For the first few months afterwards I lived with my father. Traditionally, children in Iran are the property of their father; but the same tradition permits boys up to the age of seven and girls up to nine to live with their mother. So, after long negotiations, my father agreed to let me live with my mother as long as she did not remarry.

Although my grandparents were able to support us, my mother was a very proud and independent person and wanted to earn a living. So she worked as a teacher in a private preliminary school, and in the evenings she sewed sheets for a hospital. In this way she was able to enrol me in the school where she worked – I was under six, not yet old enough to attend a state school, but my mother wanted me to have the best education possible.

Staying with my mother was the happiest time of my life. She was about thirty years old, and although by then she had already had two miserable marriages and borne four children, she was still a very lively and cheerful person. Life had not been easy for her. Her mother had forced her to marry one of her cousins when she was not even fifteen years old. Like her father, my mother had a heart of gold and an open mind, while her first husband was a very religious traditionalist from a small city, stuck in a world far removed from modern life. After a few years, with the support of her father, she was able to divorce him. Her joy was tempered by sorrow that she couldn't take her three daughters with her and was rarely able to see them. But she was still only about twenty years old, beautiful and able to start a fresh life. Unfortunately, a year later she entered into a second marriage even worse than the first. I was never able to understand why she married my father! Society's expectations, probably: an unmarried woman, especially a divorcée, enjoyed no respect and was prey to gossip. My father was about thirty years older than my mother, but he was rich and educated along Western lines.

My grandfather's name was Arf'al' Mamalek Auhei. A retired government official, he loved reading and was content with life, rarely complaining about anything. Whenever my grandmother asked for something, he would say, 'Woman, what do you want these things for? The bigger the house, the bigger the problem; more furniture creates more work and more worry. Aren't you happy as we are? When we die we'll need only a one-by-two-metre space to be buried.' And he would laugh and go off to his room, away from his wife's demands.

Radio in those days was a rare luxury. There was a big set on the first floor in my grandfather's room, and speakers on the ground floor and in the basement. When the radio broadcast a happy song my grandfather would dance and turn the volume up high so everyone in the house could hear it.

His father, my great-grandfather, was a small landowner and musician from a very small town called Ah in Mazandran, a northern province of Iran.

My grandmother's name was Fakh're Aazam, and her family name was Dolat Shahi. I used to call her 'Maman Tala [Golden Mother]' because her hair was gold-coloured; her eyes were as blue as the sky. She was from Kermanshah in the west, originally from a Kurdish family and a great one for order and discipline. She had weekly, monthly and yearly programmes for the cooking of particular dishes and the making of jams and pickles.

My grandparents lived in a medium-sized house in one of the streets at the centre of Tehran that was named after my grandfather. Along with my mother, my youngest aunt and uncle, the old family wet-nurse and I lived with them. Everyone had separate rooms except me, so I was – luckily – able to share my mother's. I spent most of my time playing with my cousins who came to visit, while the grown-ups talked and joked and played cards and backgammon. In summer, when there was no school, we put chairs and tables in the garden and had kahoo sekangebeen (Iranian lettuce with a vinegar syrup) or broad beans cooked with salt and herbs. My grandfather would put his chair in the pool and sit with his bare feet in the water. The garden was full of the scent of jasmine, which the girls would pick and wind into necklaces.

At school everyone was kind to me, and my teacher and I liked each other. Attending the school where my mother worked was not all good news, however. I had to be first in the class and get full marks in everything. When I was reluctant to work, my mother would put a pen between my fingers and press it until I said, 'OK, I'll study as hard as you want me to.'

Once, while playing by myself, pretending that I was on the second floor of a building, I fell from a chair perched on a table and broke my right arm. My mother and aunt took me into the street, and we hailed a taxi to the physician's house. It was summer, but the night was cold, or perhaps I felt cold from pain and shock. In those days, although there were hospitals and doctors in Tehran, people continued to visit traditional physicians who had no academic training but treated with herbal cures. The common belief was that illnesses were related to nutrition. Edible foods were divided into three categories: cold, warm and neutral; if you had a stomach ache, people would say 'sardiat kardeh', meaning you had eaten too much 'cold' food such as cherries, for which the remedy was something 'warm' like dates. The healer gave me a toy to play with; then, while I was distracted, he took hold of my arm and pulled, hard. The pain was awful but momentary. Then he rubbed some herbs and oils on my arm and fastened two splints tightly to them.

As we were leaving the surgery, my mother said, 'Masoud, it is late and cold, so I have called a gentleman, a friend of mine, to come give us a lift. When you meet him you'll be very polite, won't you?' I said, 'Of course, but who is this gentleman?'

'I'll tell you about him later,' she replied. Just then he arrived, at the wheel of a fine German automobile. He was about forty years old and wore a military uniform. Later I found out that he was a naval officer. He was very kind and gentle and had brought a present for me, a toy car. We spoke about my broken arm and he consoled me.

Later, my mother told me that she loved him and that they wanted to marry. She said I must tell no one, because if my father found out he would take me from her. I promised and asked whether I should call him 'Dad'. She said, 'No, you have your own dad; you can call him "Ammo Jan [Dear Uncle]".'

Ammo Jan and my mother married, and we moved into his house. He was quiet, generous, honest and hard-working. He had two children by his first wife, a son named Ghoolam five years my senior and a daughter named Shoaleh, two years younger than me. I was pleased to have a stepbrother and stepsister to play with.

My mother had to take me to my father's house every Thursday until late Friday, when she would fetch me. Although those two days were not as much fun as being with my mother, they were not too bad. Normally I had to go and see my father and perhaps kiss his hand say 'salaam', staying for a few minutes until he permitted me to go to the garden and play. Thursdays were fun, because all my relatives – brothers, sisters, cousins, aunts and uncles – came to the house for dinner. On Fridays we went to my father's orchard near Karaj, outside Tehran, where there was a big pool and a river running through the apple, peach, plum, cherry and mulberry trees. We used to climb the mulberry trees and wait until someone passed below, then shake the branches as hard as we could. Within seconds the unfortunate passer-by would be stained bright red from the red mulberries or covered in sticky juices from the white ones. We would pelt each other with rotten fruits and then go swimming in the pool. In the afternoons we would visit my aunt's orchard, which was nearby, and play there.

One Friday I waited for my mother to fetch me. When the doorbell rang I ran to my father's room to say goodbye, and he asked me where I was going. 'To my house!' I replied, astonished.

'What!?' he shouted. 'Where is your house? This is your house, not a stranger's house. Your mother has married and is living with a stranger.'

I said, 'No, he is not a stranger, he is Ammo Jan. He is very kind and I like him.'

My remark only made my father angrier and he shouted, 'Don't you have any honour? Your mother is sleeping with a stranger and you call him "uncle"? Is he my brother?!' Not understanding what he meant, I began to say something else, whereupon he told me to shut up. 'You are my son and should not have noon v namak [the bread and salt] of anybody else.' Then he asked my stepmother to take me to another room and give me a permanent bed and cupboard. I started to cry and it was at this time, I think, that I got my first slap from my father. I never found out how he had learned of my mother's marriage. Some years later my stepmother said that my aunt had told him, because my mother would be happier in her new life without me around. I could never accept this, but it was the only version of the story that I heard.

That Friday, for me, was Black Friday. I cried all night with my pillow in my arms where my mother's arm should have been. Until late in life I hated all Fridays.

My father was about sixty years older than me, so I never knew his parents. His mother was the daughter of the head of the Gharegoozloos, a famous Azerbaijani family related to the last regent of the Qajar dynasty. His grandfather was a great *ayatollah* and had two titles: Sadr'o al-Islam [Highest in Islam] – which was inherited by his oldest son, my grandfather – and Sadr'o al-Olama [Highest Among Religious Leaders], which passed to his younger son.

My father, who was born in 1896, was educated at a school in Tehran run by French priests and graduated in veterinary medicine. As one of fewer than 100 young Iranians with knowledge of French, he was engaged to serve in the Iranian gendarmerie.

During the First World War Iran was neutral, but the British and Russians refused to respect its neutrality and, on the pretext that Iran might side with the Germans and the Ottoman Empire, they occupied the country from the south and north. The newly founded gendarmerie was powerless to stop them. My father was so depressed and angry that he left home and went to Rey, a religious city near Tehran. He told me later: 'Normally when Iranians face aggression, they first take time to understand the enemy and then gradually, by subtle diplomacy, they try to change them into Iranians. This is what they did with Arabs, Mongols and Turks, but times had changed. We couldn't turn the British and Russians into Iranians. We had to find a new form of defence. But nobody seemed to have any idea what to do, nor were there enough people to make the effort. The British and Russians promised that they would leave Iran after the war, and it was fortunate that they did.'

After the war, my father, then twenty-two years old, became responsible for investigating war damages and had to inspect the entire western side of the country, village by village. Later he was sent to France to study administrative and financial management, disciplines that, in Iran, were then in short supply.

Although my father was from a religious family, he himself was not observant and did not wish us to be so. The only time I heard him refer to faith was when he told me about an accident in France, when he was badly burned and thought he might not survive. 'Do not let me die in this foreign land', he had prayed to Hazrat Abolfazl, one of the Islamic saints. 'Let me die in my own country.'

Father was very hard-working. He always woke up at five, winter or summer, and, of course, forced everybody else to wake up then too. Between six and seven was breakfast-time, and then everybody had to go to work or school. On days when we didn't have school it was hard to know what to do so early. Up to the age of eighty, my father worked at least fifteen hours a day. I rarely saw him ill or even tired. He always displayed great certainty about everything he did. Although he was rich, our lives weren't easy or comfortable, as he was always economising. There was a programme for the consumption of everything from food to heating oil, electricity to water. Sometimes ripe fruit would rot because we had already had our daily share and were forbidden to take more. In winter we shivered with cold but were not permitted to light a heater because our share of oil had been used up; we would have to do our studying under a blanket.

The walk home from school took about thirty minutes. When I was perhaps seven years old we had a severe winter, and the ground was blanketed with about thirty centimetres of snow. It looked beautiful and we children loved it because we could build snowmen and drink *shireh barfee* (snow mixed with grape purée). One day while running home, my foot slipped into the snow-covered canal that ran parallel to the street. I pulled it out, only to find I had lost my shoe. I had to go the rest of the way without it, sometimes hopping for fear my bare foot would freeze. The worst of it was wondering how I would explain it to my father. If I didn't, how was I supposed to go to school with only one shoe? There was no way round it, I had to tell him. I don't remember whether he beat me or swore at me – these things were such common occurrences that they weren't memorable – but I recall that he took me to the nearest shoe shop and bought me a pair of shoes. I would have preferred to have none at all than to have the ones he chose for me: green, two or three sizes too big, probably girl's shoes and, to my eyes, quite repulsive. He knew about shoemaking, he told me, and insisted that the shoes be hard at front and back. That they were an embarrassment to me didn't matter to him: he only cared that they should last 100 years. I had to put up with these shoes – making jokes about them before anyone else did and cursing myself for not seeing that canal – until my mother bought me another pair.

Extreme discipline and order were maintained in the house.

There were set times for eating and sleeping, difficult to circumvent even if one was ill. We were one of the first few families to own a television set, but listening to the radio or watching television was permitted only during meals or on occasions when my father decided it was important for us to see or hear what was going on. We children liked films, even silent films or ones in English, which we couldn't understand. Our liking for movies, however, was not enough to persuade us to stay in our father's company for even a minute after the meal was over. We never discussed anything in front of him unless it was as in answer to a question. We couldn't wait to be out of his sight.

Although my father was against polygamy, he didn't believe in suffering an unhappy marriage. 'If your tooth aches,' he used to say, 'what do you do? Get rid of it. If you are not happy with your wife, what do you do? Same thing.' But I never heard him imply that women are less intelligent than men, nor did he treat his sons and daughters differently. He was as keen on the education of his daughters as of his sons, and after their marriages he respected them equally. For his day and age and in Iran, he was progressive. But we could never forget what he had done to our mothers and us. He married and divorced more than ten times; I had seven half-brothers and five half-sisters – not even one full sibling. In addition, I had three half-sisters from my mother's side. According to my cousin, my father had married the beautiful daughter of the ruler of a northern Iranian province, but his father had another in mind bride for him, daughter of the head of the army and a close relative of the Shah. My father was forced to divorce his beloved wife and marry his father's choice. His first wife attempted suicide, never married again and died a few years later. My father fled to France, where he married a French girl. My cousin told me that my father said he married and divorced many different women in a constant search for his lost love, with no success.

When my father was not at home, everybody felt freer. Even my stepmother, who was much younger than he, would become more light-hearted and would even play with us. One summer day all of us – stepmother, brother and sister, servant's children – were having a water fight, when someone threw a bucket of water towards the entrance door and broke the glass. What to do? We all decided to put in money and get the glass replaced. Unfortunately father returned sooner than expected. My sister Sorya, in a flash of inspiration, told him that the cat had been about to catch the parrot, of which Father was very fond, and we had had to throw our shoes at the cat to rescue the bird. Her invention saved us; sometimes lying to him was the only way to solve a simple problem. Telling the truth usually meant a lot more trouble than we even imagined.

Father believed kindness would ruin a child. He never hugged or kissed us and insisted on being called 'Agha' (Sir). Once a year, on Norowz (Iranian New Year, the first day of spring), he would call us to his room, kiss our foreheads and give us a gift of some money. After that it was back to normal. Usually on that day more than 100 people called to see my father and say congratulations, and it was our job to prepare food and make the house ready for them.

The rest of the time he was mostly bad-tempered. He wanted us to be self-disciplined and self-sufficient. Even at the age of seven I had to wash and iron my own clothes. We were one of the lucky families that had a washing machine, but it was taller than I was and I had to stand on a chair to reach the buttons. After washing the clothes I had to pass them through an electric press to extract the water. Once, my hand went through the machine along with the clothes. I managed to switch off the machine, but didn't know what else to do. I stood there, shaking, on the chair, with my arm trapped. I didn't dare cry for help in case my father heard. Fortunately my stepmother happened to come into the kitchen. Astonished that I was not crying or calling for help, she opened the edges of the machine to release my hand then took me to my father to see if anything should be done about it, although I begged her not to. Contrary to expectation, he showed some kindness, putting oil on my hand, massaging it.

Towards others, my father displayed a different side. With guests or strangers he was cheerful, polite, sociable and friendly. He used to address even the servants as 'Agha' (Mr) and 'Khanom' (Mrs) and made no great demands on them. They were responsible for some jobs around the house, cooking when we had guests and looking after the garden, but the other chores were divided equally between us. For example, I always knew which days of the week it was my turn to set the table for dinner, wash the dishes or water the garden.

Since entering my father's home, my life had changed completely. I lost my mother, who was my protector and defender. My father didn't want me to see her again because she was married. I think it was revenge as well, because it was said that my mother was one of the few of his wives whom he loved and one of the few who had divorced him. For the first few months I kept my mother's photograph with me all the time and used to talk to it and cry and complain to it. I felt the lack of her love acutely, and there was no one to take her place.

In retrospect I have to acknowledge that my father's bad temper must be offset against his genuine concern for our future. Just before he and my mother divorced, he took us both to the outskirts of the city and showed us a plot of land. 'I have bought this land for you,' he said to me. 'What are you going to do with it when you grow up?' In my youthful innocence the only use I could see for it was as a burial ground.

'When you die,' I answered him, 'I shall bury you here.' Naturally my reply angered him, but he made an effort to conceal it – more than he would normally have done.

Of all my half-siblings, only my half-brother Esau and half-sister Sorya lived in my father's house. The others lived with their mothers or were grown up and had their own families. I felt we three children were prisoners together, sharing our misery. The only happiness we had was on Thursdays and Fridays, when we were able to see our brothers and sisters from the outside world. Saeid and Simin were about seven or eight years older than me and used to take me in their arms, play with me and show kindness. Even they were not exempt from my father's temper and were sometimes beaten or humiliated for some perceived misdemeanour. Once, by mistake, Simin made tea with cold water instead of hot. My father turned this into a drama and teased her about it mercilessly, even in front of the whole assembled family – hardly the way to treat a young lady of eighteen.

We had two garages, one of which we rented to a poor and honest man named Hussein Agha, who had migrated from his village to Tehran. At first he had slept rough but then joined together with other people who made houses out of *halabie* (used kerosene and oil cans) and lived in a 'handmade city'. Sometimes waters from the north of Tehran where rich people lived would flood their district. For children it was fun, and the women would wash their clothes and dishes in the water, as they had no running water. Sometimes they even used the same water for drinking. I was not able to understand what it was like not to have running water or electricity, or to live in such a place, but I could see the freedom that Hussein Agha's son had that I didn't have. When he moved into our garage, Hussein Agha would ride to the vegetable bazaar on his second-hand bicycle early every morning and bring back produce to sell from the garage. When my father was not in, I used to go and talk to him and play with his son, and he would often tell us stories. When Hussein Agha wanted to go to the mosque for afternoon prayers, he would ask me to look after his shop, and gave me some of my favourite Iranian carrots, which were yellow and very sweet. One day he late returning, and my father came home earlier than usual. I couldn't leave the shop unattended, but I had to face my father. When I told him what I was doing he looked surprised and said, 'So now you want to be *sabzii froosh* [a greengrocer]?!' I couldn't tell him I was looking after the shop as a favour, or that I sometimes visited Hussein Agha to listen to his stories, so I just said I went 'because he gives me a carrot'. He looked as if he was going to explode; he was shouting, 'Now my son works for a greengrocer for a carrot a day!' He slapped me, and the rest of the day he swore at me every time he saw me.

It was clear to me that my mother was powerless to stand up to my father, even when they were living together. Whenever they quarrelled and she feared that it would escalate into a beating, she would faint. She told me that the cause of her fainting fits dated back to a miscarriage she had before I was born. Still, whenever it happened, which was often, I thought she was dead. Thus I faced the prospect of her death from an early age. I used to sob uncontrollably whenever my mother had one of her attacks; then it would be my turn to be slapped. My father would then fetch a bottle of ammonia and hold it under my mother's nose. I would look on, choking with fear until, with a jerk and a loud cry, she would come round and open her eyes. The crisis would pass – until the next time.

I found out about God as a saviour in Karbela in Iraq, when we made a pilgrimage to Imam Hussein's shrine. There I saw strange people with strange clothes, who I discovered were Arabs. As usual, my parents had a fight; my mother took my arm and we went to the shrine. Crying bitterly, she told me that she was going to pray to God in front of his beloved Imam Hussein to save her from my father. She addressed the Imam and took hold of the bars of the tomb, shaking them as hard as she could. I was astonished. Eventually a *mullah* who was caretaker of the shrine came over, spoke to my mother in Arabic and pushed her out of the tomb. I was only about five years old, but this filled me with anger. I felt I had to stand up for my mother. Although her prayer had been cut short, I think she got her answer; it gave her the courage to leave my father a few months afterwards.

I felt that God had answered my prayer too, because not long after that something good happened. Despite opposition from my grandparents, my mother's youngest sister married my oldest half-brother, whose wife had committed suicide. I felt they were my defenders, and I was now able to go see my mother every week on Thursdays and return to my father's house on Fridays. Whenever I was with my mother I felt the real meaning of freedom, like a bird able to leave its cage once a week and fly wherever it wanted to. My stepfather Ammo Jan bought me new toys every week and took my stepsister and me to the playground or the zoo. On Friday evenings I suddenly changed into a religious person as well, praying that when we got to my father's house we would find he was not there and I could return with my mother to their house. Anything that kept me at my mother's house was a good thing: even pain, illness or disappointment were always more bearable there, and joy, pleasure and peace were more intense.

Unfortunately those happy Thursdays didn't last long. The Navy posted Ammo Jan to Abadan, in the south of Iran more than 800 kilometres away from Tehran. My father didn't know that my mother and he had left, so instead of going to my mother's house I went every Thursday to my grandparents', who were very good to me. Their wet-nurse, Aghbajie, was about seventy years old and addicted to opium. Because of her age she was able to get her opium free from the government, but she never received enough to smoke, so she usually ate it. If I had an earache she would smoke opium and blow the evil-smelling fumes into my ear. Once, when I had stomach ache, she gave me a very small piece of opium to swallow, and I discovered that its taste is as horrible as its smell. I could never understand why anybody would use the stuff.

'You know,' she explained to me, 'this was a present to us from the British. About 200 years ago, during the rule of Nadir Shah, we were so powerful that we could conquer India. But the kings of the Qajar dynasty were capricious, weak, unworthy and incapable. They let the British and Russians come and do whatever they wanted with our wealth and lives. The British were like serpents, *khosh khat 'o khal* [beautiful on the surface]. Nobody could see what they were doing, and most of the time they pretended to be our friends; they were polite, merciful and apparently spendthrift. Standing up to the Russians was simple. Anyone could see how brutal and ruthless they were, and everybody knew they were our enemies. We fought the Russians and easily defeated them. After the Russian Revolution they left us alone. But the British didn't leave us until they had sucked every drop of blood from us. Instead of helping us confront Russia, they forced us to sign agreements with the Russians that meant giving up the golden parts of our country. They drained our land of its lifeblood, our oil, and brought opium and tobacco to our country. They hoped opium would turn us into harmless incompetents so they could then plunder our wealth. Many greedy landowners started growing opium instead of traditional crops and they created this habit of smoking, first among intellectuals and rich families and gradually even among the common people. You could buy opium, smoke it and sell the *shireh* [burned residue] for more than the opium itself.'

This was the first time I felt some hatred towards foreigners. Later on I discovered Aghbajie was not the only one who hated the British; it was a very common sentiment. In fact, people often blamed their misery on the British. This was partly justified, but one might wonder why they couldn't see their weaknesses and inability to look after their own rights!

My grandmother told me how her father, a landowner, blamed the country's ills on the weakness of the king, claiming the British and Russians ruled the world because they had strong monarchs. He was against a parliamentary system on grounds that a Shah was a single person, easy enough to get rid of, but their so-called representatives would be a bunch of thieves whom they could not trust to act in their interests.

Her uncle, on the other hand, was pro-revolution and favoured a constitutional monarchy or republic. British success, in his view, stemmed from their parliament, not their monarchs. The Americans and French had achieved revolutionary independence, overthrowing despots. He believed democracy – mastery of their own fate – would invite security and prosperity. He was a great believer in progress, and especially keen on railway development.'Yes', he argued, 'we have slipped back a bit, but still they teach our scientists' works in European universities: Omar Khayyam's algebra, Zakaria's discoveries in chemistry, Abyssinia's discoveries in medicine. They have learned from us, and now it is our turn to learn from them and try to catch up with and perhaps overtake them ... United, we could overthrow the Shah and bring in a government to work for the people and be accountable to them, not serve the interests of foreigners.' In support of his case he recalled the *jonbash tanbacoo* ('Tobacco Movement'), when people successfully protested against the Shah's cession of tobacco rights to the British.

Neither my grandmother's father nor uncle had long to wait. Without much of a struggle, Mozafar ol Din Shah agreed to constitutional monarchy and signed it into law. (The inscription above the parliament building entrance reads '*Adel Mozafar*' [Justice of Mozafar].) Unfortunately, after Mozafar's death, his son Mohammed Ali Shah – considered a puppet of the Russians – repealed constitutional monarchy; his Russian friends bombarded Parliament and abolished the constitution.

Thus the revolution (1907–11) ignited, first in Tabriz (capital of Azerbaijan), then nationwide. People rose against the Shah and suddenly discovered how rich they were in courage and conviction, ready to sacrifice everything for their country's good. When famous revolutionaries like Satar Khan and Baqar Khan rose up, not even Russia's military might mattered. Such people would do anything for their new leaders, whom they trusted, who spoke their language, who were honest and plain-dealing. Once the revolution started, it was unstoppable; but as it evolved, traditional social bonds and loyalties were broken. Overnight, neighbours and families became bitter enemies. The quarrel between Grandmother's father and uncle turned violent. Her father believed the revolution was a British trick. It was his fate to be killed by his own brother, the pro-revolutionary uncle.

'Grandmother', I said, 'you must hate your uncle for killing his own brother!'

She sighed. 'He was a very good man. He cried for my father more than all of us together, and took care of us better than his own children. He was a revolutionary; revolutionaries live in a world of myth and legend. For them everything is black and white, life and death, nothing in between. Any obstacle to the revolution came from the forces of darkness and had to be destroyed. He could not see that real life is colourful, that one must settle for the best colours available, knowing that nothing is pure white nor the rest pure black. When you fight, you can't think about the person who is to be killed. The only thing you know about him is that his objectives contradict yours. You must kill him or be killed. So we could not hate our uncle, much as we hated war and killing.

'After the revolution my uncle had to face reality and grieve for the loss of his brother and for the fact that for the first time Iranians fought each other, when previously they had fought against common foreign enemies intent on plundering the country. Iranians belong to different religions and speak different languages, yet we had lived together in this beautiful country in harmony and peace.

'He was immensely sad. Even the revolutionaries' joy in victory didn't last long. In a way my father had been right. They did what they could to keep their newly won democracy, but I suppose the majority of people were not educated enough or ready to nurture it properly. You see, revolutionaries, intellectuals are a tiny minority. They cannot become guardians of the people's rights. If they stay true to their promises, at least they do not become new dictators, but then it is the duty of the majority to look after what they have gained. Our heroes were honest enough not to seize power themselves. So power again passed into the hands of the same old group of people who had previously ruled for 100 years, only this time in the guise of the people's representatives. Parliament became a centre for British and Russian agents. Foreigners bought popular votes and put their own stooges in power. After the collapse of the Russian tsar in 1917, Britain became the only beneficiary of Iranian wealth, and in 1919, thanks to treacherous parliamentarians, Iranian ministers were able to dictate a shameful treaty to Iran, which made us a virtual British protectorate.'

One Thursday, my mother came to collect me instead of my aunt. It was a wonderful surprise; I was, as they say, unable to move in my skin from happiness. It was my ninth birthday, and she had travelled all the way to Tehran to be with me. Instead of taking me to her parents' house she took me to her uncle's, as she had apparently quarrelled with her mother. Her uncle, a widower, lived with his mother, her sister and his two beautiful daughters – Bitta, my age, and Bittak, about two years younger. They had prepared for a party, with colourful paper decorations, paper hats for the guests and, of course, food and drink. It was one of the best days of my life: my first- and last-ever birthday party.

For the next few months I went to my great-uncle's house on Thursdays and Fridays, where I played with Bitta and Bittak and the servants' children and asked him any questions I wanted, sure of a fair and intelligent reply. Bitta went to private school, so she knew some English and could write it on her blackboard, which impressed me greatly. Although my father was richer than theirs, he did not approve of private schools and accordingly sent me to a state school, where the standard of education was undoubtedly lower. Once Bitta kissed me, which I found pleasant and strange. She also told me about sex and how babies are made. She had everything I might have wanted in a future wife, but she was much taller and cleverer than me, so I thought I stood no chance.

One day when I asked to go to my mother's house, my father asked me, 'Are you sure you want to go to your "mother's house"?' 'My mother's house' for me was a metaphor for 'freedom'; it was not literally accurate as she had not been living in Tehran for some time.

Naturally, I answered, 'Yes.'

My father became angry and said, 'Why are you lying to me? I know for a fact that your mother has not been in Tehran for the past six months, and nobody knows where you go every Thursday and Friday.'

Thinking quickly, I explained: 'When my mother is in Tehran she goes to her uncle, and instead of asking if I may see her I asked if I could go to her house.' This only made him angrier.

'Each week you leave us for two days to see your mother's uncle!' he stormed, 'and all this time you know that all your brothers and sisters and your own aunts and uncles are here on Thursdays? The answer to your question is no! No, you cannot go and see your mother's uncle any more. Last week was the last time.'

It was a dark day for me. I felt I had lost the only freedom I had, although I had expected worse. If it had been my older brother Esau in this situation, my father would have given him a beating for 'lying'.

My father preferred me to Esau, who was five years my senior. His mother married immediately after divorcing my father and after some time left Iran for the United States, so from childhood Esau was separated from his mother and did not have the weekly outlet of freedom and love that I had. Perhaps once a month his grandmother would come and visit him, bringing some sweets, clothes and money. These things were very precious to Esau, and he used to hide them from everybody. A few times we found him in the toilet secretly eating some delicacy he had hidden. This stinginess lasted all his life. I, on the other hand, always had more money than I knew what to do with, so I would throw coins to the sky and let anyone who wanted take some. Therefore I was thought to be generous. My father's sister put it this way: 'The difference between Masoud and Esau is that if you give Masoud one raisin he will try to divide it among whoever is in the room, while if you give a bag full of sultanas to Esau, he will take all of them to toilet and eat them alone.' Once Esau made a syrup with mint and vinegar, which he would eat slowly, every day, in front of us, without letting any of us taste it. I negotiated with Esau to buy some. When I tasted it, I found it was too sweet, so I asked if I could have my money back. 'No', he said. 'You have struck a deal and you cannot reverse it.' So I lost my money, but I learned that it was up to me to pay for my mistakes.

Unlike my parents, I was religious, even superstitious. Once, when I was feeling sad, Esau told me I would have to pray if I wanted to be able to see my mother's family. I said, 'Don't be silly, I pray every night before I go to sleep.'

'Prayer alone is not enough,' he said. 'There are billions of people who pray every day for things they don't have. You must do something to force God to hear you.' He said there was a particular prayer he had found, and he might give it to me one day. I became entirely focused on getting hold of that prayer. Once I saw Esau hide a piece of paper, and while he was out of the room I took it out and started reading it. But before I finished, Esau came back into the room. I held out the paper and begged him to tell me the prayer. I told him I had managed to read only the number '100'. 'All right', he agreed, 'I will tell you.' But he instructed me first to drink 100 glasses of water to purify myself, and then he would reveal the prayer. In my desperation I drank a few glasses of water but developed a stomach ache and couldn't continue. I thought I was about to be sick. 'I cannot carry on,' I said, 'but what is the next stage?' The next stage, he said, was to share my food with the dog and eat from the same plate, to show God how much I respect all his creatures.

'If you know this prayer,' I challenged him, 'how come you are never allowed to go and see your grandmother?'

'Because', he answered, 'like you, I could never fulfil all the stages of the prayer.' He added, 'In order to distribute prayers to different people, God puts conditions in front of them that are like a very large stone that nobody can lift. That relieves him from having to listen to so many people's demands.' After that, I felt that prayer was not useful at all: if it is simple, God doesn't want to listen to it, and if it is so difficult to master, what is the use?

Esau was not good at school and directed most of his talents towards deceiving our father, who used to beat him regularly and show him up for his failings in front of everyone. When Father found Esau reading his own books hidden under his schoolbooks, father decided that from then on we would go to his room each evening to study. So, thanks to Esau, we lost what little freedom we had in our rooms after school.

By contrast, I was always top of my class, which made me popular with the teachers and won me favour with my father. Although he would praise me in front of his guests, in private he gave me no privileges and still subjected me to the occasional beating. What made it worse was that people who saw only the public side of the situation were jealous of my favoured status.

In wintertime we used to sit in my father's room on cushions placed on a large quilt around a *curcy*, a square table on short legs, under which a coal fire was lit in a large pot called a *manghal*. You could keep your feet warm by putting them under the table. Among us three children there was always a fight for the place furthest away from Father. It didn't do us any good, as he would ask us one by one to come and sit next to him. Then he would ask about our studies, usually posing some particularly difficult question.

Normally Esau went first, then Sorya. If I was lucky, the questioning of those two would take so long that it would be too late for my turn and we would have to eat dinner and go to bed. Sometimes I wished to be first because watching Father put my siblings to the test and then beat them until they got bloody noses was nearly as bad for me as it was for them. And the waiting was awful. Most of the time, he asked such difficult or misleading questions that we couldn't answer them.

On one occasion I was reading a storybook instead of a textbook. My father was already displeased with Esau, so when he asked what I was reading and I told him, he spluttered, 'Why are you not studying?'

'Because I have nothing to study,' I said proudly.

'Oh! Is that a fact?' he yelled. He asked Esau to fetch my schoolbook so he could see if I had mastered its contents. But Esau, instead of bringing my book, brought another one, much more advanced than mine. Whether he did that on purpose or by mistake I never discovered. My father began asking me questions from that book, to which I obviously did not know the answers. I tried to explain but it was one of those nights when he was in a fury and was not prepared to listen to anyone. Instead, he just beat me as hard as he could. In the end Sorya had to take me to the lavatory to wash the blood from my nose. Then my father said, 'I thought I could trust you to study without my supervision. Now I see I was wrong and cannot leave any of you alone.'

The question he had asked me involved calculating the area of an ellipse. I didn't know how to do that, and after he had shown me he told me to study the relevant pages in that book because he was going to test me on the method the following day. At school during break time, I didn't go out into the yard to play, but stayed indoors studying. It was difficult material, and as I pored over the book I was choked with sadness and anger. My teacher happened to spot me and asked what was going on. With some fear of the consequences, I showed her the book and explained. As she listened, her astonishment turned to anger. She dragged me off to the principal's office and asked him to call my father and insist on an explanation. The principal, like most of the teachers, liked me. He didn't hesitate to pick up the phone and speak to my father.

That afternoon when I went home, everything was different.

Although my father would never admit his mistakes, it was clear that he regretted what he had done. He could not bring himself to look me in the eye. Painful as the inquisitions and beatings had been, the suffering had somehow been worthwhile, because he never asked about my studies again. Thereafter I always studied for myself, in my own time and free from anxiety. I concluded that good things may come from bad, and that what seems bad may contain the seeds of something good. This realization has stayed with me throughout my life.

Sometimes I felt Esau was not only jealous but actually hated me. Sorya said it was because Mother used to give me the best of everything, and in revenge he wanted to harm me.

In the basement of our old house we had a private bathroom which was large and dark, a horrible place with an oil-fired heater that had only enough capacity for one bath. It would be turned on once a week, and everybody had to bathe on that day. My stepmother would send Esau and me to bathe together, normally as the last ones in the house and late at night. The bathroom was always cold, even in summer; I would shiver with cold and fear. That was not all: people said there were spirits living in the basement. Esau used to make noises like the voices or movements of spirits, and tell the most terrifying stories. Our bathroom was also full of very large beetles. Esau knew I was afraid of them, so he would pick up a handful and drop them in the pot of water with which I had to wash myself, or even throw them at me. After bathing, we had to walk upstairs and I wasn't brave enough to do that alone; I was prepared to pay the price and wait for Esau to finish washing so we could leave together. When I told my sister she said, '*Tars bradar margeh* [Fear is the brother of death]', and told me to prepare myself for the worst and face my fear. So one evening I walked down to the bathroom, picked up some beetles in my hand very proudly returned upstairs. From then on I was able to leave the bathroom on my own and Esau didn't trouble me there any more. Gradually I learned how to disagree with my brother, not to trust him too readily and to stand on my own feet.

Once, at school, Esau came to my classroom and asked for permission to take me home early. Strangely, my teacher let me go. He had hired a bicycle.'Come on, Masoud', he said,' I want to teach you how to ride.' I hesitated, but he was not a person to resist, so I sat on the bicycle seat in front of him and off we went. On the main street, we were unfortunate enough to pass in front of Father's car at a red light. We were certain he had seen us, so we forgot about riding and the whole afternoon were thinking what to do. Esau was certain that we'd be beaten if we went home. We would have to run away; he even suggested we commit suicide. In the end, Esau said, 'Father will not beat you as hard as he'll beat me. I'll go away and find a job and never return home.' At that we parted and I went home. It turned out Father had not seen us after all, but I could not find Esau and tell him. Apparently he had not been able to find anywhere to go, so he came home late. My father was so angry with him for being late that he locked him out, and poor Esau had to sleep outside the door. Eventually we were permitted to let him in. My father wielded his whip, which always stood ready for us in the corner of the room. This time, however, Esau didn't let him continue. When my father lifted the whip, Esau grabbed the point of it and pulled it towards him, so that Father could not use it. Sorya and I were overjoyed to witness that scene. For us it was a victory of the oppressed over the tyrant. (Later, when moved from that house to a new one, Esau found the whip and threw it away with a strength powered by rage.) My father realized he could not beat Esau anymore and, fearing the loss of his authority, he permitted Esau to go live with my eldest brother in Rasht, in the north of Iran. This was a stroke of luck for Esau, who went somewhere none of us could have dreamed of. Again, I felt that something good had come from bad. Quite soon afterwards my father stopped beating us altogether.

# 2

# Absolute Rule

My father rarely talked about himself, but once he told me the story of Reza Khan's British-backed coup against Ahmad Shah, the last Qajar king and Iran's only-ever constitutional monarch. Ahmad Shah was an obstacle to the British, who wielded the real power in Iran. They wanted to get rid of him, not least because he presided over an increasingly restive population that threatened British oil interests. They wanted to install a strong but still malleable leader, and chose Reza Khan, an authoritarian Iranian Cossack officer with no ties to the political elite.

My father, then an officer in the Swedish-run gendarmerie, went on to describe the day of the coup. On 20th February 1921, he said, a warning was issued that an attack on Tehran was imminent. The armed forces were amalgamated to defend the capital. The next day, my father continued, they heard that a group of Cossacks under the command of Reza Khan were approaching Tehran from the northwest. But the armed forces were ordered not to intercept Reza Khan's men, but to open the city gates to them and surrender.

The British representative in Tehran had compelled Ahmad

Shah to appoint Reza Khan head of the army and minister of war; in 1923, Reza Khan became prime minister, and in 1925, with the help of the pro-British parliament, he deposed Ahmad Shah, abolished the Qajar monarchy and proclaimed himself king. Reza Shah chose the name 'Pahlavi' for his dynasty.

I had always thought my father a supporter of Reza Shah and when I said so, he said, 'Reza Shah was an absolute dictator and killed many who opposed him in cold blood. Many died in prison, or under torture. He came to power by the will of the British, who took most of our oil profits. Reza Khan confiscated most of the valuable lands for himself. When he came to power he was a poor army officer, who like me and all officers used to get mud bricks instead of a monthly salary, but when he left he was richest man in Iran. But he did many good things as well. Under Qajar rule we were a backward country with no hospitals, no proper roads, no railway. Electricity and clean water were luxuries reserved for the elite. Most of the people were illiterate; we didn't have a united army, so whoever was powerful enough could seize control of a part of the country. Kings in the capital thought only of their own pleasure and even if they cared about others they were so incompetent and weak they couldn't do much to change anything.'

My father said, 'Now judge for yourself how things have changed, most of it during the reign of Reza Shah. He was a nationalist, keen to take our country forward, yet the same British felt he was not useful any more and might form an alliance with the Germans in a bid to develop our country. So they started broadcasting on the BBC that he was a dictator and reminding us how brutal he was and eventually they asked for his abdication and exiled him to South Africa. Now how do you want to judge him? It is easy to read history with hindsight but you have to consider the circumstances of the time and assess what was done in the light of those.'

I remember the day of Ashorra, when I was about ten years old. On this day the betrayal and death of Imam Hussein are remembered.

Muslims, mostly Iranians, who believe that the Prophet Muhammad had chosen his cousin and son-in-law Ali and his sons as caliphs – successors – called themselves the Shi'a Ali (Party of Ali), known as 'Shi'a'. Ali was eventually elected the fourth caliph.

After his death, Hassan made peace with his father's foe Muawiya. After Hassan's death, Ali's other son Hussein refused to accept the accession of Muawiya's son Yazid to the caliphate. The people of Kufa invited Hussein to go there to mount his revolt, but when he arrived he found no one ready to come to his aid. Hussein, alone except for about seventy of his relatives and disciples, fought Yazid's army in October 680; all were killed, a tragedy known as the Incident of Karbela (the town near which it occurred).

The Incident has long since given courage and inspiration to all revolutionary Shi'i Muslims worldwide. Hussein fought not to retain an empire but to protect the main goals of Islam: freedom, equality, social justice for all and brotherhood among all Muslims. When he saw that he and his brothers in arms were going to be killed, he preferred death on the battlefield to life without freedom. Many times he warned his followers that they would most likely die, and asked them to leave his army if they were not ready to fight. It is said he used to ask for all lights to be extinguished so that whoever wanted to leave could do so without shame.

Believers mark Ashorra with demonstrations and ceremonies. Everybody wears black clothes takes to the street, chanting slogans that the *marekeh gardan* were chanting for them to copy, while beating themselves, occasionally very hard, with a sword-like weapon called a *ghameh* and with *zanjir*, metal chains fastened together. People have different views about these events: some believe it is *vahshigary* (savagery), while others sympathise and appreciate the commemoration of Imam Hussein. The self-flagellation reminds people how far they should go to defend freedom.

Usually we went to my god-uncle's orchard near Tehran, where he gave the marchers a free lunch. Each year more than 1,000 people would gather there. We went mainly out of respect for my uncle; my father disapproved of the ritual and forbade us to join in. That year my uncle, too, wanted us to stay away; something dangerous was going to happen.

Around noon I asked to accompany Esau to the bakery to buy bread, as I wanted to see the demonstration. Usually the ceremony was like theatre, with people dressed in the garments of Imam Hussein's time and bearing contemporary arms, re-enacting scenes from the past. Their slogans were not bellicose but rhetorical, almost poetic. But this time the bakery was closed, and what we saw astounded us. Gone were the sedate marchers offering their make-believe resistance to Shemer and Yazid, the rulers of Imam Hussein's day. Instead people were running, shouting 'Death to the Shah!' For us it was fun, as was anything that disturbed the routine of everyday life. The demonstrators attacked government offices, banks, cinemas and even public phones, breaking windows and sometimes setting fires. Soldiers ran after them, firing, and when they caught any demonstrators they beat and arrested them. Their conduct seemed to us so brutal that our sympathies went to the demonstrators. Without thinking, we joined the demonstration, running and shouting slogans like the others. This was the first time I had seen people beaten and killed, just as I imagined things had happened during the time of Imam Hussein. That year Ashorra was not history, but real and alive. After we had gone a few streets with the crowd, being shot at by soldiers, the demonstrators dispersed and we, too, went home. For days afterwards we talked about nothing else. I heard that an *ayatollah* named Khomeini was behind this uprising, but I did not discover what his purpose was.

That week my father permitted me to go to my grandparents' house, where the talk was mainly of the demonstration. My grandfather believed that the British were behind whatever the *mullahs* did. 'Times have changed,' he said. 'Now the Americans want to get their hands on our wealth. They have asked the Shah to change things, so he is bringing in land reform, and as a result many landowners who collaborated with the *mullahs* and the British will lose their power. The British, who are on the verge of losing everything, have asked the *mullahs* to start this riot.' My grandmother held a different view:

'After Reza Shah came to power, he proclaimed himself a nationalist and said that religion and the power of the *mullahs* were the cause of our sufferings. But I think he understood that these were the only forces that could challenge his dictatorship, so he wanted to crush them. He tried to copy Turkey's Atatürk and turn us all into Europeans, whether we liked it or not. Nobody dared oppose him and those who did ended up in the prison being tortured or in an early grave. The first thing he did was to enforce a law making European dress compulsory. Women were ordered not to wear the *chador* (veil) or the *hijab* (dark-coloured garments covering the hair, face and body), which they wore not as a matter of taste but as testament to their devoutness and chastity. People were beaten and arrested because of their clothes. Even your grandfather objected to this, saying it was not about dress, but freedom; if the Shah doesn't allow us our freedom, we might as well be in hell for all the heaven he promises. Grandfather had nothing against European dress, only against people being forced to wear it. He even bought me a hat in place of my scarf. For few days I wore it at home to get used to it. One day I went out as far as the nearest street, but I was so ashamed, I returned home immediately. Gradually I got used to it, but I know many who couldn't, and so they never left the house. So for some women the new legislation amounted to even more restriction, especially when their husbands or fathers ordered them to stay indoors.

'You see, dictators think they can do anything and for a short time they can, but their achievements are superficial and the effects run deep. They create a huge zeal for destroying whatever they disapprove of, but that fire consumes everything indiscriminately. Reza Shah wanted to rule a European country, but that meant rooting out traditions that were thousands of years old and couldn't be changed in a matter of days. When his son came to the throne he wanted to become an absolute ruler like his father. But all the real authority, according to the constitution, was vested in the prime minister, cabinet and parliament. He thought that by uniting with the *mullahs* against the intellectuals and the ruling elite, he could gain power. So he answered the *mullahs'* call to abolish laws against our religion. Once he had gathered enough power he tried to curb the *mullahs* again. What we see today are the consequences of that power struggle and Reza Shah's attempt to mould us into the European nation he wanted.'

# 3

# Cartoons and Conundrums

From the top floor I climbed out on to the roof and looked around. There was another building about the same height, a metre or two away. I knew I could jump across to the other roof, but any mistake could be fatal. The urge was irresistible: I jumped. Suddenly my anxiety and worry had been dissipated. I felt relieved and satisfied, empty and happy at the same time.

It was summer of 1963. For a few weeks my mother and Ammo Jan were living in Tehran, where I was able to see them on weekends. Ammo Jan had lost most of his fortune, and instead of living in their own house they rented an apartment. In fact, neither of them really cared much about money. They loved to play cards and gamble, and were the most generous of hosts.

Their flat was on the third floor of a building in Pastor Avenue. It was Friday, and in a few hours' time I would have to return to my father's house. I was tired of being thrown like a ball between my parents. On the face of it I had two homes, but in reality I felt at home in neither.

I stayed on the neighbouring roof for about half an hour. I became tired, and there was no point staying up there. I had released my anger and somehow protested my situation. But now that I was calm I couldn't summon up the courage to jump back onto our building. From where I was I could see the window of our toilet, so I gathered some stones and threw them. My grandmother was in there. She opened the window, astonished and frightened: how could anyone be throwing stones? They must be coming from the sky! Her face was such a picture that I immediately started laughing, and couldn't stop for a long time. The others thought it was funny too, which put paid to any idea of punishing me. One kind of punishment was unavoidable: I would go back to my father's house.

The school year had finished; I had passed my fourth-year examinations with maximum grades. So, to keep me occupied through the summer, my father bought me the fifth-grade books to read, and also let me arrange his old newspapers in his library.

After the abdication of Reza Shah my father lost all hope that the army might one day be strong enough to repel foreigners. So he resigned from the military, and with the fortune that he had inherited from his father he started a weekly newspaper called *Ansan Azad* ('Free Human'). He believed all our problems are rooted in ignorance, that if people were educated, they would not be deceived so easily, making progress and independence possible.

My father's library had a few rooms, one of which was almost full of back issues of *Ansan Azad*. Sorting and filing these newspapers took all summer. The first issue was dated one or two years after Reza Shah's abdication, and the last sometime in 1953. During this era Mohammed Reza Shah, the new king of Iran, was so young and powerless that his role in any event was scarcely traceable. The real power was in the hands of the prime minister. In a sense, then, we had a kind of constitutional monarchy, with all its weak and strong points.

From what I could see, my father's library held hundreds of different daily or weekly newspapers. He said that in Reza Shah's time, by contrast, there had been only a few, strictly controlled and censored by the government. After all, he joked, Reza Shah could think for everybody. 'We were less free but happier than in the time of the Qajars. There was some progress, and generally we were stronger than before. Freedom was a luxury we couldn't afford.'

I was about ten years old and not as easily frightened as before, but I was still not comfortable being in our basement, which was damp and dark. But father kept thousands of old books and magazines here, and it was an honour to be allowed to work with his papers, so I had to put up with it. Reading *Ansan Azad* was sometimes fun too. The serious material was hard for me to understand, but each issue had a huge, usually political cartoon. Britain was mostly depicted as a deceitful, smiling, fat man or as a dragon; Russia, perhaps as a bear; the US, as Uncle Sam; and Iran, as a lion asleep or injured by the arrows of its enemies. The people of Iran were shown as an emaciated bony man with no energy to defend himself and whose only desire is for 'a piece of bread'. The blood of Iranians was sometimes transformed in these cartoons into oil. Political intrigue was nearly always the subject.

One issue published a picture of people living in terrible conditions in Abadan. My father explained that in 1946 there had been a general strike among Iranian oil workers; he had gone there to report on the situation. The British manager of the oil company welcomed him and took him to the part of Abadan where British personnel lived. It looked like a European city, with asphalted streets lined with beautiful flowers and green lawns, large houses with private gardens and supermarkets selling the best European goods. After dinner the company gave him a private car with a driver to show him around. 'Mr Banisadr,' the driver said, 'do you want to see how Iranian workers are living in this "beautiful city"?' The contrast could not have been greater. While on the British side water was wasted for keeping grass and flowers blooming even in the heat of the summer, on the Iranian side people didn't have enough to drink. They had to collect rainwater from a metal container, which then stagnated and became infested with worms that lived under the skin and could be eliminated only by twisting them out of the body over time around sticks. All commodities were in short supply, and most people didn't have proper roofs. Company wages wouldn't even cover daily necessities.

In the summer of 1949 the prime minister took a new oil agreement, still more beneficial to the British, before the mostly pro-British parliament for approval. But the nationalists opposed the deal and filibustered until the agreement fell through. The next election was arranged such that no nationalists could be elected. But through strikes organised by Mohammed Mossadegh and members of Jebh'e Melli (National Front), plus some journalists' reports, people became aware of events. Under public pressure the government called new elections, in which Mossadegh and other nationalists were elected.

The new prime minister, a nominee of the Shah, presented the oil bill to Parliament. Although privately he found it favourable, he chose not to speak for it. Pressed by Mossadegh either to resign or to withdraw the bill, he resigned. In November 1950 Mossadegh and his friends introduced a bill to nationalize all Iranian oil production. In the atmosphere of public jubilation it was obvious that no member of parliament, however pro-British, would dare to reject it.

The next prime minister, Razm Ara, hesitated either to reject the Nationalization Bill or to defend the earlier bill. Ultimately he withdrew the latter, knowing that it was probable the Nationalization Bill would pass anyway. He also shut down many newspapers and had journalists arrested. Now I understood why there were gaps in the sequence of issues of *Ansan Azad*.

The next issue carried news of the assassination of Razm Ara. After his death Parliament approved the bill. For the first time in fifty years Iran took possession of its own most valuable commodity. The latest in the succession of prime ministers resigned after a few months, having had difficulty supporting the bill.

There were no more issues of *Ansan Azad*. I later discovered that the missing issues contained pro-Mossadegh news. My father destroyed them out of fear of the Shah's secret police force, Savak.

In the ensuing political chaos the pro-Bitish parliamentary leader challenged Mossadegh to nominate himself for prime minister. Against all expectations, Mossadegh did so; pro-British parliamentarians, confused by Emami's suggestion, thought that this was a trick to destroy Mossadegh. So most of them voted for him. The Shah was astonished when Mossadegh emerged victorious from the ballot.

The Mossadegh premiership was very mysterious. Almost nobody was prepared to talk about it, nor could I find any written literature about it. The only thing I discovered at that time was that he was overthrown by an American-British coup a few months before I was born, in August 1953. One of our relatives, Abol-Hassan Banisadr, went into exile and his brother, Fathollah Banisadr, was arrested.

All through the summer of 1963 I lived with a contradiction. In the morning, reading in my father's papers of the humiliations and troubles that had been inflicted on my country, I felt hate, sorrow and pity. In the evening, reading my beloved school history book – which to me was like an enjoyable storybook, with colourful pictures, maps and accessible language – I was inspired by evidence of Iran's strength and prosperity at a time when Britain, Russia and America were barely civilized.

October always was fun, because it meant going back to school, where I could see my friends. Our new teacher told us many stories that could not be found in our history or geography books. Another teacher taught us how to write beautifully and read the Qur'an. I loved our Prophet and our Imams (saints), but I didn't like the Arabs for what they had done to our country. Thus I could not be persuaded either to learn Arabic or read the Qur'an in Arabic. I decided to read my prayers in Farsi, too. My stepmother made fun of me, warning that God would not accept my prayers if they were not in Arabic. 'Why?' I asked. 'Is God Arab too? I'm going to pray to a God who understands Farsi.'

Iranians are Shi'i Muslims and many, because of their history or education during the Shah's time, feel hostility towards the Arabs but are also deeply religious. After the Arab invasion during the reigns of Omar and Osman, the second and third caliphs, many Iranians changed their religion from Zoroastrianism to Islam. It became fashionable to use Arabic both as an everyday language and for learned texts. Iranian scientists, writers and poets became absorbed by Arabic culture and history, and were identified as Arabs. This may have been because the Shah and the aristocracy were the sole guardians of Iranian culture. Common people were not permitted even to educate their children. One story tells of Anoshirvan the Just, king of the Sassanians, who needed money for one of his battles. His advisers suggested he borrow it from a wealthy farmer. The farmer was more than happy to lend money to the Shah, but in return asked that his son be allowed to study. The king's 'principles' came first, as education was not allowed for the caste of farmers. Rather than make one exception, he chose to look elsewhere for the money. In this sense, perhaps, the Arabs were more sophisticated than we were: their culture was less advanced than that of the Iranian elite, but it was at least owned by everybody and it was the responsibility of all to cherish it and help it to prosper. This may be why common Iranians did not resist Arabization of their society, and why those who converted to Islam did so out from conviction, not by compulsion.

As usual we celebrated Norowz, the Iranian new year, on 21st March 1964. Its origin is disputed. Some say it is the birthday of Zartosht, the prophet of ancient Iran, others that this is the day on which in the future Ahura Mazda, god of good, will triumph over Ahriman, the god of evil; when light will prevail over darkness, day over night, spring over winter. In any case, Norowz always marks the start of spring, and accordingly people wear new or at least spruced-up clothes on that day. Each family sets a table with *haftseen* (seven objects whose names all begin with the latter 's') and leave it like this for thirteen days. Normally they grow greens in a pot for the festival as a symbol of agriculture, which has been important in Iran since ancient times. We gathered in our house for lunch and afterwards went to visit relatives. One of these was my great-uncle, who at that time was perhaps eighty or ninety years old. Already a great-grandfather, he also had a young daughter of only about eighteen, and he was complaining to my father that she had appeared 'half naked' in a TV advertisement. 'Thank God I am dying and shall not have to see the future,' he said, 'but I am certain that we are all going to hell.' Next we went to visit my father's cousin, an *ayatollah* called Sadr'o al-Olama, who gave a golden coin to everybody as a new year's gift. His house was segregated: the ground floor was for women only and the first only for men. His two sons, one of whom was my brother-in-law, were supporters of Mossadegh.

After that we went to see another cousin of my father, a close relative of the Zahedi family. Ardashir Zahedi was the son-in-law of the Shah, and his father – with the help of the CIA-supported coup – became prime minister of Iran after Mossadegh but was ultimately forced to resign by the Shah, who wanted the country in his grip alone. In October 1957, the Shah appointed his own prime minister, Manuchehr Eqbal, who proudly described himself as *ghoolame'e Shah* ('the Shah's slave'). The Shah called on two of his closest disciples to establish two political parties opposed to each other, so he could play them off against each other and retain full power. At about the same time Savak, the secret police, was established. From then on complete obedience to the Shah was assured.

When John F. Kennedy, newly elected President of the United States, began to speak of democracy and social justice in developing countries, the Shah realized that he would not enjoy absolute rule without American blessing. In April 1962 he switched his allegiance from Britain to the United States, and persuaded Kennedy that he was the best person to advance reform in Iran.

In January 1963 the Shah called a referendum on his plan for land reform and other changes, called the White Revolution. Unsurprisingly, he gained the 'support' of 99 per cent of the people.

My eldest brother, an agricultural engineer, was posted as head of the Agriculture and Land Reform Ministry in Gilan, one of Iran's most fertile states, south of the Caspian Sea. I spent my holidays with him in July 1964 and heard him complain often that agriculture itself was being overlooked in the drive for land reform. The potential for growth and development was excellent, but farmers were not receiving assistance to buy seeds and hire machinery. As a result, some farmers who became new landowners, in the absence of a planned programme for agricultural development, merely became confused and ever poorer. Policies were administered haphazardly. One year we would have too many tomatoes and the poor farmers would have to sell them for as little as they had paid to buy the seeds; at the same time onions had to be imported. The next year there would be a glut of onions and the market stalls would be bare of tomatoes. The fault lay with the Shah and his devotion to his White Revolution. After he appointed a colonel to head the new Land Reform Ministry, my brother was transferred there and exchanged active work for the improvement of our agriculture for a desk at which he sank in a swamp of bureaucracy.

That summer change was evident. American products, from rice to bananas and cars, were advertised on billboards and flooded our markets. While Iranian staples were imported from the US, farmers grew asparagus – a vegetable unknown to Iranians – for the American market.

Around that time I learned two lessons about the complexity of the human character. Every month my mother would cook food and sweets and take them to the poorest areas of Tehran to distribute them among the poor. I was not so sure about my father, for whom wealth was a serious affair. Once, when he saw me giving to a beggar, he said, 'You are not helping someone in need, you are encouraging laziness. If you carry on like this you will get nowhere; you will be poor and when you find yourself on the streets begging for bread, no one will help you.' He paused a moment, then said: 'It would seem I'm giving you more money than you need!' This seemed like a joke to me: he used to give me two *rial* per day, which was the price of two sticks of chewing gum. Most of the time I did not even bother to collect it from my stepmother. My 'real' money came from my mother, who I knew would be happy to see me using it to help the poor.

I was much surprised, then, when my father took me one day to a poor district with a big lorry full of coal and other goods, which he handed out to the inhabitants. It was the first time I had seen so many poor people crowded together, in dwellings made from thin boxes or mud. Some even lived in caves in the nearby hills. It was a cold, rainy day, and children with ragged clothes were playing in the water, making a kind of small dam from which the water would run everywhere, including into their houses. When the lorry arrived, they raced to be first to receive some of the goods. I could hardly believe my eyes. Up until then sadness had been a reaction to something that might happen to me. Now I felt sadness for others and was close to tears. 'If you want to help anybody,' my father said, 'help these people. There is no need for anybody to know about it.' It was a side of him I had never seen before.

I had three half-sisters on my mother's side. In the summer of 1964, they came to visit my mother. Strangely, they were all wearing scarfs, long dresses and thick socks. 'What *are* you wearing?' my mother exclaimed. 'Take them off! You are not in Kermanshah now, you are in Tehran.' It was the first time I had seen my mother so indignant; normally she was quite flexible. My sisters declined to change their clothes, and my mother said no more about it. The youngest and my favourite, Farzaneh, was about to enter university in Tehran, but I discovered that she planned to stay with family friends instead of with my mother or grandparents. Privately she told me, 'Look, Masoud, our mother doesn't like us as much as she likes you.' At that, I went to my mother and pleaded with her. 'You don't love all your children equally', I accused. 'And if Farzaneh can't stay here, I'm not going to come here anymore, either.' My mother then tried to persuade my sister to stay with her, but we both felt her insistence was not genuine. For the first time I saw that my mother was not the angel I had always thought her to be. Even for her, personal beliefs sometimes overrode kindness and caring.

People, I then knew, were not creatures of black or white.

Interestingly, after Farzaneh had been in Tehran for a few weeks, she dispensed with the scarf and began wearing pretty dresses like the other girls, even following the latest European fashions.

# 4

# Lessons from History

One day in January 1965, when I was at my grandparents' house, we heard on the radio that the prime minister had been assassinated. My grandfather said the followers of Khomeini were responsible. After the Shah ordered so many people killed in the streets of Teheran in June 1963, Khomeini went silent. It looked as though his uprising had been crushed and he was not going to mount any further resistance to the Shah. But when Parliament, at the Shah's bidding, voted for extraterritorial capitulatory rights for American personnel working in Iran, Khomeini could not hold his tongue any longer. 'These Americans can do anything, they can rape our women and kill our young men and one cannot do anything about it. Would Americans give us the same rights in their country?' The Shah angrily exiled the old man to Turkey.

Everything was changing, but hardly fast enough for the Shah, who pledged that 'we are going to be one of the most progressive countries in the world within twenty years. Then we shall enter the era of "Great Civilisation".' Religious people, led by Khomeini's supporters, were unhappy about the changes in relationships, behaviour and dress. Their remedy, when the prime minister presented a new oil bill to Parliament, was to shoot him.

The next prime minister, the Western-educated Amir-Abbas Hovida, remained in office until near the end of the Shah's era. To the accusation that he was a puppet, he replied: 'I do not work for Parliament. I am the servant of His Majesty.'

In late spring 1965 I finished primary school with good grades. The principal persuaded my father, who was opposed to private schooling, to send me to the highly regarded Hadf High School. Soon afterwards my father bought a house in the north of the city, an upper-middle-class area. I now had to take the bus to school. Most people thought bus travel was sheer torture, but for me it was fun. The buses were always jammed so full that nobody could breathe properly, and we children used to run after them and hang from the iron bar by the entrance. The ticket collectors behaved like little gods. If they were in a good mood they would let us board; if not, they might push us out of the bus with their feet while it was moving. Once I saw a boy thrown into the street and killed.

In the summer of 1966 my father let me go to my mother's for vacation. She was then in Bandar Pahlavi (formerly Bandar Anzali, renamed in honour of the Shah), where Ammo Jan was stationed. The navy personnel there lived like film stars, with access to their own private sandy beach. Women on the beach wore two-piece swimsuits, a rarity in Iran in those days. There was a programme of nightly entertainment, with performances and gambling. Food was cheap and delicious. My stepbrother and sister and I spent the days playing, swimming and learning card games. While my mother played she used French and English words, which was considered chic. Seeing her lose so often at card made me realise how she and Ammo Jan had come to lose all their money. Ammo Jan, though second in command of the base, was office-based; I don't think he ever travelled on a ship.

That October I started my second year of high school. With my two best friends, Ghoolam from Azerbaijan and Mohsen from Kermanshah, I wrote a 'wall newspaper' to pin up on a notice board for people to read during their breaks. At the beginning it was mostly fiction, but later issues contained history and then politics. I loved books, and spent all my money on buying history books. Near the University of Tehran was a bookshop where the shopkeeper indulged my interest by letting me see books that were not on the shelves. The first few books he sold me were by Kasravi: *The History of the Constitutional Revolution*, which explained the failure of the revolution, and *What Can Be Expected From the United Nations*, which argued that the UN was a tool in the hands of the great powers to control small countries and crush their struggles for liberty or independence.

Another book was called *Varjavand Bonyad*. Kasravi disliked Arabs and resisted Arab influence on our culture and language. In this book he suggested new words to replace those with Arabic roots. In the Farsi alphabet there are many letters with similar sounds, represented by different symbols. For example, there are two different types of 'T', three different types of 'S', four types of 'Z', two types of 'H' and two types of 'GH'. Many of these letters, along with many words, are not Persian, but were introduced by invaders – Arabs, Turks or Mongols. If they were subtracted from the alphabet, the number of letters would be reduced from 32 to around 23, simplifying the writing system. The complex alphabet was the main reason for widespread illiteracy during Reza Shah's era and even now. Reza Shah wanted to adopt the Latin alphabet like Atatürk in Turkey, but encountered strong resistance among intellectuals and *ayatollahs*, who feared the loss of links to our rich history, literature and religious books. My father, while in the army, tried to address this problem in a book about how our writing system could be simplified, but met with the same resistance. Whatever the failings in our language, I was proud of it, believing it to be more progressive than Arabic or English, as it is gender-neutral. It felt funny to have to identify the gender of an object or a person or even to assign masculine gender to God. In my eyes the language proved that Iranians believed in the equality of men and women; moreover, two women had been Shah at a time when women had hardly any rights elsewhere in the world. I believed the differences between men and women in Iran were the result of Arabic influence.

At that time I also read *Mein Kampf* and other books about Hitler, none of which made much mention of his actions against Jews. All I knew was that he opposed those nations that were also our enemies – the British, Russians and later Americans – and that he considered himself Aryan and wrote of the glorious days of the Aryan race, namely the ancient history of Iran.

In autumn Ammo Jan was transferred back to Tehran and my mother bought a small house in Hassan Abad, close to my school. Hassan Abad was on a strip dividing north and south Tehran. To the north were brightly lit department stores displaying all the latest styles in clothes and home equipment, big modern cinemas showing new films from Europe and America (dubbed into Farsi), tall office buildings and banks and streets full of expensive modern cars. People dressed fashionably and girls and boys walked hand in hand, openly.

The south was quite different. Whenever I felt depressed I headed south. The Prophet said: 'If you feel depressed or unhappy or your expectations are not being met, go to the cemetery. There you will be reminded that you are not here forever, life will end and what seems so important will vanish. A few years after your death, nobody will even remember your name.' I never actually got as far as the cemetery, but the misery of the inhabitants was plain to see and forced me to forget my own problems and find a reason to live. My hope was that one day I would be able to do something for those people. That was reason enough for living. In the south the streets were dirty; canals were full of smelly rubbish; shops were small, dark and old, selling mostly second-hand goods. Even the food was second-hand. In winter a vendor would cook a kind of stew called *aash*, or tripe, on a small stove in the street. In summer he made *ghati poolo* (a rice dish). Everybody knew that the ingredients were leftovers from a restaurant in the north of the city. Still, people queued up to buy his food. Next to him he also had a bowl of greasy water in which he washed the plates after his customers had eaten the food. Close by was a *gigaraki*, who would grill strips of *gigar safid* (cow's lung) on skewers over a small brazier and sell each kebab for two *rials*. The alleys were narrow, the houses small, old and sometimes made of mud. In every room of every house lived a whole family of up to ten people. They were the lucky ones; many had no roof over their head at all. Children played barefoot in dirty streets. Everyone wore ragged clothes, repeatedly patched and mended. Men walked in front of children and women, who wore *chadors* or scarves. There were a few cheap cinemas showing old Iranian or Indian films. A half-hour walk from north to south was all it took to see the huge gap between rich and poor.

Ghoolam, Mohsen and I used to go to my mother's house for lunch and read the new books I bought every week. I was interested in newspapers as well, but rarely did they contain reliable information. There were also many weekly specialist magazines aimed at children, teenagers and women, all carrying copious advertisements, fashion pages, product news and tales of fantasy. A few newspapers and magazines discussed politics. The two main dailies, *Kyhan* and *Etla'at*, like all printed material then, were under total censorship and were mouthpieces for the government. My grandfather used to say that the only reliable information in these papers was the announcements of deaths; the articles could be read upside-down. My favourite weekly contained political satire. *Tofigh*, like my father's copies of *Ansan Azad*, was full of cartoons. One of them showed the offices of the two main parties created by the Shah, interconnected at the back, yet with members from each brawling out front. The prime minister was always caricatured on the front page, being depicted as the Shah's dummy and scapegoat. *Tofigh* invented a 'party of donkeys', which was the focus of the magazine's political barbs. Corruption was the butt of many cartoons, including one that depicted people against a background of a map of Iran, each person with his hand in the pocket of the person next to him. Even children could see how corrupt and bureaucratic the system had become. The only way to get around this was with bribery. With inflation and high rents, no official could survive without accepting bribes to supplement his salary.

It was clear from our history lessons that Iran had always been the victim of attacks and invasions by foreign tyrants and colonial powers. From the west, Alexander the Great had been followed by the Romans and later the Ottoman Empire. From east came the Central Asian Turks, the Mongols under Genghis Khan, Timurlane and later the Uzbeks and Afghans. Arab and then British invaders came from the south, and the Russians threatened from the north. Strong leaders had been able to repulse foreigners and hold the country to a path of independence and progress. Weak leaders like Darius III or Fath Ali Shah allowed the country to be taken over and progress halted in its tracks. The people seemingly didn't mind who ruled them, as long as the ruler brought some kind of peace, stability, law and order and respect for culture. Hence we were happy to accept Mongols or Turks as our kings, as long as they accepted our religion, language and culture. This attitude did not apply to the Arabs, who wanted to impose their culture on us and elicited a different kind of resistance. For the last 100 years Iran had had no foreign ruler. Yet we felt ourselves to be under foreign domination, our culture and religion threatened with suppression and gradual elimination. Mohsen, Ghoolam and I, like the Germans after losing World War I, felt that strong nationalism could unite us and save us from exploitation by foreigners and domestic tyrants. So one day we decided to create a party. We called it the Iranism Party, and I wrote a sixty-page Agenda setting out our hopes for the future of Iran.

On 4th March 1967 the daily paper carried a brief news item: 'Mossadegh dead'. Until then I hadn't even known he was alive. Nobody around me wanted to talk about him and all my information had been collected fortuitously and through the few people who overcame their fear of Savak to reveal what they knew. Next day I told my friends Mohsen and Ghoolam the news. It turned out they hadn't known he was alive either. For a short time we thought we might write up the story in our wall newspaper but we knew that our headmaster would censor it and, worse, tell our parents. So we didn't do it. In fact, we stopped writing the newspaper altogether after that.

I needed to know more about Mossadegh. I asked the owner of my favourite bookshop whether he had any books on the subject. He looked at me in doubt and fear and for a few minutes was evidently weighing up what to do. At last he said, 'Let me go and see if I have anything.' From the back of the shop he brought out an old book lacking a title page presumably torn off for security reasons, so I never discovered its title. That night I began reading it, hardly able to put it down.

This was Mossadegh's story.

After he accepted the premiership, he broke off all negotiations with the oil company and the British. In response, in September 1951, the company evacuated its technicians and closed down the oil installations. At the same time the British government reinforced its naval force in the Persian Gulf and imposed sanctions on Iranian oil.

Mossadegh travelled to New York to presenting Iran's case to the UN Security Council in an effort to overcome the financial difficulties occasioned by the oil export ban; but no financial aid was forthcoming. The British and their followers, along with the Shah's family, conspired against Mossadegh and his government, putting him under great pressure. At the end of 1951 he closed down all British consulates. To neutralise the Shah's plots, he asked for the premier's constitutional right to nominate the war minister. When the Shah refused to accept his nomination, Mossadegh resigned. In a public address he said, '... In the present situation, the struggle begun by the Iranian people cannot be brought to a victorious conclusion ... I will resign and permit someone who enjoys the confidence of the king to form a new government and implement His Majesty's policies.' Royalist and pro-British members of Parliament elected a new prime minister.

But they had miscalculated. People angry at Mossadegh's resignation poured into the streets. Demonstrations and strikes gripped Iranian cities, especially Tehran. At first the Shah called in the military, but after five days of bloodshed he capitulated and asked Mossadegh to form a new government. What became known as the 'Seyeh Tir (21st July 1952) Uprising' passed into our history as a rare instance of popular resistance against tyranny. Mossadegh appealed to the people to eschew revenge and safeguard unity and cooperation; the danger was that infighting would make people forget the goals of nationalisation of oil and independence, freedom and prosperity for the country. In the end, he said, our hopes for the re-establishment of a state equal to our glorious past would certainly be fulfilled. Although in the uprising almost 250 people were killed by the army, the whole city of Tehran – including the wealthy north – stood united. Encouraged, Mossadegh took steps to restrain the Shah and his British advocates, and at the same time instituted measures aimed at social progress. He transferred Reza Shah's lands back to state ownership, cut the palace's budget and allocated the savings to the health ministry; cut the military budget and announced that only defensive equipment would henceforth be purchased. Using emergency powers sanctioned by Parliament, he decreed land reform that established village councils and increased the peasants' share of the annual product. Through his tax reforms Mossadegh shifted the burden of taxation from those with the lowest incomes. To raise funds he printed government bonds which were widely sold; even schoolchildren bought them with their savings.

Mossadegh's reforms met with increasing resistance from Parliament, where most members were pro-British and pro-Shah. Eventually all members of Parliament who belonged to Jebh'e Melli resigned, reducing the numbers to below quorum. Mossadegh dissolved Parliament and called a referendum on the question of its abolition. A majority voted in favour, and Parliament was duly abolished. Mossadegh now felt strong enough to press ahead, no longer feeling obligated to the demands of the *mullahs*. Up to then many of the reforms were deadlocked because of opposition from religious groups, especially concerning the position of women, land issues, social freedoms and even the economy and nationalisation of big companies. But his new mandate brought him new enemies. Religious figures who had hitherto supported him suddenly changed direction and swung behind Mossadegh's opponents, calling him 'fascist'; a 'dictator'; 'worse than Hitler'.

As Mossadegh lost his traditional supporters, Royalist officers secretly planned a military coup. Commanders retired after Seyeh Tir formed a committee led by General Zahedi. They had contacts with the British Secret Service through some wealthy businessmen, the Rashidian brothers. At the same time the new American administration under President Eisenhower reversed policy towards Iran and supported Britain against Mossadegh. They sent Kermit Roosevelt of the CIA to Tehran to finance the military coup, and with his help Zahedi won over key officers in the army and created an alliance with the *mullahs*. On 19th August Zahedi, commanding thirty-five Sherman tanks, surrounded the premier's residence, looted and destroyed it and captured Mossadegh. A military tribunal was held at which the foreign minister and many others were sentenced to death and executed or imprisoned for life. The Shah, recognising how much Mossadegh was loved among the people, was clever enough not to have him executed.

How did Mossadegh allow the coup to succeed? Why did his supporters not come to his aid? Some say he'd predicted it, perhaps even knew it for certain. But his army reform had not been radical enough, and some argued that he should have pre-emptively had a few high-ranking officers killed. Perhaps he failed to realise that Iran was not ready for democracy, that his enemies would benefit from freedom more than the people themselves. Some observers went so far as to say that he should have armed the public on a par with the army, others that he didn't have a strong organisation to support him and neutralise his enemies.

Ammo Jan had the best answer. '*Ma ghabel Mossadegh naboodiam* [We were not worthy of Mossadegh]', he used to say. 'For a long time we had lived under a dictatorship, so we didn't know what to do with democracy and how to defend it. The main problem for the common people was bread, and here was Mossadegh talking about democracy and independence. One day all our streets were full of slogans like "Hail Mossadegh", and the next day it would be "Death to Mossadegh". Most people were ignorant and passive, and as a result were silent. There were some who capitalised on the situation by taking money to repaint these public slogans, changing "Death to the Shah" to read "Long live the Shah". Only they were so ignorant that they often changed just the first words so the slogan would read "Long live the Shah, the traitor" or "Long live the Shah, the criminal"!'

By now I felt I knew enough about Mossadegh's era, though I still had thousands of questions. As an Iranian I felt I could never forgive the Americans or the British for ruining the only chance we had for many years to come to have freedom and a democratic government. I hoped that some time in the future we would be strong enough at least to force them to apologise for their wrongdoing.

But this business would remain unfinished. For my generation, there was another war and another enemy to contend with.

In June 1967 the Arabs lost the Six Day War against Israel. Although I considered myself anti-Arab, I was nevertheless unhappy about their failure and angry with the Americans for helping Israel. Whatever the Arabs had done to us 1,000 years ago had nothing to do with what was happening then. Israel, it seemed to me, had no right to occupy their land force them to become refugees. Our Jewish friends told us, 'We don't approve of what the Israelis are doing there, but do you approve of what Hitler did to the Jews?' I had not known about the Nazis' crimes, which were truly shocking.

Nevertheless, I replied, 'Of course Hitler's actions are to be condemned. But do you really think that the fact that the Jews' ancestors lived in those lands gives them the right now to come from Europe and other countries after thousands of years and occupy territory that has been home to many generations of Arabs?'

'No,' they agreed, 'but what about those who were forced out of Europe during World War II and emigrated to Israel? Must they be wiped off the face of the earth?' I could see there were wrongs on both sides of the argument, but did not have the wherewithal to argue. Why were Jews and Arabs unable to live in harmony? This family, well-established in Iran for generations, eventually emigrated to Israel. They were forced out, I felt, not from hardship but from ideology; they were captives of history – but perhaps I was, too!

Our high school literature teacher, Mr Sobhhi, was an enlightened man who wanted to enhance our understanding of our heritage. From him I learned that national disasters may be self-inflicted. History is often described as written by the winners; too often the winners' crimes en route to victory are forgotten. He told us the story of the followers of Mazdak, a prophet who opposed the Sassanid caste system, believing in the equality of mankind. The reigning king, Ghobad, was brave enough to embrace change and ordered that the Mazdakians be protected, even converting himself. Zoroastrian priests were angered by this tolerance, and after Ghobad's death they persuaded his son Anoshirvan 'the Just' to rid the country of this sect. Anoshirvan ordered the Mazdakians buried head-down in the earth close to each other, so their legs would appear as a forest. Thus did this 'just' king crush a nonviolent movement advocating social progress. When, less than 100 years later, the Arabs attacked Iran preaching 'brotherhood, equality and social justice', there was no one to disagree. As a result, Iranians failed to resist them.

One of our textbooks was a book written by the present Shah called *Enghalab Safid* ('The White Revolution'). There were six articles in the 'revolution', ranging from land reform to the creation of a literacy corps, every year or month more were added. These articles were essentially meaningless. Nobody seemed to defend or believe in them. We were forced to line the streets and wave to the royal couple or their foreign guests whenever they passed, and often had to put in an extra day's schooling to make up for the time lost. My aunt, the head teacher of a school, found the whole thing particularly ironic in the case of girls, who had to attend these occasions even more diligently to show their appreciation for the emancipation of women which the Shah championed. 'What,' she wondered, 'have the men done with their "freedom" and "right to vote" that should make us so proud and happy?' Everybody with the slightest sense and understanding knew how meaningless elections were. The Shah personally approved all members of Parliament and predetermined the numbers of votes cast in any referendum or election before polling day. As a result it was the rare person who bothered to vote voluntarily. Savak spread rumours about the dire consequences of failing to get birth certificates stamped to indicate having voted. In this way they managed to intimidate some people into voting.

Although Mr Sobhhi tried to use the time we spent studying 'The White Revolution' in teaching us about social justice and even the forbidden subject of 'socialism', we found the whole area boring and hated having to memorise so much useless material.

Perhaps the only thing we learned from that subject was the precise opposite of what the writer intended. We learned that colonisation is not as simple as it used to be. Instead of reading newspaper headlines we would seek the truth in the small print. My stepbrother translated articles from the American and British media for the *Kyhan* newspaper. Most of the sources were not generally available but he used to satisfy my curiosity by passing on the news to me. Through him I learned about the Americans in Vietnam and students demonstrating against the war there. I heard about Fidel Castro and of Che Guevara, murdered by CIA agents and Bolivian soldiers. I could see the real face of John F. Kennedy, who we had thought might be our saviour. I heard about the assassination of Martin Luther King, Jr.

Gradually I formed a picture of America's role in our own and international affairs and began to understand why there was so much hatred towards the British for their crimes in Iran. From my 'secret' bookshop I obtained a book called *Miras-Khar Estamar* ('Inheritor of Colonisation') by Bahar. It explained how the British extended their empire and lost the American colonies; how Indonesia's Sukarno was murdered and Suharto became protector of American interests there; and about the illegal activities of American companies in South America. It helped me to understand what was behind the Shah's so-called 'White Revolution'. I realised that it is useless to hate invaders and colonisers of the past – Alexander the Great, the Arabs, the Mongols and even the British – while it was the US that ruled our country now, dictating orders to the king and Parliament.

# 5

# Turning Point

One day when I went to my mother's house, she did not greet me at the door. I found only my stepbrother Ghoolam in the house; my mother had asked him to take me to the cinema. I felt something was wrong. 'Where are Mother and Ammo Jan?' I asked. When he told me they were at my grandparents' house, I insisted on going there first. My mother's aunt, dressed in black, opened the door. She called my mother, who asked Ghoolam why we were there. Ghoolam replied, 'What could I do? You know Masoud: when he wants to do something, who can stop him?' My mother, half-smiling at this observation but at the same time holding back tears, took me aside and told me that my grandfather was dead. She had wanted to break the news to me more gently but now was forced to blurt it out. I went down to the basement, where Grandfather and I had often spent time together, and remembered his face, his kindness, his fine character. Apparently he had died quietly. 'Good people die easily and silently,' they say, 'without much pain'. For the next few days hundreds of people, including my father, came to express their condolences. It was the first time in many years that I had seen my parents together in the same room.

Although Mohsen, Ghoolam and I were not in the same class, and though our beliefs about history and nationalism had been badly shaken, we still saw each other and talked about our 'party'. We would hand our booklet to friends and ask if they wanted to join. About ten of our friends were attracted to our goals. One day, I found my father waiting for me at home, angry. He showed me a photograph I had taken for my photography class, of our dog wearing a copper mask of the Shah. One of my friends had printed it, and I had shown it to Ghoolam and Mohsen, but I believed nobody else had a copy. I kept everything of that sort at my mother's house, so I was dismayed. That was not all. He also held my cherished book about Mossadegh. My father asked for an explanation, telling me that one of the students had given these items to the school principal, who kindly handed them to my father instead of to the authorities. One of my 'friends' must have done this, someone who also must have had our booklet, as we didn't see it again. 'What do you think you are doing?' stormed my father. 'Do you really want to spend the rest of your life in the Savak prison – and perhaps take me with you?' His punishment was less harsh than I had expected, although he did burn the photograph and, to my great regret, the book too.

This incident was a turning point for me. Most of the things I had previously accepted as pure truth had turned to dust. Now there was a question mark over my friendships too. I was sure of Ghoolam and Mohsen, but who gave our booklet and the photograph to the principal? And where was our booklet? None of us knew. How naïve and childish we had been, not realising that what for us had been just a game meant something much more sinister in the real world. I thought I had a solution for every problem. Now I could see I knew nothing, not even anything about myself. I had to relearn, to become an adult.

After our third year of high school, we had to choose our subjects for further study. Mohsen and I wanted to be physicians. But two of my brothers were medical students, and my father said that was enough, that the country needed engineers as well. So I chose mathematics. Mohsen acted as my conscience and remained a close friend until I left Iran and we lost track of each other.

Near school there was a hawker, from whom I used to buy old books and pictures of former kings of Iran. Everybody thought he was a Savak agent sent to spy on the pupils. There was a common belief, put out by Savak itself, that one person in ten was a Savak agent in disguise. Thus everyone was paranoid and unwilling to readily trust anyone else. Even police officers were wary, and didn't go near anyone they weren't sure of. The hawker used to put pictures of the Shah and Reza Shah in front of his books and magazines, so no officer dared question him. Once he offered me some foreign magazines. 'Let's see them,' I said. They turned out to be issues of *Playboy*. Although the sale of such magazines was not forbidden, they were not sold openly, at least not to young boys like me. (Later, an Iranian version of *Playboy* was published and its office bombed.) I bought one or two *Playboys* and on Thursdays my new friend Shahram and I went with other friends to the cinema and afterwards to my mother's house, where we would look at my magazines, talk and play cards.

I still liked to follow the news. Normally there was a lot of anti-Russian and anti-communist press. I was not very fond of the Russians for their opposition to Mossadegh, their demand for Iranian oil and their recently improved relationship with the Shah. Still, if one had to choose between bad and worse, the Russians had the edge. They were socialists, we thought, and at least they were good for their own people. In general, we were glad to hear of their victories over the Americans. We welcomed news of a pro-Soviet or socialist coup or revolution and by the same token were saddened by news of any pro-American action anywhere.

Once, my father was speaking with my aunt's husband about his trip to the Soviet Union following the Russian Revolution. He told of a poor Russian farmer whose crop the Red Army wanted to expropriate. Rather than give it up he burned it, but paid the ultimate price and was shot. Hearing this, I couldn't stop myself from blurting out, 'Whatever they have done in the USSR, at least they don't have the corruption that we have here. There are not so many rich thieves on one hand and so many starving and homeless people on the other.'

My father tried to rein in his anger in front of our guest. 'So you say whoever is rich is a thief?' he asked.

'Yes', I replied. 'Otherwise how could anyone become rich in this poor country?'

'So', he continued, 'you say I am a thief as well?'

'Well, I don't say you have actually stolen anything, but buying land, doing nothing with it and then selling it shortly afterwards for a big profit is a kind of theft.'

Now my father let loose. Turning to our guests, he said, 'Listen to him! He calls me a thief!' He turned to me. 'What do you know? Do you think I didn't want to produce something, instead of buying and selling land? I tried to establish a factory to make construction materials, but was forced to sell the land because Reza Shah wanted to build a railway and needed the adjacent land. I tried to establish a paper factory with the help of a Swedish friend. Just before starting up production, we found a poor soul in the woods, crushed to death by our machine. It was a sign from foreigners against our intentions. Recently we bought land for farming fish but were told we had to give half our shares to Princess Ashraf or we might find all our fish dead. What do you think I could do? Yes, we sold the land after a few months at a profit equivalent to what we would have earned after years of hard work. But I did that in order to have some chance of carrying on!' It was the end of the discussion.

At about the same time I became conscious that people in the Soviet Bloc countries were unhappy with their governments. I read about the Soviet invasions first of Hungary and then Czechoslovakia. It was my belief that it is better to live in hell freely than to live in heaven in chains. While socialism might promise a better life, it was a detestable system where people were not free to choose their own destiny.

I loved my mother very much, so any news about her health had a great effect on me. When I heard she had a kidney problem which might mean the loss of one or both kidneys, I was willing to donate one of mine. She was touched by my offer but asked how an operation was possible when she had no money. I think this was the first time she let me know about their deteriorating finances. Every night for a week I cried myself to sleep with worry. Fortunately it soon became clear that she had a kidney stone, easily curable. Facing the prospect of living without her as my protector, I was still too young to understand the way in which my father showed his love and care for us.

Not long afterwards my sister Farzaneh called me urgently and asked me to come and see Mother, who had almost lost a finger in an electric fan. Even then, Mother was, typically, trying to laugh to hide her pain. We rushed her to hospital, where the staff demanded money before treating her. We were outraged, but there was no alternative but to accept their conditions. I went back to the house and got money. The incident alarmed us. What would have happened if we had had no money? What would poor people do in this sort of situation?

One Thursday Ammo Jan surprised me by being at home when I arrived at my mother's house. It turned out the Shah had compulsorily retired all senior naval officers and replaced them from lower ranks. A few days earlier the media had carried the story that the Shah had saved Farsi, an island belonging to Iran in the middle of the Persian Gulf which the Arabs were threatening to overrun. It seemed the island itself didn't have any value for the Shah, so some navy personnel had been stranded there without food or drink for several days. A British oil tanker had rescued them. One of the British newspapers ran an article asking, 'How can the Shah claim Bahrain when he cannot even look after his own men on a tiny island?' The Shah's action against the officers was his way of venting anger. Poor Ammo Jan, though only about fifty years old, was never again able to find suitable work; this episode marked the beginning of his decline into depression.

I didn't know much about the outside world, but like many Iranians I had a yardstick for judging international events. Any friend of the Shah was our enemy and vice versa. Everything our media portrayed as good was in fact bad, and vice versa; it brought us news about the death of Nasser in Egypt; the overthrow of Allende's government in Chile; the arrest of Papadopoulos by the Greek colonels and American involvement in Vietnam; and, indeed, of student demonstrations in the US and Europe, which were echoed in our universities. The Shah and Savak were worried about these demonstrations and strikes and tried to suppress them as quickly as they occurred, as well as crush embryonic dissent in high schools.

In one of those demonstrations two of my brothers, who were medical students in Pahlavi University in Shiraz, were arrested. One of them, Saeid, was around two metres tall, so was clearly visible in Savak's photographs of the demonstrators. They charged him with being a ringleader, claiming that he always stood on a chair and directed the others. They arrested my other brother as well, who was not interested in politics at all. Saeid was kept naked in an empty room for several days in cold weather, without proper food or drink. Worst of all, they prevented him from sleeping: whenever he tried to sleep they poured a bucket of cold water over him. My brother was lucky, as one of our relatives – a high-ranking member of Savak dealing with American and European expatriates – was able to vouch for him and prove that he had been falsely accused on account of his height.

One day as we left school we came face to face with armed soldiers and officers standing at the entrance. They were rough and brutal-looking. We were ordered to leave the school immediately. I don't know who started it but soon we were all are hooting at them. Their commander became very angry and ordered his soldiers to enter the schoolyard and attack us. Students who tried to exit had to pass through a narrow opening; as a result some fell and were trampled upon. One fat pupil who could not run quickly fell to the ground, where the soldiers started beating him. We never saw him again; I later heard from a friend that they had killed him. As soon as we could get out we ran for our lives, without looking behind us. Afterwards I discovered the reason for this commotion. The Shah had increased bus fares – as always, without realising the consequences – and the increases had taken effect immediately. Demonstrations in the universities were joined by ordinary people, whose interests were at stake, and spread to schools and streets. As a result, the Shah had to reverse his decision. It was a victory for the people, especially for students.

By the end of the 1960s Iranian society was changing fast. Lots of American serials and films were shown on television. (Curiously, my father didn't prevent us from watching them.) They became part of our culture. We spoke about them in school, and once I even heard my mother's wet nurse vowing seven *rials* to the saint Shah Abdul Azim that Rodney and Alison in *Peyton Place* would get married. People acted and talked like Americans, copied American architecture and interior design and followed American fashions. Shahram took me to a new boutique called 'Number One', where I bought clothes that were completely different from anything I had worn before: tight, light blue, bell-bottomed trousers, a close-fitting shirt and a long, waisted coat. I bought shoes in Western-style boutiques too and let my hair grow longer. All the young people did the same – that is, in the north of the city. The boundary between south and north was sharper than ever. If I walked towards the south wearing my 'Number One' outfit, everybody would look at me strangely and make remarks about me under their breath.

One day my friend Farokh asked me, 'Do you want to become a man?' He took me to a district in the south of Tehran called Shaher No ('New City'). All prostitutes had to operate within the walls of this so-called city. Two policemen guarded the entrance, stopping anybody under age from entering: we had to dress older than we were. The fifteen-minute taxi ride showed me scenes I had never seen or even imagined. People walked impassively by a dead man lying in the street; children sold hashish and opium; outside old, derelict houses, men in rags, women clad in *chadors* and barefoot children bought and sold every kind of object. The policemen at the gate allowed us into the city, which consisted of two or three parallel dead-end alleys. Farokh knew a house with younger women. To see these poor women, aged from about fifteen to forty, depressed me. The thought of having sex with any of them made me sick. I told Farokh I wasn't going to 'become a man' this time. I just waited for him to finish his business so that we could get out of there as quickly as possible. Somehow I knew then that I could never accept sex without love.

My personal appearance opened up a new area of disagreement with my father, who did not approve of the colour of my clothes or the length of my hair. I didn't want to antagonise him, but at the same time I wasn't about to be seen as old-fashioned by my friends. I found a way around this problem. Each morning I brushed my hair hard, pushing it behind my ears, and put on clothes my father approved of. I kept my fashionable clothes in the servants' room by the front door. After saying goodbye to my father, I would go to their room, change my clothes and rebrush my hair. On my return from school I would do the reverse before going to greet my father. This worked well until one occasion, when I rang the doorbell and my father himself opened the door. 'Where have you been and why do you look like this?' he demanded.

I felt this was a turning point, so before he could say anything else, I said, 'I have just come to say goodbye!'

He was taken aback. 'Where are you going?' he asked.

I replied, 'Where I can be free, or at least have the freedom to wear what I like.'

'And where is that?'

'I don't know,' I answered feebly. 'Perhaps my mother's house.'

'Your mother's house?' he repeated. 'Doesn't she or her husband feel ashamed to see you like this? Doesn't she ask you to cut your hair?'

'No', I said, 'but if she did I would certainly cut it.'

'Oh!' he exclaimed. 'Is that a fact? So, if she asks, you will cut your hair, and if I ask, you grow it even more?'

'Yes', I said defiantly, 'because if she asks me for anything, she has a reason for it and persuades me that it is in my interests. But you ask because you want me to act according to your tastes. If all of us acted according to the tastes of our parents, we would still be wearing animal skins and living in caves!'

My father was clearly hurt by this conversation and indicated that I should say no more and go to my room. For some time afterwards we didn't speak to each other. I stopped sharing meals in the house. I even started buying oil separately for my heater. For lunch I would go to my mother's house, and for dinner I would take something from there and eat it in my room. After a while my brother and his wife visited us. They came to my room and said my father had been saddened that I would obey Mother and not him, but that he was old and couldn't really help treating me like a child. He was sorry, too, but couldn't be expected to admit it. 'Come downstairs, kiss him and forget about everything,' they said. I did so, and after that it was an unwritten law that we didn't discuss our differences. He pretended not to notice my appearance, and I wore what I wanted.

Despite daily anti-Arab (and in particular, anti-Iraqi) stories in the media, we were now inclined to be pro-Arab – more because of the Shah's propaganda against them than because of our common religion: any enemy of the Shah had to be our friend. Although no Arab country and few Muslim countries had diplomatic or cultural relations with Israel, Israel had an economic-interests section in Tehran and our sportsmen regularly competed with theirs. In April 1970, as part of an Asian football tournament, there was a match between Israel and Iran in Tehran which Iran won 2–1. People interpreted this victory as a victory by Muslims over Israelis and, later, over the Shah. Everybody was in the streets except the army and police, so no one could stop us giving free voice to our jubilation, shouting slogans against Israel and the Shah and saying things that for a long time had stuck in our throats. We celebrated until dawn, relishing our one night of freedom.

At the beginning of the school year, we heard that a few of our students had been arrested because of long hair and 'improper' dress. We were shocked. We knew that we were not politically free, but at least we had enjoyed personal freedom. Now it looked as if even that was under threat. Apparently the chief of Tehran police, acting on the Shah's orders, had raided some rich hippies' houses. Going a step beyond the Shah's wishes, he ordered the arrest of any boy with long hair. Obviously he believed he would earn praise for his action. Unfortunately the Shah did not appreciate initiative on the part of his officers; he wanted obedient automatons who would not think; that privilege was for the Shah alone. For his pains, the chief of police was sacked.

On 8th February 1971, all the front pages were covered with news of the defeat by the Shah and Savak of 'Marxists' and 'terrorists'. Thirteen young men armed with rifles, machine guns and hand grenades had attacked the gendarmerie post in the village of Siakal on the edge of the Caspian forests and were killed. This attack, later to become famous as the 'Siakal Incident', sparked eight years of intense guerrilla activity. Although the affair was a military fiasco, the Feda'ian, the group born after this incident, took it as a great propaganda victory that a small band of determined men could frighten the whole Pahlavi regime. Unsuprisingly, the day of the incident went down in Iranian history as the birthday of the guerrilla movement. As if to confirm the importance of the Siakal Incident, the Shah followed up the executions with a series of dramatic measures. He launched a major propaganda war against the guerrillas, accusing them of being atheists, agents of the illegal communist Tudeh party and tools of the PLO and Arab imperialists. He rounded up fifty-one left-wing intellectuals in Tehran, none of whom had Feda'ian connections; declared a week's unscheduled holiday for universities in Tehran; and outlawed as an international conspiracy the Confederation of Iranian Students, based in Europe and North America. He also increased government salaries, decreed the current year in honour of civil servants, raised the minimum wage and declared that 1st May would be celebrated throughout Iran as Workers' Day.

The final year of high school passed very quickly. I was very depressed about having to say goodbye to my friends, who were scattering to destinations far and wide. I wanted to get the exams over with as soon as possible, so I did little more than the bare minimum and then left. Accordingly I got decent but not brilliant grades.

School may have been over but I was not sure about what I wanted to do. I knew my father could not decide for me. Not that he didn't want to, but there was a new system of examinations for admission to universities, including private ones. The results would determine which university a student could go to and which subjects he or she could study.

As I was afraid I would not pass that examination, Ammo Jan suggested that I take the Navy entrance examination as well. They would send us to the US for further education and pay the highest salaries from the start. I said, 'You know what I think about the military! How can I join up?'

'Don't be a fool,' he replied. 'Who says you have to join the Army? After you've done your training in America or Italy or Britain, you can leave the military and stay there, like my son and his cousin. I will be your guarantor.' My brother in-law, who was a general in the Air Force, suggested about the same time that I join that service. When I went for interview, I was amused to see so many Americans there and signs on doors restricting entry to Americans. I passed both examinations, so at least I knew that I would not end up without a job or a future like hundreds of thousands of high school graduates.

It was the beginning of the summer. My good friend Farzad and I were preparing for the university entrance examination by revising all the subjects we had studied over the previous three years. It was hot, and we studied day and night in my mother's house. One day my mother said, 'Enough is enough. If you study any more, you will go mad and I'll have to take you to Amin'ol Dolleh [the hospital for the insane].' She asked Farzad and me to accompany her to see my aunt. Farzad declined. 'Maybe we should spend some time with our families for a change,' he suggested, 'and forget about studying. Whenever I see you I remember chemistry formulae and I probably make you think of the laws of physics.' I went with my mother. Some of my aunt's neighbours were visiting as well. My aunt's husband said, 'There is no need for you to stay with your mother and ruin our game of cards by winning it. You should go to the living room and be with the other young people.' There I was introduced to the neighbour's sister Anna and her cousin. The moment I saw Anna I felt something was wrong. Later on I discovered what the trouble was. I was in love.

# 6

# Dicing with Destiny

*Some consequence, yet hanging in the stars,*
*shall bitterly begin his fearful date with this night's revels;*
*and expire the term of a despised life, clos'd in my breast,*
*by some vile forfeit of untimely death:*
*But He that hath the steerage of my course direct my sail!*
–William Shakespeare, *Romeo and Juliet*

Franco Zeffirelli's *Romeo and Juliet* was in the cinemas. I think I saw it eleven times, with my sister Farzaneh and with friends, and eventually several more times with Anna. I loved films; my true ambition was to be a director of historical or romantic films. For me, life itself was a kind of film, directed by God or nature, with human beings playing their roles in stories written before birth. Though the plot is fixed, the details are in the hands of the players: it is their talent and will that determine the outcome, good or bad. I never minded seeing the suffering of characters as long as the story had a happy ending. Somehow this was the formula I wanted for my own life.

I had first seen Anna at the end of the pretty Tehran spring. She was a year younger and the most beautiful girl I had ever seen or ever would see. Her long hair was dark brown and waved like the sea. She wore a short red skirt and a shirt with red and white stripes. Everything about her appealed to me, but most of all her free spirit, lovely smile and quiet sincerity. Although I was in the middle of preparing for the most important examination of my life, I invited her and her family to our orchard in Karaj the following day. Luckily my father was away and, peopled by Anna's family and my mother's, the orchard ceased to be a place of torture as it was when my father was there, and instead became a paradise. Life is often like this: we think happiness lies in changing our outside surroundings, whereas the only thing that needs changing is what goes on in our hearts and minds.

Before lunch we decided to climb the mountain behind the orchard. Anna's shoes were not right for climbing, so during our descent she went more slowly than the others. I naturally hung back with her. Forthright as ever, I told her I loved her. Strangely, she was not surprised and replied that she loved me too. She asked to be sure to pass my examination or we would have problems with her family, especially her mother. That day I was flying. Suddenly the sky was bluer, the grass greener and the fruits in the orchard more delicious than ever. From then on I could not stop thinking about Anna, yet at the same time worried more about the exam result that could bless or ruin my future with her.

After the exam I stayed with my mother for a month, during which I was with Anna most of the time, walking and talking in the streets of Tehran under a hot summer sun or weeping as we watched *Romeo and Juliet* and *Love Story*. When I was not with Anna I talked of nothing else – to my mother and Farzaneh, if my friends were tired of listening.

Eventually the results of the university entrance exams were announced. Out of any ten students only one would be accepted. I was thrilled to see my name among the latter. I was admitted to the science department of the National University of Iran, and my friend Farzad to the Aryamehr (Industrial) University, perhaps the best in the country. For the next month or two I had to attend some preliminary courses, but my mind, as always, was on Anna. I thought if I could persuade my father to let me to rent a room close to the university, I would be free to see her whenever I wished, and there would be no need to tell him about her. Of course he didn't agree, but fate had something else in store.

On Friday 2nd August 1971, Anna and I decided to ask my
mother to approach Anna's family for approval of our union. My
mother and Anna's mother were at my aunt's house, so we left
them alone to talk and went to Anna's sister's house across the
street. After a few hours we decided to return to hear the good
news we hoped would be waiting for us. The road was unlit and
always busy, especially on Fridays. As we crossed, a car ran into me.
I don't know how long I was unconscious, but when I came to I was
in the middle of the road with many people around me. My first
thought was, 'is Anna all right?' I looked around and saw her lying
in the road. I tried to go over to her but I couldn't move. Soon the
pain made me lose consciousness again. The next time I opened my
eyes we were at the local clinic. Anna was awake. She looked at me
and asked how I was, but I wanted first to know how she was. The
truth was that nobody, not even the doctors, knew how we were.
They were waiting to move us to a hospital, and in the meantime
were injecting us with morphine to kill the pain and make us sleep.
The next time I woke up I was in the same room, but found to my
horror that Anna wasn't there. My mother told me she had been
moved to the hospital, which had agreed to take her because her
brother-in-law was a physician. To take me into the same hospital
they were asking 10,000 *toman* in cash. My mother didn't have that
kind of money, and my father was not in Tehran; they called him,
and after a day or two he returned to the city and joined us.
Eventually they moved me to the hospital but they still would not
give me a bed. My father had never had one of his cheques refused,
and was annoyed that the hospital demanded cash. It took another
few hours before he could get the cash and return to the hospital.
During that time I was left lying in the entrance with no treatment
for the pain.

I had four fractures in my right leg and arm, a broken upper
arm and a few broken ribs. When I regained consciousness after
surgery I found my entire body except for my left leg and hand in
plaster. My first question was about Anna. My mother told me she
was fine and was in the next room. My father was silent, waiting to
talk to me. He asked whether I was in a lot of pain. I thanked him
and apologised for all the trouble I had caused. But how was Anna?
I knew he was the only one who would tell me the truth. She had
had a small blood clot in the brain, he said, which had been
successfully removed, but she was still in a coma. Both of her legs

had been broken and had had to have platinum pins put in. Now that I knew the facts, I had to know the prognosis, so I asked to see Anna's mother. I felt her face would tell me how bad things were. When she appeared at my bedside, she recited the facts as my father had done. I asked if my mother had talked to her of our proposed marriage. 'Don't think about these things now,' she said. 'Nobody knows what is going to happen. It is possible she may be paralysed or ...'

I interrupted her. 'This is why I am asking you now. I want to let you know that nothing can change my love for her.'

'Even if she is paralysed?'

'Nothing,' I repeated. She laughed and said,

'*Ansha'Alleh* [May God will it].'

The next day I heard that Anna was conscious, and insisted on seeing her immediately. After a long battle with everyone, I succeeded in getting my bed wheeled into her room so that I could visit her. She was lying on her bed like an angel, dressed in white with her head swathed in a white bandage. She smiled when she saw me, and asked, 'How are you?'

'I am the happiest and luckiest man on earth, lying in the room next door, waiting to marry you as soon as possible.'

Throughout our stay my mother and hers were constantly with us. Then one day Anna's mother didn't come to see me. My mother said she had gone home to attend to something. The same thing happened the next day. I sensed something was wrong, but nobody would tell me what. When I asked to see Anna again I was told the nurse would not allow it. This only heightened my frustration and anxiety. So, I waited until I was alone and then tried to make my own way to her room. But as soon as I raised my leg I fell to the floor and lost consciousness. When I woke up I discovered I had had another operation.

Seeing me still mad with worry, my mother had no alternative but to tell me the truth. There had been some kind of disagreement between Anna's family and my father, and they had decided to break off our engagement. At the same time, a relative of Anna's had proposed to her and her family had accepted. In addition, her grandmother believed that the road accident was a bad omen for our marriage. Out of obedience to her mother, Anna had bowed to the decision.

I was stunned. Not until my friend Farzad repeated the whole story to me did I begin to believe it.

I was transferred to another ward, perhaps in the hope that I would forget Anna. My relatives and friends continued to visit regularly, hers more rarely but when they did they were like messengers from Paradise. My poor mother was distressed about my condition and state of mind. She tried to get me to eat special foods, which she cooked every day – when, I don't know, as she was with me all the time. Unable to sleep or eat and unwilling to smile, I often reduced her to tears. She kept telling me that I had to eat to get well. Only then might I be able to change the situation.

With my father I was polite, but he knew that I seethed with anger towards him. When the time came for me to be discharged, I chose to go to my mother's house. I never found out how culpable he had been in my reversal of fortune, and he was not one to explain himself. But somehow I felt he understood love and respected those who were in love. Mother and Ammo Jan did everything to please me. They made a room for me in their living and dining rooms, as I was still encased in plaster and unable to sit or stand. I was dependent on others for everything.

My grandmother came to sit with me every morning. She was very intelligent, and I could talk to her about everything. She told me about the preparations for ceremonies to mark twenty-five centuries of the monarchy in Iran. Thousands of triumphal arches decorated with lights and flowers graced the streets of Tehran. Shopkeepers had been forced to paint their shops and install lighting on the facades, to display flags and of course pictures of the Shah and Queen and to contribute to the repair of the pavements outside their premises. Some people were required to put lights and flags on their houses. The real extravagance was visible in Shiraz and Persepolis, where food was being imported from France and elsewhere for banquets for visiting royalty. Everyone knew that people in the south were going hungry, and that this celebration was not for them but for the enjoyment of the Shah and his guests. All through the summer and autumn of 1971 the talk was of the celebrations. The Mojahedin, a resistance group, tried but failed to disrupt the proceedings; most were arrested and imprisoned. Students were at the forefront of strikes called to protest the celebrations.

In addition to conversations with my grandmother, Farzad

called on me every day, and we often talked late into the night. Another regular visitor was my stepsister's husband, Hassan. He had worked his way up from nothing to own a textile factory, but was anxious to dispose of it. The Shah had ruled that part-ownership of a factory had to be given to full-time workers. Owners were therefore reluctant to employ full-time staff, who would ultimately take over. The result was that both sides lost: workers could not find secure full-time employment and employers had no incentive to train workers and could not rely on those they had. If the Shah owned a factory, workers wouldn't dare to claim anything, but in a small business workers' rights were paramount. Listening to Hassan, I could see how the 'White Revolution' had killed the national bourgeoisie as well as agriculture. The Shah worshipped at the altar of capitalism, but even that could be sacrificed easily when his interests were at stake.

We watched the Shah's festival on television. It was obviously meant to demonstrate his wealth and power to the world. The people counted for nothing in his eyes; their only role was obedience. He and his wife became the butt of many resentful jokes. When the Shah stood by the shrine to Cyrus (the first king of Iran) and said, 'Sleep, Cyrus, as we are awake,' the satirists mocked him with, 'Sleep, Cyrus, while we destroy everything you built' or 'Sleep, Cyrus, so that we can sleep too'. Another joke had the Shah and Queen Farah flying from Tehran to Shiraz. The Shah suggested Farah throw 100 *toman* from the plane to make somebody happy. Farah said, 'Why not throw out two fifty-*toman* notes and make two people happy?'

The pilot turned round and said, 'Why not throw yourselves out and make twenty million people happy?'

More than anything else, I wanted to write, but my right hand was out of use. One day Farzad brought me a pen and a 200-page notepad and suggested I try writing with my left hand. I started with poems and moved on to short stories. My first was a simple piece called 'Aghaz and Farnaz', about love turning to hate.

*When Farnaz leaves Aghaz for a richer man, Aghaz commits suicide; but before dying he asks the stars to fulfil a wish. The wish is that Farnaz should suffer at the hands of the one she loves most, so that she will learn what love really means. When Aghaz dies his soul transmigrates into the body of Farnaz's child. One night*

*Farnaz's son, in a fit of insane anger, entes her room while she*
*sleeps and stabs her in the eyes with a fork.*

Although the story had echoes of my relationship with Anna, the horrific ending did not reflect my feelings for her: the next day I noticed that Anna's photograph had been removed from a table next to my bed. I shouted at my mother, for the first and last time in my life, and then apologised. We both cried, and she put the photograph back in place. I had not been able to get out of bed for almost two months.

I expressed my physical and mental suffering in my next story, 'And He Became God'.

*A man loses his senses one by one. First he finds he cannot move. He is young and wants to walk and run in the rain among the fallen yellow leaves of autumn, but he can't. Then he loses his sight. He wants to see the beauty of his loved one, the twilight and the red sky at dusk, but he can't. Eventually he can no longer hear, neither the music of the rain or the song of nightingales. He turns his unseeing eyes to the sky and cries out, 'God, oh God, why? You may as well give me a heart of stone – unloving, unloved, which cannot feel the difference between the soft touch of the beloved and the sharp claws of a witch – as leave me with a heart that cannot distinguish between the sweet song of a nightingale and the screech of an owl.' With that his pain vanishes and all his senses return, but his heart has turned to stone and the joy has vanished along with the pain. Although he can walk and talk again, there is no difference for him between mercy and compassion, misery and enjoyment, laughter and tears. He stands still and says, 'Now I have become God'.*

I had no desire to be God; but neither could I stand still and do nothing.

One of my friends was Sohila, a very beautiful girl from a rich family. As children we had spent a lot of time together, but we later lost touch until 1970, when we were both at the same university and resumed our friendship. As I had no secrets from my friends I'd told her about Anna from the beginning. One day I asked if she would do something for me. 'Of course,' she said. 'Anything.' I asked her to find Anna's new address, buy a present for her birthday and take it to her with a card from me. Next time Sohila came to see me, she brought a letter from Anna thanking me for the present but asking me to forget her. She wrote, 'It was our destiny not to be together.'

I wish you the best of luck and success. I hope one day you will find someone to love and be happy.' Sohila was very upset on my behalf.

I was beginning to hate the word 'destiny'. I was determined not to be ruled by it.

When they took the plaster off my body and left it only on my leg, I decided to resume going to university. My friend Farokh was prepared to drive us in every day, and Ammo Jan kindly lent us his car. After three months the plaster cast on my leg came off too, and with Farzad's help I started learning how to walk again. Now I was ready to do something to overcome 'destiny'.

I was friendly with Anna's older sister Manna, and through Sohila I contacted her. We arranged that I would help her with her schoolwork, and soon we were seeing each other most days of the week. She said Anna had forgotten me completely and wanted to marry the relative who had proposed to her. In those days a man's profession was his most important asset if he wanted to marry, and I was up against one who had nearly qualified as an engineer, while I was a first-year student. Our family backgrounds were similar but he had the advantage of being related to Anna, which was considered an advantage.

Apparently Anna was surprised that the lovely Sohila was only my mouthpiece, and wondered why I would not consider marrying her instead. 'Sohila is my friend,' I told Manna. 'I have asked her to relay my message to Anna, to tell her that love is not something that can be measured by beauty, wealth or education. You can't buy it or sell it. You can't exchange it. Love has a separate life; it is born, lives and grows. Sometimes it gets old and dies. But just as human beings are not for sale or exchange, neither is love.' The strength and sincerity of my feelings must have impressed Manna, for she invited me to the house one day – ostensibly to help her prepare for an exam. For the whole of that day, my heart hammered in my chest. At the house, Anna's mother reacted as though nothing had happened since I last visited. Anna was surprised but did her best not to show any feelings for me. After a few hours, which are a blank in my memory, Manna suggested I ask Anna out. I could see no point in doing so, as it seemed clear that her love for me had died. Perhaps she was in love with her fiancé or even lost the capacity to love at all. Manna ignored my objections and seized the initiative. Loudly, in front of everyone, she said she was tired of studying and asked if we could go to a movie. When I nodded she turned to Anna and asked her the same question. Before I knew it, I was sitting in the cinema next to Anna. Of the film, I took nothing in. I wanted to take Anna's hand, but my hands were as cold as the dead. Eventually I summoned up courage to take her hands, and kissed them. She didn't withdraw, but she still betrayed no emotion. We went to a restaurant afterwards, and I told her during dinner how much I loved her and again asked her to marry me. She said she needed her mother's permission to do anything, that I should ask her. I thought, 'so be it!'. The next day I had an appointment with Anna's mother. She said a proposal had to come from my father, not from my mother or me. Also, as her other son-in-law was a doctor, I would have to have a PhD. Moreover, we would have to wait until Anna finished high school.

This posed quite a dilemma. I hadn't had any contact with my father for several months. How was I supposed to ask him something like that out of the blue? His house was his kingdom, so I knew I had to see him on neutral territory. I asked if could talk to him privately. 'Of course', he agreed, 'I shall ask everyone to leave us alone in the room.'

'No', I said, 'please, let us meet in the street. This is our last chance for us to talk together as father and son.'

He was so surprised that he forgot to demur. Perhaps he was afraid of losing me again. Perhaps he loved me and wanted our former relationship reinstated. Perhaps he recognised my superior willpower, and the love that was its source, and felt that surrender was in order. When we met near Anna's home he had tears in his eyes, and I too had to wipe away mine as I hugged and kissed him. I told him what I wanted from him and he agreed readily. As soon as Anna's mother could see us, we went to their house. My father was gentle, calm and charming. He proposed on my behalf and they accepted. Now that I was engaged to Anna, my misery was ended, but I had other worries. I was way behind in my studies and had to think about earning enough money to marry Anna.

I never found out what happened to the poor man who had hoped to marry Anna. I heard a rumour a few years later that he'd died in an accident.

# 7

# Learning, Licences and LSD

The National University of Iran is beautifully located in the north of Tehran, close to the village of Evin (site of the infamous Evin Prison). On a small hill on campus was a single tomb said to be that of a *seyed* (a descendant of the Prophet). Looking to the left from the top one could see Evin,with its higgledy-piggledy houses and narrow alleys and the sad façade of the prison. To the right one could see Tehran's most fashionable and expensive residential areas. It was clear that the right existed at the expense of the left.

Unlike students at other Iranian universities, those at the National University were not very active politically. Hence, when students at Tehran University or the Industrial University were on strike and many other universities were closed, ours stayed open and operated as usual. It was modern, with beautiful buildings, tall trees and wide lawns. After lunch in the refectory, which was unbelievably cheap, we often used to lie on the grass in the sun for hours until the next lecture. Relations between students and lecturers were as informal as in European and American universities. On the other hand, like the other universities it had guards, introduced a few years earlier at the start of student strikes.

Students throughout the country considered themselves the vanguard of the same poor class of people from whom the guards were drawn, and the mutual hatred between the two groups awaited an opportunity to manifest itself physically. Our university was an exception; students and guards occasionally even exchanged polite smiles. This may have been because the guard commander was a mild man. All that was soon to change when confrontations between students and guards led to beatings. Savak had a policy of changing university guards every few months to avoid fraternisation.

At Norowz Anna and I went for a trip to Kermanshah in the west of Iran. It was our first trip on our own and, having little money, we travelled mostly by bus or hitchhiking. Compared with Tehran Kermanshah was a village, with low-rise buildings, small shops displaying cheap, old-fashioned goods and hardly any traffic. Most of the women wore *chadors* or scarves and the men wore either Kurdish dress or worn, long-outdated suits and hats. It was my grandmother's city, and somehow I felt at home there. I saw many people with blond hair and blue eyes, just as the ancient Greek historian Xenophon had described Iranians. The inhabitants seemed poorer than in Tehran but happier, perhaps because there were fewer class divisions or threats to their traditional way of life. From Kermanshah, with its mild spring weather, we went to Ghasr Shirin, where it was as hot as a Tehran summer. Meanwhile, only fifty kilometres away in Hamedan, it was snowing.

There we found that many people earned a living by smuggling goods into the country and selling them at inflated prices. At that time there were verbal clashes between the Iranian and Iraqi governments, but for the people living along the border on both sides this was irrelevant as they were both visually and culturally indistinguishable.

Finding my own happiness with Anna somehow intensified my awareness of other people's misery and of the uncertainty and lack of freedom hidden underneath the beautiful trappings of the Shah's regime. Writing stories provided a refuge. Among the stories I wrote during this time was 'Spider's Web':

*A butterfly flies among the flowers and trees in springtime. Everything looks perfect to her, until suddenly she falls into a spider's web. Now, though she can still see the sunlit flowers, it all looks different as she is not free to fly and she must await her destiny, which is to be eaten by an ugly spider.*

Ammo Jan and my mother were in an ever-worsening financial situation. Inflation rose daily, and they were not able to live on their income. Having sold all the carpets in the house, my mother was now reduced to selling the house itself and moving into a rented flat. I wished I could help. I had received insurance money for the accident, but it was not enough to contribute towards her expenses. More keenly than ever, I felt the hardship that comes with being 'poor' in a newly materialistic society. I expressed my feelings in a story called 'Goldsmith'.

*A nugget of gold complains to Goldsmith that he has lost his soul, the stone from which he was mined. He was happy living with his soul, and begs Goldsmith to reunite him with the stone, in return for granting one wish. Goldsmith's wish is to live in a 'city of beauties', where people are judged by their looks: ugliness is a crime, punishable by banishment or imprisonment in the handsome king's dungeon. Goldsmith soon comes to see the real ugliness beneath the superficial beauty. Gold grants him one more wish, and he wishes that the king become as ugly as his soul. As soon as his subjects see how hideous the king has become, they revolt and send him to his own dungeon.*

By summer of 1972, I had no choice but to take a job. I didn't want to ask my father for money, never having asked him for a penny; my pride wouldn't permit me to start now. A cousin who owned an engineering company offered me a job drawing construction plans. For 600 *toman* per month, I worked every day after university until ten in the evening and all day Thursday. Having no car, I rarely got home before midnight.

Nevertheless, this meant I could ask Anna to marry me, and we could start living together. According to Islamic law, the consent of the man and the woman is all that is required for them to contract a marriage; the services of a *mullah* can be dispensed with. So we married ourselves by reading the appropriate sentences from the Qur'an. We found a single room in a house near Anna's family home. To use the toilet we had to pass the landlady's room, which we found embarrassing and tried to avoid as much as possible. But we were happy being together and independent.

At work I made friends and learned a lot by watching the

engineers, notably how to design central heating systems. From
being a draughtsman I became a designer, with a corresponding
rise in salary to 900 *toman* a month. But when our landlady's
husband returned from a trip, we were evicted and had to find
another place to live. The new flat had two rooms plus a small
kitchen and toilet, neither of which, unfortunately, had a ceiling or
hot water. The rent was 600 *toman*, so every month we were left
with only 300 *toman* for other expenses. We had nothing. My
grandmother bought us a carpet, which we put in the room we
dignified with the name 'living room'; I found four car tires, which
we painted, lined with cushions Anna made and used as chairs. A
lorry tire painted and topped with a sheet of glass became our
dining table.

Being fond of Shakespeare's plays, I was loath to miss any of the
film versions. Grigori Konzintsev's *King Lear* had a strong effect on
me. The night I saw it, I stayed up and wrote a story until morning,
putting down the last lines just as dawn broke. It was in verse and
called 'Azad Shah' ('Free King').

*A hundred barefoot old men and women leave their town, each*
*carrying the best part of the body or soul of a human being to the*
*desert in order to construct the perfect human being who will*
*become their king. In turn, his breath in their bodies will transform*
*them into beautiful, strong and loyal soldiers, and together they*
*will bring peace and justice to the world. But their jigsaw king soon*
*falls in love with a beautiful woman. One day she says sadly, 'How*
*can our love endure? Day by day I become older and uglier, yet you*
*remain ever young and handsome.' He divulges his secret to her*
*and she immediately starts singing the magic song of the old*
*people. With her singing the magic evaporates: the king*
*disintegrates into pieces of human flesh; his soldiers become*
*decrepit old people on the verge of death and all their achievements*
*vanish.*

*The old men and women again bring new pieces of the best*
*human minds and bodies and gather in the desert to recreate their*
*king, who will be more perfect than the last because he will be*
*invulnerable to personal emotions …*

I was immensely pleased with the story and simply had to wake
Anna and insist she listen while I read it to her. By now she was
used to my writing at night, when everything was quiet and I could
think and feel clearly.

I worked my way up to the position of site engineer in the company and had sole responsibility for the air conditioning system in two huge tower blocks in Pahlavi Street. One day I saw a worker named Yadollah beating the sole of his foot with a stone, stanching the blood flow from a nail that had pierced it. Yadollah came from a village where, after land reform, he had become part owner of a plot. He hadn't known how to manage or cultivate it, but was able to sell it to its original owner and with the proceeds move to Tehran with his family – where, however, he spent all the money on the first few essentials. I would chat with Yadollah whenever I was on-site. He complained about everything in Tehran: the polluted air, the traffic, the cost of living. In his village he and his family had worked, eaten and slept together. Now he had to leave home every morning at five to reach the building by eight, and after working until six or seven in the evening he rarely got home before ten. Worse, he saw no prospect of any improvement in his circumstances. People in the north of the city had lost their faith, he said, and soon we would witness the resurrection of Imam Zaman, the promised saint who will appear on earth to save human beings from misery and injustice. His father had told him that when men and women wear similar clothes, when a cross can be seen on every tall building, when some people have so much wealth that they don't know what to do with it and others are so poor that they have nowhere to sleep and nothing to eat, then the resurrection of Imam Zaman would occur. He pointed to the television masts on top of all the buildings and said, 'There, those are the promised crosses.' He pointed to the hoarding depicting a half-naked woman on the cinema over the road, and at the modern men and women dressed in clothes indistinguishable from each other. 'My father was right,' he said. 'We will see Imam Zaman very soon.'

After a few months the company I worked for declared bankruptcy as a tax dodge. Our wages were halved; we now knew what it was to be poor. We had just enough to pay the rent and the bills, but often had no money for bus fares. We used the public baths, and constantly shopped around for the cheapest goods. At least for us it was temporary. I would find a new job and when my studies were completed, we would be able to improve our standard of living. (It was not long before my eldest brother found me another job in a building company.) For people like Yadollah and his children, there was no way out.

Iranian universities were becoming more and more politicised, especially after President Richard Nixon's trip to Iran. When his car passed the halls of residence of Tehran University, students threw stones. This was the start of widespread raids by Savak agents on students' homes and the random arrest of many students. My old friend Mohsen, a medical student, was raided by Savak in the middle of the night. 'They banged on the door,' he said, 'nearly frightening the poor landlord to death. In my room, they threw furniture and books everywhere. I doubt they even knew what they were looking for. When I asked them, saying I could perhaps help them, they told me to shut up. Then they started collecting books – any book with a red cover. Some of my medical books had red covers. Luckily they were borrowed from the university library, so I reported their loss to the library and said, "Get them back from Savak if you can!"'

Generally students were anti-American, on the grounds that America supported the Shah. The main problem was lack of freedom. We hoped that with democracy we would be able to regain our independence. Although all American governments were to be despised, recent history had given us cause to hate Republicans even more than Democrats. The Watergate affair was thus greeted as good news as it represented the failure of Nixon, who was considered a close friend of the Shah. Our dislike of American policy towards our country didn't turn us all into revolutionaries. On the contrary, most students shunned the idea of armed struggle and only a minority would have supported revolutionary groups like the Mojahedin or Fedai'in. The assassination of a few Americans and some high-ranking army and police personnel by the Mojahedin didn't cause jubilation among us; they did us harm, bringing only more guards and restrictions to our universities and more suppression and censorship to society. But perhaps revolutionaries welcomed this on the grounds that suppression raises awareness and readiness for revolution. By contrast, we were hoping in the short term to see the abolition of Savak and the university guards, and in long term democracy and a just society.

In March 1973, Anna went to visit her father in Bandar Abbas for Norowz. In her absence our apartment seemed very large and empty. To keep myself busy, I decided to paint it. While painting the ceiling I fell, and the tin of paint emptied over my head and body. When I saw my reflection I was reminded of Charlie Chaplin's films, and started laughing. The weather was still cold, and I didn't want to scrub the paint off with cold water on the balcony. I was wondering how I could bring myself to walk down the street looking like that when my friend Farokh and his girlfriend Mehri dropped in. After laughing heartily at my predicament, they kindly helped me along to the public baths. Farokh and Mehri were from Azerbaijan, both writers and students. Farokh worked in the archives of the state radio station. Most of the time we three talked politics. Farokh's view on censorship was that, instead of bothering to censor all books, the state forced writers and publishers to censor their own work with the result that nowadays publishers were taking a stricter line than the government. One of my cousins was a poet. She enjoyed reading my stories and said that if I would let her change parts of them, they would be publishable and the book could be a great success. I discovered that the things she wanted to change were those that were closest to my heart, without which it would not be my book any more.

I was soon promoted to site engineer and supervisor. I knew nothing about civil engineering, but I learned quickly by experience. The difficulty was getting there. At that time even second-hand cars were expensive and so scarce that one could buy a car, use it for a few years and then sell it for a profit. Production did not match even internal demand, and to compound the problem the Shah wanted to promote 'industrial exports', so most production was exported to neighbouring Arab countries. Eventually, with help of Ammo Jan, I managed to buy a *Jyan* (Citroën).

The next hurdle was to get a driving licence. Friends helped me to learn to drive, but passing the test was a huge challenge. The examining body was the Tehran police. First one had to overcome a series of bureaucratic obstacles. The authorities wouldn't accept a photocopy of my birth certificate, so I had to go to another government office to get a handwritten copy – not one, but twelve of them. Then there was the official eye test and the official photograph, after which I had to get evidence from the local police that I had no criminal record. At the test office itself hundreds of other people were waiting, desperate for a licence because their job depended on it. The examiners didn't have enough time to process everyone properly, so they lined us all up in the street, found an awkward parking spot and gave us each a few seconds to park the car there. Thus only the lucky ones, or those who happened to have a lot of parking experience, passed the test. Of course, knowing how to bribe the examiner or being friendly with someone in the police force could solve the problem instantly. But I failed the test a few times, and each time had to wait some months before retaking it.

The penalty for driving without a licence was 1,000 *toman* and three months in jail. I had to drive because of the constant need to travel between my job, home and university. Once I was flagged down by a policeman. Knowing I would be asked to show my licence, and that I couldn't afford to go to jail for three months, I just drove off as fast as I could. I knew my registration number would be spread throughout the city's police network. The next time I was stopped, I wasn't able to get away. Instead, I put a twenty-*toman* note inside my vehicle document and passed it to policeman. He was unexpectedly open about taking money, saying twenty *toman* wasn't enough, I had to pay fifty. This was the first time I had ever bribed an official. Soon I found out that bribery was essential to get anything done in Iran.

Another form of corruption I encountered concerned tendering for contracts. By law, all construction work had to be put out to tender to all engineering companies. In my company, the notices came to me. Strangely, I would receive them all just one or two days before the reply deadline. When I complained to the manager, thinking someone in our own company was holding onto them too long, he laughed. 'You don't know anything about this country, do you?' he said. 'You can't learn these things at university. Nobody is holding onto these documents. The big fish receive the documents with plenty of time to put in their bids, even enough time to buy cheap materials and sell them to the government at higher prices. But we small fry just get the crumbs.' One project consisted of piping fresh water to a new town. Instead of building a small bridge over the river to take the pipe from the source of water to the town, the construction company took the pipe along the river bank to an existing bridge and all the way back down the other side. This made the project a few million *toman* more expensive and nicely enhanced the company's profits.

With the Arab-Israeli Yom Kippur war in October 1973, oil prices increased sharply. The concomitant increase in Iranian income meant nothing to ordinary Iranians, as the proceeds went mainly to American arms manufacturesr or certain influential individuals, including the Shah's family and entourage. Instead we saw a rise in inflation and more hardship.

Since the previous year the Shah's propaganda machine had been promulgating the idea that he had fought the American oil companies and won. There was some truth in that, but for us everything that emanated from the Shah – even the truth – was received as lies. His propaganda only generated more hatred for the regime. His advisers may have known this, but as he was an absolute ruler, they neither bothered nor dared to force him to see reality. Meanwhile, his ambition seemed to be to 'own' a strong (i.e. heavily armed) country. So he bought sophisticated weapons at whatever price was asked, which no Iranian even knew how to operate. He bought extravagant numbers of planes when there were too few pilots and inadequate facilities for training more. Whom were we going to fight? No one dared pose that question to him. We could defeat the Iraqis without these weapons, and we stood no chance against the Soviets even with them.

As military investment rose by 300 percent, the Shah declined to spend money on any project whose beneficiaries were the people. With the oil money he could have built houses, hospitals and schools, without adding to inflation. He could have rebuilt the poorly maintained roads and railways. He could have encouraged agriculture to feed the hungry.

One of our company workers built a house on cheap, unused land. I helped him to obtain inexpensive materials. Not long after he moved in, I found him distressed: because his house was outside the city boundary, city councillors had destroyed it. He was forced to return to his previous home in a shanty town. I could imagine his thoughts when he saw plans for the luxury houses we were building for the rich, and how readily the council granted planning permission for them.

During this period my mother seemed eaten up with sadness and worry, a cigarette instead of the customary smile on her lips. She and Ammo Jan were in debt, which all his wages went straight to paying off. Eventually they were forced to give up their rented flat and live with my grandmother. As they were proud people it went entirely against their grain, but they had no alternative. I wished I could help them, but we were even worse off, though because we were young and in love we did not feel the hardship of our circumstances so keenly. Grandmother graciously told everyone that my mother's move was at her insistence, as she was alone and ill and needed somebody to look after her. She had much respect for Ammo Jan and was careful not to do or say anything that might show him in a bad light. I remembered when he owned several houses; now they were living as house guests and could not even call the furniture their own. However, even that barely acceptable situation didn't last much beyond my grandmother's death from a stroke. Somehow I sensed some tension between my mother and uncle. He was worried that she and Ammo Jan would remain in the house. I felt it was shameful to worry about his inheritance at this sad time, and I said so. Everyone agreed, but no one dared challenge him, as he was a brigadier general in the army. But Mother and Ammo Jan felt uncomfortable living in the house after Grandmother's death, and moved out to a cheaper flat in a poor area until another aunt of mine invited them to stay with her.

At university I made new friends, among them Hussein, who had previously studied in Britain and was accordingly accepted without having to sit the entrance examination. A few years later I introduced him to my sister Sorya, and they married. He would speak about the freedom people enjoyed in Europe, especially the younger generation. He told us about Speakers' Corner in Hyde Park, London, where people get up on soapboxes and say whatever they want against the government or even the Queen. It struck me as strange that in a capitalist country people were free to buy Marx's *Das Kapital* and to talk about communism and socialism openly. I was also interested to hear about student unions and the power they exerted.

With my friends Shams and Qumarth I sometimes went for lunch to Evin, where there was a coffee house. Many villagers used to go there too. We would sit on a blanket spread on a wooden platform in the yard next to a pond and have the only dish on the menu, *dyizee*. This was the traditional meal of the poorest people, although it was quite a treat. It was a stew made from a small piece of meat with a lot of fat, a few potatoes, some peas and onions.

Each *dyizee* was cooked separately in a small jar. The cook poured all the ingredients into the jars and sealed the tops (sometimes with mud), then leave them for a few hours in the oven. It was delicious; one couldn't cook the same thing at home. The coffee house was almost opposite the prison, hence university and prison guards came there too. While we ate lunch there was no animosity between us, but as soon as we were back on campus the guards went to one side and we to the other, and we looked at each other like age-old enemies. Although the area was full of secret police, gendarmes and guards, and the penalty for selling certain narcotics was execution, in this and another village nearby, one could easily buy anything from hashish to opium. As a matter of fact, it seemed to be government policy to get students addicted to narcotics so that they would cause fewer disturbances.

Drugs were freely available in Tehran. In parks and on the streets, even in the northern sector, young boys would approach people, offering hashish or opium. Using drugs was a way for young people to escape the bitter realities of life – the competition for university, the difficulty of finding a decent job, overcoming obstacles to marriage and general insecurity. In all these areas the lower-and middle-class young without any connections were the main losers.

One day Hussein took me to a place far out of town, in the middle of nowhere, to a house where about twenty or more people, young and old, lay on rudimentary beds on the ground, half-asleep. I was almost stoned just breathing the air in that room. There were braziers full of red coal and pairs of men using an implement called a *negarie* for smoking opium residue. One man (the 'host'), would blow into one end of the *negarie* and the other (the 'customer') breathed in the smoke from the other end. The walls of the room were stained dark from smoke; the beds looked greasy and dirty, used again and again by different people for years. Although I was always keen to try something new, I couldn't bring myself to lie on one of those beds or put that pipe in my mouth. It was all I could do to wait for my friends, and by the time we left my head was spinning and I felt sick.

We tried opium once at a party, but I thought it was bitter and smelled bad. Another time my friend Faried brought us a white powder he said was cocaine. He prepared some of it on foil and we all smoked it through a straw. If I had known that the powder was in fact heroin, I would have hesitated, knowing how easily one can become addicted. Luckily it just made us sleepy. When Faried asked me what I thought, I said, 'Well, my problem is that I don't have enough time to sleep, so you'd better give me something to keep me awake.' We laughed; it was the last time he brought us anything like that, but I later found out that he was addicted to heroin, which eventually claimed his studies, his wife and his life. It seemed that what he and other addicts I knew lacked was a reason to live, a sense of being useful and a player in life's game. Our generation suffered from this problem – we who were taught to think and asked not to think.

One day Qumarth and Shams came to our house with two small tablets they said were LSD. Well, I thought, they can't be any stronger than heroin, they'll probably just put me to sleep. We each swallowed half a tablet. It didn't make me sleepy at all; on the contrary, I felt wide awake and full of energy. After half an hour we all felt likewise: everything seemed to be moving and changing. Hanging on the wall of our living room was a poster of a half-naked woman and man in a jungle, and now they seemed to be dematerialising and disappearing into the trees. The flowers on our patterned carpet came alive and burgeoned wildly. We became weightless, we could jump from our third-floor window, we could even fly ... and to prove it we spread our arms wide and wafted around the room. Suddenly Shams said, 'Maybe we're dead and that's why we feel like this.' We were in a limbo between the real and the unreal. How could we know if Shams was right? We decided if we could communicate with the outside world, that would be proof that we were not dead. Fortunately at that moment our neighbour rang the doorbell and asked to borrow some salt. Anna gave her some and the neighbour went away, registering nothing unnatural about us. But we were still not sure, so we agreed that Qumarth, who seemed more clear-headed than the rest of us, would call my friend Farzad and ask him over to our house and help us. We had no phone, so he had to go to a shop across the road. Thank God he used the stairs and not his newfound ability to fly! For one second I closed my eyes, but I could 'see' as clearly as with open eyes. Then somehow we were all flying, not in space but in time. Time was going backwards, and I could see the whole of history flashing before my eyes. We went back to the beginning of time until we ceased to be human, becoming simply four separate sparks of light which merged together and became one.

There was a tremendous feeling of liberation. All my tension and fear dissolved, the heavy carapace of self-protection crumbled and fell away. We were free from our bodies and souls, one and together, nobody and everybody, nothing and everything. I sat in the middle of the room and babbled with inexplicable joy. The only thing I could see was light, brilliant and pure, perhaps the beginning of creation. When I opened my eyes, it was the lamp on the ceiling I saw: Farzad had rushed over to see what had happened and switched it on.

It was an unbelievable experience for all four of us. The joy I felt was like nothing I had ever known before. Yet the episode also showed me my vulnerability for the first time, so I never tried to repeat it – although it became my ambition to find the same feeling in the real world, not just for a few seconds but for life.

Though I was happily married and working hard, I felt I needed something else. I tried to learn classical guitar, but had no talent for it. I listened to the teachings of an Indian guru, but had no faith in them. So I stuck to writing stories. At that time I was in the middle of writing a long story called *Pier Zad* ('Born Old'), about a man who dies and is reborn, but instead of starting young he returns as an old man and grows younger until he eventually disappears into the nothingness before birth. Writing that story helped me explore lots of issues in my own life, among them the search for a system that ensures a secure and decent life for everybody.

Once a month Anna and I would go see my father. I still brushed my hair back behind my ears so that he wouldn't see how long it was. Of course he did see, but it was one of respectful gestures that strengthen a relationship. Although I was not much older than the boy he used to order about, his attitude towards me had totally changed. He respected Anna and me, and whenever we met we had serious conversations about politics or family matters. He still rated the progress and prosperity of the country above democracy and freedom and felt, compared with the time of the Qajar monarchy, that things were good and Iran was to become a great civilisation. His only complaints were about corruption, bribery and overwhelming bureaucracy, but he couldn't accept that the Shah's hand was visible in all these problems.

Sometimes he still took me to his favourite room or the library to show me his old handwriting books, photographs or stamp collection, taking the trouble to explain in detail the background to any newly acquired drawing or artwork. Once he told me he had given many of his books to the new library established by Queen Farah, and that they were going to name one of the rooms there after him. Another time he said he had funded the building of a school, also to be named after him. I think this was his way of leaving something behind to be remembered after death.

While recognising that Anna and I were married to our own way of thinking, my oldest brother felt it was time for us to have a conventional wedding. I presume the whole family thought the same but kept silent, as they didn't dare meddle in our private life. We hesitated. We loved our life as it was and knew perfectly well that after marriage we would be obliged to have a big house like other married couples had, along with expensive furniture and all the trimmings. We would have to endure the usual rituals like the giving and receiving of gifts on special occasions. Like it or not, we would have to become rich. The pressure was such that we began to feel that we had no alternative. Once we had agreed to a formal wedding, my father and Anna's mother haggled about the dowry and the trousseau. We found this amusing but unimportant; we had each other, and that was all that mattered to us. Our concern was to get the ceremony over with as quickly as possible.

It was summer 1974, and the weather was very hot. Nobody helped us with the preparations: we had to find everything ourselves, and all the accoutrements had to match the expensive standards of our families. We had to buy diamond rings, a wedding gown and suit, silver candleholders, mirrors. We had to have bread specially baked for the occasion and sugar confections made. We had to arrange food and drink, a photographer, invitations. On it went, until minutes before the ceremony itself. Even in the middle of the ceremony somebody came and asked me where to put the ice. We were so tired that while the meal was in progress I slipped away to snatch a few minutes' sleep. Many of our relatives gave us gold rings, necklaces and coins; my father gave us a costly carpet and later half the house, which from childhood had been in my name. We didn't know what to do with the gold items, so we put them all in the bank. As for the house, which was huge and in an expensive neighbourhood in the city centre, it had been let perhaps ten years earlier. There were sitting tenants who could not be removed without legal action, and the rent was frozen at its original level, which meant it was worth almost nothing. (This was one of the advantages of living in a rented property.) After the wedding, our lives went on much as before, and we managed to avoid being caught up in all the customs in which married couples normally participated.

In March 1975 we drove to Bandar Abbas, over 1,000 kilometres away, to visit Anna's father. On the way we came across a huge building in the middle of the desert, around 500 years old. Although it was hot outside, the interior was kept cool and pleasant by a cold spring in the basement. It was a resting place where travellers could refresh themselves, and made me realise how much things had changed. We commissioned lengthy reports and surveys, employed engineers and inspectors, spent vast amounts of money on the latest equipment and still were not able to build something like that. The main airport roof had even collapsed because of heavy snow. How sad! Perhaps Iran had risen and fallen, materially and spiritually, in step with the kind of ruler it had. Who made that beautiful desert building? Where are they now …?

This was my first visit to Bandar Abbas, a city named after the most powerful king of the Safavid dynasty. As the Shah had decided to situate the main naval base in the Straits of Hormuz, this city was set to become more important. Accordingly, we found the road leading into it in perfect condition. It was a place where the gap between rich and poor was even more evident than elsewhere; many inhabitants were deprived of their basic needs, while others enjoyed lives of luxury up to the highest European standards. On the way we saw a number of women in the middle of the road, sweeping it. We asked Anna's father what they were doing. 'They are so poor,' he said, 'that by sweeping the road they can gather up some grains that have been spread by the wind on the road from lorries carrying shipments.'

# 8

# Exit Fees

In March 1975, after an agreement between Iran and Iraq over the Arvand River ended hostilities between the two countries, many leaders and fighters among the Iraqi Kurds came to Iran as refugees. These people had hoped, with the Shah's help, to achieve some kind of autonomy. It was sad to the Shah abandoning them now that he had achieved his goal.

Doubtless they felt betrayed. After this victory, the Shah created a single party called Rastakhiz, or National Resurgence Party. To ordinary people it meant nothing, as all political parties simply pawns in the Shah's game. The way they were run was so blatantly artificial, one wondered why the regime didn't bother to make the system look a little more acceptable to the public. The Shah and his prime minister cavalierly sacked people and designated parties. We were completely indifferent to this new single-party system. In fact, we were relieved to see the pretence of democracy end, exposing the real face of the system to the world.

This was a move by the Shah to confirm his ownership of the country. In a broadcast on national radio and television published also in the newspapers, he said, 'We must straighten out the ranks of Iranians. To do so, we divide them into two categories: those who believe in the monarchy, the constitution and the sixth Bahman Revolution [the 1963 declaration of the White Revolution] and those who don't ... A person who does not join the new political party or believe in those three cardinal principles to which I referred ... is either an individual who belongs to an illegal organisation or is related to the outlawed Tudeh Party, in other words, a traitor. Such an individual belongs in an Iranian prison or, if he desires, he can leave the country tomorrow without even paying exit fees. He can go anywhere he likes because he is not an Iranian, he has no nation and his activities are illegal and punishable according to the law ...' Such tactics are common among dictators to force people into 'choosing' their rule.

Many Iranians neither agreed with him nor opposed him, wanting to join neither his party nor a revolutionary group. The Tudeh Party had little support, being seen as Soviet puppets. But now the Shah threatened people with the labels of 'traitor' or 'foreign mercenary'. He was dividing the country into black and white. Those who were not with him were against him, against the country and the people. Most Iranians caved in and joined the new party, although doing so was meaningless. All its creation did was to intensify people's hatred for the Shah and his system.

That summer Farzad and I went to the Festival of Art in Shiraz, organised by Queen Farah. There were contributions from all over the world, but it was difficult to get tickets, which were restricted and expensive. We managed to see an open-air play (from Southeast Asia, I think). The players, half-naked, mingled with the audience, where passers-by could also see them. I found it unbelievable that they could do something like this in front of Muslims. In fact, the whole city had turned into a kind of quasi-European street theatre, peopled by visitors and tourists behaving exactly as they pleased. Nobody had bothered to ask what local people, especially the more traditional ones, thought about this.

The Shah and his queen were keen to demonstrate their leanings towards Western culture. Those who opposed him, therefore, automatically turned their backs on Western ways. Whereas all previous uprisings in Iran had been nationalistic rather than religious, Islam became the motivating force for freedom as the

Shah also appropriated the symbols of nationalism. Many young people became increasingly religious, openly demonstrating their commitment to Islamic religion and culture. Female students started wearing the *chador* in a kind of passive defiance of the Shah. Although I had nothing against Western dress, I couldn't help admiring the strength of those students' beliefs and resistance. In my final year at university the number of students who prayed regularly and wore beards increased sharply.

During the winter of that year, when the universities were closed, we travelled widely, visiting Yazd, Kerman, Bandar Shapur, Shiraz, Ahvaz, Arak, Khomaien and other cities. Our travels showed us the two faces of Iran. In the smaller cities like Yazd or Kerman, hardly anything had changed in the last fifty or even hundred years though they were provincial capitals. Likewise most of the small towns and villages except perhaps in the wealthy north; many of them had no running water or electricity. In the industrial and tourist centres like Isfahan and Shiraz, however, the signs of modernisation were evident: high-rises, wide streets, prosperity. Often we saw villages submerged under floodwaters, where residents regarded such calamities as normal and expected no assistance from the government. Graduates from Tehran were sent to do their military service in those villages, which only generated feelings of envy and desperation among the local populace and fuelled sympathy for revolutionary groups.

Throughout 1975–76 prices rose daily. At the same time expectations had been raised, mainly through access to Western culture via radio and television. Now there were many middle-class people who were not prepared to live without such consumer goods like electrical appliances and cars. But these were in short supply, and expensive. Knowing the high price of Iranian oil sold on the international market and the benefits that accrued there from to the ruling elite added to the general resentment. There were daily shortages of one thing or another: meat one day, bananas the next. The government started importing goods more quickly, sometimes even by air. A new movement against the Shah's regime, Negative Resistance, came into being, resisting, for example, the consumption of imported meat which religious leaders decreed was *haram* (forbidden), as the cattle had not been killed according to Islamic law. In response, the government announced that they had

sent some *mullahs* to each place of export to supervise the
slaughter of cattle. Negative Resistance also opposed the
government by spreading rumours and making political jokes.
Government response was sometimes so naïve that it gave rise to
yet more jokes, as when one official advised those who couldn't
obtain fresh fruit to have fruit juice or compote instead. It evoked
Marie Antoinette's remark that if the French people had no bread,
'let them eat cake'.

To combat shortages and inflation, the Shah ordered the
creation of an organisation of students from the Rastakhiz Party
who would check shops to control prices and expose the hoarding
of goods. Unsurprisingly, this measure made matters worse,
undermining the relative prosperity and security of shopkeepers
and stirring up hatred between them and the students. The Shah's
covert purpose may have been to defuse political activism among
the students by aligning them with the government. Whatever the
reason, the result was that the fight against corruption merely bred
new forms of it.

As I approached the end of my university course, two
momentous things happened. One was that I had offers of
placement at universities in England to study for a master's degree;
we decided to move there. The other was that we discovered we
were going to have a baby. Although Anna and I were essentially
happy with both developments, I couldn't help but worry about the
new responsibility combined with a move to a foreign country
about which we knew nothing, and where and there was nobody to
help us.

We sold our belongings. Funnily enough, we sold the car,
television, hi-fi and carpets for the same prices as we had paid for
them several years earlier – and the buyers were all delighted to be
getting a bargain! We then paid off the outstanding university fees.
With the rest of the money and my father's gift of rent for a flat, we
would be able to support ourselves in the UK. In June 1976 we said
goodbye to family and friends at the airport in Tehran and flew to
London.

The first few weeks there were horrible. Although we were free
from the shadow of the Shah and Savak, we missed everything
about Iran, especially the people. We had to decide which offer of
admission to accept, eventually choosing Reading University.

Once I started the English course I made new friends from different parts of the world: Tomas from Spain, Estavros from Greece, Daniel from Venezuela and several from Chile and other South American countries. Our origins were far-flung, but we had much in common and often talked politics. One day I teasingly asked one of my Chilean friends what they had done to the great Allende. Without a second's pause, he answered, 'The same thing you did to the "great Mossadegh".' According to him, the other Chilean students on our course were members of Chile's secret police; he was very careful not to criticise their government in front of them. With our Greek friends we spoke about the regime of the Colonels, which ended in July 1974, and with Tomas about the dictatorship of General Franco, which concluded with his death less than a year earlier. In September the death of Mao Zedong saddened most students, who appreciated him as one of the last revolutionaries and saw no truth in what his 'imperialist enemies' wrote about him. We Iranians had specific reservations about him, as he had held discussions with one of the most hated individuals in Iran – Ashraf, the Shah's twin sister. But opposition to him and his ideas in the Western and Iranian media made him acceptable to us. Such thinking tended to blind us to the obvious wrongdoings of other leaders like Cambodia's Pol Pot. For us, the failure of American aggression in Vietnam meant that they would now have to think twice about supporting dictators in developing countries.

With the new academic year I made new friends, among them Mahmud, a PhD student and fellow Iranian. He and his wife were religious Muslims, following Islamic dress and customs. When we were at their house Mahmud tried to avoid speaking to Anna or, if he had to address her, to avoid looking at her. We found this strange and insulting at first, but realised that this came from their religious observance, and started to follow suit when we were in their company.

They were trying to recruit us: Mahmud told us about the Iranian cleric Ali Shari'ati and the opening of a mosque called Husseiniyeh-i Ershad, at which Shari'ati spoke. I was interested to learn that the Shah had been forced to allow this degree of freedom to the people. Later, I discovered that his intention was to distract the younger generation from communism, his main worry. Mahmud gave us some books by Shari'ati, which illuminated in simple terms the connections between religion and everyday life, between religion and science, history and politics and, most importantly, between individuals and their state of mind. He recognised that many traditions and beliefs were alienating young people. Having taken no interest in religion for the past few years, believing it to be mere superstition, Anna and I now started reading Shari'ati's books and learning from them.

I was with Anna throughout her labour. Witnessing her pain, being unable to alleviate it, was among the most difficult things I had ever had to do. I'd had a kidney stone for a few months, but the pain of that was much easier to endure than watching Anna suffer.

She gave birth to a beautiful daughter whom we named Sarvenaz, the name of a beautiful Iranian tree. Sarvenaz soon became shortened to Sarvy. My main hobby at that time was photography and making Super-8 films. To Anna and the natural world – autumn leaves, swans dancing on a frozen lake, a butterfly, a flower opening – I now added a new subject, our pretty Sarvy – waking up, being fed and throwing food everywhere, having a bath.

Generally we experienced kindness and generosity from British people. When I said as much to Mahmud, he was displeased, and reminded me what the older generation of these same people had done to us and how much Britons were still benefiting from Iranian oil and other resources. 'They can afford to be generous, as they get their wealth from our pockets. British oil companies, businesses and factories have become so rich from years of exploiting countries like ours. They spend most of it on themselves and the fraction they spend on foreigners who come here is negligible. If Iranians had access to the wealth of our own country, I could tell you how kind and generous we would be.'

# 9

# Revolution

One day a pamphlet in the student union building caught my eye. It had the name and emblem of the Mojahedin on it and described the activities of that group in Iran. I mentioned it to Mahmud, who told me some of the history of the group. The Mojahedin was founded in 1965 by six former members of the Liberation Movement under Mehdi Bazargan (the first prime minister after the 1979 revolution). Mohammed Hanifnezhad, the oldest and central figure of the organisation and an agricultural engineer, was born in 1938 to a clerical family in Tabriz, capital of Azerbaijan. The bloody massacres of the 1963 uprising were a turning point. The Mojahedin, along with other revolutionaries including the Fedai'in, concluded that the old ways of opposing the Shah's dictatorship – street protests, labour strikes and underground networks – were bankrupt, and that new means of resistance were called for: guerrilla warfare. The first strategic handbook of the Mojahedin was called *Mobareze'a Chiest?* ('What is the Struggle?'). It focused on training responsible members who would be informed about the different areas of struggle and become effective leaders. The main enemy was identified as worldwide imperialism, with American imperialism foremost. Imperialism has three main characteristics, it argued: its aim is to swallow the whole world; no human relationship can exist between imperialism and people under domination; it can be defeated from within or without – it is a paper tiger. The main ideological works of the Mojahedin were *Shanakht* ('Knowledge and Understanding'), *T'akamul* ('Evolution'), *Rah'a Anbia, Rah'a Bashar* ('Path of the Prophets, Path of Human Beings'), *'Nahzat-i Husseini* ('Hussein's Movement'), *Tabi'ian Jahan* ('Explanation of the Universe') and *Dynamism of the Qur'an*.

The Mojahedin began their military operations in August 1971. Their first operations were designed to disrupt the extravagant celebrations of the twenty-five-century anniversary of the monarchy. Savak recruited a member of the Tudeh Party and used him to infiltrate the Mojahedin, enabling the arrest sixty-six members. In subsequent months, the group lost all its original leadership through executions or street battles. Despite these heavy losses, it survived and found new members. In 1975, the Mojahedin was faced with an internal coup by members who wanted to change the organisation's ideology from Islam to Marxism. Some who refused to accept the change were expelled, and later one of them, Sharif Vaghafi, was killed by the Marxist wing.

Although I applauded their courage and self-sacrifice, I was not inclined to accept their way of thinking. I think Mahmud realised this and, instead of giving me more literature about the Mojahedin, he gave me more books by Shari'ati. These continued to impress me with their descriptions of Islam's respect for individual rights and freedoms, defence of the oppressed and preaching of compassion and mercy. For the first time I understood the philosophy behind such Islamic rituals as prayer, fasting or the Hajj. Shari'ati's writing solved for me the contradictions between religion, logic and science.

That spring I heard from Mahmud that Shari'ati had died of poisoning in London. Although it was never proved that the Shah had had him killed, everybody accepted this version of events without hesitation. I wished I had known he was in London, that I could have met the great man.

With the drop in demand for and price of oil, the financial

situation in Iran worsened. The Shah needed a scapegoat, and targeted the government and prime minister. For the first time, he let the government be publicly criticised; in August 1977, he decided after twelve years to dismiss his 'loyal servant', the prime minister Amir Abbas Hovida. American-educated Jamshid Amouzegar, mastermind of increasing oil prices, was appointed instead.

The Shah went to Washington to persuade President Carter's administration to support him and his actions. Iranian students took the opportunity to demonstrate in front of the White House and the police sprayed tear gas to disperse the crowds. The wind blew some into the Shah's eyes, which made it look as if he was crying. It seemed symbolic. There seemed to have been a change of mood among the Western powers, who had come to realise that they could not keep the Shah in power any longer.

Politics became a frequent topic for discussion with Mahmud and other Iranian fellow students. It was in September that Mahmud mentioned Khomeini for the first time and said that he would lead the revolution against the Shah. This was too much for me to swallow. A *mullah* leading the revolution? I burst out laughing. I had known about Khomeini since childhood and had some respect for him as one of those rare people who opposed the Shah. Even so, I had never seen him as a potential leader. In fact, I had never encountered a good or intellectual *mullah*. Many reputable people said that all the *mullahs* thought about was 'their belly and what lies below it' (i.e. sex). But Mahmud's prediction, incredible as it seemed, struck fear into me.

A long time earlier I had written a story about a young man searching for truth.

*He finds a stone on which is engraved, 'Whoever captures* parandeh' a azadi *(the freedom bird) will come to know the truth about life'. He searches for the bird; when he finds it he shoots an arrow and kills it, believing the bird carries the message of truth physically. But with the bird's death, the sun goes down and night falls. The earth splits open, and from the fissure emerge ancient men, thousands of years old, dressed in black, who have come from the underworld to rule the world of darkness. The poor young man searches anew, this time not for freedom or truth but for brightness and sunlight. To succeed he must overcome those dark-clad ancients who have waited for millennia in the centre of the earth for their time to come.*

I was tired of the Shah and the Iranian regime and like many Iranians wanted a change. But I wanted neither a communist nor a religious revolution. My ideal was a constitutional monarchy with the type of government we had seen under Mossadegh. The American and British media were putting out contradictory statements, suddenly calling Shah a dictator but appearing to offer vehement support to the Shah (like David Owen, the British Foreign Secretary). Jimmy Carter travelled to Iran, calling it an island of peace and stability. These favourable remarks were totally belied by what we experienced on the ground. Much later we learned that they stemmed from confusion on the part of the Americans and the British about the position of the Shah's regime and its chances of survival.

On 6th January 1978 *Etla'at*, one of the two main Iranian newspapers, published an article about Khomeini, calling him the 'black reactionary', the same epithet by which the Shah referred to him. Three days later, theology students from the holy city of Ghom (near Tehran), wearing *kafan* (burial shrouds), poured into the streets in a demonstration against the Shah. The Shah's police and agents of Savak, whose experience of public demonstrations had been limited to those in praise of the Shah, fired on the demonstrators and killed a few of them. This was start of the revolution. No doubt the leader of the revolution was chosen on the same day. For Iranians *shahadat* (martyrdom) was not just a term used of people killed defending the worthy causes. *Shahadat* was much more than that; it was an ideology or a philosophy, with roots going back to Alexander the Great. Examples of religious leaders killed by their rulers abounded throughout history. Martyrdom as a philosophy is deeply embedded in the Iranian subconscious. It is why the Shah did not kill Mossadegh.

Shari'ati's books discuss and venerate *shahidan* (martyrs), who, in his terms, do not die and therefore must not be mourned. Instead, the family and friends of the martyr are to be congratulated, as he is going to heaven where, according to the Qur'an, he will be judged on equal terms with messengers of God.

To mark the lapse of forty days since the death of the Ghom martyrs, a ceremony was held in the northwestern town of Tabriz in which more people were killed. The BBC and Iranian radio both reported it and later Khomeini delivered a message about it. We knew that Iranian radio was not to be trusted. We had learned how to interpret the media: we knew that when news was short it meant something bad was happening. No news meant a lot of news. Conversely, a lot of news meant no news. Newscasters on Iranian radio and television were so hated that we often felt we could kill them with our own bare hands. Not only they were issuing lies and denying reality, they were also denigrating people's reputations and goals.

Another forty days after the Tabriz incident, there were demonstrations in most major cities including Isfahan, Shiraz, Yazd and Ahvaz. So vociferous was the activity in Isfahan that the Shah had no option but to announce the imposition of martial law there. From then on the revolution was unstoppable, with small and large demonstrations throughout the country. Symbols of the Shah's rule were attacked, including Western cultural imports like cinemas and banks, which had made the fortunes of the ruling elite at the expense of the common people.

Khomeini announced that the Shah was not the legitimate ruler of Iran, and that people should refuse to pay taxes to him and his government. In an attempt to discredit him, the Shah's supporters said Khomeini was not Iranian, but born of an Indian woman and thus Indian himself. Nevertheless, Khomeini's taped messages, sent to Iran and distributed through *mullahs* and mosques, succeeded in reaching the ears of people on the street within hours. It was said that there were now almost 85,000 theological students and over 100,000 *mullahs*. Khomeini spoke in simple language, understandable to all. He made clear statements with examples ordinary people could relate to and used slogans around which people united.

Never known as a great decision-maker, the Shah now badly needed someone to tell him what to do. Most of his acolytes were people who had learned to obey unquestioningly, to admire and flatter him and give unstinting loyalty. In their eyes he had attained such a position of authority that he could teach foreign leaders, including the Americans and the British, how to run their countries. Who dared to tell him what to do? But to order mass killings required supreme self-confidence, which he lacked, or the protection of allies in the USA or the UK, which was not forthcoming. As a result, he advocated contradictory policies. On one hand, he showed muscle by establishing martial law in various cities and ordering his soldiers to stand firm against the demonstrators. On the other, faced with the people's strong resolve, he had to back down and grant concessions, like replacing the head of Savak (a favourite) with someone more acceptable.

In June I graduated with a MSc in Engineering Mathematics, having enquired at several universities about studying for a PhD. I was offered places at Leeds, Loughborough, London and Newcastle-upon-Tyne. We weighed the options. Living in London was very expensive; Newcastle was too far and too cold. Having visited Leeds and Loughborough, we decided we preferred Loughborough. Just then we received an invitation from my cousin Hussein, who lived in Edinburgh with his wife and daughter and studied medicine. On our way to Edinburgh we decided to visit the department at Newcastle for an interview. It was a beautiful sunny day and we went to the seashore. It had been years since we had been able to play on a sandy beach. I made a sandcastle for Sarvy, who was learning to walk.

The interview was very positive. I liked my prospective supervisor and the subject of my proposed research project was interesting and useful, straddling the departments of Engineering Maths and Chemical Engineering with the possibility of solving some of the problems in Iranian oil refining. Anna liked the city, which she found more lively than Loughborough or Leeds, with particularly friendly people. We stopped in Newcastle again on our way back from Edinburgh, this time to accept a place at the University and fill in application forms for accommodation. In the end we found a comfortable semi-detached house to rent in an open space, with a pleasant landlord and neighbours.

Whenever I thought about our decision to stay in Newcastle, I felt it was destined. If it had not been for the invitation from my cousin, or the fine weather that day, or the remarks of the supervisor about the usefulness of my project, the whole course my life since then might well have been different.

In August 1978 we heard two items of important news. One was very sad: a cinema in Abadan, southwestern Iran, had been set on fire and more than 600 people had been burned alive. According to BBC Persian news, Khomeini announced that this had been the work of Savak agents intent on undermining the revolutionary acts of the people. Iranian radio, meanwhile, claimed that fanatics or Islamic Marxists had been responsible. We knew enough about the workings of the propaganda machine to be sure that Savak were the perpetrators. Reporting the news promptly and in detail meant it must have been planned ahead. In responding to genuine breaking news, Iranian radio would have to go through various channels until it reached the Shah, then wait for his reaction and announce his response. This could take days. Furthermore, other groups like the Mojahedin and the Marxists laid the blame on Savak. So the case was clear, although who was ultimately behind this dreadful deed we could not know.

The other news was about a change of government. The Shah had chosen Sharif Emami as his new prime minister. Some said he was chosen for his links with the British, as the Shah felt that, unhappy with his oil policy, they were masterminding the revolution. Others said he was chosen because of his close ties with some *mullahs*. Whatever the reason, the appointment didn't solve anything. Emami changed the imperial calendar back to the old Islamic one (reversing an act by the Shah); ordered the closure of all wine shops and casinos; freed most political prisoners; ordered the arrest of some of the most hated ministers; increased the wages of government employees; and removed Reza Qotbi, the Queen's relative, as head of the national radio and television network.

Khomeini saw through the appointment immediately. A few days afterwards he broadcast a message, saying, 'Within the past fifteen years and especially in the past few months, the Shah has killed many innocent people. Now he has employed a new satanic trick. We must listen to the people. They are not calling for the temporary closure of casinos and respect for *aghaian* (religious people). They are saying that they don't want the Shah and the Pahlavi dynasty. It is essential that the holy Islamic movement be pursued until this tyrant regime is brought to an end.' He warned factions of the movement to avoid any split in their ranks and urged them to unite more firmly than ever against the regime.

It was clear from the Mojahedin bulletins on the notice-boards in Reading and Newcastle universities that the opposition was indeed split. The right-wing factions were not asking for fundamental changes and were ready to compromise with the regime and be satisfied with some minor political reforms. The faction on the left was not prepared to accept anything less than total overthrow of the regime. The leadership of this faction allied themselves with Ayatollah Khomeini.

On 7th September Emami announced the imposition of martial law in Tehran and twenty-three other cities. The following day, when some people unaware of the new law gathered in Tehran's Jaleh Square, soldiers fired on them and killed many. The regime announced fifty-nine deaths; the opposition put the number in the thousands. News of 'Black Friday' was announced around the world. The official Iranian Radio, by contrast, pretended nothing was happening. Rumours were rife: it was said that the soldiers were not Iranians, but Israelis the Shah employed to fight the rebels. The Shah, meanwhile, claimed that the leaders of the demonstrators were from the PLO.

I found a leaflet advertising a demonstration at the student union. We joined about 300 people for it; unlike at Reading, many students were active in Newcastle and the surrounding towns.

At the beginning of October Iraq's Saddam Hussein answered the Shah's call and expelled Khomeini from Iraq to France. The Shah wanted him far away from Iran and the religious circles of Iraq. But the expulsion had the opposite effect. Now we were able to see and hear our new leader every day on our own televisions; people in Iran, too, had frequent access to him through Persian-language radio broadcasts from Europe and America. From then on he was also able to respond much more quickly whenever the Shah got up to his tricks.

In the Chemistry department I met Yahya, another Iranian, who had the same supervisor as I. He was in his final year. His wife Nasrin, a pleasant Baha'i woman, was also a student at the university. Anna and I began socialising with them. Nasrin worried about the prospects for her family if the resistance came to power, and we reassured her that all the political forces lined up against the Shah had 'democracy' and 'independence' as their primary aims – although in truth the slogan 'Islamic republic' was beginning to be heard as well.

In the Engineering Maths department I had another Iranian Baha'i for a colleague who, like Nasrin, worried that if the demonstrators came to power they would kill the Baha'i. According to him, it was against Baha'i religion to involve themselves in politics, although I pointed out that this stance is itself a political policy. He was a clever and genuine person with whom I got on well, and we agreed on almost everything except politics. Another colleague was John, from Tanzania, son of a Muslim father and a Christian mother, who considered himself a Christian. He and I learned a great deal from each other about the politics of our respective countries. My third colleague was an elderly Japanese professor who was forever reading and did not communicate with us at all, except perhaps to thank us profusely if we made him a cup of tea.

With the start of new academic year I saw more and more Iranians in the student union arguing about politics. The Marxists and the Muslims would take opposite sides in discussions about various passages in the Qur'an, the former finding them unbelievable, the latter insisting that the stories were completely true. Having read Shari'ati's books, I had learned how to interpret the Qur'an; on one occasion I stepped in and tried to explain what a certain story was meant to convey. As the newcomer, everybody was curious to know me and my political affiliation; they fell silent and listened respectfully. This in itself was unusual. Generally, in those days, nobody listened to anybody else: they loved arguing but were not interested in responses. I seemed to have made a good impression with my intervention, as they all turned to shake my hand. Suddenly I found I had some friends there.

At that time I still did not consider myself an adherent to this or that faction. I was listening and evaluating, so as to find my own way. Our friends covered a spectrum of views. Paviz and his sister Mino were far-left supporters of the Fedai'in guerrilla organisation, but sympathised with the Marxist faction of the Mojahedin (still using the same name as the Muslim faction) and other Marxist organisations. Ahmad, Mojgan, Aliraza and Mohammed, followers of Shari'ati, used to sell Mojahedin books that they received from the Union of Islamic Societies – until the Mojahedin split from that organisation in a bid to create a separate body. These people became closer to us than the others. Some, like Faried, were in between; they were hoping to see the Mojahedin and the Fedai'in united. On the far right there were Vahid, Jafar and Darvish, who supported the *mullahs* and were also receiving materials from the Union of Islamic Societies. Apart from them there were some outcasts like Babak, who was a member of Tudeh, and a few who were pro-Shah. We suspected them of Savak affiliations.

Most of the time the pro-Shari'ati/pro-Mojahedin and pro-Fedai'in groups gathered at our house to catch the news on television and radio and then discuss what we had heard. Disagreements were many but essentially friendly and moderate. The main point of contention was Bazargan. Sometimes Ahmad defended him, with my support, while those inclined to Mojahedin thinking were silent and the Fedai'in supporters called him a liberal and a bourgeois. In my innocence I thought at first that to be liberal was a desirable thing, but I soon learned that the word was used as a term of abuse and so instead of calling Bazargan a liberal I began to describe him as a social democrat and nationalist. During this time, the left generally won the day. It wasn't possible to lean further to the left than Khomeini, and in consequence everyone admitted his leadership without question.

As a rule, we would not reach consensus when Anna called us to dinner. Then the talk switched to her wonderful cooking, and political argument was forgotten. Sometimes Anna joined in our discussions but generally she took a more pragmatic interest in what was going on in Iran rather than in abstract theorising.

Often during these discussions I wanted to explode with exasperation and frustration. My interest was in the revolution itself, not this infighting between factions. This disunity obstructed progress. Fanatics like Jafar were particularly infuriating. One day he said that people in Iran had seen a picture of Khomeini on the moon. Trying to nip the inevitable fight in the bud, I said, 'This is the kind of rumour that is good for the morale of the people and bad for the morale of the soldiers.' '"Rumour"?' he repeated, offended. 'What do you mean, "rumour"? The image was there. Millions of people saw it.' My intervention had had the opposite effect from that intended and just led to an argument between Jafar and myself. Others looked on, doubtless laughing inwardly at these two PhD students engaged in an idiotic dispute about the moon.

Almost every other week there was a demonstration or meeting by University and Polytechnic students, normally organised by Darvish and Asghar. Darvish, who after the revolution became the head of the Pasdaran (revolutionary guard) in one of the northern provinces of Iran, was always the last person willing to demonstrate yet the first to find a speaker and shout slogans against the Shah. As a result, it was Asghar who did most of the work. Ashgar, the brother-in-law of Masoud Rajavi (one of the leaders of the Mojahedin), was executed by the new regime a few years later. The pro-Tudeh students, still without guidance from their mother Communist Party in the Soviet Union, had no official stance and therefore could do nothing but look on in silence.

One day I heard that my cousin Abol-Hassan Banisadr had been invited to deliver a speech in Newcastle. Several hundred Iranians came to hear him. Afterwards I introduced myself. It was the first time we had met, as I was very young when he left the country. I invited him to our house and he gladly accepted, refusing to go anywhere else on the grounds that 'I must see my cousin after twenty years'. Two of his supporters and some of my friends came as well. Discussion centred on the differences between Marxism and Islam and why Banisadr thought Islam was more progressive than Marxism.

That evening someone called Tehran to get the latest news. He reported that there had been a demonstration there and that fifty people had allegedly been killed. 'Fifty?' said my cousin. 'When they say fifty they mean five hundred. No one can know how many people are killed in all the different streets.' Then he asked his friend to call Paris and see if Khomeini has issued a statement on this incident. The caller said, 'I hear 500 people have been killed today? Of course the real number may be much higher – perhaps even 5,000.' I was astonished to hear how a number could grow so fast in the course of two conversations. 'Ah, well,' I thought. 'This is a propaganda war too. The Shah hides many of his crimes and people have to deduce what they can't see from whatever they can.'

That same evening we watched the television news and there was Khomeini as usual, allowing a visitor to kiss his hand. 'Why does Khomeini let people do that?' I wondered. 'And what is our guarantee that he won't change into something like the Shah?'

My cousin replied, 'He's an old man. He can't stop people who want to kiss his hand. He can't change their habits in a single day.' Then he added, 'We ourselves are the only guarantee we have for our future. If Khomeini were to change into something like the Shah – which is doubtful – we should have no alternative but to oppose him too.' Somehow that answer satisfied me, and from then on I put aside all my doubts and became an advocate of the revolution and of Khomeini.

By November popular demonstrations and activities had reached such a pitch that the Shah was obliged to change the government again. This time he chose a military man to save him, General Azhari. In a rare speech the Shah said, 'The Iranian nation has risen against tyranny and corruption. The revolution cannot but be endorsed by me both as monarch and as an Iranian.' He ended by declaring, 'In this revolution of the Iranian nation against colonialism, tyranny and corruption, I am at your side.' We had to laugh wrily to hear the Shah's talk about tyranny as though it were perpetrated by others and he too were its victim. We also couldn't help wondering what Azhari, a pathetic old general whose strength had always been obedience to the Shah would make of this revolutionary speech, and how people could take him seriously.

Needless to say, during Azhari's premiership the popular revolution, far from fading, grew by leaps and bounds. Demonstrators who came face to face with soldiers started putting flowers into their rifle barrels, shouting, 'Army brother, why are you killing your brother?' The result was that fewer and fewer soldiers were prepared to shoot people, and many actually ripped off their army uniforms and joined the demonstrators. Popular slogans became more virulent, some promising 'death to the Shah' or 'death to America'. The Mojahedin and other revolutionary organisations were unhappy with the practice of giving flowers to soldiers and believed that the only useful language was the language of force. At the time Mojahedin policy was to support Khomeini vigorously in order to keep popular morale high and prepare people for further sacrifices.

In order to expose the latest tricks of Azhari's government, Khomeini ordained that everyone should go up to the roof their house and say, '*Allah'o akbar* [God is great]'; the implication being that people should fear God and no one else. The next day Azhari spoke on the radio, and while the sound of the slogan was undeniable, he claimed that it was not the voices of the masses chanting but a tape recording played by a few individuals. A day later there was a spontaneous rally, where the demonstrators sarcastically chanted a different slogan: '*Azhari bechare'a inham navar'a, navar ke'a pa nadar'a* [Poor Azhari! Is this a tape as well – a tape with feet?]'.

In those days our main worry was that the Americans would not permit Iranian democracy and independence and might stage a coup and establish military rule. So our main slogan outside the country was, 'Iran the next Vietnam, US get out of Iran.' Inside Iran the slogan was, '*Azhari bechareh, Iran Chile namish* [Poor helpless Azhari! Iran will not turn into another Chile].'

At this time there were major strikes by government employees and oil was in short supply, causing domestic hardship. The G7 countries decided that they were not able to keep the Shah in power any more, that they would have to engage with Khomeini and his advisers to find a way to solve the Iranian crisis. An American committee under George Ball simultaneously reached the conclusion that the Shah had no choice but to resign and leave the monarchy to his son or a regency council.

The Shah was trying to find a prime minister who would be acceptable to the people, in order to leave matters in his hands and depart the country. But nobody was willing to take the job. It was both funny and sad, and a complete reversal of the situation of a year earlier. Even Azhari had accepted his appointment as a matter of obedience only.

By now I was spending most of my time in support of revolutionary activity, as well as studying and giving tutorials to undergraduate students, for which I received a small salary.

Anna was now attending meetings and demonstrations, bringing Sarvy, who was learning to say a few words and sentences. One thing she had learned to say was, '*Marg bar Shah* ['death to the Shah'])'! Our English neighbour felt it sad that a child of that age should learn to wish for someone's death. We agreed with her, but said, 'This is the reality of life in Iran and she is an Iranian. Soon we will return to Iran and she will have to adapt to the rights and wrongs of the situation there.'

Sarvy wasn't the only one who was changing. I was no longer interested in writing or taking photographs; we no longer went to the seaside, although we were very fond of the sea in any weather. I, who had always objected to any kind of personality cult, now admired Khomeini, with his angry, serious face. I even put up a poster-sized picture of him in my study. One day Sarvy came into the room and saw the poster. She confused 'hail to' with 'death to' and said, 'Death to Khomeini!'. Reflexively, I smacked her. Poor Sarvy had only been trying to please me, and ran from the room crying, leaving me very sad and remorseful. It took some hours before I could get her to laugh and forgive me with a kiss.

At the university there was an Iranian society run by supporters of the Tudeh Party, and an Islamic society organised by Malaysian and Indonesian students. In our view they were very reactionary. They were opposed to translating the Qur'an, and for a time resisted permitting female students to pray at the university mosque. They said that putting a photo of Khomeini in the mosque was blasphemy and often claimed that he was not a Muslim but a communist. Later I discovered that their antipathy towards Khomeini was not ideological but political: like us in recent years, they were afraid of their own secret police and of their president, Suharto. On a personal level, they actually admired our courage and commitment and wished to emulate us. For our part, we were proud of our revolution and our leader. Soon the tide began to turn in our direction. Muslims began taking our leaflets featuring Khomeini's messages and buying pictures of him and copies of Shari'ati's books in translation. When we bought goods like *halal* meat from Pakistani shops, we were treated with respect; sometimes the shopkeepers waved aside our tendered payment or gave us large discounts. Eventually some non-Iranian Muslims started attending our meetings and demonstrations.

Some students went to Paris to meet Khomeini. I couldn't afford to do that, but I never missed his speeches or interviews. He always talked about democracy and freedom. In one speech he said, 'The Shah claims he is going to give us freedom. Who is he to give us freedom? Freedom is given to human beings by God.' He said all should be free to worship any way they wish, and communists had the right to have their own political party. In an interview with Netherlands Television in November 1978, he said, 'The regime that replaces the Shah's regime will be fair, to a greater degree than any you will find in a Western democracy. It is possible that our ideal democracy is similar to Western democracy, but the democracy we want to establish does not exist in the West. Islamic democracy is more advanced.'

The issue of the status of women in Islam gave rise to

considerable disagreement with our communist friends. There were passages in the Qur'an that were difficult to defend: that a man may have more than one wife, that he may beat his wife as punishment, that a woman is entitled to only half the inheritance of a man and that the value of a woman's testimony is also only half that of a man's. So when Khomeini proclaimed that a woman could even become president, it was quite a victory for us *vis-à-vis* the communists. On the other hand, though my allegiance was entirely to Khomeini and the Mojahedin, I was uncomfortable with some of their behaviour, such as holding group prayer sessions in public places and advocating Islamic dress for women. Anna didn't conform, nor did either of us want her to, but we sometimes felt she was frowned upon for this reason.

The Mojahedin members in London asked us, via Ahmad, to set up a committee of supporters in Newcastle. I didn't know much about the Mojahedin, but their philosophy seemed indistinguishable from Shari'ati's. I worshipped the same martyrs they did. I observed their vehement support for Khomeini. Through the only ideological book of the Mojahedin movement I read, *Shanakht* ('Understanding'), I discovered that certain beliefs and contentions that Marxists claimed as their own were actually prefigured in the Qur'an and in the works of Imam Ali and the Iranian poet Molavi. But I still did not know what economic principles the Mojahedin advocated. Once our old friend Behzad came to stay with us. It was the fashion of the day for everyone to ally himself with a particular political group, and Behzad introduced himself as a supporter of the Fedai'in. For the first time we quarrelled about our beliefs, though neither of us knew much about what we were defending. He asked us out to the pub for a drink, but we declined, as we had become observant Muslims. He swore at God and attacked religion, 'the opium of the masses'. Then he announced that all talk about religion is in fact just superstition. We soon discovered we could not have any meaningful conversation together. He said it was a good thing I was going to support the Mojahedin, who were very close to the Fedai'in and believed in socialism and communism. I was in favour of democratic socialism at the time, but opposed to proletarian dictatorship, which normally went hand in hand with communism. So I disagreed with him strongly. 'You don't know much about the

Mojahedin,' he said accusingly, 'so how can you support them?' He was right. My ignorance shamed me, so when Ahmad asked me to set up a committee I put to him some of the questions on my mind. I soon found that I knew more than he about many areas, including the Mojahedin's ideology. To fill the gaps in my knowledge I set about finding as many books as I could about the Mojahedin, among them *T'akamul* ('Evolution') and *Rah Anbia* and *Rah Bashar* ('Path of Prophets' and 'Path of a Human Being'). I also felt that we needed our own organisation at the university, so I asked some Indonesian and Malaysian friends, along with our Iranian friends, to join us in establishing a new society we called the 'Iranian Muslim Society'.

On 6th January, after Azhari suffered a number of heart attacks, the Shah appointed a new prime minister, Shapur Bakhtiar – the only one willing to accept the premiership. The announcement was followed immediately by another saying that he was no longer a member of the National Front. I confess to shedding a few tears when I saw Bakhtiar's picture under the photograph of Mossadegh instead of the Shah's. At last, Mossadegh had found his true position in Iranian history and even the Shah's government had to acknowledge it. Unlike other prime ministers, Bakhtiar did not bow and scrape before the Shah. In my eyes it was another victory towards toppling the giant. Bakhtiar abolished Savak; freed all remaining political prisoners; guaranteed freedom for all political parties and newspapers; promised fair and free elections; and asked to meet Khomeini. His promises seemed to answer all my dreams and, in pragmatic terms, to be the only way to stop the bloodshed. For me, human life was to be valued above all else. The Mojahedin took a different view. Their interpretation of events was that the choice of Bakhtiar as prime minister was another trick perpetrated by the Shah. They rejected his government and announced that 'all who join this administration are inferior, worthless traitors, who, when public awareness and activity are at their height, are helping the Shah to breathe again'; the new regime had reached a compromise with imperialism and rendered all bloodshed and sacrifice fruitless. Bakhtiar was seen as a powerless servant of the Shah. Only days later we heard the happiest news of our lives: the Iranian newspapers ran banner headlines reading, '*Shah raft*' ('The Shah has gone') or '*Shah farar kard*' ('The Shah has escaped').

On 1st February, while still rejoicing over the Shah's departure from Iran, we heard about Khomeini's return to Tehran. When we saw the news broadcast on the student union television, we Iranians jumped from our chairs, hugging and kissing each other. The British and other students looked at us, bemused, wondering why the return of an old man to Iran should make us so happy. We could see millions of people gathering to welcome him. Khomeini's answer to a journalist about his feelings on seeing his county and his people after an absence of fifteen years: 'Nothing'.

Very quickly Khomeini appointed Bazargan as prime minister at the head of a provisional government: further good news, although it gave rise to disagreements between the pro-Fedai'in supporters and those on our side. I believed we had to give our full support to Bazargan to overthrow the regime and solve the problems facingthe country. The big worry was what America might do. But the US was trying to persuade Iranian generals not to mount any coup against the revolutionary government due to take power very soon. Our time seemed taken up with following the news and discussing Iran's future. Even Tudeh Party supporters became proponents of the revolution and were seeking to associate themselves with us. They distributed leaflets containing the text of Khomeini's speeches, posted his photograph all over the place and joined us for meetings and demonstrations. From 7th to 9th February we hardly breathed as we waited for the outcome of the showdown between men of the Shah's special armed force and air force personnel. At the end of that period the result was a clear win for the revolution. Bakhtiar, like the Shah, chose to leave the country and Bazargan became the sole prime minister. Our joy knew no bounds. Tyranny had gone! Freedom had come! Or so we thought. We were soon to discover how wrong we were – a misapprehension that had implications not just for our generation but for those to come, not just for Iranians but for many others around the world.

# 10

# Tehran First and Last

With the success of the revolution, political activity declined. We all had to work hard to catch up on the time and effort lost.

Sarvy was growing fast and starting to talk, switching between Farsi and English and sometimes confusing them. I had everything one might wish for: I was married to a most understanding, kind and beautiful woman. I had the sweetest child. I was in my final year of study, which could secure our futures, a pleasant home, a car ... True, I worked late every day at the university, but every night I returned home to love and warmth.

Although since adulthood Anna and I had been nominally Muslims, we were now trying increasingly to act according to Islamic values. At parties we would proudly announce that we didn't drink alcohol because of our religious beliefs. Once we met a couple from Libya, both postgraduate students, from whom we felt we could learn a lot. At the time we thought that anybody – including Libya's leader himself – who talked of restoring Islam as an ideology had the same values as Shari'ati and Bazargan. But we were surprised to learn that these people were political refugees, opposed to Qaddafi's regime; we realised they were like pro-Shah Iranians, who had to flee the country, and that we had nothing in common with them. Instead of love, unity and brotherhood, we sensed the barriers of anger and hate caused by ideological differences.

Less than two weeks after the victory of the revolution we heard about the first disagreement between the Mojahedin and Bazargan's provisional government. Rajavi had attacked Bazargan and questioned him about two of his people and their relations with America, including the speaker of the government. Like many Iranian intellectuals, I loved and respected the Mojahedin for their courage and self-sacrifice. We regarded Bazargan not only as prime minister but also as a teacher, with the Mojahedin as his ideological inheritors. We were proud to introduce ourselves unequivocally as supporters of the Mojahedin, and I became a member of the local committee of supporters. But now the first crack appeared in the unity of the revolutionary forces. The Mojahedin were behaving like other ultra-left groups. This ideological disunity was echoed among the Iranian students around us – even those who at the start of the revolution had been like brothers, united against the Shah's tyranny. Now supporters of different Marxist groups and even some Mojahedin supporters were vehemently attacking the leaders of the revolution. Only the most progressive *ayatollah*, Talaghani, and Khomeini himself were exempt from accusations of collaborating with imperialists and with America. Less than a month after the revolution, some people calling themselves Hezbollahi ('followers of the Party of God'), self-proclaimed Muslims who branded the Mojahedin as Marxists, had attacked Mojahedin centres in several cities. Mojahedin there had been beaten and ejected. Strangely, these people also accused Bazargan of collaborating with imperialism. A few days later there was news of fighting in Kurdistan and Torkaman-Sahra between the Pasdaran and supporters of various revolutionary groups.

Soon we all had to take sides. Supporters of different groups rarely talked to or even greeted each other. As Bazargan later said, the unity of revolutionary forces disappeared with the departure of the common enemy, the Shah. I was attacked not only because I defended the provisional government and Bazargan, but also for supporting the Mojahedin. Supporters of other Marxist organisations claimed that the Mojahedin were silent on many issues unless they felt their own interests to be at stake. They declined to defend other organisations or speak out against political killings. Only on the issues of America and imperialism, which they felt were good propaganda issues, did they criticise the government. So it was said.

Thus the new Iranian year didn't bring as much joy as we expected. A referendum was called for 1st April, posing the choice between an Islamic republic and a constitutional monarchy. For many of us this was a spurious choice. While we all rejected the latter, we were not necessarily willing to accept the former. All other revolutionary and some national groups like the National Democratic Front boycotted the referendum. The Mojahedin's position perfectly reflected my own. They suggested changing the wording of the question into one on the abolition of the monarchy in Iran and postponing the selection of a name for the new republic until such time as the National Assembly decided on a constitution. They also announced that, as Muslims, they would naturally answer in favour of the first choice, but with the proviso that an Islamic republic meant a state that would ensure freedom and justice for all, including non-believers in Islam or even in God.

On the day of the referendum most of us travelled to Manchester to vote at the Iranian consulate. It was the first time I had been there since the collapse of the Shah's regime. It had totally changed and felt like a second home, where everybody called everyone else 'brother' or 'sister'. I asked where could I pray and was shown to a large room. While praying I felt happy; it seemed to me that this new republic was going to be a land of freedom and brotherhood.

The vote was overwhelming: 99 percent of voters said 'yes' to an Islamic republic. It was the first and perhaps last free and (almost) fair election in Iran's modern history, and the first and last time I voted. After the referendum the views of the various groups diverged sharply. Hezbollahis attacked women without the *hijab* (veil or scarf); their slogan was, 'you wear a scarf or you get hit on the head'. Some *mullahs* now demanded the return of the *Shari'a* (traditional Islamic law), which had rarely been practised throughout Iranian history. Such practices as stoning, slashing and cutting off limbs were considered barbaric and denounced as pre-Islamic Arab laws unrelated to Islam. Beneficial principally to men, they were deeply entrenched in society and could not be changed – in fact, they remain today as they were 1,400 years ago. However we balked, such practices had already been instituted and our laws and judiciary system were going backwards fast. The Hezbollah slogan, *'hesb faghad Hesb'ol llah, rahbar faghad rohol llah'* ('the party is the only party of God, Khomeini is the only leader'), implied no freedom for anybody except members or allies of the group: you were either with them or against them – a sentiment beloved of dictators throughout history, echoed in the Shah's famous statement, 'either you are with us or you should leave the country'. Their activity was beginning to predominate. Soon the movement included the entourage of Talaghani, who was respected and loved as *padar* ('father') by people from both ends of the political spectrum. Hezbollahi kidnapped his sons, and in response he closed his offices and was not seen in public for some time. The public reaction was one of anger and dismay. The Mojahedin, by revealing what had happened and denouncing the reactionaries' actions against Ayatollah Talaghani, now regained some of the popular support they had lost by criticising the provisional government. As a result, the reactionaries retreated and freed Talaghani's sons.

Nobody criticised Khomeini himself. He was loved and revered, and everyone hoped he would live to see the success of the revolution. For some time there was no good news from Iran. The revolutionary spring was short-lived, and one could detect the popular temperature rising. I could not approve of what was happening in the name of the revolution and Islam, but we were afraid of Khomeini becoming a second Allende. It was time to return to Iran to see events firsthand.

It was July 1979, exactly three years since we had left home – three crucial years, which had changed millions of Iranian lives forever. We tried to show Sarvy, young though she was, our joy at being on home ground. Out of respect for the new Iranian culture, Anna wore a scarf on the plane, which Sarvy found a little strange.

As we disembarked, a delightful breeze touched our skin; we wanted to kneel down and kiss the blessed soil of our country. At the airport, a few familiar faces were to be seen, but the majority of the staff were Pasdaran, young men with beards, dark green clothes and shoulder-slung rifles. Thanks to our name and kinship with Abol-Hassan Banisadr, one of and new regime's most popular faces, we were whisked through official controls. Outside, Anna's relatives waited with my mother and Ammo Jan. It was a joyous and emotional reunion, full of questions and smiles, tears, hugs and kisses. We felt as though we had been away for centuries.

Tehran was a strange city we barely recognised. The walls were daubed with slogans, barriers built to resist the army during the revolution blocked some streets and street names had been changed to obliterate memories of the Shah and celebrate the martyrs of the revolution. Pahlavi Street had become Mossadegh Street, which we found intensely moving. Most of the women had discarded their high-fashion clothes for dark veils, and formerly clean-shaven men in ties wore beards and buttoned shirts. The Reza Shah statues had all gone. People no longer seemed afraid of the traffic police. In fact, it was perhaps the other way round, as police treated people with a new politeness and respect. We witnessed a minor car crash; in the old days, the drivers would have got out and sworn at each other, maybe even have come to blows until onlookers or police separated them. Now, to our amazement, they shook hands, kissed and exchanged addresses and telephone numbers. It seemed as though the revolution, like a patient teacher, had educated people, bringing 100 years of advancement in the space of one year. At my mother's house we watched Islamic TV and listened to the new Iranian radio. For the first time we heard the names of Mojahedin martyrs. The new regime was proud of them and had named many universities, hospitals and public places after them. Martyrs are, after all, the main pillars of the Shi'a faith.

But, as Ammo Jan said, 'unfortunately the good and the bad have both been burned. We miss some of the good things.'

When we visited my father, he apologised for not meeting us at the airport. 'I am rarely able to go out,' he said. 'I don't know much about the new customs. I cannot drive any more as nobody respects the old traffic laws. Nowadays anyone who does not like something from the old times says it is *taghoti* (pertaining to infidels and enemies of God) and rejects it immediately without substituting something better for it.' At lunch, as he was about to pour us a glass of wine, I apologised and said that, as we now considered ourselves Muslims, we couldn't drink. His smile suddenly changed into a look of sadness. He shook his head and said, 'So now you are Muslim and those who drink wine are not?' All through lunch he argued that wine is part of Iranian culture and figures large in our literature. 'All our intellectuals, writers and poets were good Muslims and at the same time they drank wine, as do many ordinary Iranians. We have never had a problem with alcoholism in this country. Anyway', he continued with some anger, 'Islam has accepted many backward Arab traditions and forced us to accept them. Why can't we keep one "backward" tradition of our own?' He laughed and changed the subject.

His house was different too. The statue of the Shah in the hallway had gone, as had the fine silk tapestry. His former servants now had their own houses in the same area. So my father, stepmother and sister Nazi lived alone and had to maintain the household by themselves. After a while, we went out together. On the bus he put a question to me – the first time he had ever treated me as an equal, or even as someone whose opinion might be sought: 'Do you really think these *mullahs* are good for our country?'

'Well,' I replied, 'I think the revolution was not intended to bring in the rule of the *mullahs* but the rule of the people.'

He didn't let me continue in this idealistic vein, instead asking, 'What will you do? Will you stay? Or are you going back to finish your studes?' Unusually, he did not follow up these questions with observations that suggested his own view and implied the answers.

'I don't know', I said, 'Everything is changing so fast, and I want to be part of those changes. Although I do have some doubts about the direction of the new government.' He asked me about our relative, Abol-Hassan Banisadr. I had nothing good to report: the Mojahedin had accused him of calling them *eltaghatii* (people who have combined two ideologies, in this case Islam and Marxism), and Stalinist. We didn't object to the designation 'Stalinist', as Stalin was a revolutionary and his name meant 'man of steel'. My father said, 'I am going to make an appointment for you to see Banisadr and tell him your concerns. Perhaps you can get some answers to your questions.'

The next day I called Mohammed, my second-closest friend in the UK Mojahedin. The first was Aliraza, who, although younger than Mohammed and me, was our guide in the Mojahedin's ways and indeed symbolised it for us. He was unfailingly calm and patient, logical and honest; he worked tirelessly for the cause. His uncle was a minister in the provisional government whom he never hesitated to criticise for bad decisions. Aliraza's father was a high-ranking revolutionary. Aliraza, Mohammed and I had jointly decided to return home to judge events for ourselves. Aliraza had not yet arrived, so Mohammed and I went to Behash't Zahra, a new cemetery where most of the revolutionary martyrs were buried. There we met two of his friends, both Mojahedin supporters. They took us to the newly built tomb of the Mojahedin's founders, then to other graves – each marked with tributes carved in stone and tended with dried flowers or plants. Each headstone bore a picture of the deceased. From these pictures, stretching in their thousands in parallel rows, one could tell that the martyrs of the revolution were mostly young, of school or university age. One of Mohammed's friends pointed to them and said, 'You see? Our generation paid the price of this revolution, yet others are claiming it as their own. How many *mullahs* can you see among these martyrs?' he continued. 'Yet they are the ones who control everything and don't let us say a word. Where were in the government and revolutionary council, like Banisadr or Yazdi or Ghodbzadeh, during the revolution?' The Mojahedin say it is forbidden to grieve for martyrs, but it was hard to suppress our tears. Later we realised that our sorrow was not for the dead but for the living.

We went on to the University of Tehran, the heart of the revolution. The weather was very hot, and it was almost noon. Hundreds of people stood in small groups discussing and arguing to and fro. The debates were loud and lively, but not abusive or violent. They seemed a healthy symbol of the adulthood of our society. In one circle was a discussion about the Mojahedin's use of the phrase, 'In the name of God and the heroic people of Iran'. Why, someone argued, did one need to link God with any other entity? This was dualism. A Mojahed (singular of 'Mojahedin') replied that many crimes had been committed in the name of God, whereas the will of the people alone was not always to be relied on. Thus it was right to act in the name of God, for the good of the people.

Outside the university walls thousands of books carpeted the street, ranging from Marx, Engels and Lenin to Shari'ati and Bazargan, plus texts from various organisations from the far left to the far right. In between the books were other things for sale, including cassette tapes of Motahari and Shari'ati, ice cream and sandwiches and cartoons, some depicting Khomeini as an angel driving out the Shah, shown as a devil. I asked Mohammed's friend what he thought of that cartoon.

'What can I say?' he said. 'He is the leader of the revolution. He sees all the unjust actions of the reactionaries and some revolutionary guards, and remains silent. Does silence mean approval? For many, it does.'

Still, for me the joy of being in the new Iran and seeing the achievements of the revolution far outweighed the disappointments. The university was open; the armed guards had gone. There was free speech, freedom of the press and no censorship. A new culture of trust and respect was evident. The revolution could not be judged by the actions of some individual club-wielders and hooligans.

The following day, Friday, we attended prayers in the same place. Everything was completely changed. It was two hours before the prayer hour, but it seemed millions of people had poured in to the area and were sitting or standing, walking or even running, trying to find the right place to pray. The university itself was full to bursting and the streets were crowded with people queuing in parallel lines. Anna had to leave us and join the women's lines. Some people prayed on the streets, others on pieces of cloth. The weather was very hot and some people had brought cold water and sweets which they offered around. The *imam* leading prayers that Friday was Talaghani. There were loudspeakers everywhere, so we could all hear him, even if we were some distance away. It was a moving scene. Although prayer demands total concentration on God and God alone, still I could not help noticing with some elation the discipline and unity of the people around me.

Afterwards Mohammed told me that Aliraza had arrived. I had an appointment with my nephew Reza, himself a nephew of Abol-Hassan Banisadr, and I suggested to Mohammed and Aliraza that they join me on a visit to the office of the *Enghalab Eslami* newspaper owned by Banisadr.

Greeting Aliraza, I told him how glad I was to see him in Tehran and suggested that with the help of my relatives at *Enghalab Eslami* and his uncle's support we might be able to do something useful. At this he looked at me angrily and snapped, 'Do you know what are you saying? Do you realise how opportunistic and status-seeking that suggestion is?' His admonition shamed me so much that for the rest of the day I could barely speak with him. At the newspaper we met my relatives and the other staff, most of whom were young and seemed honest and hard-working. The *mullahs* were creating problems for them as well, but as they were not contradicting Khomeini and the revolutionary council as sharply as the communists and Mojahedin did, they were freer to go about their business. They were critical of the communists and the Mojahedin, painting them as a pseudo-left wing whose actions and words not only failed to solve any problems but also gave more ground to the far right, forcing Bazargan and Banisadr into a corner. Aliraza disagreed with them hotly and some fierce argument ensued, in which neither side made any inroads into the other's beliefs. I took Aliraza's part and, as a result, declined the offer of a press card granting me admission to restricted places so as to judge things for myself.

When we left, Aliraza told us there was going to be a demonstration in support of Sadatti, a high-ranking member of the Mojahedin who, after the revolution, was designated 'the first political prisoner'. He had been arrested and tortured a few months earlier by some unofficial revolutionary guards and was now on a hunger strike in Evin prison, having been neither charged nor tried. Reza joined us, although he kept apart from the column of demonstrators. Anna came too, marching with the women.

The route of the demonstration was from the University of Tehran to the Palace of Justice. I had never seen so many people in a demonstration. Most were young, down to primary-school age. Members of the Mojahedin and their supporters, wearing a red armlet, maintained discipline. Banners bore images of Sadatti, Khomeini, Talaghani and the martyrs of the Mojahedin. Along the route, bystanders looked puzzled, unable to understand what the demonstration was for – the Shah had gone, a revolutionary government was in power. Then, from the middle of the road, we saw and sensed other people around. From whispers amongst the demonstrators, we realised that they were reactionary club-wielders. On closer inspection one could see that many of them hid a piece of wood or club under their coats or had their belts in hand. Then we heard the voice of a woman standing on the pavement and swearing loudly and repeatedly at the demonstrators: it was the famous Zahra Khanom, spokeswoman for the club-wielders.

As we neared the Palace of Justice, they launched their attack. Our orders were to keep the discipline of the lines at any price, not to react to the beatings but remain passive. The reactionaries beat the demonstrators with their belts and clubs, kicking, punching and throwing stones. The Mojahedin guarding the demonstration joined hands and stood before them, so that they bore the brunt of the beatings; but they were not many, and at best they could protect only the women. Some of us, including Aliraza, Mohammed and I, joined hands with them. We managed to reach the Palace of Justice, where we were due to hear an address by Reziae's Mother, mother of four martyrs. I expected the Hezbollahi to fall silent out of respect for her, but on the contrary they started swearing at her too. Soon they received reinforcements and their attacks increased. We could see blood around us. Then the smell and sound of gunfire told us that the revolutionary guards had arrived on the scene. By now the circle of defence was broken in many places. A man left us, shouting, 'This is impossible. We have to answer these bastards in the only way they can understand.' The voice of Reziae's Mother from the loudspeaker mixed with the sounds of shots, blows, swearing and the screams of the injured. The presence of the revolutionary guards forced the demonstrators to flee in every direction. Some demonstrators had found garden gates open and ran to take refuge.

An hour or two had passed; I was bewildered and terrified by what I had seen. The worst of it was that I didn't know where Anna was. I wandered the streets looking for her and at the same time, deep down, searching for the lost revolution on which we had pinned all our hopes. I think those club-wielders and revolutionary guards were the final messengers who pushed me into the arms of the Mojahedin. Almost before I realised it, their actions had decided my destiny. I remembered what my cousin Banisadr told us at our house in Newcastle: 'If they don't respect the freedoms and rights of the people we will fight them the same way we fought the Shah's regime.' Where was he now to see these supposed guardians of freedom and civil rights? In a revolutionary council, 'collaborating' with the same criminals who were responsible for this savagery. In this way, my mind was made up about him as well.

At Anna's parents' home I found her calmly awaiting me. I told her how worried I had been about her and how desperately I had searched for her. 'I learned again how much I love you', I said. In the living room were Anna's cousin Mohsen and his wife, both Mojahedin supporters. I recounted my few hours' horrified tramping the streets, spilling out all my anxieties about the reactionaries' and revolutionary guards' behaviour. It had taken me only a day to see how easily one could be killed or lose loved ones in this city. They laughed. 'For us it is a part of daily life. We are used to it, only we can see that it is getting worse and worse.' Mohsen was one of the nicest and most honourable people we knew, so to find him among supporters of the Mojahedin gave us more courage and determination to follow their path. His mother, he said, was a fanatical follower of the *mullahs*, and had threatened to curse him if he did not reject the Mojahedin. This was the last time we saw Mohsen; a few years later we heard he had been executed by the revolutionary guards, and that his mother had refused to visit his grave or mourn him.

The next time I saw my nephew Reza was at my sister's house. His father-in-law was Minister of Justice in the provisional government and his father, my cousin, was the provisional government's public prosecutor. As with other posts, there was a parallel 'public prosecutor' in the revolutionary administration. I asked him why the provisional government was doing nothing to curb the behaviour of the revolutionary guards. He said it had no power in this respect: all the power was in the hands of the revolutionary committees and other bodies. It was the revolutionary prosecutor and court that decided the fate of the people.

A few days later I left for Zahedan, about 1,600 kilometres south of Tehran, to see my oldest and closest friend Farzad, now a lecturer at Baluchistan University. Although it was the capital of the province, Zahedan was in very poor shape, consisting mainly of mud houses, except at the city centre. Strangely, unlike in Tehran, the government buildings – even the Savak offices – were not burned or damaged. 'The revolution came to this city very late,' Farzad explained. 'Even the statue of the Shah in the centre of the city was knocked down only a few days ago, and not by a popular mob but by university students and lecturers. People here are so poor that their only concern is how to find food for the next day. They can't think about politics. They say the Shah is gone, and Khomeini is the new Shah. As you can see, class differences are not very evident here either. So many people feel that things are as they should be. Anyone who becomes a bit richer soon moves on to another city; those who remain are leaders of tribes who have the respect of their own tribesmen.'

At the university campus, which was unusually modern and attractive, I met some lecturers who were Mojahedin supporters.

'The programme of the Mojahedin and some other revolutionary groups,' they told me, 'is to introduce themselves by going to villages and helping people improve their living conditions. For example, here we are trying to lay a water pipe, so that villagers can have clean water for drinking and cultivation. But the *mullahs* are obstacles: in one village the *mullah* told the villagers that the work had been carried out by communists, and that the water was *najass* [religiously unclean], so nobody wanted to use it. Eventually, when we left, the villagers dug up the pipes and stole them. For the Fedai'in and other communist groups the situation is even worse, and they're grateful if they get away with their heads still on their shoulders. The biggest obstacle, though, is poverty. People are so poor that they don't believe intellectuals like us might come and work for them for free. They have difficulty trusting us; we don't have enough time to live amongst them and let them get to know us. Yesterday we took some tools to one village and today when we were due to start work we found that the villagers had stolen everything. While we were working, they watched us suspiciously. We look rich compared to them. Well, we can't do anything about the way we look, but the result is that mostly they regard us with hatred rather than love.'

The next day, in the city centre, I wanted to buy a bottled beverage from a shop as we were unable to drink the dark, smelly water that came out of every tap in town (even at the university). The shopkeeper asked if I wanted to drink it there or take it away. It was a strange question for me; I answered that I wanted more than one to take with me. At that he said he had none to sell. The same thing happened at a second shop, and when I went empty-handed to Farzad's car he told me where I had gone wrong. 'People here are so poor, nobody goes and buys a few beverages; normally the price of a bottle is more than the drink itself, so when you want to buy the drink you have to pay for the bottle as well. When you asked for a few, the shopkeepers must have thought the price of bottles was going up but they didn't know how much to charge, so they couldn't sell you any until they discovered what was going on. I'm afraid we won't be able to buy any drinks today, here or maybe from anywhere else. You single-handedly pushed up the price of beverages. Now everybody will suffer for a while.'

Many people made a living selling smuggled goods, from alcoholic drinks to sex magazines. Farzad said, 'Here everything is for sale, even children.' In that situation, I reflected, who could talk to these people about democracy? Even Mojahedin supporters were considering leaving the area. 'It is almost impossible to work here', they said. 'Apart from the *mullahs* and the poverty, the leaders of the tribes don't want us here. So we achieve almost nothing at the end of the day.'

A few days later I returned to Tehran. I heard from Anna's brother Hussein, who called himself a Fedai'in supporter, that the Hezbollahi were planning to attack Mojahedin bases. The following day I went to the Mojahedin's main centre in Mossadegh Avenue, formerly the office of the Pahlavi Foundation. People crowded around the building, most of them worried supporters wanting to see what they could do to defend the centre. Some of my Newcastle friends worked there, including Masoud, who took me inside and gave me a copy of the first issue of *Mojahed*, the official organ of the Mojahedin. He told me the latest news. 'The issue of Sadatti is getting hotter every day. They can't prove he is a Soviet spy, but nor can they admit their mistake and free him.' Masoud Rajavi and Mussa Khiabani, the Mojahedin's highest-ranking members, had met Khomeini and, instead of kissing his hands as was usual, kissed his face. Khomeini had asked them to defend Islam against the Marxists.

Reactionaries had attacked Mojahedin centres in various cities. This one had not been attacked yet, but they were prepared to defend it and would not surrender easily. Masoud introduced me to a high-ranking Mojahed, who asked me about my relationship to Banisadr and others in the provisional government. When I told him about our visit to the *Enghalab Eslami* office and my refusal to accept their press card or meet Banisadr himself, he said we had been wrong, and that I could help the Mojahedin a lot by doing so. Then I asked his advice about staying in Iran or returning to England. Perhaps he realised that I was not politically mature enough to be of use in Iran; perhaps he also saw how terrified I was by the events surrounding the demonstration. 'Go back and finish your studies,' he said, 'and help our brothers and sisters in England.'

# 11

# Blood and Hatred

We knew our financial circumstances in Britain would be tight, that we would have to be thrifty and live on what we got from the rent of our apartment. But we decided to return. Saying goodbye to our parents and friends was difficult. With tears in my eyes, I told them we would be back in a year or two. How could I know that this was the last time I would see and hold them? How could I know that this was the last time I would see my beautiful country and have its warm air in my lungs? If I had known, would I have ever been able to tear myself away? Never!

During our stay in Iran I had bought as many Mojahedin books as had been published. The material was heavy both in quantity and comprehensibility. It contained a new vocabulary to deal with the Mojahedin worldview, a whole new culture and system of thought.

In a tiny book called *Rahnamodha'e Be'a Javanan Enghalabi* ('Advice to Revolutionary Youth'), I found definitions of people like Anna and me, who had grown up during the Shah's regime and become 'stupefied' by the Western culture that suffused our education – to the extent that they became rotten and corrupt. Revolutionaries were defined as those who had rejected this education, rejected fake heroes like Bruce Lee, and instead sought real heroes among the people, learned about the Mojahedin and emulated their qualities in daily life.

The lesson was very clear: We had to forget our past, learn everything from the very beginning. It struck me, reading this book and another about the lives of some Mojahedin martyrs, how selfish I was, how wasteful my life had been and how corrupt and dirty my mind and heart were. While I enjoyed myself, thinking about love, marriage and life's pleasures, the Mojahedin were suffering torture and fighting, under the harshest conditions, against the Shah's tyranny. Up to then I believed my character, if not perfect, was at least not wholly bad. It had served me as a kind of immune system against the outside world. But now, according to Mojahedin teaching, it was itself under attack and had to be neutralised. I knew that to become worthy was not the work of a day, month or even year, that it was as difficult a task as any battle ever fought.

I chose to characterise myself as a Mojahedin supporter. Instead of judging their actions, I judged myself according to whether or not I was complying with their teaching. Instead of judging the rights and wrongs of political events according to my own logic, I tried to understand them according to the logic of the Mojahedin. The more I read their literature, the more I was ashamed of my past fecklessness and ignorance. I knew I had to work to change myself. Fortunately our friends in Newcastle, if no worse than me, were certainly no better, and our experiences in Iran had given us a slight advantage.

The first issue of *Mojahed* was very interesting. I particularly liked an article about the responsibility of writers to be sincere and truthful, and another about Khomeini, depicting him clearly as the leader and guardian of the revolution. I had reservations about the issue of Khomeini's attacks on certain newspapers, which focused mainly on leftist activity and reactionary brutality. It represented a move on Khomeini's part against freedom of the press, which was at heart against freedom as a whole. Another issue that bothered me concerned execution orders issued by the revolutionary courts. However evil the activities of the Shah and his ministers, I could not defend any kind of execution, especially when carried out on people without proper trial. In my view it was a long way from the 'Islamic justice' we wanted to introduce to the world. I was not happy to see the Mojahedin approving these executions and congratulating the prosecutors and judges, demanding more decisive action and more executions. I understood, however, that my view stemmed from the education I had received, which the Mojahedin called corrupt. I knew it took time to learn to think and hate anti-revolutionaries as they did.

That summer, in the hope of returning to Iran as soon as possible, I worked very hard and finished my research. In September Anna's father, whom I liked very much, visited us. He was with us less than a week when a cry from him woke us one morning. He had heard from Iranian radio that 'Padar' Talaghani was dead. We also wept when we heard. It was one of the saddest events of my life. Talaghani was a barrier against the reactionaries, a defender of democracy, progress and the rights of people, including minorities. Whatever wrong happened in Iran, we looked to him to put it right. He had everyone's respect – the reason, perhaps, why the reactionaries didn't like him. His death represented the end of any hopes of a compromise that could unite the different factions of the revolution.

On 4th November 1979, a momentous event took place: a few Iranian university students seized the US embassy in Tehran, taking sixty-six hostages and calling themselves 'student followers of the Imam's line'(*Imam*, meaning 'leader', was a common reference to Khomeini). They demanded that the US extradite the Shah, then receiving cancer treatment in an American hospital. The hostages were held for 444 days. Many things changed, including Iran's politics and reputation abroad.

As Mojahedin supporters we could not oppose the students' action; since the victory of the revolution there had scarcely been a statement or article by the Mojahedin that did not condemn imperialism and American activity in Iran, Vietnam or elsewhere. The Mojahedin and other revolutionary groups criticised the provisional government, including Prime Minister Bazargan, for his lenience towards America and even sometimes accused his associates of collaborating with imperialists. The Mojahedin were very proud of their anti-American actions during the Shah's regime, even boasting of the number of Americans they had killed. At the same time came news of the occupation of the American consulates in Isfahan and Tabriz (two major cities in central and northwest Iran) by the Mojahedin themselves. This news confirmed to us that the hostage-taking had the support of revolutionary groups, including the Mojahedin. Later, we found out that the Mojahedin were unable to hold the captured American consulates against the revolutionary guards. Personally, although I believed that international norms had to be respected at all costs, I could see that the students had acted out of revenge for illegal American acts during the previous twenty-six years, including a CIA-organised coup against Mossadegh; foreign-embassy personnel shouldn't involve themselves in the internal affairs of their host country, yet the Americans gave no sign of apology or regret to Iran for their transgressions.

There followed what was called the second phase of the Iranian revolution. We had to put aside our normal lives again, including our studies, and concentrate more than ever on politics. Most of the time Iranian students gathered in the student union building or the mosque, exchanging news and information, discussing these with people of other nationalities, explaining, defending and interpreting events. Unlike the first phase of the revolution, when we had almost universal support, many opposed us this time. Some Muslims even reminded us that in the history of civilisation, envoys were safe from aggression in their host countries, even in wartime, and embassies were sometimes used as sanctuaries. On the other side were sympathisers with Allende in Chile, Sukarno in Indonesia and the Palestinians in the Middle East; many Latin American and African students; and some on the British left, for whom the embassy attack was a response to American bullying around the world and a vehicle for their hatred of America.

In general Iranians received bad, one-sided press, and as a consequence faced hostility from the British public, even from former friends. Some began to call themselves 'Persian', trading on general ignorance and the positive associations of Persian carpets and cats.

In those days Iranian Muslim students in Iran and abroad were divided into 'Islamic societies' – supporters of the regime and especially of the *mullahs* – and 'Muslim Student Societies', known as 'MSS', which supported the Mojahedin. Unlike the MSS, Islamic societies were not unified in their policies or actions, as each was under the influence of a different faction of the regime.

After some time Iranian students began to reunite. A few days after the hostage-taking, there was a demonstration organised by

Islamic societies in Manchester. It was interesting to see students who did not belong to any group, along with supporters of the Tudeh Party and people of other nationalities, all taking part. Public reaction was hostile. Shouts of 'Go home, you bloody Iranian' were common; one construction worker urinated on the heads of the demonstrators from the top of a building.

Afterwards, the organisers contacted me, wanting me to represent them in our area. The Manchester organisation supported Banisadr and was thus keen to maintain connections with me. Aliraza, at first, said nothing about this; then, probably after contacting a Mojahedin representative in London, told me that I had acted wrongly: I should not have attended the demonstration or created an organisation in Newcastle to support such activity; I should disconnect myself from them immediately. I couldn't agree. I saw how sincerely the Mojahedin were showing solidarity with the students responsible for the hostage-taking. They even demanded that the embassy be converted into a museum of American crimes in Iran. Every article in *Mojahed* was about imperialism and the fight against it. One article even went so far as to suggest a ban on computers as they made us dependent on the US and other imperialists. They announced that in defending the country against American aggression, their forces would be under the command of the revolutionary guards. It was not acceptable to me that the policy of Mojahedin supporters abroad should differ from that of the lead organisation inside Iran. Having read and learned from *Mojahed*, I could see nothing wrong with what I had done. I felt it was my right to demand some sort of explanation. Aliraza said we were not to question the policies of the organisation, merely to obey, and when I referred him to an article in *Mojahed* about the right to ask questions and criticise the organisation, he replied that that was for ordinary people, not supporters and members. I suggested this was his own position, to which he answered that I should go to London and speak with Mojahedin representatives there.

It was my first visit to the London Mojahedin base – a very simple apartment in the centre of the city. In one room a few people sat around a table, translating articles from newspapers. At five o'clock they announced a break, and tea, biscuits and oranges were served. My first impression was of a homely and harmonious place in which everything was communally owned and everyone fulfilled their responsibilities pleasantly and efficiently; it seemed like heaven on earth. I met Hussein, a Mojahedin representative who impressed me with his politeness and patience. He explained that, as a sympathiser of the organisation, I would have to follow the line put forward by its representatives. It was not satisfactory to go by what we read in the paper, as that was often inaccurate. Later I learned that, according to the organisation, 'hostage-taking' was not an act of anti-imperialism but a policy conducted by reactionaries against true revolutionaries and the liberal faction of the regime. This action forced the premier Bazargan to abdicate, and weakened and disarmed the revolutionaries, especially the Mojahedin, in their real fight against imperialism.

From then on I was a recognised organisational sympathiser of the Mojahedin. Instead of interpreting Mojahedin policies through their paper, I could consult Mohsen, a student in Leeds, who was my *masoul* (official representative of the organisation) responsible, I later learned, for all the Mojahedin supporters in northern Britain.

Although in the first few weeks after the victory of the revolution, the Mojahedin (like many other leftist organisations) attacked the provisional government and Bazargan himself for allegedly 'paving the way for the return of America'. They soon discovered that their main enemies were not the so-called 'liberals' – Bazargan and his government – but the 'reactionaries', the *mullahs*, who controlled the revolutionary council, committees and guards. When the Bazargan government resigned, the Mojahedin were not satisfied. From then on another verbal battle raged, not between them and the reactionaries, but against some of the revolutionary organisations including the Fedai'in, who'd been closest to the Mojahedin since the struggle to remove the Shah. While the tactics of many factions lined up closely, ideologically they were at daggers drawn.

We had many arguments with our Marxist friends over which faction of the regime the revolutionaries should side with. The Mojahedin believed that, although the reactionaries were less friendly towards imperialism than the liberals, classwise they were more backward than the Shah and the liberals, so their opposition to imperialism was not progressive but regressive. On our side the argument was that reactionaries were unable to solve twentieth-century problems, and would eventually need help from imperialists.

The main exponents of the liberal-versus-reactionary debate were the Tudeh Party, who defended reactionaries. The debate caused confusion, and eventually split the ranks of Iran's largest Marxist organisation, the Fedai'in. Divisions followed in all progressive and left-wing, Muslim and Nationalist organisations. Old friends became enemies. The Tudeh Party got the blame, especially from intellectuals and revolutionaries.

The line that had emerged between the Mojahedin and the reactionaries since even before Talaghani's death soon changed into a red line of blood. When a constitutional assembly was elected, the Mojahedin – in a coalition with four other organisations – nominated their own candidates. They knew the reactionaries would not let even a single member of that coalition be elected; their objective in participating in the elections was to reveal how monopolist the reactionaries were. The results were a foregone conclusion, and after Talaghani's death the outcome could not be anything but a regressive constitution. The assembly's most outrageous decision was to give power to Khomeini under the title of *vilayat faghieh* ('superior religious guidance'), a position that ranked above everything and everybody, including the people's votes and the country's laws. I heard from a supporter of Bazargan that the idea was not even Islamic, but derived from Greek philosophy, combining democratic thought with ancient wisdom. According to Islam, all rights of government come from the people and nowhere else. Bazargan even wanted to abolish the assembly, but Khomeini himself stopped him.

When in November there was a referendum to approve the constitution, the Mojahedin declared a contradiction between the Islam they knew and the constitution written and approved by the assembly; thus, they would not vote. At that point Khomeini announced that nothing in the constitution contradicted Islam. The Mojahedin found themselves confronting Khomeini on a religious issue, which was tantamount to denying his position as *imam* and *ayatollah*, an expert on Islam. The reactionaries responded by calling the Mojahedin not by their own name – which means 'warriors of the people and the faith' – but *monafaghin*, meaning 'hypocrites', and branding them worse than infidels, who would one day all have to be killed.

The Mojahedin soon realised that to oppose the reactionaries they needed to arm themselves. The moment came for the

Mojahedin to reorganise militarily when, in reaction to the American threat, Khomeini asked for the creation of a twenty-million-strong army. Soon the Mojahedin showed their military preparedness with parades in the main streets of Tehran and other cities.

Reactionary activity against the Mojahedin continued at a high level. Near the American embassy they had set up a 'tent for unity' – to be interpreted as unity against the Mojahedin, not against America – and used it as a base from which to attack Mojahedin properties, including a clinic. Kidnappings, beatings and murders of Mojahedin supporters and members were commonplace. They published fake literature with Mojahedin logos and slogans, accused the Mojahedin of raiding a bank and claimed to have found opium and pornography at a Mojahedin centre. They spread rumours of splits within the organisation in an attempt to undermine its credibility. The immediate effect was to strengthen our support for the Mojahedin, who, in retaliation, were doing everything possible to prove that the reactionaries were monopolistic and mercenaries of imperialism. While Talaghani was alive, the Mojahedin went to him for help in exposing the actions and motives of the reactionaries. After his death, they liaised instead with Ahmed Khomeini, son of the *ayatollah*, particularly with a view to demonstrating that Khomeini himself was not only aware but perhaps even approved of what was going on. They wanted to force Khomeini to show his real face. After the death of Talaghani, who was the Mojahedin's first choice as presidential candidate, they nominated Khomeini so as to contain him within a political role rather than have him act as a free agent above the law and the people. But Khomeini refused to stand, moreover, asked that no *mullah* stand either. The Mojahedin, in early January 1980, nominated Masoud Rajavi.

We threw ourselves into canvassing and campaigning to get Rajavi elected, generating leaflets and posters and engaging in debates and speeches. Our activity was magnified hundredfold by Mojahedin supporters inside Iran, where some suffered beatings, torture and death at the hands of the reactionaries. Some among us felt guilty and helpless, and sought the blessing of the Mojahedin for revenge attacks on members of Islamic Societies.

Rajavi drew support from a wide spectrum, including ethnic and religious minorities, writers and poets, revolutionary groups and Talaghani's widow. He stood on an anti-imperialist, anti-reactionary, pro-revolutionary platform that rejected capitalism or an intermediate solution such as Egypt and Somalia had adopted, and instead aimed for a monotheistic anti-exploitation approach. There were many calls from the reactionaries for Rajavi to withdraw his candidacy on the basis that he did not accept the country's constitution. The Mojahedin countered that, if elected, he would work within the framework of the constitution. Before long Khomeini openly sided with the reactionaries, announcing that anyone who had not voted in the constitutional referendum could not stand for president. Accordingly, Rajavi, who was the only candidate to whom this applied, resigned. Khomeini's edict was a blow for us who had hoped that what was happening in Iran had nothing to do with Khomeini, that he would keep the promise he had made in Paris not to involve himself in politics as the spiritual leader of the country.

Rajavi's departure was a very sad day for us. It seemed that whatever we had done had been in vain. More importantly, the sacrifices of the Mojahedin in Iran had been in vain too. Now we knew who the real leader of the reactionaries was, and that there would be no political or peaceful solutions – the reactionaries would accept nothing less than a total monopoly of power. We regarded the episode as a failure. But the verdict of the organisation was that it was not a failure, nor a withdrawal, but a victory. We had demonstrated the reactionaries' monopolistic ambitions to the people more clearly than ever. (Privately, the Mojahedin were saying we had also forced Khomeini to come forward and reveal himself.)

In the event, my cousin Banisadr was elected as Iran's first president, which influenced my political life in significant ways, more bad than good, ever afterwards. He won by a landslide, polling eleven million votes out of an electorate of fourteen million. The runner-up won two million votes. The candidate of the newly established, reactionary Islamic Republic Party, was unable to gain even a million votes, despite the support of some Marxist organisations including the Tudeh Party, who were siding with the reactionary faction of the regime against the 'liberal' faction now headed by Banisadr.

# 12

# Learning How to Think

In February 1980 it was decided that the MSS should reorganise to deliver the Mojahedin's objectives abroad more efficiently. Mohsen, my *masoul*, came to Newcastle and explained the changes. As a result, four of us were appointed to form the leading council of the society in northeast England and Scotland. Mohammed and Ebrahim had been close friends of mine since the revolution, and there were few differences of opinion between us. Davood was from another city and 'modestly' claimed a working-class background. In the Shah's era, education and wealth were symbols of status and importance. In the new political thinking, coming from a poor or working-class family meant one was more revolutionary and progressive. Poverty and even ignorance were honourable credentials. I was from an educated family, a cousin of the president, head of the liberal faction of the regime. I was married with all the middle-class attributes, including a PhD. My behaviour – conversation, logical thought, concern for human rights, even politeness and unconditional love of democracy – all branded me, in Davood's eyes, as a liberal bourgeois and therefore member of the exploiting class. Worse, I had no revolutionary background and

knew little about the history, culture or songs of the Mojahedin, or
the names of their martyrs. To avoid conflict, I said as little as
possible during our council discussions, except when I had to speak
out on behalf of Mojahedin sympathisers.

In fact, none of us knew much about Mojahedin ideology,
especially as it differed from that of other Muslims and Marxists.
For me it was enough to know that they supported democracy,
independence and progress; as long as they held to these principles,
I was happy to follow. But when Davood told us that the Mojahedin
believed in the dictatorship of the proletariat, I couldn't hold my
tongue any longer. We argued the issue hotly, Mohammed and
Ebrahim looking on without taking sides. Davood was merely
parroting his inadequate knowledge of Marxism, and I was
defending my own liberal views; nothing either of us said had
anything to do with Mojahedin beliefs. At one point, regarding
exploitation and the inevitable final class war, I mentioned a
documentary I had seen recently about the Fiat factory, where
computers and machines did all the mechanical work. My
argument was that in the very near future there would be no
proletariat left to defend; the main problem would be
unemployment. This would invalidate the Marxist definition of
exploitation and prediction of the final class war. Davood made no
reply, but jokingly said, 'Perhaps that is why we are against the
computerisation of society. That is something that must be done
after the class war!' Later, I discovered the Mojahedin's view on this
matter. For the 'proletariat' they substituted the Islamic term
mostazafeen, or 'oppressed', and they foresaw a final battle
between the oppressors and the oppressed.

'In the country of the blind, the one-eyed man is king.' Ignorant
though we were, Mohammed and I were each lecturing to and
'educating' half the Mojahedin sympathisers in our area. We were
supposed to be learning from Mohsen during our two-day stay in
Leeds each week. However, Mohsen believed in action rather than
theory, so we rarely had any lessons or even discussions. Our
knowledge came from the weekly Mojahed and from Mojahedin
books.

Among our textbooks were a few that played a significant part
in changing me from a political supporter of the Mojahedin into an
ideological one. The most important was a book called The

*Dynamics of the Qur'an*, which answered many of my questions about Islam and the Qur'an. For example, I learned that the Prophet believed change had to be achieved by evolution, not revolution; hence he had been unable to institute his desired changes immediately after his victory. He had a twofold strategy for turning people away from bad traditions and customs. First he encouraged good practice; he could not, for example, instantly abolish slavery, but he introduced hundreds of grounds on which slaves could be freed, which meant that eventually there were practically no slaves left. Second, he put obstacles in the way of bad practice, draining away its lifeblood and eventually killing it, as with the stoning of women for adultery.

The Qur'an generally promoted incremental over radical change. The lowly position of women in society and their absence of rights could not be reversed overnight. So, as a first step, their testimony was to be accepted as lawful. Second, they could begin to inherit from their parents – even if only half as much as men.

Learning about two issues – *mohkamat* and *moteshabehat* – helped me to understand the Mojahedin's interpretation of Islam. *Mohkam* laws are permanent and inalienable, like everything that relates to God. *Moteshabehat* laws are those governing daily life, interpreted in accordance with the times and society. They can be changed inasmuch as the changes do not contradict any *mohkam* law.

Then there were *nasekh* and *mansookh*. Some laws in the Qur'an were introduced for special situations and have been changed, rejected or neutralised by later laws. A new law is called *nasekh*, and the old one, *mansookh*.

These concepts got me thinking. It was clear to me that certain laws in the Qur'an relevant at the time of the Prophet were now outmoded. But who should determine which laws were *mohkam*, *motashabeh*, *nasekh* and *mansookh*? The answer was surely a progressive Islamic expert, specifically our own *ayatollah*, who was supposedly an expert not only in Islam but also in modern science and knowledge. Yet time seemed to have stood still for these 'experts', who remained engaged in the scholarship of earlier ages, studying Greek philosophy and mediaeval science.

Thanks to the modern interpretations of Shari'ati, Talaghani, Bazargan and eventually the Mojahedin, I could see a new face of

Islam that was not only fully compatible with modern knowledge (including the theory of evolution) and behaviour (like respect for human rights), but was also more complex, complete and democratic than any other ideology, capable of answering questions where other ideologies including Marxism failed. Once more, I was able to defend Islam without hesitation and wholeheartedly call myself a Muslim.

Another text that was equally important to me in a different way was a tiny book describing the organisation and principles of the Mojahedin and the rights of those within it, characterised as 'centralised democracy'. It set out the circumstances under which members were permitted their own thoughts and questions, and when they had to obey and suppress doubts: this, according to the book, was the scientific model of any revolutionary organisation.

As explained in the first few pages, belief in something demanded an understanding and acceptance of both its content and its form. Content without the correct form was harmful, as was form without the correct content. A simple example was offered: 'However thirsty you are, you can never be refreshed by drinking water from a sieve. On the other hand, drinking oil from a glass will accentuate your thirst rather than kill it.' Now that I was a believer in the ideological content of the Mojahedin, it was equally important to understand and accept its shape.

The book went on to explain that the Mojahedin was based on centralisation and democracy. The first without the second would lead to despotism, while the second without the first would turn it into a liberal-bourgeois organisation, not a revolutionary nor a Muslim one. It was possible to reconcile these two elements by respecting seven golden rules. One was to recognise the experience and capabilities of the organisation's vanguard. Another was to maintain brotherly trust. A third was to examine doubts about the actions or decisions of someone within the organisation, especially a *masoul*, to see if they were 'scientific' – that is, based on clear facts rather than feelings or guesswork – or 'unscientific', that is, spontaneous or illogical. 'Unscientific' doubts later became a sticking point with me. The rule prevented me – and many others – from criticising the wrongdoings of the organisation, because self-criticism had to precede criticism of others. The most important of the seven golden rules concerned the right of members to ask questions and make suggestions, upon which the central committee would gather relevant information, evaluate the issues and announce their decision to all members.

Although sometimes we later held elections to prove to outsiders that the organisation was democratic, we understood that voting was a meaningless, liberal-bourgeois practice and that it was right that nominations to posts be from the top down, made by the vanguard. Another important principle concerned the 'right to know'. Again, unlike in liberal organisations, the individual was allowed to know only things that related to him and his responsibility within the organisation. Often we were told, 'there is no need for you to know this'. An individual's ideological merit could be measured and redefined by the vanguard.

We had to study several other books on the history and politics of the organisation and guides to understanding its ideology, which told us to focus not on the 'how' but on the 'why' – for example, not *how* the twelfth Imam, Imam Zaman, lived for more than 1,000 years, but *why* such a man had to appear at a certain time in history in order to save people from inhumanity and oppression.

This was called the philosophy of hope, a belief that whatever happens and however despotic the rulers, goodness and right will always win in the end. The irony of this position was that if oppression and inhumanity prompted the Imam's appearance, then these evils, giving rise to good, could not be so bad after all. In the present case it was argued that the Mojahedin would not win or, that if they did, they would be overthrown or become oppressors themselves. Otherwise the Imam would not appear. The answer was: it was not the quantity of oppression that was important but its quality; as time went on, inhumanity would diminish but also become more complex. Exploitation in modern times is certainly less severe than in the days of slavery, but being more difficult to identify is also more difficult to resist.

A short book titled *How to Think* explained how to avoid 'intellectual', unscientific and anti-revolutionary thinking. Under the Shah we had grown up liberal and bourgeois. The book's first lesson taught that being liberal was tantamount to being anti-revolutionary, imperialist and an enemy of the organisation, society and country. To be called a 'liberal' was the worst possible insult, although after the ideological revolution the Mojahedin

believed they had rooted out liberalism and the word 'ordinary'
took pride of place, followed by '*borida*' ('severed'). Politically the
Mojahedin sided with liberals against reactionaries, but
ideologically they were closer to reactionaries; to be liberal was
unimaginably bad...

Apart from these books, we had to read from the Qur'an every
week, which I found difficult and in fact never mastered. At the end
of each week we had to read *Mojahed* and discuss the articles.

During the first few months of 1980 the Mojahedin held various
election gatherings, one at Tehran University attended by more
than 200,000 people; one in Rasht, the capital of the northern
province of Gilan, with 300,000 people; and another in Tabriz.
Rajavi, the main speaker at all these meetings, concentrated on
exposing reactionary activities and the regime's shortcomings in
the struggle against America. He was a compelling and moving
speaker. I soon put aside my belief that the organisation did not
centre on individuals and realised that Rajavi was, at least, 'first
among equals'. He was clearly not just the spokesman for the
organisation but, along with Mussa Khiabani, one of its highest-
ranking members. His picture or statements often headed the
organisation's papers. At meetings large pictures of Khomeini and
Talaghani were hung at the far right and far left of the stage. In the
early days it was customary not to display pictures of a living
Mojahed, but at election time the practice changed. From then on
posters of Rajavi and Khiabani, and later of Rajavi alone, were
hung centre-stage. The custom of impersonally hailing a 'Mojahed
brother' also gave way to 'Hail to Rajavi'. Still, altogether nothing
implied that the Mojahedin was anything but the most democratic
and freedom-loving organisation we had ever seen in Iranian
history.

During the elections, the speeches and communiqués from the
Mojahedin mostly concentrated on the monopolising tactics of the
reactionaries, their fraudulent practices and so on. The object was
to show how oppressed and innocent the Mojahedin were. In
Mojahedin thinking, the weak, oppressed and martyred were right
and the oppressors – the rich and powerful – were wrong. Our
commitment to the Mojahedin was such that we no longer actually
listened to or tried to evaluate what was actually said. We had
made our choice.

Every weekend we four council members from the northeast went to Leeds to meet with Mohsen. Ten council members from other regions also attended. Here we sifted through the news about Iran and America in the newspapers, already translated by our colleagues in the regions. We compiled two digests – one in Farsi, another in English – to be sent to the mother organisation in Iran. We called this the '"News of Iran" job'. Mohsen had his own way of making us more 'revolutionary', with a regime in which we had to sleep rough, work on the floor and eat sparsely and poorly. Admittedly, it alleviated our sense of guilt *vis-à-vis* our brothers and sisters in Iran, whose hardship was far greater, but working on the floor for hours usually left us with backaches rather than with solutions for revolutionary problems.

I never spoke about my own financial problems, as everybody thought we were rich. However, the situation worsened to the point where we had to sell our carpet, then our car, then other items, too. When Mohsen asked why I sold my car, I lied: 'Well, it was part of my bourgeois past, which had to go.' Without a car, living far from the university and city centre, we faced more problems including time pressures. During exam periods most of the news translators were out of action. Anna and I had to do their job, as 'News of Iran' had to be prepared as usual. I was unconvinced of the value of much of this material, from far-flung countries or published in newspapers with tiny circulations, but by now I had learned not to question or complain.

We were required to attend an MSS seminar in Essen, Germany. This was our first experience travelling as a family and living in a Mojahedin commune. There were about 200 people from different countries, some, like us, couples with children. Chores were shared in communal fashion, in a way reminiscent of reactionary culture. It made us realise that they too were Islamic, and that we shared certain customs that differed from those in Western bourgeois culture. The atmosphere at the seminar was warm and friendly. We felt at one with these people, united in our common sentiments and cause. The lectures given on different topics by the delegates were of a high standard.

Every morning for an hour we had an open-air communal exercise session, despite the cold weather. I discovered that being a revolutionary would compel me to do things I had never done before: exercise was one of them. I developed a severe case of influenza and had to remain bedridden in a sick room. Brother Reza, one of three founders of the MSS abroad, was suffering likewise, so we had company for a few days. He was a man in his late thirties and an archetypal Mojahed: gentle, patient and educated. In the course of one of our conversations, I confessed some of my fears to him. I could never be a true Mojahed, I said, as I am weak and unable to endure hardship and suffering. He asked me to give him an example. I chose the most harrowing one I could think of: that of Talaghani, whose daughter was raped before his eyes.

'Who wants to torture you?' he asked. 'Do you have anything to hide? Have you valuable information someone might want to extract from you?' I smiled sheepishly. 'Look,' he said, 'to be a Mojahed you don't have to think in terms of torture and martyrdom. Yes, you should know they could be part of our struggle. Just be sure that before you get to the point where you are holding any valuable information or responsibility, you are ready for whatever sacrifices may be required of you.' I felt relieved and reassured; his words stayed with me for the rest of my organisational life. I realised it was pointless to worry about the long term; if I was too concerned about preparing for the final steps I would never find the courage to take the first one. I confided in Reza that compiling 'News of Iran' was irksome and time-consuming. When Mohsen next enquired about its status, Reza said, 'You all seem so busy preparing "News of Iran" that you can't do anything else! Is that true?' Later I discovered that others had the same complaint. It appeared that Mohsen was keen to pursue this venture because it made him look good, especially as the digest went straight to Iran – perhaps even to Rajavi himself.

Later Reza asked me if we were going to hold elections. It seemed a strange question, as I had thought the Mojahedin didn't believe in elections. He explained that we were not Mojahedin but, as MSS, sympathiser organisations outside Iran. Our constitution required that an election be held for members to sit on the council of each branch. I was glad to hear this, and to know that my democratic inclinations in this respect did not stem from my 'liberal tendencies' but were shared by the Mojahedin.

In one meeting at Essen a row blew up between the normally

mild-mannered Reza and members of the audience. He accused them of belonging to the pseudo-left and supporting those who had mounted a coup in the organisation. When he tried to defend himself, he was asked to leave the room and never call himself a supporter of the Mojahedin again. None of this made sense to me or to the rest of the audience, for that matter, but I took away the message that it was better to remain silent if one had questions or doubts.

While we were in Germany we dressed according to the current fashion among Mojahedin supporters, in an American or German military overcoat (which raised a few eyebrows). We sang rousing Mojahedin songs whenever we were in a group.

On our return to England Mohsen told us that preparation of the 'News of Iran' had been divided between us and London. He also told us we were going to have an election. After some time Mohsen was transferred to London; somebody from London was sent to become our *masoul*.

From Iran we received transcripts of the speeches of Rajavi on the subject of creation, the transition from earth to heaven, awareness and interpretations of the basic principles of Islam. He clearly explained the essence of monism; the duality of popular and divine sources of leadership; human beings' accountability for their actions; the universality of divine law; and the aim of creation – to evolve towards a Godlike state.

Rajavi's speeches attracted many new sympathisers to the organisation and gave him a higher public profile. He was pictured in the paper presenting a rifle to Yasser Arafat, who was much respected by Iranians. Many of us cut the picture out and hung it on our walls. Rajavi's thoughts and sayings also found a prominent place in the paper. During the Shah's time, when it was announced that the imprisoned Rajavi was not to be executed, the Mojahedin praised him and hailed him as a living martyr. Now, the 'reactionaries' decried him for not having been executed along with other leaders of the Mojahedin. They issued a booklet called *Monafegh Aval* ('The First Hypocrite'), claiming he was saved from execution by the Shah's regime by collaborating with Savak. Rajavi was Enemy Number One, they claimed. This barrage of negative propaganda succeeded only in increasing Rajavi's popularity enormously.

# 13

# An Arrow in the Eyes

After the first month of the Iranian New Year we faced a new challenge from the reactionaries, who wanted to monopolise everything, launching what they called (following Mao Zedong) a 'Cultural Revolution'. Universities were at the forefront of political action. Unfortunately, after the revolution, unity among the students evaporated and they split into several societies, each supporting a different political organisation. The Islamic Societies, as supporters of the regime and generally also of the newly established Islamic Republic Party, were, for us, reactionaries. Ranged against them were the Muslim Student Societies, who supported the Mojahedin. Additional societies supported the Fedai'in or one of the tens of new smaller Marxist organisations. These organisations had, in almost every university, their own offices with printing facilities, so they could continue to operate safely irrespective of world events. We called this situation 'an arrow in the eyes of the reactionaries'. Since the hostage-taking, Islamic Societies had become more aggressive, and were now powerful enough to remove lecturers or even the president of a university by alleging collaboration with Savak or the US. Although they had greater power and resources, they lost out numerically to the other groups, which were on the whole anti-reactionary. Thus the Islamic Societies often had to plead for help from Hezbollah or the regime's leaders.

In March 1980, Khomeini announced in his New Year's message that universities must be cleansed of saboteur elements. The leaders of the Islamic Republic Party followed suit over the next few months, talking of a cultural revolution in the universities. This sparked off fighting among students from different factions. Many universities were taken over by groups opposed to the regime. During Friday prayers Khamenei, the speaker of the Revolutionary Council, gave three days' notice to all students to leave university premises. This meant that students would come under attack, even from ordinary citizens obedient to the Revolutionary Council. The MSS announced their departure from all university premises. But supporters of other organisations remained to defend their rights. The result, inevitably, was bloodshed. At Tehran University, 500 were injured and at least 5 killed; at the University of Ahvaz, 700 injured and at least 7 killed; at the University of Gilan, 600 injured, 7 killed; at the University of Shiraz, fifty buildings demolished ... in all, thousands of students were injured, hundreds arrested and many killed – even before the three-day ultimatum was up. The Mojahedin asked Banisadr to mediate in order to help the students. It was the end of an era in which university students were free to engage in political activity. What the Shah was unable to achieve in almost twenty-five years with his horrendous Savak and armed university guards, the new regime – operating at a time when students were disunited and had no popular support – was able to do in a single month.

The so-called Cultural Revolution was the source of new quarrelling among students abroad. We, as Mojahedin supporters, were accused of being rightist and of surrendering to or even collaborating with the regime!

Alongside their attacks on universities, the reactionaries attacked Mojahedin bases in such cities as Shiraz and Mashed, killing and injuring many. Even when American helicopters landed in the northeast of the country and it was very probable they would attack Iran, the main concern of the reactionaries was getting rid of the Mojahedin and what little freedom remained in the country.

If America is the great Satan, they said, the Mojahedin are the great traitors. The situation infuriated and frustrated us, but we could do nothing.

Parvin, a young woman assaulted by reactionaries on Labour Day and losing her eyesight as a result, was sent by the organisation to Britain for treatment. From her and her father we received first-hand information about events in Iran. The only way to survive, they said, was to suffer the beatings in silence. If one could afford it, one bought a helmet. Parvin's father was so proud of her that he was even prepared to lose her and would distribute sweets at her funeral. It made me think about my own wife and daughter. I knew I couldn't bear to lose them. I believed I could suffer torture or die, as long as I knew they were safe. I drew comfort from the fact that they were likely to be safe in Britain and that family, friends and above all the Mojahedin would look after them if anything happened to me.

On 12th June 1980 Rajavi drew his largest audience ever for his last public speech, in Amajadiyeh Stadium in Tehran. The title of the speech was 'What is to be done?' and in tone and content it was quite different from any other he had previously given. Although we were not able to witness the great event itself, still we scarcely moved or blinked as we watched the videotape. His speech started with some sentences from the Qur'an, building to a crescendo in which he cried, 'Every night a star is drawn to the earth, and this sorrowing sky remains drenched with stars ...' Outside there was the noise of gunfire from the revolutionary guards. With emotion he said, 'History will follow its course and, in the end, it will reveal who is the oppressor and who the oppressed. We shall remember these words of Nasser until eternity. Let the bullets fly! We too, we too, will bare our chests as shields.' At this he pushed up his shirt to allow bullets to be aimed at his heart. The audience was burning paper to neutralise the effect of teargas bullets fired by the revolutionary guards. They all stood and chanted, 'Hail Rajavi'. He quoted again from the Qur'an, promising with determination to achieve a society in which there were no distinctions of class, no exploitation, no ignorance, no repression. He prayed to God for acceptance. Then he read a moving Palestinian poem:

*In the name of a God who rends the oppressor asunder*

*An old man who does not weep or mourn or sorrow,*
*Ceaselessly uttering, 'Do not grieve, do not grieve.*
*My child is martyred, my child is martyred.*
*With his own blood, he has opened the way to immortality.*
*And I am blessed, and I am blessed.*
*I raised him for such a day ...*
*This is the way that is eternally proud.*
*In the name of the life, never grieve.*

Then he returned to the Qur'an before exhorting: 'Now, tell them to fire! Yes, you mothers and fathers, do not grieve! The club-wielding hoodlums, the guardians of the night, will be rooted out. But let me ask of these blossoms nipped in the bud, "For what sin were they slain" [a Qur'an verse]?' He spoke about freedom of expression and of association. He said, 'There is one thing I want to make very plain: that for every Mojahed arm they break, ten more will appear in its place, and for every Mojahed eye that they gouge out, 100 eyes will open up in its place, and for every Mojahed heart that is torn to pieces and every head that is broken, 1,000 noble hearts and heads will spring up in their places. That is the logic of revolution. That is the logic of evolution. That is the logic of Islam and the way of God and the way of the people.'

He finished with these uncompromising words: 'What response can we give? Haven't we torn our society to pieces for long enough? ... They [Mojahedin sympathisers] ask us why, after getting nothing in response to our complaints, we have fallen silent. What response can we give? What can we do ? What is to be done? ... Let me remind you of Imam Ali's warning that the day of revenge of the oppressed is harsher than the cruelty of the oppressor. This is the response we give to those who threaten to throw the Mojahedin into the sea: "Gentlemen, just make sure you don't just sink into the quicksand of imperialism in the process."'

His message was clear. He warned that Iran was in danger of becoming another Lebanon, where civil war raged and the army was paralysed. Was this our future? Did we have to witness the moral and material destruction of the country?

His speech was the most threatening ever delivered against the regime. The likely outcome was a regime-initiated civil war. The Mojahedin no longer seemed to be taking action to avoid it.

Perhaps they felt they were ready and welcomed it. The meeting ended in violence, when the revolutionary guards came to blows with the police and the Hezbollahis. A close associate of President Banisadr later announced that the police had been in complete control until the revolutionary guards had arrived with teargas and bullets. Khomeini's son Ahmed defended the rights of people to express their ideas freely and demanded that the authorities put a stop to the activities of the club-wielders. Many believed his position might reflect that of Khomeini himself, and took cheer from it.

A week later, Banisadr revealed an Islamic Republic Party plot to bring about his downfall; the Mojahedin had tipped him off. This collaboration between the Mojahedin and Banisadr, and the Mojahedin's obvious intention to split the regime ever more deeply, was abhorrent to the regime. Khomeini could no longer remain silent. Sure enough, he went on television to deliver his bitterest and sharpest attack on the Mojahedin ever. Without naming them he called them *monafaghin* (hypocrites) and said that the main enemy was not the US or Soviet Union, but in our midst. To neutralise the influence of Talaghani and his son, both Mojahedin supporters, he added, 'Even some people close to me have been deceived by them.'

His speech signalled the end of the legality of the Mojahedin. When Khomeini announced he was not going to read the *Ayandegan* newspaper any more, the paper's offices closed. Everyone could guess what would happen to the Mojahedin. In a pre-emptive move the Mojahedin, without referring to Khomeini's speech, quietly announced the closing of all their centres around the country and the cessation of their paper. They broke off contact with us abroad. We were left to our own devices.

We were keen to show the video of Rajavi's speech and discuss it, but the London section of the MSS told us to hang fire, as they had an important message for us from three founders of the MSS. The message, delivered on 28th June, was that all Mojahedin centres were occupied by the revolutionary guards. Somehow, the organisation's documents – including the names of members and contacts – had fallen into the regime's hands. They advised us to disconnect ourselves from Iran and be aware that the regime might try to contact us under some pretext. Our instructions were to break off all telephone and postal contact with the organisation in Iran; if we received any calls from Iran, we were to say that our *masouls* were in Iran, and they should speak with them. We were told to use the summer to improve ourselves as revolutionaries by reading and reflecting on the events of the past few months, to try to understand why the Mojahedin were now in deadlock and what the future of the MSS might be. They said they would let us know what was going on as soon as possible.

This message turned us to stone. Afterwards, everyone sat in silence. When we did speak, we couldn't say anything sensible.

The next day I called Aliraza, who was then in Tehran was working at the Mojahedin headquarters. I told him what had happened. He said, 'Those three founders of the MSS who delivered that message have had problems for some time. After Khomeini's speech they raised some unacceptable doubts, and as a result they are no longer members of the organisation.' He asked me to contact other branches of the organisation and decide collectively what to do.

A week later all MSS members met in London to discuss these contradictory messages. According to the Mojahedin, the MSS founders were seekers of rank and position, had switched their allegiance to Khomeini and were thus ex-Mojahedin. We now had to choose between them and the Mojahedin. If we decided to remain Mojahedin supporters we had to consider whether to expel those three from the MSS. While we wrangled over possible changes to our constitution to take account of this, one member interrupted us with the news that Reza (one of the founders) would arrive from Iran in a matter of hours, and we could hear his view and then decide. Having heard what was going on, he had immediately taken a flight from Tehran. After he arrived and had started to address us, Davood stopped him and asked him to let us finish making our decision first. We then received a further message from the Mojahedin advising us not to listen to any arguments until we could hear both sides. That meant waiting until a representative of the Mojahedin could join the discussion. Those of us who considered ourselves Mojahedin supporters were to step outside the room so as not to be biased by hearing only one side. I believed privately that I was perfectly capable of making my mind up by listening to only one view, but after trying to justify my thinking and persuasion from others who said that I should set an example, I decided to step outside.

Some years later, when I had left the organisation, I found out that MSS founders took issue with the Mojahedin not only at that juncture but on many other occasions as well. They believed Rajavi's recent speech had been wrong and leftist, and was pushing the organisation to choose between taking a stand against Khomeini and fighting a civil war for which it was unprepared, or surrendering everything to the reactionaries. They felt the organisation was undemocratic and had been monopolised by Rajavi.

One criticism of the Mojahedin was that the founders of the organisation were right-leaning. Being right-wing and liberal now became more taboo than ever and everyone wanted to prove himself more left-wing and radical than everyone else, without knowing how to do so! Of the four MSS branches in Britain, the Newcastle branch under my tuition was clearly the most 'liberal' and 'bourgeois', while the Manchester branch, being mostly under Mohsen's influence, was the most 'radical' and 'left'. (Once, the council members – including Mohammed and me – went to a meeting in Manchester. No sooner had we stepped inside than we were subdued and whipped by the host members. We were shocked and astonished, but learned that this was part of their *khood sazy* (self-improvement) programme, preparation for facing the Iranian situation. As there were no club-wielders, they reasoned, they had to do it themselves. Consequently they whipped visitors for anything – someone who had not fulfilled a responsibility, or wasn't good enough, or was simply late for an appointment.

As part of their fight against bourgeois liberalism and their commitment to collectivism, they were sleeping rough, eating rough and living rough. For example, their lunch consisted of some pasta with a little tomato purée, rarely meat or fruit. The food was served on a tray and everyone had to eat from it, without benefit of individual plates.

Back in Newcastle we were obliged to emulate some of Manchester's 'good practice'. I balked at introducing whippings. Instead, we agreed to learn self-defence. Our karate class was a comic parade: twenty of us, including women with scarves, all with unsuitable clothes and unfit bodies; one can imagine the face of our trainer when he saw us for the first time. In class we had to run in a circle and then jump on each other's bellies – the men avoiding the women and vice versa, of course. I personally had not taken any exercise in my life, yet in a matter of weeks I, and others like me, were supposed to transform ourselves into fit and able karate experts. Our poor trainer doubtless suffered immensely.

By then our base had moved from a middle-class section of Newcastle to a poor and rather rough area of the city, partly because of financial problems, partly because of transport. We were supposed to leave our bourgeois lives behind and work on ourselves to become better revolutionaries. To that end, it was suggested I live with others to share costs and collaborate. I was not ready for this change. I saw my family as a separate entity, and wanted to keep it that way. Deep down, I clung to the idea of ownership. 'Ownership is a natural human need,' Bazargan had written. 'But if some people eat more than they need and become unhealthy, we do not remove their stomachs. Similarly, if people are greedy and amass more money than they need, you have to control them, not abolish the right of ownership.' Nevertheless, we agreed to move as close as possible to the base and share cooking and mealtimes with the other members. To make life hard for ourselves physically was something we did artificially and at some cost. Mental pressure, on the other hand, was completely real and ever-present, and caused at least one mental breakdown among us.

At the end of July 1980 the Shah died. We watched scenes from his funeral on television. President Anwar Sadat of Egypt and his old friend Richard Nixon walked behind his coffin. Many Egyptians appeared present, but not many Iranians – not even those who once called him 'the shadow of God' and who, thanks to him, lived abroad in great affluence. He had lived long enough to see our misery. I wondered whether the country's decline caused him regret in his last days, or whether he had tried to justify himself, believing he had attempted to create a great civilisation in Iran that the people had not been ready for. Anyway, he was the only person who could unite us: we joined together in hatred of him. Now he was dead, and Iranians were more divided and hate-filled than ever.

# 14

# The New Martyrs

With the outbreak of the Iran-Iraq war, there was a demonstration against Iraqi aggression in Newcastle. We Iranians again put our differences aside and united against the foreign aggressor. We were attacked by an organised Iraqi mob, and there were beatings. After that, the MSS organised a demonstration in London which many other groups, including supporters of the Tudeh Party, joined.

The slogan we chanted was, 'The US plans, Saddam attacks, down with the US'. At that time Saddam Hussein was a favourite of the West, including the Americans and British; human rights in Iraq were not mentioned. Iranians were the 'bad guys', the Iraqis the 'good guys'. The Mojahedin announced that they would defend the country on the battlefield, but not in the same contingents as the revolutionary guards and the army. This led to accusations that we were collaborating with the Iraqis. Our members met their deaths at the hands of Iraqis, guards and Hezbollahis. About the same time I received a letter from my youngest sister, one of the very few relatives and friends with whom I still communicated. She knew of my activities and had some sympathy for my goals, but she accused the Mojahedin of acting out of self-interest. They helped people, she said, but their aid came with the organisation's emblem, to remind people where it had come from: did I find this kind of behaviour Islamic? I never answered her, and soon I lost this last connection with my family in Iran.

Then came news that the American hostages might be released. *Mojahed* claimed it had all been a plot against revolutionary organisations, notably the Mojahedin. It ran the slogan, 'Death to imperialism – long live freedom'. In any case, the hostages were freed and, as Bazargan said, 'in this issue only the Americans were true winners. After losing face because of the Vietnam war, they could now gain some international credibility ... On the international scene Americans could portray their enemy as barbaric and uncivilised ... and themselves as champions of humanity, democracy and freedom.'

The relationship between Bazargan and the Mojahedin was complex. Masoud Rajavi, in a *Mojahed* interview, accepted Bazargan as one of the teachers of the Mojahedin. On the other hand, the Mojahedin had been the first to attack him, and in doing so had paved the way for an assault on him by reactionaries which brought about his downfall. Rajavi pointed out that Bazargan was an honest man, opposed to dictatorship, and the first intellectual to make the link between Islam and science. There was interesting article in *Myzan* (Bazargan's newspaper), which was essentially an open letter from Bazargan to both the Mojahedin and Hezbollahis, pointing out that their similarities were much greater than their differences and that the conflict between them was threatening the future of the country and helping our enemies. Each called the other 'reactionaries', 'hypocrites', 'mercenaries of imperialism', and each believed they had a monopoly of the good and the right. Both had accepted Khomeini as Imam and both followed the Fedai'in in attacking the provisional government. Marxism had influenced both movements, which were anti-capital and monopolist, unwilling to share rule with other parties. Both called themselves enemies of America and were against step-by-step progress, calling it treachery. 'If you are revolutionaries', Bazargan urged, 'this is a real revolutionary action ... I ask you to accept each other as Muslims and brothers ... sit and talk, resolve your differences.'

This open letter was reprinted in *Mojahed*, inevitably with a rejoinder. The Mojahedin did not agree with Bazargan's ideological viewpoint, nor did they accept a share of the responsibility for the situation we were in. They had always been ready to talk, they said, but their offers of reconciliation were answered with whips and clubs.

*Mojahed* appeared weekly again, published clandestinely and distributed at great risk on Iranian streets by sympathisers. Many sellers were attacked, beaten, arrested, even murdered, in numbers ranging from one or two to several hundred every week. Each issue of the paper published details of those killed, along with pictures of tortured bodies. One showed a militiaman with cigarette burns on his back in the form of the words 'Long live Khomeini'. Documentary evidence of tortures and murders was systematically supplied to Banisadr, and sometimes extracts were printed in *Enghalab Eslami*, his newspaper. At last, voices of protest were heard. Some famous people, including clerics, spoke out against the activities of the revolutionary guards and the Hezbollahis. As a result, Khomeini was forced to nominate a committee to investigate the 'allegations of torture'. After many months examining thousands of documents and witnesses, the committee delivered its predictable opinion that there had been some wrongdoing and *tanbie'h* (chastisement) but 'certainly not torture'!

As we were no longer able to receive *Mojahed* directly from Iran, it was decided to reprint it in Newcastle and circulate it everywhere else except Iran. This became part of our job. Most of the work was done by one of our members, Hussein, a very young university student whose commitment was such that we often found him dead to the world in the printing shop, having worked for days without a break. The rest of us shared in the folding, packing and posting of the printed papers. At this time I had to spend one day a week in Edinburgh, one day in Middlesbrough and one day in Sunderland, giving lectures to our supporters there and helping them solve problems, including internal conflicts that arose from sharing everything. To see our supporters in those cities helped me to forget my own problems and reinforced my commitment. It also brought me closer to them than to my brothers and close friends. There were also meetings of our members and supporters in Newcastle and long weekly executive planning meetings.

Communal living certainly made life difficult. About fifteen people lived together, and most of the time sympathisers were there as house guests too – each with their own character, habits and wants, which often didn't match up. None of us was an asylum seeker, and we received no state benefits. Nor did we receive money from Iran, and so we made do with the meagre earnings of the few of us who worked. As a result some supporters and members were driven to cheating and even stealing. We had to consider how to respond to these issues. Should we punish people who didn't conform or do their job properly? Was expulsion a means of keeping the organisation pure?

Events in Iran were accelerating. Khomeini, as commander of the army, appointed Banisadr head of the armed forces. Banisadr consequently won some popularity among army personnel. In line with his liberal policies, he confronted reactionaries more openly and intensively, even supporting the Mojahedin and allowing Rajavi to arm for self-defence. Mojahedin members attended all Banisadr's public appearances. On 5th March 1981, while Banisadr spoke at his last public meeting honouring Mossadegh, the Hezbollahis as usual laid into his listeners. Banisadr ordered their arrest, and many were beaten and arrested by other members of the crowd, mainly Mojahedin members. Of those arrested, most were members of the revolutionary guards or the Islamic Republic Party. As Banisadr had now publicly declared his allegiance, the battle between his government faction and the reactionaries now reached its peak. The authorities were gearing up to try the president instead of the club-wielders.

Around this time a Mojahedin representative came to Britain to give us guidance. At home they were under pressure and had to find creative solutions to their own problems. Some of their members' and families' lives were in danger; perhaps they also wanted to pave the way for sending them out of the country. We met the representative in London and he described events in Iran, including how they had been able to back Banisadr and encourage him even against Khomeini; how they had been right to support the liberals against the reactionaries; how, contrary to what we had heard from the founders of the society, the regime and its supporters were in deadlock and the Mojahedin were more popular than ever and ready for action. The regime could not win, he said. If it chose to fight the Mojahedin, it would lose. If it chose to maintain the status quo, the Mojahedin would continue to attract new supporters and the regime would lose more popular support. 'Without any doubt,' he said, 'the regime must choose the former alternative. Banisadr has to make the most important decision of his life. He must choose between us and the regime.'

I was puzzled by what he said about Khomeini. He said we had known from the beginning that he was a reactionary and that sooner or later he would show his true colours. We had only to be patient and wait for that. I could not accept this. If I had known he would be as he was now, I would never have supported him at the beginning of the revolution; if anyone had known his real nature and failed to say so, that person betrayed not only the people but also his conscience. I always believed the Mojahedin did not know him – in one of his articles Rajavi had written that 'the real nature of any human being is so complex that God alone is aware of it'. How, I asked, could we call Khomeini 'Imam' and leader, when we knew he belonged to the reactionary front and would ultimately take us back 1,000 years ...?

I didn't receive a straight answer. Somehow the representative managed to give everyone the impression that I was defending Khomeini by claiming he was not reactionary. They began reminding me of Khomeini's approval of many murders, etc. I lacked the self-assurance to argue, so I said nothing. After the meeting the representative drew me aside and said quietly, 'Khomeini is going to join the anti-popular front soon'. I started to say that this had not been my question, but he smiled, thumped me on the back and said, 'You have to work hard, you know how much we need people like you!'

I returned to Newcastle with many questions in my mind. If everything had been predicted by the Mojahedin, why had they spoken out so strongly against imperialism, which meant weakening the liberals and strengthening the reactionaries? Most of the arguments used by the reactionaries against the liberals had come from the Mojahedin, who in that sense were the reactionaries' teachers. Why had the Mojahedin not thrown all their weight behind the provisional government? Why let people think they accepted Khomeini as Imam and leader of the revolution, even leader of the Islamic revolution? Were they really hypocrites, as the reactionaries said? Already the Mojahedin in their inner circles were calling Khomeini worse than the Shah. If they knew that, why had they chosen him over the Shah? Were they really opportunists, as some Marxist organisations claimed?

Definitive answer came there none. I chose the wishful thinking route. I decided that I preferred to believe Rajavi's words and that the view that I had heard expressed was that of an individual member and not of the organisation.

In Iran the Hezbollahis wanted revenge for what had happened at Tehran University. There were more arrests, whippings and killings of Mojahedin than ever, all featured in *Mojahed* as new martyrs. Banisadr spoke out publicly against the reactionaries with increasing frequency. He called for a referendum, implying that Khomeini's judgement was no longer enough and that the people must decide.

Protesting against the killings of their members, the Mojahedin organised a huge demonstration in the middle of Tehran at the end of April. Over 100,000 people attended. But the assaults on members did not stop. The number of officially arrested Mojahedin supporters now exceeded 1,000. Less than three years after all political prisoners had been freed, a new wave of political prisoners now existed, to our shame. The reactionaries enacted regressive changes, such as passing the law of *ghasas* (religious punishment according to ancient Arab custom) – including whipping, beheading and stoning. They publicly hanged a man charged with smuggling narcotics. Needless to say, the Mojahedin and liberals opposed such laws.

On 2nd May 1981 the Mojahedin wrote a polite and humble letter to Khomeini asking to see him. Its intention was to force Khomeini into a corner. If he agreed, he would face several hundred thousand people opposed to the regime. If he refused, the Mojahedin could claim they had done whatever they could to prevent more bloodshed, whereas Khomeini, as leader of the revolution, hadn't even bothered to meet or hear them. To their surprise, Khomeini replied. 'Hand over your arms,' he said, 'and there will be no need for you to visit me. I will visit you and will be at your service.' The Mojahedin appealed to Banisadr, as executive head of state, to guarantee their safety and the application of law and order in the country so they could hand over their weapons. But Banisadr was no longer able to guarantee his *own* safety.

Banisadr published some documents against the reactionaries, after which the Justice Department, which was under their control, ordered the closing of his newspaper. In one of its last communiqués Banisadr wrote, 'The giant of dictatorship is coming', and warned people to resist it. He was now in hiding most of the time; the Mojahedin announced that his life was in danger. A bill was presented in Parliament to force Banisadr's abdication.

On 20th June 1981, without any prior public announcement, the Mojahedin organised their largest demonstration ever. By all accounts, 500,000 Mojahedin and supporters poured into the streets of Tehran. According to the Mojahedin, this day was a turning point in Iran's history. It certainly left its mark on the lives of millions. In later years events were organised for the same day, the tenor of which was joy and celebration, not sadness and rebellion – a day full of laughter, dancing, singing and mutual congratulation. The message was that the Iranian regime, by rejecting and refusing to share power with the liberals, had shown that it would not accept freedom at any price; that those who killed people in the streets of Tehran could no longer be considered as belonging to the people's front and were exposed as the country's worst enemies. Within a few months, the Mojahedin had advanced so far as to brand Khomeini – now no longer Imam, leader and father – as worse than the Iraqis, the imperialists and the Americans, an enemy of humanity, a murderer, *dajal* (deceiver), the Old Fox, Hyena ...

How many people were arrested, beaten, injured and killed that day? God alone knows. The regime itself was quick to publicise the names and details: they wanted to inspire maximum fear. In fact, in the confusion, real guards were killed by mistake, along with Mojahedin wearing guards' uniforms, men and women, old people, children ... Few of those arrested were brought to trial. Those who were faced trumped-up charges like possession of salt and pepper (to throw in the eyes of pursuing guards) or two-*rial* coins (used in payphones).

What was Rajavi's real intention? Was the event meant as a 'final warning' to the regime? Or was he hoping to march, with the Mojahedin spearheading the crowd, on the Jamaran, Khomeini's residence, and overthrow the regime? Was he a winner because a total massacre was avoided? Or a loser because he had been unable to rally sufficient forces to overthrow the regime then and there? Was he simply acting as a Muslim revolutionary, doing everything possible to avert bloodshed and war? This was what we all believed and continued to believe.

Whether the final bloody war started there or whether 20th June was merely the point of no return on a path that had been travelled for some time no longer matters. What is clear is that the Mojahedin were going to defend themselves from then on. A few days later we heard that an explosion had destroyed the headquarters of the Islamic Republic Party. About 100 people died, including Behashti, the head of the party, members of parliament, ministers and many of the leading lights of the regime. Of the key decision-makers, the only survivors were Rafsanjani and Khamenei. The perpetrator was a Mojahedin infiltrator. The Mojahedin never publicly accepted responsibility for the explosion, although they benefited from the political fallout.

A surprise election was called to vote in a new president and prime minister. Shortly afterwards I heard a report that Banisadr and Rajavi had left the country for Paris. I rejected this news vehemently; we used to criticise the Tudeh Party's leadership for fleeing to the Soviet Union after the 1953 CIA coup. This was the main reason we embraced members of the Tudeh Party as revolutionaries and martyrs of the people and reviled their leaders as traitors. I found it plausible that Banisadr had been sent to Europe for his own safety but could not believe that Rajavi would abandon Iran. Our leaders were not like those of the Tudeh Party. Yet that day, while in Sunderland lecturing our supporters, I saw with my own astonished eyes televised pictures of Rajavi and Banisadr arriving at Paris's airport. Later it was claimed that the politburo had sent Rajavi abroad to introduce our resistance movement to the world and to save him for the revolution and for the people. At the time people – stunned by the news of the explosion – did not question Rajavi's and Banisadr's departure. There were rumours the Mojahedin had infiltrated everywhere, into all the regime's offices; even that they had put a bomb under Khomeini's bed and said, 'We can kill you as easily as this but want you alive to account for yourself at the people's trial'. There were many among us who thought victory was imminent. The organisation itself assured us unequivocally that Rajavi and

Banisadr would return to Iran in triumph within a year at most. We thought of ourselves and the Mojahedin as honest and steadfast people who kept their promises and held to strict discipline. Consequently nobody questioned their statement.

During this time we were asked to distribute Banisadr's letter to Rajavi and the joint declaration of their coalition. This departed from our previous stance towards Banisadr. The organisation tried to persuade us that we had to support the coalition to avoid the creation of an anti-revolutionary front by Banisadr, Bakhtiar and others. It was especially difficult for me to follow this new line as I was responsible for forming relationships with other groups opposed to Banisadr. My name alone put me under suspicion of being pro-Banisadr.

In his letter Banisadr had written that, after reading the Mojahedin's literature, he had gained a new understanding of their beliefs and reviewed his old opinions about them. He implied that he had been wrong in calling the Mojahedin 'Stalinist' and their ideology a mixture of Islam and Marxism. Just as the Mojahedin had to find a way to justify to us their position *vis-à-vis* the coalition, I guess he had to do the same thing to his followers.

A few weeks after the arrival of Rajavi and Banisadr in Paris, we were asked to show our defiance of the Iranian regime and our condemnation of the executions taking place there by mounting a public hunger strike. About twenty members from our region and many more from other sections started a hunger strike in Trafalgar Square. We remained there for about a week. During the daytime we talked with passers-by and explained the situation in Iran. There had been enough anti-Iran and anti-Khomeini propaganda around for people to be sympathetic to our cause, politicians and even police included. In our conversations we maintained as liberal a position as possible. Our members no longer met with left-wing groups and our understanding of the IRA and Sinn Fein had changed: we were told that their actions were wrong, that they should express themselves through political means. The poster associating the Mojahedin with Sinn Fein was banned from display, remaining copies of it collected and burned. Banisadr's support reassured people that we were liberals, not communists or Muslim extremists. People took our literature and donated to us generously. Our faces, yellow from hunger, and our well-documented accounts and photos of the regime's atrocities no doubt helped. Now, unlike previously, we felt a sense of solidarity with others. Even among ourselves, we forgot about our anti-imperialist slogans. Every night during the hunger strike, as the streets were very cold, we went underground. Homeless people living there, angry that we were taking their places, sometimes tried to force us out or quarrelled with us.

Every night, after making sure everybody else was asleep, three *masouls* and I went somewhere else to talk about the next day's programme. One night a bunch of xenophobic thugs attacked us. I was slower than my colleagues in running away and was left at the mercy of the gang. They beat me so viciously that my right shoulder was broken. I lost consciousness with the pain; when came to, I saw all my friends standing around me. Some of my attackers had been captured but I declined to file a complaint at the police station. We had enough enemies, and didn't need one more. The hunger strikers maintained their vigil for a while longer but I was invalided back up to Newcastle.

# 15

# Occupations and Demonstrations

A week or two later came our next order: we were to occupy the Iranian embassies. I felt this was a bit radical. Our society was now organised more or less along Mojahedin lines. Each section had its *masoul*, nominated from London, from whom we took all our orders, which were straightforward, short and usually without much detail or explanation. The excuse for issuing this kind of order was that we were at war; everything had to be kept as secret and brief as possible. It seemed to me, however, that occupying the embassies ought to be our final act outside Iran, and would normally signal the regime's imminent collapse. 'Do you think we are at that stage?' I asked my *masoul*. He smiled. 'This is not an isolated act,' he assured me, 'and it will be done at the same time in all countries. It won't take much time, perhaps a day or two, and we'll leave the embassy as soon as we have relayed our message to the media.' My broken arm confined me to Newcastle to continue our routine work, but I had to recruit people to go to London. We were not supposed to tell them their precise destination or purpose. Many Iranian embassies were captured simultaneously, making headline news in several countries. In that sense it was quite a successful venture. I felt ashamed for questioning it. I was obviously wrong and misguided not only ideologically but also politically and in terms of action.

From then on physical confrontations between ourselves and supporters of the regime occurred constantly in Britain. Our area was famous among regime supporters as an area of *monafaghin* (i.e. Mojahedin) but Manchester, by contrast, was clearly under their control. Almost every week there were fights between our supporters and theirs. Eventually we decided to teach them a lesson. We got permission from the police to have a standing demonstration in front of the Iranian consulate in Manchester almost every week. By now most of our full-time members and supporters were in prison as a result of the embassy takeover; it wasn't easy to find enough people to go to Manchester, especially as usually afterwards fights were organised between the two sides. This happened regularly for a couple of months, but the situation in Manchester changed as more Iranians lost their illusions about the regime and stopped supporting it, adopting a more neutral stance instead.

On 30th August another piece of news shocked everybody and gave us new confidence that the regime was about to collapse. An explosion had taken place at the president's office in Tehran, and both the new president and prime minister were killed. Along with regular assassinations, including of many *mullahs*, there were more and more executions of prisoners – among them Sadatti, who was sentenced to ten years' imprisonment but was killed in this new wave of indiscriminate, hasty executions. Once more the regime proved that it had no respect even for its own laws. Among those executed were political figures of all stripes and many people under the age of eighteen, along with their elderly parents. News of executions became part of our daily lives and came so fast we scarcely had time to mourn our dead. A new phase in operations began with suicide bombings. The first of these came on 11th September. The bomber, Majid Niko – a young militiaman – was killed along with his target, Madani, a *mullah* and representative of Khomeini in Tabriz, plus seventeen revolutionary guards. Losing our young brothers and sisters was very painful, but the deaths of important figures in the regime at their hands gave us cause for jubilation rather than mourning. Steeped in a culture idealising martyrdom, we paid the highest respect to those we felt had made the ultimate sacrifice for democracy and independence, comparable to the honour accorded kamikaze pilots of World War Two Japan.

The activists who had gone to London for a one-day demonstration after the occupation of the Iranian embassy had been arrested and imprisoned for a few months; many had their lives turned upside down by this, and had to abandon their studies and become political refugees.

In many respects the MSS network mimicked the Mojahedin, to which it was ideologically very close. Its hierarchy and system of roles and responsibilities, like that of the *masoul*, was based on the Mojahedin's much more complex structure. The high level of personal commitment was similar too, in that a member of a supporting organisation was expected to work full-time for that organisation and be prepared to sacrifice everything to it, including his life – just like a Mojahed. Full-time adherents of the MSS were divided into members, designated 'O', and sympathisers, 'S'. Anyone who supported the Mojahedin but was not working full-time for the society was termed a supporter (*havadar*, or 'H'). I was *masoul* of all those classed as 'S' and of any other supporter in our area.

I believed the system was unfair to people working as hard as the rest of us but uninvolved in making decisions concerning their daily lives and work. I pressed for a change in the rules, basing my arguments on the Mojahedin's literature and appealing to their commitment to democracy. The executive council in London responded directly with two questions: Did I accept the authority of the council, and did I agree to whatever they decided? My answer to the first question was 'yes', as I knew the council had the blessing of the Mojahedin, who nominated the *masouls*. As to the second question, I knew I must do whatever was asked, but that didn't mean I had to agree to whatever they said. In the past I had sometimes disagreed with their decisions and been proved right. I asked our *masoul* to let me think about the second question and give him my answer the following day. He pre-empted me by asking to see me that night and advising that 'it will be better if you don't come to the base for a while'. He was, in the politest way, expelling me from the society.

The next day I stayed home. The official explanation for my expulsion, given to a puzzled Anna and to sympathisers in other cities for whom I was the *masoul* and teacher, was that I had a liberal tendency in running the organisation which was at odds with the framework of the Mojahedin. One day all the full-time supporters turned up at our house in a show of solidarity and support, having heard of my dismissal and been told not to ask questions.

A year before this event, my old and dear friend Shams had, as a result of conversations with our group, decided to settle in Newcastle and join us. Another friend, Nadir, a young man intensely devoted to the Mojahedin but frustrated by his inability to contribute effectively to the cause while abroad, had asked to go home. We protested that we needed him and his vast fund of knowledge to teach others, but he insisted. His brave death in an operation a year later profoundly affected everybody – especially Shams, who had been very close to him and who then redoubled his efforts for the organisation. As a reward, he was appointed to the Newcastle executive council. From then on our relationship changed completely, as personal friendship within the organisation was strictly forbidden and considered a clear sign of liberalism. Whatever the Mojahedin's public stance, liberalism was anathema within the organisation; it was a weakness of which both Shams and I were accused. Shams therefore didn't know much about my problems with our *masoul*. He was instructed by the London council to explain my situation to our supporters, one by one, and forbidden to visit us. This was difficult and painful. Sarvy adored her 'Uncle Shams' and he too loved her, yet it was now his duty to stay away from us and try to undermine me in the eyes of all – particularly those who had been learning about the Mojahedin from me. Perhaps his personal feelings prevented him from condemning me as vehemently as he was expected, but the outcome was that many of our supporters felt some animosity towards him and more sympathy towards us. Soon our representatives in Edinburgh, Sunderland and Middlesbrough, plus many supporters in different cities, left the society's base and were more or less living with us in our tiny two-bedroom flat.

A representative from London came to our house to speak to those who were with us. He told them there was a difference of opinion between the organisation and me which, being under the direction of the Mojahedin, was obviously not about to change; hence I would have to be the one to change. As for the supporters, they were instructed to return to their jobs and not ask questions, as this was a private matter between them and me.

Except for two members, everybody decided to stay put.

I could see that, on the one hand, my principles were binding me. On the other hand, if I did not return and accept whatever they instructed, then most of our local supporters would also stay away from the base. The work would not get done, and I would be blamed for paralysing our area and splitting the society at a critical time when we were on the verge of overthrowing the regime.

# 16

# Executions

We now received a lot of news about the Mojahedin's activities inside Iran, in the form of 'resistance cells'. The regime seemed bound to fall: Iran, at war with Iraq, had already suffered many defeats along its western borders; most of its assets had been seized by the US; and relations with other countries had been broken off. It was internationally isolated, and the Mojahedin had killed many high-ranking figures. A new coalition between the Mojahedin and Banisadr, the National Council of Resistance (NCR), had attracted many new faces, even if they didn't have much public support or influence. An important partner in the NCR was the Kurdish Democratic Party (KDP), the largest Kurdish group, with many combatants and part of Iran under their control. Some intellectuals, smaller parties and the National Democratic Front were also members, as were the association of university professors and the association of bazaar traders. International support for the new coalition rose quickly, thanks to the hard work of Mojahedin supporters and the cachet of the Banisadr name. In the beginning support came only from small, local organisations and leftist groups, but gradually bigger names like the British Labour Party and the Socialist Party in France came into the fold.

In October 1981 the Mojahedin announced a new policy of 'armed demonstration', with the slogan 'Death to Khomeini'. By now, they said, no one could have any more illusions about Khomeini's true nature. It was necessary to break the hold he had over the population. They claimed that in the new presidential election to replace the murdered incumbent, only three million people had bothered to vote. The regime claimed the true number was sixteen million, even more people than voted in the first presidential election. At the start of the new academic year Mussa Khiabani, the commander of the Mojahedin inside Iran, exhorted students to abandon their studies and consider 'the resistance' their education, which implied joining 'armed demonstrations', where Mojahedin members and supporters distributed clandestine publications under the watchful eyes of armed colleagues. As well as demanding Khomeini's death, they shouted, 'Death to reactionaries!' and 'Death to imperialism!' Naturally, many clashes ensued, followed by deaths, injuries, imprisonment and executions.

The executions were perpetrated with equal vigour by both sides. The regime was particularly fond of public hangings, even of fighters already ill or injured. A 'religious order' went out mandating that 'as virgins cannot be judged on Judgement Day and sent to hell, young girls must first be married before being executed'. Thus, in prisons, young girls were systematically raped by guards before being executed. The law that sanctioned this barbaric practice was *sieghe* (short-contract marriage). Another *fatwa* (religious order) permitted the blood of prisoners to be drained before execution and given to war victims. Rapes of young girls and boys, and of sisters and wives in front of their menfolk, were very common. Torture was used to extract information from prisoners.

Every week there was a chart listing the latest executions of members and supporters of Mojahedin and other groups. In December the numbers rose sharply. It was difficult not to be moved by the photos and letters of those executed. Among them was the will of a young militia girl, Giti'ol Sadat Joze. She wrote:

> *I kiss your face from far away and send my regards to everybody, among them my dear, kind mother, she who gave her whole life to us, she who burned like a candle and lit our*

*lives. And my lovely father, who devoted his life to our well-being. I ask God to give you all patience and endurance. I have missed you all, including dear Mr Mansur and naughty little Nasser and all our other relatives. I have missed them all badly. Dear mother, please tell them all that I chose this path with honour and pride ... and with hope that my unworthy life will be part of the price of freedom for all those now oppressed. ... God willing, I hope one day you will see that just society. My dear mother, I beseech God, you should not cry for me. Any time you want to cry, remember how I am suffering because of that. I ask you, instead of listening to other people, for once just sit and think. I wish I could see you all once more, first because I have missed you very much and also because I want to tell you about things I have seen here in prison. I wish I could see you and tell you about them, and then perhaps you would believe me.*

Elsewhere, reaction to the bloodshed was equally strong. An Italian woman publicly burned herself in protest at the killing of children in Iran. Some Mojahedin supporters were inclined to follow suit.

Rarely did any prisoners receive the benefit of a fair trial. Those who were tried sometimes showed breathtaking strength and defiance, even embracing a sentence of execution. One young man not yet eighteen years old, Daryosh Salhshoor, was invited by the judge to plead for lenience in view of his extreme youth. Far from doing so, he said:

'... From the beginning when I chose this path, I was ready for any accusations. I am a follower of Imam Hussein, whom they accused in Karbela as well. They called the Prophet Muhammad mad and Imam Ali an apostate. Why should I be afraid, if I am following in their footsteps? ... I know the verdict of this court. Many of my friends were executed. I will go to meet them ...'

Caught between discarding my beliefs and principles and neglecting my responsibilities for resistance against tyranny, I decided to refer to the Mojahedin themselves. I wrote a lengthy letter explaining my dilemma, asking them to guide me. I informed my friends and colleagues, proposing to take no action until I received the Mojahedin's answer. MSS policy was to isolate us as much as possible, not to let us do anything in the name of the Mojahedin. Once, at a demonstration in London, it was obvious that many members and supporters had been told not to talk to us. Old friends turned their backs on me. One, who apparently didn't know about my situation, came forward with a smile but was intercepted by one of the organisers, who pointed at me, saying, 'He is a traitor and you shouldn't talk to him!' It was sad and strange to experience such things. Naively, I believed that those policies were decided by the MSS, and had nothing to do with the Mojahedin.

Although I had not been brought up to see life as black and white, the events of the previous few months forced me to see the Iranian regime as totally 'black' and the Mojahedin as completely 'white'. It was impossible for me to accept that the Mojahedin could be wrong. My only worry was that my bourgeois tendencies, selfishness and impulse to avenge what had been done and said to me might influence my decision about what to do next. I tried to force myself to be patient.

# 17

# The Sadatti Society

I had been under extreme pressure to be politically active during the previous five months but my hands had been tied as punishment for rebelling against the MSS. Almost two months had passed since the date of my letter to the Mojahedin, and I had received no answer. Sometimes, when the MSS could not prevent it, we attended their public activities – among them another hunger strike held in London at the start of the winter. We were treated as outcasts and banned from distributing materials; we sat apart from the others, in the cold weather, on the pavement, speaking only with each other. Even at night we had to sleep in our own corner.

Seven amongst us were full-time advocates of the Mojahedin. We lived in a small two-bedroom flat and spent most of our time together, joined for a day or two each week by some ten or fifteen others. Our sense of uselessness, the impact of the news from Iran and, in some cases, family pressure to resume normal lives created problems of their own. I felt the responsibility especially keenly, most of all towards young people whose lives and motivation were going to waste. Eventually we formed our own organisation in support of the Mojahedin. During those few months of activity we had been able to use everybody's talents to prepare materials, including posters, banners, leaflets and booklets, in the hope that they would prove useful to the MSS once we were permitted to return. This programme let us feel we were not wasting our time completely. I wrote another letter to the Mojahedin, enclosing pictures and photocopies of these materials. Again I asked for their guidance, adding, 'If in a month's time we have received no answer, we will need to conclude that our problems are too small compared with the major problems you are facing at the moment and that you have no time to deal with them. We feel we have been forgotten, and that we must make our own decisions to solve our problems. As the policy of the MSS is currently to isolate us, we have no alternative but to establish our own society to support the Mojahedin actively.' Another month passed with no reply, nor any change in the behaviour of the MSS towards us.

We decided to start operations on 11th February, the day of the victory of the revolution. We thought our first act should be a hunger strike. To avoid any conflict of interest with the MSS, we decided not to be active wherever they were active enough: we would complement, not compete with them. We called our society Sadatti, after the name of the regime's first political prisoner, who was executed. We also decided to publish a newspaper with the same name, again, to complement the MSS paper.

But on 8th February we heard unbelievable news in the British media: Mussa Khiabani, Ashraf Rabia'i (a high-ranking Mojahed), Rajavi's wife and several other members and leaders – including the sister of Ahmad Reza'i, one of the Mojahedin's founders – had been ambushed and killed by the revolutionary guards. We were unable to cry or even speak from shock. Nobody knew what to say or how to mourn. These were not ordinary martyrs of the revolution; the popularity and legitimacy of the resistance movement depended on their leadership. We all had personal affection for these people – especially Khiabani, whose popularity almost equalled Rajavi's and whose honesty lent credibility to the movement.

The incident raised many thorny questions: how could we claim we were going to overthrow the regime when we were not able to look after our own leader inside Iran? How was this unstable regime able not only to bear the loss of its high-ranking members and to continue its war with Iraq but also strike us at this level?

We all wanted to be alone. Some went outside, others stayed at home. I went to a nearby park with a lake where, I often thought, the swans swam like angels. I could do nothing but gaze at the lake, my mind a blank. I became aware that I was crying when passers-by looked at me strangely. When I returned home, somebody asked me what we were going to do. I told her I didn't know, and asked to be left alone in a room for a few hours.

I searched my soul. By then everything was prepared for our hunger strike at the University of Edinburgh, the first act of the Sadatti Society. Should I now forget all the principles I stood for and tell everybody to go back to work? Should I do so myself? Had I been fair to my colleagues? Should I admit the whole episode had been my mistake and apologise? To help me to think, I started drawing a large picture of Khiabani and hung it up like a banner, from ceiling to floor. Then I wrote about who Khiabani was and what he had done during his short life. I decided to put the alternatives to everyone and ask them collectively to choose one.

In the middle of the ensuing discussion somebody corrected me, saying that the principles to which I adhered were not mine alone but held by all of us. If I had to apologise for something I didn't believe was wrong, they would have to do so equally. Was our previous decision practicable? In the end we decided it was. The Sadatti Society came into being and we held our hunger strike under the banner of Khiabani.

During the next few months we held several meetings, demonstrations and exhibitions in cities where we knew the MSS would not be active. Although we opposed the Iranian regime and supported the Mojahedin and the NCR, our activities were banned by the MSS, which put it about that our actions helped the regime. We published replies in our paper, often referring to articles from *Mojahed* and recalling that supporters of the Mojahedin, according to Rajavi, were allowed to have minds of their own and were not expected to be dictated to word for word by the leadership. To make sure we were not out of line, we sent reports and pictures of all our activities to the Mojahedin without ever receiving any response.

Each issue of the MSS's magazine carried at least one interview with Rajavi, usually very informative pieces that elucidated, for example, why the provisional government was named the

'Democratic Islamic Republic' when the goal was to achieve a separation of religion and politics. In one interview he called Khomeini's regime even worse than the Shah's or imperialism. We knew little about his position within the Mojahedin and rarely saw other names from the organisation except when he appointed Ali Zarkash its commander-in-chief inside the country. Then, in a letter from the central committee offering condolences to Rajavi for the martyrdom of his wife and Khiabani, we saw for the first time his new title as the chief spokesman for the organisation (*masoul aval*).

In winter Anna told she was expecting our second child. I didn't know whether to be sad or happy. We loved Sarvy very much; she had brought us such joy that we couldn't imagine sharing that love and happiness with another child. I guess I was not ready for that. Financially, our future was bleak. We had no country to go to, no savings, no income or job. Although I was in my final stages of studying, I wasn't keen to finish. I knew the degree would be useless in my future. Besides, as I rarely had time for anything, studying was the last thing on my mind. We were fighting the Iranian regime without moral or material support from our mother organisation. Moreover, I shouldered responsibility for our members, who looked to me for solutions to personal and political problems.

I felt somehow indignant at the news, as though Anna had decided to have another child by herself. I wondered how the person I loved most – and who loved me most – could fail to understand the pressure I was under. Our departure from the base had been as much her decision as mine; it was she who had invited the others to leave the base and move into our home. But I had hoped for more understanding from her in the wake of this decision. Obviously, she was not happy. She wanted more privacy, more of my time and care – all completely understandable, but well above my ability to give at the time. To others I seemed capable and strong, but in reality I was torn between two loves and responsibilities.

For years Anna had shown all the love, affection and tolerance anyone could want. She accepted the hardships in our lives, even though she was not especially interested in politics. She had not been a revolutionary or activist, but for me she became one. Now, after suffering months of intense pressure, she wanted her life and husband back. Jean-Paul Sartre had posed the choice between 'looking after an ill mother or going to war to defend the home country'. His answer was direct and correct. One must choose the latter, as without country there cannot be family, and one will lose both. At this time the story of two young militia girls appeared in the Mojahedin paper. One, in a suicide attack, had killed Khomeini's representative in Shiraz and twelve revolutionary guards. Before the operation she had written of her eagerness to die paving the way for others: 'I don't think I am the owner of my existence. It belongs to God, the people and the Mojahedin.' Yet here I was, paralysed between the wish for a private life and my responsibility towards my country and people.

Anna, perhaps because of her pregnancy, was becoming recalcitrant, angry and unwilling to help. We rarely spoke and were not even sharing the same room. Certain of my decision to put duty to country first, I left her to decide what she wanted to do. I showed her less kindness and attention, to let her know that she could not change my mind by appealing to my love for her. Before long, others realised the difficulty of our situation and suggested that we think of relocating to larger premises. We moved into two apartments in a semi-detached house in Gateshead. The practical part of Anna's problem was now solved, but not questions about the future. I imagine that she, too, was in a state of deadlock, but what could she do? She could not return to Iran; she was pregnant and vulnerable. Perhaps she considered divorce, but how? Her love for me had not changed to hate, especially as she could clearly see the difficulties facing me. She could only reproach me for loving my country more than her or for spending more time on my responsibilities rather than on her ... although she knew how, ultimately, it was the course of history that ruled our lives. Nevertheless, even in the new house we lived essentially as strangers.

To attract international support, the Mojahedin changed their appearance, stance, slogans and even their literature. Consequently, they were very cautious about reiterating previous positions, especially those against the West and America. one rarely saw their 'Death to imperialism!' slogans; these were generally for domestic use, with a view to attracting other revolutionary groups to the NCR. MSS members no longer wore American military overcoats.

Some switched to suits and ties, and could even be seen talking to liberals and conservatives. Unlike the MSS, we continued to support our ideals, and a perhaps-imaginary Mojahedin organisation that was pure, honest, freedom-loving, independent and anti-imperialist. We announced our intention to publish our paper in English. No doubt it was this, along with our determination to carry on supporting the Mojahedin despite any obstacles, that forced them to take notice of us.

One day I received a telephone call from someone who identified himself as top-ranking Mojahed Mohsen Reza'i, brother of many martyrs. I laughed and said, 'Please don't joke, I am too busy'. I assumed it was a friend playing a trick. After a few moments I realised he really was who he claimed to be. I began stammering. For me all Mojahedin members were angels: pure, faultless. Receiving a call from one of them was like being called from Heaven. 'How is everybody?' he asked. 'What are you doing? Do you have any news from home?' Then he told me he had heard about our activities, and that we had made some mistakes – first, in choosing the name of Sadatti for our society, as the regime claimed Sadatti was opposed to the Rajavi's leadership. Then he said if we wanted to continue doing what we were doing, we should accept advice, as well as permission before printing anything in the name of Mojahedin supporters.

I replied that we had never had any intention of having a separate organisation, but had been forced along this path: 'We couldn't just sit back and do nothing at this decisive point in our history. To be active we needed means and materials. The MSS was not prepared to let us to distribute its materials, so we had to produce our own.'

I felt he had a different impression about us. Perhaps he had been told how selfish we were, how liberal and pro-Banisadr; perhaps he had thought us anarchists. He seemed taken aback at first, but then absorbed what I was saying and realised he was not dealing with some rebel but with an honest sympathiser imbued with love and respect for all Mojahedin, including himself. Gone was the questioning. Now, in gentle but decisive tones, he was commanding: we must forget everything that had happened and return to work at the MSS base. They were part of the Mojahedin. Their actions and requests had to be considered as though they were the actions and requests of the Mojahedin. We must obey the orders of anyone appointed our *masoul*.

I replied, 'Everything you say is fine by me, but it has to be agreed collectively. I will have to ask the others.' He conceded, saying that any time we were ready to obey this Mojahedin (not MSS) order we could return. Until then we had to cease all political activity. 'How can we do this?,' I asked. 'We feel responsible, and ideologically we know that being passive means working with the enemy. You are asking us to waste energy that belongs to the people, the Mojahedin and God.'

'Well,' he said, 'sometimes action is more damaging than beneficial. If you consider yourselves Mojahedin supporters, you must obey this order. Otherwise you are free to do anything you like. But you should not call yourselves Mojahedin supporters and enjoy the support people give you on behalf of the Mojahedin.' He appeared to believe we were getting financial help. I explained how we had spent all our savings on our activities and had not received help from anybody else. I promised to send him a financial report detailing all our income and expenditure.

Afterwards we held a meeting, at which I said that my inclination was to obey the Mojahedin and return to the MSS, but that I would follow the group's decision. They were not prepared to forget the past, however. They needed to know whether we had been right or wrong in principle. In that case, I said, we must do nothing until we are told what to do.

When Reza'i next called me, I explained the situation and asked if he could arrange for a Mojahedin representative to come and persuade them to follow Mojahedin orders.

Mussa, from the Mojahedin, along with my old friend Ebrahim (now in charge of the MSS in Britain) duly came to meet us. I kept silent. After Mussa's address, people started asking him one question after another – sharp, clear questions, mostly about the basic rights of sympathisers and the relationship between leadership and members, democracy and freedom. Mussa seemed either unable or unwilling to answer. He listened and launched into a lengthy speech, as the Mojahedin customarily did when circumventing the truth or forcing listeners to swallow a bitter reality. He spoke of the tortures that had been inflicted on our brothers and sisters, of members in Iran who had no homes and were separated from their families, sleeping in trenches or underneath cars at night with only scraps of bread to eat. Eventually, he said, 'When part of a body has rotted, it must be cut out and discarded. It is painful; once it was healthy and functioning perfectly. But its disease might infect and destroy the rest of the body. Removing it is the only remedy. This is what the Mojahedin have done with some of their members.' My heart was in my mouth. Everybody got his message: I was the rotten part that had to be excised. I was angry and hurt, as indeed were the members, who began leaving one by one. Even Mussa seemed upset; perhaps he was just doing his job, saying things without believing them.

Once or twice in a lifetime, you get a chance to see reality with great clarity, to hear the truth, however bitter, to think rightly and make the correct decision, however difficult. That was my day, and those few seconds of silence were my moment. As Mussa sat with us drinking tea, I went over to Ebrahim. I said,

'This was not right. Even if what he said was right, this was not the right time. He was here to attract these people to the organisation, not push them away. They can't accept that I was just a rotten piece of the MSS. He thinks I have deceived and brainwashed them, and that he is responsible for reversing that. But the questions they are asking, which used to come just from me, are now their questions too. So if I'm rotten because of my beliefs, well, so are we all!' Ebrahim looked sad and said nothing, his silence signalling that he agreed with me.

Then I said, 'You know perfectly well that whatever I did and said came from my education and my understanding of Mojahedin teachings.' His expression turned to anger and he snapped,

'When will you forget about those things you have read, forget your idealism and face reality? You must accept things, including the Mojahedin, as they are, not as you wish they were or think they should be. Please forget the reading, see the real Mojahedin. Accept them and let us work together to get rid of Khomeini. After that there will be plenty time for other things.' His words were like a hammer banging on my head – but instead of awakening me, they knocked me unconscious.

That was my moment. But instead of opening my eyes and seeing reality, I closed them and refused to see anything. Instead of opening my ears to the truth, I closed them so as not to hear any more. Instead of forcing myself to think, I shut my mind to all doubt and questions. The moment passed, and I had wasted it. Suddenly the castle of my hopes crumbled to dust. I lost my trust in the written word. I decided not to read any more books; for all the time I was with the Mojahedin, I rarely did.

The group's decision was clear. We had been told not to do anything, to attend only public activities of the MSS. The *masoul* would call us if they needed our help.

# 18

# Back Within the Fold

And so we were back to the bad old days, with nothing to do. I held myself responsible for all that waste of energy and talent and felt more paralysed than ever. Now I could not even encourage anyone to read books, as I had lost all faith in written work. I couldn't ask them to do anything. 'What for?', they would inevitably ask. Our future as a group was finished; as individuals, everything was up in the air. We sent all our political materials to London, which helped us feel useful. But it was hard to keep morale up. Some of us had private lives and could continue to work as usual, but others had burned all their bridges and could not go back and resume their work or studies. A partial solution was to exercise early in the mornings, something I had always been too lazy for. But we went out daily and performed military-type exercises, much to the suspicion of our neighbours.

A small backyard garden we created also helped pass the time. Friends came from other cities to help and to tell me their problems. I empathised with them but also became anxious about giving them the right advice. I was thinking of leaving university, but my supervisor warned that this could ruin my future. I told him events in Iran made it hard for me to concentrate. He said, 'You have finished your research. The only thing left is to type it and hand it over, then prepare for an oral examination, which I know is not difficult for you.' He urged me to at least continue computer programming, which could be used or sold to help the resistance. Some friends believed that obtaining my doctorate would be beneficial to the movement and for the future of Iran. But I was reluctant to return to my studies when there were talented, young people around me who had to be saved from deviating from the course of being a revolutionary and a Mojahed.

A turning point came with the news of the Israeli invasion of Lebanon. There were heartrending reports of the killing of Palestinians in Lebanon. Throughout the Shah's era, a time of friendly ties with Israel, we developed special feelings for the Palestinians, reinforced by Mojahedin literature. To see them murdered was like seeing Iranians murdered by foreigners. Rajavi issued a communiqué demanding that Khomeini, if he really cared about what was happening in Lebanon, let Mojahedin supporters cross Iranian borders and help the Palestinians defend themselves against the Israelis. We believed Khomeini was not only *not* anti-Israel but also the Palestinians' worst enemy. Rajavi wanted to show how strong the Mojahedin in Iran were; he promised to send 100,000 combatants to Lebanon. This statement pleased us all greatly. There followed a communiqué from the MSS saying that all their members and assets were under PLO orders, and announcing that they would join the Palestinians in their struggle. Ebrahim called us for the first time since our meeting and asked us to draw a banner, prepare some materials and participate in a large demonstration in support of the Palestinians. It was good to feel useful again.

After the demonstration I called our friends together and made strenuous efforts to persuade them to forget the past and return to the MSS. I loved each and every one of them, and could no longer bear to see their lives going to waste. This time, when they argued, I argued back We finally decided to surrender and return to the MSS. I wrote to Reza'i, who accepted our offer. Later he asked us to take responsibility for something very special and secret. It was an honour and privilege. We were going to receive the MSS newspaper and send it to various addresses, not of Mojahedin supporters but of ordinary Iranians. To make it difficult for the regime to trace, we would post them in different kinds of envelopes, with different stamps, from different cities. We were also asked to join regional MSS members and supporters in selling *Iran Liberation*, the daily English edition of their paper.

Rajavi spoke on the anniversary of the NCR's establishment and also summed up the achievements of the first year of resistance, including support gained at international levels and recognition of the atrocities perpetrated by the regime. He mentioned that more than 2,000 high-ranking members of the regime had been killed by the Mojahedin, and much of the atmosphere of fear created by the revolutionary guards had been dispelled. Soon, he said, the resistance would enter its final stage: overthrowing the regime. He placed the blame for the war with Iraq squarely on Khomeini alone, adding that the Mojahedin were true Muslims who symbolised honesty, resistance and self-sacrifice, the true descendants of Iranian revolutionaries like Mirza Kuochack Khan and leaders like Mossadegh. It was blasphemy, he said, even to suggest that they did not have the people's full support, whereas the regime enjoyed so little popular support that Khomeini's death would precipitate its collapse. He forecast victory in the 'short term' – within one to three years, paid tribute to the Mojahedin's many sacrifices and recognised the pain of those who had lost loved ones. 'It is very painful,' he acknowledged., 'Many of them have decided not to remarry, but I advise them, and bachelors, to marry.'

He himself married three months later. His bride was Banisadr's daughter (which meant I could now call him one of the family). His marriage raised some eyebrows; Rajavi's martyred wife, a symbol of Iranian women's resistance, had been dead for less than a year and his colleagues were suffering in prison and dying in the streets. Clearly it was a political move. The Mojahedin wanted to strengthen ties with Banisadr by making their leader his son-in-law.

During the previous few months I had been able to spend more time with Sarvy, collecting her from school and playing games with on the walk home. Anna and I still loved each other, but were both proud and hesitant to make the first move towards ending the bitterness between us, perhaps each waiting for the other to give in first. Without saying as much, Anna made it clear she wanted her life and husband back. I wanted her to realise that we could not reverse the clock. Ours were not the only lives changed forever; the lives of all Iranians had changed, and the repercussions would outlive us, perhaps for generations.

One day I returned home to find her gone. Apparently she had felt her time was due and called a taxi to the hospital. When I heard this I rushed immediately to the hospital, but it was all over when I arrived: I discovered we had a son. We named him Hanif, after Mojahedin founder Hanif-Najad. Hanif's arrival obliterated our differences and restored our love, but I felt ashamed that Anna went through the pregnancy and birth alone, without the comfort of her husband by her side. From then on we were extremely busy and equally happy. Although good and bad news assailed us daily, we felt we were doing something tangible, sharing the responsibility for resisting injustice, oppression and inhumanity. Now our time was divided between preparing magazines for posting and joining teams of newspaper sellers. Anna returned to work. She was not tied to Sarvy and Hanif thanks to an array of willing childminders among our friends.

Out on the street, the response to our cause was positive and heart-warming. People stood in the rain to listen to our stories, often with tears in their eyes. Once, while selling newspapers in Darlington, I noticed some skinheads looking at me. Having had that bad experience in London, I didn't ask them to buy a paper. Then one of them approached and asked what I was doing. A little nervously, as I did not know his intentions, I explained the situation in Iran. He looked sad, and asked what they could do to help us. Apologising that it was not enough, he asked me to accept the few pounds he had on him. He also wanted to know if supporters of the regime attacked us. I told him about recent incidents in London. 'OK,' he said, 'from now on, any time you're in Darlington, we're going to guard you.' I was impressed and grateful, but also didn't want the presence of 'guards' to make people hesitant to talk to us. So I thanked him, telling him we didn't want to take up their time. But I could not persuade him; for the next few months, whenever we were out on the streets of Darlington, we had our skinhead protectors.

Needing money for stamps and envelopes, we got permission to set up a business. Then we wracked our brains examining all the options; someone suggested we buy a van and make doner kebabs to sell in the street. We bought an old ambulance and converted it. There were only two kebab outlets in our region then, one Turkish and the other Iranian. Somehow, by observing, we learned how to make kebabs, and later even developed our own recipe. We used a small, second-hand mixer for the meat. When the big day came, what we could only offer ugly, deformed kebabs, unprofessionally chopped vegetables and improvised sauce. That night the number of workers in our van far exceeded the number of customers. But soon we found a good site in Durham, and gradually learned how to do everything properly. In no time many people in Durham were introduced to the joys of kebabs, thanks to us. We acquired some loyal customers, some of whom travelled long distances to buy from us, and were even able to buy a second and then a third van.

As the Mojahedin was under financial pressure then, earning money was the first priority for all supporters. I was informed that our section would become a section of the MSS, and I would be responsible for Scotland and northeastern England. They asked the previous *masoul* for that region to hand over his responsibility to me. We now worked with everyone who had chosen to work with the MSS during the time we were separated from it. We were all jubilant; although the Mojahedin had never told us whether we were wrong or right, our present situation was clear proof their faulty judgement. My own new *masoul* was an old friend, and we met each week at different locations. I noticed the organisation's practices had changed. Instead working on the floor, people were using chairs and tables. They still shared plates between two at mealtimes, but the communal tray had vanished. Although the main decisions still came like revelations from above, which nobody dared question or deviate from, there were now councils responsible for minor jobs and members shared in some low-level decision-making. In each base men and women had their own rooms in which to rest and sleep. One thing had changed for the worse: the sharing of information on the basis of 'need' rather than 'right' to know. Need was decided by the *masouls*, who seemed to cherish secrecy more than ever. There were now separate bases for members, full-time and part-time supporters. The MSS wanted me to rent another flat for members, so as to separate them from supporters. I resisted for weeks, arguing that it was not practical in our community as we all worked in the kebab van and had to have the same status, without secrets from each other. Besides, people had more incentive to work harder when they felt a kind of family closeness. My protests were to no avail and I did rent another flat, but I didn't keep the place as secret as I was supposed to.

We had certain daily rituals to perform. In the morning, we had 'matins'. Standing in ranks like soldiers in front of pictures of Rajavi and Khiabani and the emblem of the organisation, we sang a Mojahedin song and hailed the Mojahedin. There were also some military-style drills to perform, like turning right or left or walking or running on the spot. Although I, as *masoul* or section commander, was supposed to lead the session, I was hopeless at learning the right manoeuvres and usually asked my deputy Mohsen or Anna to conduct the proceedings instead of me. The 'ceremony' sometimes went on for a long time and was very loud, which created problems – including complaints from the neighbours and uncontrollable fits of laughter that gripped some participants. With the permission of my *masoul* I moved this ceremony to our base for supporters so they could join in. For some, 'matins' gave added incentive for work, as well as reminding them of our people inside Iran and Kurdistan. For others the whole thing was a joke. But all members had to fill in a form each week reporting their activities, including whether they had missed any of these ceremonies (with explanation); if they had prayed daily; if they had read the weekly MSS paper, especially Rajavi's messages and interviews; and whether they had written a report of self-criticism. At the week's end I collected these reports and took them (mine included) to the meeting with my *masoul*.

Although our contributions to the organisation's coffers were more than those of any other branch and sometimes equal to all of them put together, the organisation habitually asked us for more. When I asked if we could retain our income for two months to start a new business, I was firmly told 'no'. I therefore asked our supporters to borrow money to rent a shop, promising to return it within a year. I didn't tell the organisation about the loan, as I knew they would demand it sent immediately to London. We rented some premises, applied for a change of use and turned it into a kebab shop. Only then did I inform my *masoul* about the loan. After a month or two, the shop began yielding the extra income the organisation demanded.

One day I was asked to go to London with Anna, Sarvy and Hanif. I was surprised, as I had not received such an invitation for some time, more so for the invitation as a family. Try as we might, we could not guess the reason. We went to one of the MSS bases, where many familiar faces greeted us kindly; gone, the hostility of the previous months. We continued to the base of the *masoul*. I didn't know her name, having no 'need' to know. It turned out her nickname was Mahnaz. She was a member of the Mojahedin, as was now required of the head of each society. She had all the qualities we expected of a Mojahedin member. Her room was on the second floor, and few people were allowed there. There was evidently a 'rank separation' not only between members and supporters but even among members, who could not visit and often didn't even know about other bases.

At lunch I was given a ball of pressed bread, so I could join in the Mojahedin prison inmates' game. The idea was to throw your ball at other people or, better still, aim it into their teacup or dish to splash them. Childish though it was, the game broke the silence and created a fun atmosphere. Sarvy enjoyed it more than anyone. Visitors from other bases imported this custom to Newcastle, where it was very popular until it got out of hand – players received black eyes from being hit by the balls. By order, the practice ceased everywhere.

Mahnaz spoke of the financial crisis in Iran and explained that often the choice was between money and the life of a Mojahed. Unfortunately, most of the time they sacrificed a life because of shortages. It was therefore the responsibility of everyone to help in any way possible. We were directed to call our relatives and parents and ask them for help, using whatever pretext could arouse their compassion and make them generous. It was suggested I call my father and tell him I had a brain haemorrhage and needed money to travel to Sweden for treatment. I was appalled. How could I call my father after three years without contact whatever? In my whole life I had never asked him or anybody else for money. Now I was being asked to lie to my parents, which went wholly against the grain. Besides, I was not sure my mother would be able to handle news of my 'illness'. When I mentioned these concerns to Mahnaz she preached at me for about an hour, reiterating the dire urgency of helping our brothers and sisters in Iran. I had heard that the

Mojahedin believed the end justifies the means, and here was proof. Mahnaz's admonitions were effective, making me feel ashamed of my reluctance to oblige, which might result in Mojahedin deaths. We called Iran, and Anna spoke to my father, saying that I was too ill to talk. We asked for few hundred thousand *toman*, quite a large amount in those days. He said he needed a few days to obtain the funds. When Anna called him again, he said he had asked one of the most famous Iranian medical professors, a relative of ours who lived in Paris, to visit me in London and oversee my care. My father, prepared to pay whatever it cost, wanted me admitted to the best hospital available. We faced a major dilemma: what were we to do with this professor? We could not avoid giving our phone number to my father, and soon afterwards the professor rang and asked for me.

The situation was difficult and disturbing, but also quite funny. The house members queued for the phone to spin their unlikely yarns to their own parents. One couple said they wanted to get married, whereupon their parents in Iran wanted to meet each other and share a suite at the ceremony. The family of the 'bride' wanted to attend the wedding of another couple who told a similar story. One man claimed he had killed someone in a car crash and needed to pay a ransom to avoid going to prison. Another, whose family lived in London, said he was giving up politics to open a shop. His parents were so happy that he was resuming 'normal life' that they would gladly have handed over any amount. They asked to see the shop, and he gave the address of our shop in Newcastle; his parents travelled north to haggle with us over the price! Our shop was successfully 'sold' not only to his family but also several times over to other members'.

But my case seemed intractable. I didn't know what to do. Eventually I told Mahnaz it would be better if I spoke with my father and told him at least part of the truth. I called and said my condition was not as bad as the doctors had thought, but that I was facing a situation I could discuss only when I saw him, as the phones were tapped and I worried that the regime would create difficulties for him if they were to find out about it. I reminded him that I had never asked him for money, and that if this were not important I would not be doing so then. 'Trust me,' I said. 'I will explain everything when we meet.' He seemed happy to hear my voice and, reassured that my life was not in danger, promised to send the money.

Following our return to Newcastle I was instructed to encourage other members of our branch to raise funds. Among those I believed I might approach without lying was my old friend Farzad. When I phoned him, he was very surprised and pleased at first, but as soon as I mentioned the Mojahedin, his tone changed. He cursed them, accusing them of being responsible for all our misery. 'They are reason why we have the present regime,' he said, 'and they are the reason so many people are suffering now.' His words hit me hard. In Iran, after the revolution, he introduced me to his friends who were Mojahedin supporters. We spoke a lot about the organisation, and his attitude was favourable. Obviously his view had now completely changed. It was the end of our friendship. I had always thought nothing could destroy it, but now I clearly saw how beliefs could come between us. I began dimly to understand how Gillani, the prosecutor of the regime, could sentence his sons to execution and how, by the same token, his sons were prepared to kill him. I began to understand how that mother in Iran had informed on her son and was, as a result, designated 'mother of the year'. I could see the animosity between brothers and old friends. Ugly, hateful it certainly was, but it was an unavoidable facet of contemporary Iranian behaviour. Anything was permissible under the cloak of 'belief'. Ideology overrode everything else.

# 19

# Private Griefs, Public Atrocities

Once, while in London, I was asked about the private lives of our Newcastle supporters. Were they single? Did they have girlfriends? What was the nature of their relationships? I had to admit I was ignorant about these matters. They often talked to me about their private problems, but I paid attention to them only insofar as it enabled me to understand advise.

For members we had strict rules that included 'no sex before marriage'; 'total commitment to the organisation'; 'no relationships outside the organisation'; 'no fun'; 'no private time'; 'no outside work'; 'no private ownership'; even 'no reading of material from outside the organisation'. These rules were unwritten and unspoken, but they were essential guidelines in assessing a person for membership. If somebody qualified but had one of these 'bad habits', he or she would be advised to get rid of it and to observe full Islamic tradition: collective prayer, fasting at Ramadan, abstaining from alcohol and pork and so on. Women had to observe the Islamic dress code: long dresses and scarf covering the whole body except the hands and face. If an applicant failed to discard his private interests or habits, which we called 'attachments', he or she would lose membership of the MSS without even being informed. Among them was my old friend Shams, who was abruptly transferred to our section from London, having lost his membership. I knew Shams well, as a sensitive person with a love of music and reading, attributes that could work in his favour within the framework of the organisation if they took the direction the Mojahedin wanted, but that would count as 'destructive', 'bad' or even 'dangerous' in other circumstances.

Having been alerted to the question, I discovered that most of our male supporters had girlfriends. Some of them were open about it and others found ways to hide it; one pretended to be ill and have a doctor's appointment out of town whenever he wanted to see his girlfriend; another invented an important family problem that had to be resolved immediately. For many, this was the biggest or even the only obstacle in their way to becoming a member of the organisation.

I personally liked them and wished to see them all become Mojaheds. I cared nothing about their private situations, yet I often had to spend weeks trying to persuade them to solve their 'problems', to either forget about love and sex before marriage or marry their girlfriends. Those who decided to marry found me presiding over the ceremony, acting as a *mullah* and reading verses about marriage from the Qur'an – coached beforehand by Anna so I could read them correctly. With practice, I could soon conduct the ceremony without much nervousness. Even the dowries were alike; all I had to remember was to change the names of the couple.

The weddings didn't solve everything. Many of the non-Iranian wives found it difficult to accept their husbands' total commitment to the organisation and their lack of normalcy and privacy. The only solution was to involve the new spouses in our way of life. So we organised special lectures in English to teach them our beliefs and ideology, and set them to work selling papers or helping in the kebab shop.

From December 1982 *Mojahed* was published again, instead of the MSS weekly paper. Again the news was full of executions and tortures – children, whole families, fighters. As the atrocities of the regime were not limited to revolutionary groups, we had everyone's sympathy. According to some estimates, between two to four million Iranian refugees flooded into European countries, especially West Germany: the biggest emigration of Iranians during its whole 2,500-year history. Many brought horrible stories with them. One refugee told of witnessing a woman having her lips cut by revolutionary guards as a punishment for wearing lipstick; others spoke of women arrested for being insufficiently covered. One family's son was executed by mistake; the guards returned the victim's body to his family, saying, 'Good news: as he was innocent, he is going to heaven as a martyr of the Islamic cause.' One dreadful report described a ten-year-old girl swimming in her family's private pool when their neighbour, who could see her from above, informed revolutionary guards that a naked woman was in full view. The guards stormed the house and the poor child sentenced to 100 lashes in public. Nor did the story end there: the girl's father was shot dead trying to stop the guards from whipping his daughter. The girl was left partially paralysed, and her mother lost her mind.

It seemed children were the main victims in the new Iran. There were many reports of children used on the front lines to clear mines, with the promise that they would go to heaven when they died. They were covered with blankets so that their fragmented body parts would not be visible scattered around the area. According to one newspaper published by the regime, forty students from one school alone lost their lives on the battlefront. Martyrdom was an honour. Muslims would gladly compete for it, and envy others who had attained it. Khomeini had decreed that children as young as ten could be send to the front lines without parental consent. This was another reason why many families wanted to flee the country.

On our side, however, there were many children we considered exemplars of wisdom, and who willingly sacrificed themselves for the cause. Thirteen-year-old Ebrahim, executed with his fourteen-year-old brother Bahman, wrote a letter printed in *Mojahed* describing his belief in revolutionary Islam and that 'death with honour is better for any Muslim than life with shame and disgrace. … I ask my parents not to be sad because of me, and continue their correct and dignified lives with hearts full of hope. I assure them that right and truth are the final winners.' Ebrahim's letter inspired us, as did the case of seventy-year-old 'Mother Zakeri', who refused a blindfold for her execution, saying she wanted open eyes so as to see the rightness of the Mojahedin. Her crime was helping her son escape from revolutionary guards. When her interrogators asked his whereabouts, she replied, 'Can't you hear him? He is everywhere, in all cities, all cemeteries, all jails. My son was the one in the next cell, executed a week ago; he was the one firing his machine gun at you ... all resistance fighters are my sons.'

On 9th January, in Paris, Rajavi met Tariq Aziz, Iraq's foreign minister and deputy prime minister. We had often defended our organisation against allegations of collaborating with Iraq. But after this meeting we came to recognise Khomeini's sole responsibility for prolonging the war while Iraq was ready to make peace. Two months later the Iraqis accepted an NCR peace plan, whereby Iraqi forces had to withdraw to international boundaries and Iraq had to accept the terms of a 1975 peace treaty with the Shah, plus pay reparations for the damages inflicted on Iran. Our leader had pulled off a remarkable feat, given that the Iranian regime was arguably kept in power only by the war: once they ceased hostilities they would immediately be overthrown. Not everybody agreed with this analysis. Some in the media, among supporters of the Shah and Bakhtiar and leftist organisations, thought Iran had sold out to the enemy and that the Mojahedin were collaborators. Outside Iran there were groups supposedly opposed to the regime but in fact united with it against the Mojahedin.

Rumours were rife about disagreements within the NCR. We rejected them as anti-revolutionary gossip until we read an MSS union representative's report to Rajavi. It cited the record of the MSS activities, backed up with impressive statistics detailing the acquisition of support from 447 organisations worldwide, as well as from 707 international personalities and 387 labour unions; the organisation of 1,000 meetings in various cities, 400 press conferences and 7,000 political meetings; and the publication of the MSS paper, *Iran Liberation*, in eight different languages every week. The author criticised our partners in the NCR for providing no help and pouring salt in our wounds. He was supposedly speaking on our behalf, yet we knew nothing about such offences. Years later I understood this Mojahedin trick: when they wanted to criticise their partners, they would hide behind their supporters and members.

Rajavi, responding to the report, praised supporters for their hard work and sacrifices and called us 'Mojahed' – an honour indicating that we were members of the Mojahedin 'family' but warning that, as the organisation had raised its expectations of members to the highest possible level, we would still be considered supporters, not members. He advised us to restrain ourselves, avoid conceit and hypocrisy and be patient.

## 20

# Kebabs, Kisses and Kurds

Our *masouls*, and some articles in *Mojahed*, spoke increasingly against Banisadr. I felt I was under some kind of surveillance, perhaps to see how sympathetic I was towards him. It was said that Banisadr had joined us because he thought we were strong enough to overthrow the regime in a matter of months. Soon he discovered how wrong he was, especially when Khiabani and Rabia'i were killed and he lost all hope of returning to the presidency of Iran. If it had not been for Rajavi's marriage to his daughter, Banisadr would have split from us much earlier: '*filesh yad hendeston kard*' (literally, 'his elephant has remembered India [where it came from]' – that is, Banisadr wished to return to Khomeini). Meanwhile Banisadr wrote to Khomeini, demanding that Khomeini stop committing crimes and return to the promises he had made in Paris. Banisadr insisted his letter was just and useful: if it changed anything it would be for the good of the country and if not, it would expose Khomeini even more starkly as responsible for all the bloodshed. The Mojahedin didn't accept this logic, arguing that the time for such letters had long passed. A river of blood now flowed between us and Khomeini, which nothing could wash away.

They demanded Banisadr's expulsion from the council, and in late March 1984, duly got it.

We were warned that this might lose us some of the international support we enjoyed. To prove otherwise, Rajavi asked that our diplomatic activity be increased. Our people in the society's diplomatic section persuaded Britain's Labour Party to invite Rajavi to London. Of course, it was kept secret from us; we learned about it only upon seeing his photo in *Mojahed* with Labour leader Neil Kinnock and other high-ranking officials. In an interview with BBC radio's Persian broadcast, Rajavi was asked if our increased political activity was to compensate for the organisation's shortcomings and loss of support inside Iran. He vehemently denied this, saying, 'These are the accusations of our enemies, former followers of the Shah and supporters of Khomeini'. He cited various activities that the organisation had pursued in Iran and reiterated that Khomeini's regime would soon be overthrown. The reporter continued his hostile line of questioning; this and other coverage evinced a hatred of the Mojahedin that made the BBC our number-one enemy in the media. Soon the organisation banned interviews with it by any member of the Mojahedin and, later, of the council. Anyone who disobeyed was considered a collaborator with British imperialism and with Khomeini's regime.

Perhaps to increase my motivation and to test me even more after Banisadr's expulsion, I was ordered to go to Paris. Everyone remarked how lucky I was, and how much they wished they could go.

Three brothers and two sisters accompanied me on the trip. They all considered it a privilege to visit our Mojahedin comrades in Paris, especially Rajavi. We were warned to be very security-conscious. In case we were being followed, we were instructed to bend over every now and then and, under the pretence of tying our shoelaces, look between our legs at the street behind. Such measures were joked about in London, but had to be taken seriously in Paris.

Along with crowds of other supporters, we thronged in to Rajavi's residence in Auvers-sur-Oise, near Paris, to hear his speech on the anniversary of the martyrdom of sixty Mojahedin leaders and members on 2nd May 1982. Many *masouls* were there, each competing for the best vantage points as near as possible to Rajavi. I was surprised at how many of them knew me, although I did not know them. They had evidently read reports about us. I marvelled at the excitement everyone showed at seeing Rajavi in person. Admittedly, I didn't listen too closely to his speech, as I knew it would be printed in *Mojahed*. I didn't realise I would later be asked about it and be embarrassed by my ignorance. At the end of Rajavi's speech, to my astonishment, the audience started running to greet him. As I stood there stock-still, one of the sister *masouls* gestured to me to join them. I did so, feeling that I had been a fool not to follow the crowd. The following day I was to meet Tahereh, the *masoul* who had signalled to me; a few months later she became *masoul* of our society in England.

I was asked to send a videotape of our work in the kebab shop, so societies in other countries could copy our success. The video showed scenes we regarded as normal – customers kissing, drunks – and before we knew it we were ordered to close all our vans and the shop at ten p.m. (before pub closing time) and not to sell pork. Why these matters had suddenly become an issue puzzled me – the higher-ups must have known about them for a long time. We complied, and as a direct result suffered a drastic drop in our sales. But however much I pleaded, there was no change of policy.

To plug the gap in our income, I was asked to send everybody on sponsored walks. These walks-for-charity (in this case a Mojahedin charity) had been suggested by the wife of a supporter, who noted the popularity of sponsored walks as a fundraising tool in general. Supporters were generally not keen on them, but their objections were labelled 'immoral' by the leadership, and soon sponsored walks became the sole source of our income.

Our people would go on sponsored walks in the morning and work in the shop or vans during the evening. Some customers were angered by the change of hours, even attacking our van in one city. We instituted measures to defend our boys. Still, fights broke out and people were injured. We were on the verge of changing from selling kebabs to individuals to producing and selling frozen kebabs to shops, when I was told I was to be transferred to London.

I attended a meeting headed by Tahereh and her deputy, in which we were told that 'to change yourselves and become new people and walk the Mojahedin path, you must obliterate your past'. To begin with, we had to burn all our non-essential papers and writing materials. Apart from its ideological purpose, this action had security advantages as it ensured the destruction of documents relating to the organisation that might be dangerous. I was supposed to verify that others did likewise. In fact. the organisation was changing its whole attitude towards the past, and wanted all old Mojahedin literature eradicated. They had already asked for old books to be handed in, and for some time none of them had been obtainable at public meetings.

This paranoia did not trouble me much. What bothered me was whether I wanted to change myself and wipe out my past. It was the moment of choice. I could not keep everything and pretend I was transforming into a Mojahed; I had to choose Mojahedin teaching over my own logic and desires. The Mojahedin represented the only viable future for a free, democratic Iran, and to fight alongside them one had to be a Mojahed. Perhaps it was not so much a choice between past and future as between my belief in freedom and democracy and my personal life. But if I chose the latter, how could I guarantee a future in which my children could live normal, self-respecting lives? Our homeland was being morally and materially destroyed. We had been granted political asylum, but I didn't want to live in the UK permanently or see my children grow up as non-Iranians. I had only one option; putting my family first meant dedicating myself to securing a democratic homeland for them. I had to change myself and go towards the future. I had to burn my past. All my treasured materials had to be burned: my handwritten notes about the Mojahedin taken from their books and papers; all my work from the Sadatti Society; all my university papers; my PhD thesis and MSc dissertation; my high school notes; my research on mathematical models of thought; letters from my friends and parents. Then, my stories ... those stories that had been my chief mode of expression in times of turmoil and doubt, that had given me solace and insight, that I had shared with my wife and closest friends ... I burned them all and gave my university textbooks to one of our supporters to sell. This was my goodbye to the past. Little did I know it was still a long way to the final goodbye.

The deputy head of the MSS came to Newcastle to check whether we had burned all our written materials. Some of my colleagues, panicked by the news of imminent inspection, burned items they needed for their daily work and documents related to their status in the UK. One, who was very fond of his classical records, was so focused on saving them that he accidentally burned all his old documents including his degree and birth certificate.

Every week our colleague Ali Akbar would travel from London to Newcastle to collect kebabs for the London shop. Instead of meat, he often brought us videos of Mojahedin activities inside Iran. One of these recorded a medical team of Mojahedin working in Kurdish villages under the control of the KDP. We were proud to see them working under such difficult conditions, helping ordinary people, even performing operations and relieving long-standing problems.

When Ali Akbar made his last visit before being posted to Kurdistan, we accompanied him to London and left behind not only most of our belongings but also a city that had become our second home, along with many friends who were closer to us than our own family, who were virtually of my own flesh, with whom we had shared many sad and happy times, secrets and dreams. Ali Akbar did his best to cheer us up on the drive to London by telling us stories from Kurdistan. There was one about a donkey: our boys there were working very hard, he said, perhaps fifteen or sixteen hours a day, and expected other creatures to do likewise – including the donkeys used to carry loads from mountain to mountain. One of these was said to be exhausted and dying, so they left it behind. Several months later, when they went through the same village, they saw the same donkey carrying wood for the villagers. 'Immediately, our four legs borrowed another four and made their getaway!' Ali-Akbar laughed, his white teeth glinting beneath his thick black moustache. In London he dropped us at a base where we would share five bedrooms and a living room with three other families. He wished us well, saying he might not see us again. He was right. A few months later we heard he had been martyred in Kurdistan. A meeting was held to honour him and, although I grieved for his loss, I couldn't help laughing as I recalled the donkey story and his perpetual broad smile. I reminded myself to be happy for him, as he was in heaven and was probably telling the same story to our other martyred colleagues. At that time more than 100 members and full-time supporters worked at various London bases which, except the one for supporters, were almost identical in interior design. In the living room of each there was a picture of Rajavi, Khiabani and Rabia'i, in front of which we made our morning 'devotions'. There were no pictures of heroes like Mossadegh or Shari'ati, nor an Iranian flag (still considered a symbol of the monarchy). Work started at the same time each day and finished whenever people felt so inclined, although it was considered bad form to leave before ten at night even if there wasn't work to be done. As a result, people preferred to sleep on the premises, myself included. Thus, although we worked near each other, Anna and I rarely met except for Saturday nights when we were obliged to go to our 'rest bases', ready to join the Sunday morning communal clean-up. After cleaning the rest base we had to do the same at our work bases, then perhaps watch an educational video or hear an announcement by Sister Tahereh, head of the society. When these duties were done we were free to return to our rest base to see to personal chores like washing and ironing. Obviously, in this crowded programme, there was rarely any space for family gatherings or playing with children.

The children, in any case, attended a play school where Anna was in fact the supervisor. I always regretted not sharing ordinary pleasures with Hanif, like reading bedtime stories. Only at public meetings did I share his caregiving him with Anna, and the only thing he would later remember about me was my efforts to keep him quiet on those occasions. I lurched constantly between tender, fatherly affection and self-reproach for not being 'revolutionary' and 'Mojahed' enough. How could I think about my own children, who were well-fed and had a place to sleep, when millions of children in Iran and especially those of our brothers and sisters were denied their basic needs and rights. Showing kindness to our own children was a luxury we had to avoid – a clear sign of personal attachment. I worried less about Sarvy, as she had benefited from the warmth of a family during her early life and by now knew very well how to adapt herself to organisational life, drawing on the support and affection of a variety of people.

# 21

# Paying the Price

I knew Anna found her work boring and frustrating. By contrast, her job in Newcastle had carried some responsibility. We could not talk about this, however, as our jobs were to be kept secret even from spouses. This so limited our opportunities for conversation that I began to feel that we were losing each other. But what could I do? It was a price we had to pay for the freedom of our country. Sarvy did not complain either, realising that complaining would not solve anything, and her only reply would be a lengthy lecture about the situation in Iran and the suffering of children there. Hanif was understandably content, as he was not particularly close to me; during my frequent and extended absences he could sleep with his mother as well as passing the entire day in her company.

In London I was to be secretary of our SW (sponsored walks) branch. This was the society's most important section: our main income derived from walks. (Later, some of the walkers became runners; later still, both walking and running were superseded by other activities. But the section retained the title 'SW'.) I felt this was a sort of trial period for me. The job was much simpler than my previous posts. Instead of being *masoul* to twenty or thirty

people, I was *masoul* of only one, my old friend Hussein. Instead
of organising and worrying day and night about the shop and
kebab vans, besides the normal activities of the branch, I now had
only to gather information about the SW work, sift it, determine
how much they had earned and report back to our happy-go-lucky
*masoul*, Jamil. At the end of each week I had to attend a meeting
with *masouls* of other branches and feed back to them. The job
was so easy that my biggest worry was how to fill Hussein's time
and prevent him from becoming bored. We were both from
Newcastle, and had reputations for being recalcitrant and
stubborn. I think the leaders wanted to see if I had any leanings
towards Banisadr. Perhaps this was why I was transferred to
London; or maybe they didn't want a repeat of the Sadatti Society.
Presumably they kept us under surveillance to see how much we
had changed.

Gradually, however, as I read the reports of our members' daily
work, I started enjoying my job very much. It brought out a whole
range of emotions. The reactions of people towards our cause were
unbelievable. Sometimes they sent us letters and even gifts – small
donations from their savings, words of sympathy and
encouragement.

Once I received a heavy package. In it were a few stones, a letter
and a cheque. It was from a woman in northwest England. In the
letter she wrote, 'Every week I see your people, rain or snow, cold
or warm, almost always dressed inadequately, selling your
newspaper and asking for help. To see them out there tirelessly
promoting their beliefs leaves me in no doubt that I must help you
as much as I can. I am not rich but I give whatever I can afford. But
that is not all: gradually they are becoming part of my life.
Whenever I read your weekly paper I feel I am crying and laughing
along with your people. Last week when I was walking by the sea I
found these stones, standing strong and solid; not even the sea with
its might and greatness was able to move them. I remembered you,
and somehow felt certain you will win. I hope one day I can visit
your lovely country in peace and freedom from every kind of
dictatorship...'An Italian poet wrote in the newspaper *La Stampa*
of his train journey and his customary wait for the Iranian handing
out his paper with a modest and gentle smile. Another issue carried
a drawing by a Brazilian artist of the face of a man in pain as a

dagger is driven through his head into his body. It was accompanied by a poem paying tribute to the 'warrior on the path to the people's liberty', suffering until the final victory without a moment's rest.

But there were obstacles. The weather was the worst. Then, our boys were often arrested on charges of obstruction. Our placards allegedly blocked the pavements, plus our representatives were too persistent in approaching people. (I suggested to the police that we hang our posters on sandwich boards and walk about instead of standing still. They agreed, and we complied.) Later we had complaints that our photos were disturbing, especially to children. I suggested them in a small file to show to members of the public upon request. Hussein and I made what we called 'the album', which became the only aide to our outreach work.

We all were under enormous pressure to increase our earnings. Sister Tahereh cleverly convinced us that raising funds was equivalent to believing in Mojahedin philosophy. Unlike her predecessor, who communicated very little, Tahereh spoke to everyone but was severe and entirely uncompromising. She enforced her will even on people in other cities. I think she truly believed the end justified the means. She set a minimum amount for each person to earn per day and warned, in all seriousness, 'If you haven't earned this minimum, don't bother returning to base.'

Our methods of making money were sometimes very imaginative. One guy used to stand on the street looking at the sky. When enough people had gathered around him wondering what was he looking at, he would ask them to listen and seek their help. By this means he sold up to 300 papers per day, earning a healthy £200. Some people worked the trains and buses, or knocked on doors. I once obtained the £50 I was short of for the day from a Pakistani who invited me to dine with his family and promised me the money if I could prove Khomeini's actions did not accord with Islam.

Sometimes deception was the only way to escape Tahereh's wrath, like lying about the amount you had received in the form of cheques. Another trick was to retain surplus money received on a good day and then declare it on a day when you hadn't earned the minimum. Anyway, it was better not to divulge that you had earned more, because Tahereh was likely to raise the minimum expectation to that level. The police hassled us too, sometimes denying us permission to operate in certain places. We called some areas 'burned', which meant people knew us there and would avoid us. Tahereh vetted the weekly bulletin I wrote in which I mentioned good sites and practices. Often she would censor passages.

Once, she said, 'You are worried about what people think of us, while I am concerned with our leadership's and organisation's thoughts about our income.'

I said, 'I am worried that if we continue like this we will 'burn' all areas, and there will be nowhere left for us to work.'

She laughed and said, 'Don't worry, soon we will be in Iran and it will not matter if we leave a 'burned' country behind.'

The organisation's financial record was printed in *Mojahed* annually. The total yearly income was 717,945,453 *toman*, or $12,820,454 – including $3,225,112 from loans – but the expenditure was such that the organisation ended up being short $1,539,183. The base where I worked was the central base, and as Jamil was away most of the time, normally I was supervised by Tahereh. Hussein was in a similar position; he was at the same base, and received orders from Tahereh without my knowing. I led a sort of double life. My best times were when I was very busy, my worst when I had nothing to do. I tried not to think or read, not to talk much and ask questions or make suggestions only rarely. I began to hate myself for the envy, rivalry, fear and anxiety I harboured, and for such traits as exhibiting my abilities and conservatism. Every Friday a private council meeting was held. I assumed they discussed us members as well as other important matters. One thing they certainly did was force us to compete with each other. Tahereh would sometimes emerge from the meeting and praise the achievements of others. I have no doubt she said similar things to those with whom I felt I was competing.

One Sunday we were required to watch a video about Yaghobie, an old, high-ranking member of the Mojahedin. For some reason – perhaps because of his attachment to his wife – he had lost his position in the organisation. He claimed that they were undemocratic and controlled by Rajavi's gang. The video showed a Mojahedin meeting in Paris at which Rajavi was elected chairman of the meeting by all except Yaghobie. Afterwards Rajavi asked Yaghobie to discuss his objection. I could not agree with Yaghobie's accusations, which did not seem well-grounded, but it was painful to see how the meeting's members interrupted and attacked him. For the first time I saw a side to Rajavi I did not like. He could see this old man was unable to defend or express himself in that situation, yet showed no mercy and made no attempt to stop others from attacking him so unreservedly. Rajavi even seemed to take pleasure in the plight of his former colleague. Tahereh, as usual, asked what we had learned from the video; we were all to comment. My remarks were unspecific and bland: 'Attachments', I said, 'are like a disease. If one doesn't cure it immediately, it will become chronic and eventually kill our revolutionary soul.' The real lesson I had learned was: 'Never question the organisation; never criticise the leadership, even a high-ranking *masoul*. In organisational work be as conservative as possible and in executive work be as active as possible.'

In October 1984 another mobilisation was announced under the title of 'Oppose the war – death to Khomeini'. We were told to be as active as our Iranian counterparts, to continue our work and fundraising but also to contact our friends and relatives in Iran and ask them to perform actions to help precipitate the overthrow of the regime. As far as I could see, the only person I could call for such a purpose was my dear old mother!

It had been four years since our last contact, so my first problem was shame. Not only was I to phone and ask her to put her life in danger, also to have this conversation in front of our *masoul* – in my case, the deputy of the society. How on earth could I show my emotions, my love for my mother, in front of the *masoul* and not be labelled as someone with 'attachments'? The *masoul* was Fazeleh, notorious among us for her forbidding look, bad temper and bitter words. Her rare smile was ice-cold. She was highly judgemental and equally unwilling to admit error herself. During one meeting with her I presented the Newcastle section's record of earnings. She immediately attacked the new *masoul* for raising too little income. I was astonished, as I knew the team's income was pretty good. Eventually I realised she was evaluating the wrong set of figures, confusing the number of hours worked with the amount of money earned, and pointed out her mistake. She looked at me angrily and said, 'Even so, their record is very bad!' And she continued to insult and belittle her victim. This was the woman who would be watching me phone my mother to ask her to write slogans in the streets of Tehran for us.

When I called my mother, it was as if someone had made her a gift of the whole universe. She laughed and cried and spoke loudly all at the same time – and thank God! For she expressed all emotion for both of us. I remained poker-faced, lest I jeopardise my position *vis-à-vis* my *masoul*. However, Fazeleh heard her as well, and wrote on a slip of paper: 'Say something to stop her. Tell her you must think about the expense of the telephone call.' To change the subject I asked after Ammo Jan. She began crying even louder, saying, 'Your Ammo Jan is dead!'. Now I was in big trouble, bottling up my emotions, stopping her from crying, saying something comforting. I simply was not able to continue that telephone call, not in that situation.

I said, 'God bless him. I am shocked, I can't talk, I shall have to call you again soon. But I want to ask you something.'

She replied, '*Ghorbonat beram*' [I am ready to sacrifice myself for you]. What do you want?' I told her. She was confused, and asked, 'But how? I am an old woman! I haven't done this sort of thing before. I don't know how, or what to write, or what I should write with!' I told her to buy oil paint, hide it under her veil and, when nobody was around, write the slogans I gave her in the street.

Fazeleh wrote me another note: 'Ask her to keep a record and end the conversation.'

This was my last conversation with my mother, whom I loved more than anyone. A few weeks later we had to call our relatives again to ask what they had accomplished. When I called my mother's number, my aunt answered, crying when she heard my voice and saying, '*Ghorbonat beram, ghorbonat beram*'. Through her sobs she said she was unable to speak, and asked my brother to talk to me. 'Masoud', he said, 'Mother is gone. It was easy and painless.' For a few seconds I was silent. 'What do you mean?', I demanded. 'We spoke a few weeks ago and she was OK.'

'No,' he said, 'she wasn't. She was very ill but didn't want to alarm you, so she didn't tell you anything. She died three days ago. We are gathered here for her third-day ceremony.' I could not say anything, let alone cry, not only because Fazeleh was watching to inspect my reactions, but also because I was numb, as though all my logic and feelings had stopped working. I don't remember what I said, but doubtless the words were meaningless. I am sure I said 'goodbye'. Goodbye to everybody! Goodbye to my childhood and

all my family in Iran! It was my last conversation with any of them.
Did I cry? I don't know. If I did, Sarvy told me later, it was not
obvious, though apparently I talked to her about my mother's
death. Hearing about the deaths of people close to us, of the
execution of our friends, such as Ali and Nadir and Ali Akbar and
Ali Reza, had changed us from normal human beings into
something else. We were not 'insensitive' or 'emotionless', but our
emotions were being put towards the service of others, unknown
others, unseen others, who were also people. Or perhaps the truth
was starker and my heart had turned to stone.

Ammo Jan and my mother had apparently both died of heart
attacks. After his death she had no interest in living without him.
Perhaps she had been waiting to hear from me before feeling free to
die.

The next issue of *Mojahed* had an eighteen-page spread with
colourful maps of Iran and Tehran, and the results of the
mobilisation: 1,023,813 slogans written or distributed, 67
government vehicles destroyed.

Rajavi congratulated us on our hard work, but the week had
shown we were capable of doing more. We were asked to send
many members to Paris and Kurdistan, including many of my
Newcastle friends. Several of them were later killed in battles or left
the organisation.

My position changed too. I was appointed a member of the
council and SW *masoul* in London. By now I had perhaps
demonstrated my commitment, distancing from my past –
especially my liberal and individualistic tendencies – and that I did
not support Banisadr. Previously I had envied council members and
felt bad about it, but now that I was elevated to that level I found it
was not worth much. I was pleased to have more responsibilies,
however, as it meant having less time to be alone and feel sorry for
my family and myself.

In February 1985 I was sent to Manchester for a month to
mobilise supporters for a planned demonstration celebrating the
martyrdom of Khiabani and Rabia'i. That day we received the
latest issue of *Mojahed*, which contained the puzzling news that
Maryam Azodanlu had been inducted as *hamradif masoul aval*,
equivalent to first *masoul* (co-leader) of the organisation.

What did it mean? We had never heard of this title and didn't
know much about her, though some of us remembered her name

among the nominations for parliamentary elections by the Mojahedin a few years earlier. We read *Mojahed* eagerly to find out what was going on. The paper carried a message from Rajavi along these lines: 'Among all our heroic sisters in the organisation, Sister Maryam Azodanlu, after the martyred Ashraf Rabia'i, is the most capable ... This is the choice of the organisation's politburo and central committee, symbolising a new era for the Mojahedin along the road to social freedom for women.' The message ended with his congratulations to the Mojahedin for this decision and to Maryam and her husband, Mehdi Abrishamchi, and his advice to us to listen to her orders and counsel.

We were told to distribute sweets among supporters. While pretending to rejoice, we were still in the dark about the significance of this announcement. What would happen to Ali Zarkash, Rajavi's deputy and successor? Who was now second in command? We had to wait and see; I had learned by then not to be curious about changes in the organisation's structure. In any case, I could see no connection between this change at the top and my day-to-day work, and I was sure my *masoul* would tell me privately if so. How wrong I was. That simple news was followed by another big story, which not only changed the organisation completely but also our lives.

In the next issue we read:

SEPARATION OF MRS FYROZEH BANISADR FROM MOJAHED BROTHER MASOUD RAJAVI

After seven months' separation, Mrs Banisadr announced her divorce from Brother Masoud Rajavi, in accordance with the rights given to her by Brother Rajavi ... Brother Rajavi refused to consent to the separation for several months but with much sorrow was now bound to accept it.

The originator of that news item was 'the Office of the People's Mojahedin of Iran, Paris 12th February 1985'. It was obvious, in the rift between the Mojahedin and Banisadr and the sharp articles against each other in their respective papers, that the marriage could not survive. Anyway, its original *raison d'être*, to keep Banisadr in the council, had long since disintegrated.

# 22

# The Marriage of the Century

On 17th March 1985 we were summoned to the council room for a meeting with Sister Tahereh. We were surprised. It was Wednesday, and council meetings were held on Fridays. The room was narrow and austere. The only furniture was a large, rectangular table flanked on both sides by two long benches, which were so uncomfortable that before each meeting we would scramble for seats by the wall to ease the inevitable backaches brought on by long sessions.

Once all twelve or thirteen members of the council were present, someone brought tea and biscuits. 'Let's eat something sweet', said Tahereh. 'I have some very good news.' Obviously something important had happened. Perhaps there had been a victorious operation inside Iran! Perhaps Khomeini had died! Perhaps ... Our minds ran quickly through the possibilities. Tahereh stood to read a communiqué. Fazeleh, her deputy, rose as well, a clear signal for us to follow suit. We stood to attention like soldiers, listening intently.

'In the name of God, the Merciful, the Compassionate. In the path of God and the people, willingly and with satisfaction, we have accepted an ideological and organisational imperative, which is the will of God and of the Iranian people's new revolution. Observing all religious customs and requirements ... we have decided to marry. Signed: Maryam Rajavi and Masoud Rajavi.'

In a loud voice, Tahereh said, 'Mobarak bashad [congratulations]!' and applauded. Bewildered, we joined. There followed a deathly silence. 'What's wrong?' she asked. 'Why are you all standing there stiff as boards? Don't you have anything to say?' She turned with a questioning look to Fazeleh, who had obviously already heard the news, and then rapidly focused on the person sitting beside her and demanded to know his thoughts. As confused and stunned as the rest of us, he smiled limply and said,

'Well, I don't know what's going on, but since Brother Masoud has made this decision, I am sure it is very good news.'

'Won't you offer your congratulations?' she demanded.

'Well, of course', he replied, and with the smile still fixed to his face he said 'Congratulations!' loudly.

'Have you any questions?' she asked.

'Excuse me, but who is Sister Maryam Rajavi?' asked the man sheepishly. Tahereh laughed and said, 'Don't you know? Sister Maryam Rajavi is co-leader of our organisation!' He swallowed hard.

'But Sister Maryam Azodanlu was ...' Tahereh finished his sentence for him:

'... the wife of Brother Mehdi Abrishamchi.'

'Yes ...'

She laughed again. 'Why are you stammering? Your face gone white! Has something snapped in your mind? Have your male prejudices been offended? Don't worry. No religious principles have been violated. They divorced a few weeks ago, before this news was announced.' She was silent for a few moments. Then she asked him if he still wanted to offer congratulations.

'Well, I still don't understand, but yes, of course, congratulations, many congratulations.'

Before asking the next member what he thought, she read the message again.

'Of course congratulations are in order,' he said. 'I'm sure that whatever decision the organisation makes is for the good of the people and the revolution.'

Tahereh put the same question to all the council members, one by one. Some offered their congratulations without hesitation. Others, less cautiously, protested that they had not understood the news fully, but would still congratulate the newlyweds.

The more conservative elements like me said, 'I don't know, I will have to think about the news to understand it fully.'

Then Tahereh read us a message from the politburo and central committee. It was very long, and because I was sitting on a bench with no support I had to stand every so often to relieve the pain. It began with a sentence from the Qur'an: 'Those who relay messages of God are afraid of God, and are afraid of none but God. This is enough to consider God the sole judge, the one who paves the way.' Then came the usual opening passage of Mojahedin communiqués. This time, in addition to 'in the name of God and the heroic people of Iran, in the name of the martyred Mohammed Hanif-Najad ...' the politburo had added, for the first time, 'in the name of Maryam and Masoud Rajavi'. The only living people who had ever been named in the prologue to Mojahedin messages were Khomeini and Talaghani.

The message continued with a long list of Rajavi's achievements: how he had saved the organisation from a Marxist coup in 1975; how he had fought against right-and left-wing tendencies in the organisation; how he had fought Khomeini and revealed his true nature to the people. We believed that all important organisational decisions were made collectively, but were now told it was Rajavi who had founded our militia, stood up to the Tudeh Party's sedition in the name combating 'liberals and reactionaries' and chosen the correct tactics to oppose them while other organisations fell into the Tudeh's trap and lost everything. It was he who had reorganised the Mojahedin over the past two years and stood against those who wanted to destroy them ... The message declared that, 'while the organisation was scattered around the world and enduring immense pressure, under the wing of Masoud's leadership we became more united than ever.'

The signatories to the letter claimed, on behalf of the members, that 'we in the organisation laugh at those who accuse us of hero worship, and look at them as a wise man looks upon the foolish'. A few sentences about Rajavi's personal sacrifices followed. He was the first Mojahed to have volunteered for a 'suicide mission', naturally rejected by the organisation; it was he who, imprisoned under the Shah, had inspired fellow inmates to resist their jailers; and it was he who had inspired thousands of Mojahedin to go to prison and accept martyrdom in the fight against Khomeini. Rajavi was also portrayed as a champion of women's rights. It was thanks to his leadership that the Mojahedin had appointed Maryam co-leader, the highest position a woman could gain within a revolutionary organisation.

The message continued, saying that Mehdi Abrishamchi and Maryam were in love and had no problems in their marriage, but volunteered to divorce to permit the union of Masoud and Maryam. The marriage had been advised by the politburo and central committee, to deepen the 'great ideological revolution' and avoid the 'difficult contradictions' between leader and co-leader who, although *na mahram* [an Islamic term for those who must not touch or see each other], had to work closely together. Their joint leadership without marriage would have been 'mere bourgeois formalism'. Had Rajavi not divorced his wife, the Mojahedin would have had to accept the disadvantages of the joint leadership of the unmarried Masoud and Maryam. But since Fyrozeh Banisadr divorced him, there was no reason for the organisation to deny itself the advantages that could be gained by this marriage. The idea was inspired by a sentence in the Qur'an about the Prophet's marriage to the recently divorced wife of his adopted son. Furthermore, although Mehdi and Maryam had made a supreme sacrifice by divorcing while still in love, Masoud had, in accepting this marriage, made even greater sacrifices. His was described as 'much more than a heroic action'. Had Rajavi not been able to accept the marriage, he would have demonstrated that he did not have the capacity to lead the organisation.

Since my return to the society I had trained myself not to bother about organisational news, which was relevant only if it affected my daily work. But this announcement concerned me deeply. By this time I knew perfectly well that sex, love and marriage meant little to the organisation. I feared they might have decided to order couples to separate whenever such a change would serve their interests. If so, what would happen to my own marriage? But I was put at ease, believing this ideological revolution applied only to the leadership.

I was certain Tahereh would turn to me first for a reaction to the politburo's message. 'Well', I began, 'I'm now in a position to offer congratulations. I now understand that this is one of those rare actions taken by the vanguard of the people to open a new way for the evolution of mankind.' Then I offered a few examples. I was ignorant of the example given in the message about the Prophet, but no matter. I repeated it, and added the examples of Imam Hussein's departure from Mecca during the Hajj (it was customary to remain during the pilgrimage) and the story of Ashab Kahaf, who went with a dog (an animal considered *najass* [unclean]) to a cave and slept there for centuries, a result of which the dog was blessed. These examples saved not only me from further questioning, but also others who followed me.

Having found adequate logical and religious reasons for the marriage, I decided I didn't need to think about it any more. How naïve I was! This news marked the beginning of a new era in the organisation, the 'ideological revolution'.

While Tahereh read the message, Fazeleh cried uncontrollably; this astonished us, but appeared not to trouble Tahereh. Once she finished questioning us she addressed Fazeleh, who, between sobs, explained how the divorce and remarriage had changed her completely. She launched into a catalogue of unreserved self-criticism. Fazeleh, who could never acknowledge even her most obvious mistakes, was suddenly revealing her most secret wrongdoings. She spoke of her selfishness and pride, and how they affected everyone in the organisation.

Tahereh showed no mercy or affection, saying to Fazeleh: 'But you know that you are still a long way from changing. You know that you must still work very hard.' We wondered what she meant. For the first time, I pitied Fazeleh. I had often disliked her for her negative qualities, but would never want to see her humiliating herself in front of us all. Tahereh turned back to us and said, 'You, all of you, must revolt as well. You must each kill your old selves and become new people. Either you change yourself completely or you leave the organisation.' From now on our only concerns would be to contemplate 'ideological revolution'. Our immediate task, she said, was to write reports about our past, our 'old' selves. That evening, the same scenario was repeated – this time at a meeting for all members where another council member criticised herself publicly.

I realised something serious was afoot that would change everything, and I became uneasy. But I couldn't imagine might be coming. I couldn't relate the changes in Fazeleh to the news of Rajavi's marriage, and the more I tried to solve the puzzle the less it yielded its secret. When Anna expressed bewilderment, I told her to rely on her instinct: 'Apparently this revolution is about the freedom of women,' I said. 'Perhaps as a woman you will be able to understand it better than I.'

Over the following weeks, it was rare to see anyone smile or laugh. At our New Year's celebrations the next day, our supporters staged a comedy. Many in the audience laughed, but whenever I looked around I could see members of the organisation deep in thought, bitter smiles on sad faces.

We no longer worked very hard. Our supporters did much of the sponsored work and almost all the cooking. The hardest part of my job was being responsible for fifteen to twenty supporters. I had to keep morale up and answer their questions when I was anything but cheerful and enlightened myself. One night after returning from the supporters' base, I was told another meeting had been called. This was not a council meeting, but the first of a great many bizarre gatherings that came to be known as 'revolutionary meetings'.

When I arrived, I saw that Anna and a few other sisters were present. The men sat along one side of the room and the women along the other, with Sister Tahereh in the middle. Everyone was crying, including a young council member, discussing his sex life. Sex was a great taboo for us. We had never spoken of it except to our *masouls*, especially not men with 'sisters' present at a public meeting. But no one made any attempt to stop him. He admitted he was attracted to Sister Tahereh. I couldn't believe my eyes or ears. I could never imagine, still less accept, that any of us men could have sexual feelings for our 'sisters' – not only because of the strict morals observed in the organisation, but also, to be frank, because of the way they dressed and their behaviour, which was much rougher than any man's.

When he had finished another member jumped from his seat, rushed towards him and slapped his face, hard. He showed no reaction, although his sobbing continued as it had throughout his confession. A satisfied smile appeared on Tahereh's face. She told him to sit and to write down what he had said. Then she looked at me.

'Why are you so surprised? Do you think you're better than he is? You're worse. You are all worse than each other.'

She asked if I had anything to say. I replied that I had written down whatever there was to say. (I had recently submitted a report containing all my secrets, including my thoughts when I watched the videotape of Yaghobie; my feelings about not being a council member; and much else besides.)

'Rubbish! You have said nothing; what you have written is naïve and childish. Many simple members and even supporters, who have no need for this revolution, have criticised themselves more severely than you! You must work very hard ... Do you know that Anna has revolted, and gone further in the revolution than you?'

She knew where to aim her barbs and she did so skilfully. She knew how much I loved my wife, how worried I was about losing her. If Anna had revolted and I had not, then she would remain in the organisation and I would have to leave. I would lose everything. Looking back, I think this was what she wanted to hear from me, but I could not see it then. I just sat and searched my memory for something about myself that would be accepted as a revolutionary revelation.

As soon as Tahereh felt my desperation to revolt, she left me alone and asked another man about his revolution. He confessed that he humiliated his wife. When he let drop that she was 'bony', Tahereh's face clouded with anger. She stopped him.

'What a pity your wife is not here! I would ask her to give you a few slaps to the face!' She looked around. 'Is there no one here zealous enough to teach him a lesson and slap him? But why bother asking? You're all alike. You all think of women as sex toys!' Then she ordered one of the younger members, who was supervised by the man confessing, to stand up and slap his face as hard as possible. He obeyed.

As people rose one by one to confess, Tahereh studied my reactions and from time to time directed remarks at me. My temperature seemed to rise; I was unable to think, and desperately embarrassed. It was as though I were sitting there naked with everybody watching me. Tahereh chose her moment carefully and pounced: 'What's happening, Masoud? Is your icy logic melting away? You thought you were clever and talented! Do you see your real self now? That when it comes to ideology you're just a fool?' She was right; at that moment I was like a two-year-old. All my logic, my powers of understanding, my facility with words, were gone. I wished I had something to confess, that I was attracted to a woman, anything, to save myself. But the harder I searched for some untold offences, the less I could recall.

Tahereh asked me yet again whether I had anything to say. Suddenly I, too, began to cry. My words were garbled, but I begged her not to throw me out of the society. I told her I couldn't live alone and would rather kill myself. I spoke of my childhood, how lonely I'd felt without my mother, how painful it was and how terrified I had always been of loneliness. I could see everyone, including Anna, watching me strangely and perhaps with pity. At the time it seemed like I was the only one in such a pathetic situation, although everybody else was in the same plight or worse.

Tahereh interrupted me, instructing me not to do anything but think and write.

A few days later we received a videotape of the New Year's celebrations at the Rajavi residence. There were nearly 200 people present. The mother of five martyred children of the Reza'i family spoke first:

'When I was summoned to a gathering to receive important news, I thought I would hear of another martyrdom, this time of my youngest son, Mohammed. I was preparing myself to say, "God bless him"... When I was told of the marriage of Masoud and Maryam, my heart almost stopped ... I blame myself for not having the same power of sacrifice as they. Five of my children have been martyred; I see all of them in Masoud. I want to congratulate you, Masoud, Maryam and Mehdi, for your ability to sacrifice ...'

Then Rajavi got up. He spoke first at length about the organisation's history, under the Shah, during the revolution and under Khomeini; how correct its predictions about people and events had been. He said: '"Divorce and marriage? It is madness, amazing, radical, imprudent and unwise." This is as when we stood against Khomeini, when everyone advised compromise with him. As when, against the advice of many, we met the foreign minister of Iraq in the same place as we are now. Today you are astonished again. It is like pouring boiling water on your head! Yes, this is a way of testing you all. We want people of steel. We seek a new standard of power and ability. Everybody, including our farthest-flung supporters, must be cleansed of all reactionary tendencies and demagoguery.

'If you are in, you must make it clear first to yourself and then to the organisation. There are many who claim to have feeling for the freedom and independence of our country, but how can it be measured? It can be measured according to the level of each person's sacrifice. The organisation has been shaken violently. We want to prepare ourselves for the next ten years. If we do so, we will be prepared to meet the challenge of the next two years, namely the overthrow of the Khomeini regime. Mojahedin who pass through this furnace will be more steadfast, more steely and more resistant ...' Then he held up two wedding rings, which had belonged to Maryam and Mehdi, and said, 'These are the highest and fullest symbols of sacrifice. Can anyone see these rings and not weep? Pity on you if you put any price on these rings. Can you put any price on love?'

He then expounded on the freedom of women: 'As long as even one woman remains imprisoned by her sex, all men are imprisoned, too. The freedom of women is the freedom of the whole society ... Whatever has happened is not Maryam's problem or mine. It is everyone's problem. You must all resolve it.' Then he read a few sentences from the Qur'an about the story of Mary and the marriage of the Prophet to the divorced wife of his adopted son.

Soon it was Mehdi Abrishamchi's turn to speak. He congratulated Masoud and Maryam 'with all my cells, skins and blood vessels'. Then he said, 'If it were not for Masoud, we would all have deviated, and have been lost forever ... I wish we each had 100 lives to sacrifice, not just one.' Then he referred to Masoud's past sacrifices, adding that, 'whenever I met Masoud, I wondered what kinds of sacrifice fate has in store for him. Execution, torture, he has already seen it all, in prison. On 20th June he prepared us all for another Ashorra [when we might all be killed, like Imam Hussein and his followers]. He lost his wife, and the enemy captured his child; he had to marry his last wife to keep Banisadr in the NCR and then divorce her. When marriage to Maryam was suggested to him, I found my answer. He had to face allegations and malicious accusations from counter-revolutionaries. But that was not all ...'

Then he faced the crowd and said, 'Be honest! Say what was in your heart. Did you understand his actions? Did you not curse him? Did you not swear at him? Did you not want to kick him?... Be courageous, say what you thought. Then you can know yourself... I know you will cry, feel your life turned upside-down. This is an ideological move. We must all pass through this furnace and melt away our filthy parts ... Then we can find ideological brightness. Then all will become true members of the Mojahedin.'

Everyone wept as he spoke. As usual, Tahereh surveyed us carefully for our reactions.

# 23

# Ideological Revolution

While we were deep in battle with ourselves (as Muslims call it, *jihad akbar* [the great holy war]), our external war gained momentum as well. Apart from our fight with the regime, which by now was mostly in Kurdistan, we were locked in a political battle with 'anti-revolutionaries' and 'leftist' organisations outside the country. The newspapers published by the Iranian community in exile all discussed the marriage. Some made a joke of it, others condemned it as 'immoral', 'dishonourable' and 'shameful'. Even leftist groups, who supposedly did not care much about Islamic values, criticised the Mojahedin in exactly the same terms. Because of recent support for the Mojahedin by US congressmen, they also accused us of collaborating with imperialism – the same imperialism, as they reminded, to which we had been so opposed in the past.

On another front, after a series of defeats in Kurdistan, the KDP and Mojahedin (who had fought alongside them) withdrew from almost every city and most villages under their control to the Iraqi side of the border. Of course, *Mojahed* spoke of the heroic actions of our combatants without much reference to the outcome. We were not told the worst: as a result of its defeats, the KDP opened peace talks with the regime, and in November 1984 we read an unprecedented item in *Mojahed* questioning the KDP's action. In our view it was outrageous for a party to be a member of the NCR and also negotiate with the regime. Only a few months had passed since the revelation of Banisadr's letter to Khomeini, which resulted in his expulsion from the NCR. We sensed the end of our coalition with the KDP was near as well. Their own claim was that, as a local organisation controlling part of Kurdistan, it was their duty to negotiate with the enemy over the safety of ordinary people. But the Mojahedin insisted that 'between us and the regime there could be only a river of blood'. Eventually, in April 1985, the NCR issued a resolution warning the KDP to break off its talks with the regime or be expelled. They chose expulsion. Following them, a few smaller organisations and personalities resigned, although the National Democratic Front represented by Dr Matin-Daftary (Mossadegh's grandson) and a few members of one of the Fedai'in offshoots of remained in the NCR. It was obvious to everyone but ourselves that politically the Mojahedin had failed to create the broad coalition Rajavi had promised: the sole reason for his absence abroad and 'heroic departure' from Iran.

We were not too concerned about splits or about condemning dissidence. We repeated to each other that the NCR was Rajavi's means of staying on the political scene in Europe and America and nothing more. Its main use was to deceive the Americans and Europeans against thinking of us as the same Mojahedin responsible for assassinating American citizens in Iran or coining violent slogans against imperialism. We were part of a national alliance, with a liberal and democratic appearance and programme. As Rajavi had said in different circumstances, it was the Mojahedin and their supporters who had shouldered all the work of the resistance. So getting rid of unwanted partners was cause for celebration, as it set us free from divergent tendencies and the need to share power with people who 'did nothing for the revolution'. As one of the *masouls* put it, 'It is good to get to know these people while we are still fighting tyranny. If they were to wait for victory before they showed their real faces, God knows what price we would have had to pay. So in a way we must thank God we did not succeed in overthrowing the regime earlier.'

Being in charge of the sponsorship work, I was under great pressure to raise money and slept very little. Most of our supporters were deeply involved in the 'ideological revolution' and had many questions about it to which I had no answer. I myself was breaking up inside, but had to keep up appearances. Only when I was alone could I could indulge in self-pity. I was desperate. To me, love and marriage were so natural and necessary a part of my life that I completely failed to grasp that this was the very area that I was to think and write about.

One day I was called to the main base where I was offered sweets, a cup of tea and words of congratulations. 'What now?' I wondered. It transpired that Mehdi Abrishamchi had married the sister of Mussa Khiabani, although only a few weeks had passed since his divorce. I had come to hate the word 'congratulations' and the false smiles that went with it. But I controlled myself and did what was required. By now I knew what love and marriage meant in the Mojahedin, and how far my emotions and thinking were from their requirements.

Perhaps deep down my violent antipathy towards news of this kind stemmed from an anxiety that I might find myself in this position. I feared they might order Anna to separate from me and marry someone else, then ask me to marry one of the sisters. After all, Anna had had her ideological revolution, and I still struggled to follow her. I did not go to our rest base anymore, sleeping at the work base every night, even on Sundays. In truth, I was not able to face Anna. I didn't know who she was anymore. Perhaps the ideological revolution had changed her so much that we could not live together; perhaps she no longer loved me ...

I was ashamed not to have had my own ideological revolution. *Mojahed* was full of members' accounts of their 'revolutions', which I would read anxiously to find a direction for my own. But far from helping, some of these added to my confusion. For example, Mansur Bazargan, an old Mojahed, wrote that the impact of the news on him was greater than the news of 1971, when the organisation 's founders were executed, or the news of 1975, when an internal Marxist coup precipitated a major split. Rajavi's example had inspired Bazargan to the ultimate heights of self-sacrifice.

'With this news,' he wrote, 'all my blasphemies and class

tendencies were burned ... Masoud, if for following and helping you they burn me and give me life again, repeating this 100 times, I will not stop supporting and following and helping you... '

These were like the words of one Imam Hussein's followers before Ashorra. But what use were they to me? How could this exaggerated idealism help me? Other statements, though very simple and poetic, still couldn't show me any kind of mechanism for revolting.

One sister wrote, 'My head aches so badly that I feel only tears will wash the pain away. I feel this room, house, city are too small for me. I want to fly and find new love. My eyes cannot see properly, I don't know what am I writing. I know only that you, Maryam, are my ideological symbol. Tears stream from my eyes, everything blurs in front of them. I am revolting from within. I feel if I don't write for you I will explode ... Let me burn myself in your holy fire! ... Let me, Maryam, sacrifice myself for you and Masoud! You are the symbol of a nation in chains...'

Another sister wrote, 'Dear Maryam, I swear to God that with all my existence I feel your path is the path of all messengers of God, from Abraham to Moses to Jesus the Spirit of God ... you are breaking deadlocks ... I am sure that not only we but future generations too will worship you for what you did ...'

Not only was I far behind my fellow Mojahedin, I was even incapable of seeing things foreigners could understand. A French woman wrote, 'For me the Mojahedin were always not only an Iranian organisation but an international one, as the divine message that inspires them is for all human beings ... fighting Khomeini and his regime is a means of uprooting reactionary systems everywhere ... Such systems do not recognise freedom of choice for women and thus deny them human rights. They want to change women into sex objects and merchandise ... They stand in the way of evolution and, by chaining women, prevent humankind from reaching freedom ... this is why the Mojahedin's ideological revolution has universal dimensions ... Dear Sister Maryam, for me you are an infinity, you are the beginning and the end. You are the flower of the holly tree, which has roots very deep in the earth, as deep as the history of suppression of millions of unknown women ... As God has given the power of reproduction to any flower, you are the fruit of that flower, which has benefited from the sun [of knowledge], to be born in the spring.'

*Everyone must revolt ideologically. Whoever does not, cannot call himself a Mojahed.* This slogan, written in large print, was hung in many living rooms in our bases. Nobody could escape this 'revolution'. As our base was the largest in London, each week for one, two or even three days we prepared it for 'revolutionary meetings'. On the day of a meeting everything else was put on hold – no work, no cooking, even no sleep for day or two. The meetings were no longer limited to members of the council. They were compulsory for all society members and not even illness could excuse one from attending. Our meeting room held thirty to forty people comfortably, but sixty to seventy would gather there, sometimes for a few days. Sitting on the floor was itself a form of torture, and on top of that there was only one toilet and almost no break in the proceedings. But the physical miseries of those gatherings were nothing compared to the mental pressures.

At times a guest member of the Mojahedin would attend our meetings. Once Reza'i came. In his speech he emphasised the special position of the leadership, i.e. Rajavi. He posed the question, 'If all the members of the organisation, including Mussa Khiabani, were he still alive, decided on something and Rajavi decided otherwise, whom should we follow? The majority, or the ideological leadership …?' Rajavi's position in the organisation was like that of the Imam's for Shi'is. The answer could only be, 'We would follow him!'

But that was at odds with my own 'liberal view'. So I answered, 'I would follow him but ask for an explanation.'

'What if he refused to give one?'

'Well, I would accept his word, but a seed of doubt would be sown in my heart, so if the scenario were repeated, the seed might grow and in the end I might reject all his words or be forced to leave the organisation.'

When he put the same question to others and received many similar answers, he started to lecture us. He told a story about Moses and the prophet Elijah. Moses wished to accompany Elijah on a journey. Elijah accepted, on condition that Moses follow him without question, whatever he did. En route Elijah committed a number of puzzling and apparently sinful acts, such as making a hole in a merchant's ship, which then sank with the loss of many lives, and destroying the house of an old woman. On each occasion, Moses expressed his abhorrence and demanded a reason for the act. Elijah simply reminded him of the condition and said nothing more, until at the end of the trip he explained each action – for example, when the old woman's house was destroyed, her two young children died from cold. Had they remained alive they would have become repressive rulers, murdering hosts of people.

From this story Reza'i concluded that an ideological leader has a much deeper, broader and more universal vision than the understanding of an ordinary follower permits. He may see and interpret things in a way that cannot be explained at the time, that may indeed seem illogical and irrational; yet time will prove his correctness. Therefore the follower must obey his leader not based on understanding but on total trust. He added that we had observed our leader in very difficult situations and later learned how right his decisions had been. Because of ideological vision deriving from his experience of pain and suffering, sacrifices and accumulated wisdom, he was far in advance of any of us. In conclusion he said, 'Even without a close encounter with Masoud and perhaps with little knowledge of the history and ideology of the Mojahedin, you have all accepted him as a leader and follow his orders even if they contradict everything else. But because you have accepted him with your mind and not with your heart, although you accept his word you may still harbour doubt. This might be satisfactory when following a political leader. But as we are talking about an ideological leader, it is far from satisfactory. To follow him not only politically but ideologically, you must accept him not only in your mind, but in your heart. You cannot do this unless you first open your heart to him. You should have no secrets from him. No boundary should separate you from him. He must be the one and only, the closest person to you. To reach this close relationship, you must work hard, beginning with the expression of all your contradictions and secrets, especially those concerning him.'

I thought that by this time I knew what I was aiming for and how to get there. After much effort, I would find minor untold secrets or contradictions and, by writing about them in my weekly 'ideological report' or 'revolutionary report', feel that I had succeeded in revolting. But one look from Sister Tahereh, one sarcastic remark or straight reproach, showed me how wrong I was.

In one meeting a brother confessed to an encounter with a

prostitute. Anna jumped up from her seat, hurling a string of insults at him, finally saying he should leave the room and never again face any of the sisters then present. I was shocked to see Anna so angry, offensive, cruel. It was the first time in thirteen years I had witnessed her abusing anybody. This incredible change convinced me that she had indeed had her ideological revolution. Like others in the meeting whose revolution had been accepted, she no longer criticised herself, attacking others instead. When she spoke about herself it was to help others revolt, to explain how she had reached that stage and who had inspired her.

I began to lose all hope. One *masoul* told me I was so dependent on logic and the understanding of my 'mind' that I was unable to see and understand from my 'heart'. During one of the meetings I was so desperate, so angry with myself, my 'mind' and my 'logic', that, alone in the toilet, I started banging my head against the wall and cursing myself. I knew I would lose everything, perhaps even my mind, if I didn't revolt. I would have to leave the organisation, separate from Anna who, perhaps as a result of revolting, would go to Paris or fight in Kurdistan. I would lose my political goals along with my private life. At one point I felt my only option was suicide. But I thought of Sarvy and Hanif, and knew that I could never inflict on them the shame of having a loser and a wreck for a father.

Noticing my catastrophic situation, Sister Tahereh called me to her office and asked why I did not revolt like the others.

'Do you think I don't want to revolt?' I cried. 'But', I added feebly, 'I don't know how.'

She merely laughed and said she pitied me. 'You are an able person, are you not? You studied for a long time, have you not? You have read many books ... but you are incapable of doing a simple thing that many less able, less educated, much younger than you have accomplished in a single day ... You must have an untold secret that has turned you to stone, made you heartless. You must confess it and set yourself free. When you feel there is no barrier between you and the leadership, then you will be able to revolt; then you will be able to see him with your heart and feel him with your whole being. Then you can be unified with him.'

My darkest and most tormenting memory (or, as such things were known, 'contradiction') was of sexual molestation in my childhood. I had never spoken to anyone about it and had put it out of my mind. Now, freed from all secrets in my political life, I was forced to remember this deepest secret. How could I speak or even write about it? In Iranian tradition, as perhaps universally, this is the worst demon of all and perhaps the most dishonourable. What would happen to my dignity, my honour, my position among friends, comrades and – worst of all – my wife and children? For several days, perhaps weeks, the question engulfed me. Everything else was forgotten. I ate, drank, worked and talked it, even in my sleep. I imagined the faces, even the thoughts of people close to me when they heard this revelation. I felt the shame and loneliness I was about to experience.

But what choice did I have? Either way I was about to lose everything. However, at least I was no longer confused, puzzled or stupefied. It was hard, very hard, but it was the solution! To get to the central base from our own, I had to pass through a park. During that sad and frightening spring, I once lingered for an hour or two there, watching ordinary people: children playing ball; smiling couples walking hand in hand talking; a girl jogging; a man riding a bicycle; an old man smoking a cigarette; and an old woman feeding the pigeons. How beautiful ordinary life was, and how far I was from it! The flowers were as sweet as ever, birds sang, butterflies danced and bees sucked their nectar. And here was I, sunk in the swamp of my misery. Suddenly I felt nothing worse could happen. I might be left alone like the old man or woman, smoking or feeding pigeons. At that moment I could not see anything positive about myself – not the good things I had, my youth, health, knowledge, capacity to build another future ... I had become a worthless – no, a shameful – commodity. I remembered an old Persian expression: 'fear is the brother of death'. So I had to fight my own fear and at the same time prepare myself for the worst.

I found the courage to write about my dark secret. Suddenly, instead of feeling heavy and immovable as a mountain, I felt as light, beautiful and free as the butterflies in the park. I felt no restrictions, no fear of the future, no complex about the past, no questions, no problems. I felt no need for anything. I was rich, strong, happy.

These feelings were as real as I was. They were crystal-clear to all who knew me. I had revolted, had my own 'ideological revolution'. Immediately afterwards I felt the gates of my heart opened to everyone and everything. I felt more capable than ever of loving and giving. I could love God, all existence, all human beings; my country, my people, my leaders, my *masoul*, my colleagues, those who worked under me, my family, my wife, my children. My heart had expanded to encompass all this love and still have room for the love of many more unknown things. I could even love and admire Sister Tahereh, who had mercilessly humiliated me and aimed to crush me by destroying my self-esteem.

Now perhaps I was able to understand Masoud and Maryam, who had done what they thought was right and necessary in the face of entrenched attitudes to the position of women in society. Their enemies said they had married not because the revolution demanded it but to satisfy Rajavi's sexual desires. They said he had stolen his friend's wife. They accused him of breaking codes of morality and honour, of bringing disgrace not only on the Mojahedin but on all resistance forces against Khomeini – indeed on all Iranians and all humankind. Those of a more political cast of mind argued that the leader needed to create a crisis to distract attention from his failing policies, including his defeat on various battlefronts, in cities and in Kurdistan; the loss of many supporters and members, either through execution or imprisonment or because they had ceased to believe and be active in the cause; and his failure to create a broad coalition. Others claimed the Mojahedin had changed from a broad-based, popular organisation into a cult, and that the marriage between Masoud and Maryam was a means of testing the trust and faith of their followers as many gurus did.

Whatever the truth, in our view a prehistoric taboo had been broken: a woman had been given the choice between her ideological belief and commitment to her marriage and child, and had chosen the former. For a man to have behaved like this had a long and respected series of precedents – men who had married their foe's daughter to prevent bloodshed or married into a new faith. But for a woman this was the worst crime that she could commit. In fact, nobody was talking about Maryam's role in the affair. Mostly she was regarded as some sort of commodity exchanged between two men. All she had to do was prepare to be reviled for it.

In reports of their 'ideological revolution', some said that they were inspired by Maryam's courage to face their own fears and weaknesses. But my case was the complete reverse. First I faced my own fears, then began to understand Maryam's struggle. I wrote along poetic letter to her, proclaiming that I saw her in my own revolution. I described her as a candle and myself as a moth wishing to dance in her flame. I wanted to burn myself alive in front of everyone, as testimony and tribute to her true revolution against the exploitation of women by men everywhere around the world.

As usual, we had to prepare for the demonstration of 20th June. I was sent north to recruit for the event, as well as to attend a meeting in Paris. Additionally, we had to persuade rich Iranians to help us financially, especially with the expenses of those who were travelling to Paris (many of whom were penniless). The task was not as easy as previously. Then everybody had just one question: 'When are we going back to Iran?' Now the question on everyone's lips was about the ideological revolution. Was it going to prolong the revolution, as ordinary people couldn't understand it and considered it corrupt?

Hard work and persuasiveness notwithstanding, we attracted only 600 people to the demonstration. Later, Tahereh demanded a breakdown of attendance figures between London and those coming from elsewhere. Because our ideological commitment was gauged by the numbers we recruited, everyone searched for a way to fudge them: one enterprising recruiter had persuaded a group of unemployed miners from the northeast to join the demonstration for a free day's sightseeing in London; another 'accounted' for his group by counting the number of seats in the buses and assuming each one had been filled by a demonstrator. The result was that the total allegedly coming from outside London far exceeded the actual attendance; the London figures reached into negative integers. The recruiter for London jumped from his chair and exclaimed: 'You mean I not only didn't recruit anyone, including myself, but actually turned away people from other cities!'

But Tahereh's face-saving creativity – which included counting passers-by as demonstrators – let us claim 1,200, and we were spared the accusation that we had lost support because of the ideological revolution. However, in Manchester I saw the extent of this loss quite clearly. The number of those prepared to call themselves Mojahedin supporters had dropped dramatically. In the past, people had felt indebted to us because of our fight for their country. Now they were aggressive, even rude. Even close friendships could not offset the pressure of the ideological revolution, and members were leaving the society too.

We were pleased with the quality of the demonstration, however. We had five people dressed in white to symbolise the 50,000 martyrs of the revolution, and fourteen people in prison garb to symbolise the 140,000 political prisoners held in Iran. We had a few people made up to look like Khomeini and his revolutionary guards and others playing music, and we ended with a play about the situation in Iran and the desired future, namely, a popular uprising, the freeing of prisoners and the killing of Khomeini and guards. The poor 'guards' were beaten so realistically that they complained of aches and pains for days afterwards. A number of members of the Labour and Liberal Parties spoke. The new chant of 'Rajavi-Iran, Iran-Rajavi' implied that Rajavi was equal to Iran, although we had to work hard to get even our closest supporters to repeat it.

Not long afterwards, we received a video and an issue of *Mojahed* full of beautiful pictures of Masoud and Maryam surrounded by flowers at their wedding. From then on this day was celebrated not only as the anniversary of the largest-ever demonstration by the Mojahedin in Tehran, but also of this wedding which took place exactly four years later.

That issue of *Mojahed* was treated like a rare commodity. All the members displayed the photographs on their desks, pocketbooks and briefcases to demonstrate their love for the leadership and the depth of their own revolution.

That issue also contained moving speeches and hundreds of messages of support for the Iranian resistance such political organisations as the British Labour and Liberal Parties and many individual members of parliament, including Conservatives. There were letters of support from major French political parties, various European government parties and fifteen American congressmen.

It seemed up to 2,000 guests had assembled to witness this 'historic and moving' event. In the front row were people from every walk of life and sector of society – sportsmen, army officers, families of martyred Mojahedin – and the stage itself overflowed with expensive flowers. The bridal couple sat near a table, Masoud in a dark suit as usual without a tie and Maryam in a simple white dress. Critics said the lavish ceremony was as wasteful and inappropriate as those that occurred during the Shah's era.

The ceremony began with a speech from Maryam paying tribute to Ashraf, Rajavi's martyred first wife, defending Rajavi against allegations of selfishness and explaining the reasons for their marriage. She addressed questions she said had been raised by their union: 'Some ask, "what happens if one of you dies?" ... I say, if Masoud dies, he is alive in me! ... Some ask about family values and the welfare of my daughter. I have to say, when there are 50,000 executions and 140,000 political prisoners, when there are many unsupported families and children, how could Mehdi or I think of ourselves or our child?' She said it was her right to divorce her husband, and that it was she who had proposed to Rajavi.

Then, for the first time in Iranian (and Islamic) history, Maryam as a woman read the Qur'an marriage sermon. Afterwards, Abrishamchi was the first to congratulate the newlyweds, followed by the parents of Reza'i, the families of other martyrs and sport champions who presented them with their medals and trophies.

Then it was Rajavi's turn to give a long speech, incorporating an allegory based on the classic Persian poem by Attar of the *simurgh*, a flock of thirty birds seeking a mystical phoenix representing communion with the divine and 'discovering' that it is really themselves (in Farsi *simurgh* 'phoenix' and *si murgh*, 'thirty birds'); in Rajavi's version, it was Maryam in whom this glorious revelation was manifested.

Rajavi then began refuting the accusations of his foes and said, 'This is a new birth, an explosion. I ask you to come with me to infinity! First, judge me! Accuse me, if you will, of being a disgraceful, capricious person who has stolen his friend's wife. If found guilty, it will be good for the people to be rid of a leader like me. But if I am exonerated, you must come to my aid and put your hands in mine to destroy Khomeini and bring peace and freedom to our country!'

His voice rising with passion, Rajavi exhorted the people to self-sacrifice. They should seek to 'burn, burn, die, die' in the fire of love of freedom. They had to die and be reborn, not from their mothers' wombs but from Maryam's. No one who had not been reborn could call himself a Mojahed. Standing, he came to the climax of his speech. 'What is the message?' he cried. 'Yes, I have come to sacrifice myself and my organisation and my generation for the sake of the people's freedom. A thousand times they have drilled into my heart, a thousand times they have put the rope to hang me round my neck, a thousand times they have lashed my body. Yes, I am the people's Mojahedin, I am hundreds of thousands, I am the representative of infinite generations. I have come to sacrifice myself for the freedom of my chained people. *Hal men nasar a yansornie* ['Is there anyone to help me?' – a famous plea from Imam Hussein]? Who could fail to be moved by this? Who could fail to chant rapturously, *"Ba Masoud, ba Maryam, mijangiam ta akhar!"* [With Masoud, with Maryam, we shall fight until the end!]'

After watching the video, we had to revolt again, accusing Rajavi of anything we could think of and judge him, making him our mirror as he had ordered, thus accusing ourselves of the same crimes for which we were trying him. Then we were supposed to identify our class tendencies. It was difficult. Most of us wrote pages of reports naming, describing and rationalising our class tendencies, giving examples from our past. From our analysis we were to deduce whether we were closer to the Shah or to Khomeini. In 'ideological-revolutionary' meetings we had to go to a board and divide it into two columns, writing 'old' at the top of one and 'new' above the other, then classifying and entering our old ways of thinking and behaving and our attributes after the ideological revolution.

The next demand was to show the videotape of the wedding to as many people as possible, so that everyone would see how welcome it was. We even recruited people to travel to London to watch it, many of whom rightly thought this a ridiculous waste of their time. People dreamed up all sorts of ruses to get out of attending meetings – a stark contrast with how things had once been.

A few weeks later it was announced that Brother Mehdi Abrishamchi, a hero of the revolution, would visit London to help people conclude their individual revolutions and return to normality and stability in a higher dimension.

To meet Abrishamchi in person was considered an unbelievable honour. The thought of him talking to each of us and certifying our private revolutions drove us mad with excitement. The meeting was to take place at our base, of which I was the *masoul*, so I was especially apprehensive. When he entered the room, accompanied by two bodyguards, we applauded for almost half an hour until our hands turned red. He turned his back to us and faced the pictures of Masoud and Maryam to show that our applause was not for him but for the leadership, then started clapping too. He opened the meeting by asking for a volunteer to tell the story of his or her revolution first. Immediately all hands went up. A long, emotional session thus began, which continued for nearly three days without any sleep.

It was summer, but for Iranians accustomed to hot summers, it was like spring. The meeting room doors were wide open to the garden, and one could see flowers, birds and children playing games, untroubled by anxious adults. In the room we were far removed from reality or, as we called it, 'alienated and exploited imaginary life'. With each story of misery, misfortune and dependency we would weep, sometimes so loudly that the walls of the room shook. Sometimes, when told the story of a friend's revolution, we would clap heartily for many minutes. We would laugh loudly and sing one of the Mojahedin anthems or a love song. Later I learned that our neighbours thought we were mourning the death of a close relative and tried to show understanding. They even looked after our children.

Although after the end of each speech my hand, like many others, shot up, deep inside I felt I would rather die than talk. By now I had written everything down and often prepared myself to talk; but it was still difficult to imagine confessing my dark secret in front of everybody, including Anna and people for whom I had responsibility.

Eventually Mehdi asked me to speak; but first, he said, 'I have a question. You asked in your report to be permitted to burn yourself. May I ask why?'

I replied, 'Well, thanks to the "revolution", I have seen my filthy past and I hate it with all my being. I want to burn so I can be born again as fresh and as clean as a baby from Maryam.'

He asked more questions, which I answered, crying and wanting to talk. But he said, 'I praise this Banisadr's courage. Not the other Banisadr [my cousin, the ex-president], whom I hate, but this Banisadr, who has been born from Maryam.' He applauded me and the others followed suit accordingly. I had really been ready to talk, but Mehdi said he had read my report, that there was no need to repeat myself.

Soon it was Anna's turn. Again he silenced her, asking if she was ready to divorce me. She began crying loudly. A few rows back, I was crying too. After a long pause she said 'yes', and he asked me to stand answer the same question. I said 'yes' too. He asked us both to remove our rings and give them to him. He showed them and said, 'Yes, these rings, like many others, symbolise the Mojahedin's sacrifice for the freedom and independence of our country. May God accept them.' He repeated the procedure with a few other couples. Then he asked us all to rise and, to more weeping and enthusiastic applause, he married us to our spouses in the name of Maryam and Masoud.

There were still a few who had not had their 'revolution', among them Behnam, a high-ranking member of the council who was videotaping the proceedings. Suddenly he started banging his head, hard, on the camera. Blood spurted everywhere. Behnam was under immense pressure to have his 'revolution' and didn't know what to do. Perhaps, like me, he had been driven to desperation. People jumped up to stop and help him. He said nothing in that meeting. Some time later, I believe, he had his 'revolution'.

Abrishamchi then singled out Sharif, one of my charges, and asked him why he had not revolted. Sharif could not answer. What was bothering him most? Again he had no answer.

Eventually Abrishamchi said, 'You're a chubby guy, aren't you?'

Sharif looked down at his potbelly and said, 'Oh, you mean this? Oh yes, that's right.'

Then Abrishamchi said, 'You're chubby, but you're a Mojahed. We have flabby Mojahed, bold Mojahed [here he indicated himself], blind and deaf Mojahed ... but those are not the adjectives that describe us; they are the values of people outside the resistance. Here you are measured by your sacrifices and honesty as a Mojahed.'

The meeting ended with singing, led by one of the bodyguards, and the usual chanting of 'Iran-Rajavi, Rajavi-Iran'.

Afterwards I was called to Abrishamchi's room. Did I think Anna was ready to go fight in Kurdistan? Presumably he wanted to know if I was ready to lose her. I replied, 'I don't know. Before this revolution, my answer would have been "no". But after the revolution I hardly know how to judge her.'

Once our revolution was over we were told to go to our rest base more often and spend more time, at least few hours a week, with our families. Anna even went to Frankfurt to visit her mother, recently arrived from Tehran, and I joined her. But we were recalled to London that same day to hear some important news.

The news was that most members of the society were to leave for France or Kurdistan. The official line was that, as the result of the revolution, our capacity to accept responsibility had been magnified 100 times; each of us was now capable of doing the work of several people. Those who remained, including me, now would work much harder. From then on I was to be deputy head of the society in England. I was sorely disappointed, as I didn't want to remain in an 'empty' London. I would rather have been with my old friends in Kurdistan. But I had no choice.

A few weeks later we received an order to mobilise and move most of our supporters and members to Bournemouth, as Maryam was going to attend the annual conference of the Labour Party there. Here we encountered enemies of a different hue, namely Tudeh supporters and various Fedai'in seeking to 'disclose and reveal the true face of the Mojahedin'. We were afraid they might hurl objects at Maryam's car. As it happened, our presence there was so overwhelming that it seemed more like an Iranian conference than a British political event. In addition to Mojahedin and other left-wing Iranian groups, right-wing groups (including supporters of Bakhtiar) were also present. Debating with them, refuting their accusations in front of Labour Party members, reinforced our conviction that we were in the right. Our opponents were evidently more worried about the possibility that the Mojahedin would come to power than about daily crimes committed by Khomeini.

We were invited to Maryam's hotel for an audience with the woman we thought of as our saint, our prophet, our heavenly angel. Sarvy was with us, and I was glad she would be greeted and kissed by Maryam. It was the custom then to drop one's own name and adopt the name of a hero or leader. When Maryam mentioned the letter I had written to her I asked her to change my name. 'Of course', she said. 'What do you want as your new name?' I said I wanted to change it from 'Masoud' to 'Masoud'. At the time I had no idea of the dreadful mistake I was making in appearing to want to emulate the glorious Rajavi. But, smiling serenely, she granted my request and everyone applauded me. Many times over the next few years I begged my *masouls* to let me change my name again, but each time they refused, leaving me with this shameful sign of my 'ignorance' and 'arrogance'.

A few of us were summoned to a meeting the following day with Mohadessin, a high-ranking Mojahedin official. Sister Tahereh was also present. Mohadessin explained the Mojahedin's ranking structure. He told me my rank was now 'SF-1' (foreign sympathisers-1'), the highest among supporters, but lower than that of a sympathiser in Iran, where one's conviction could be tested by facing the revolutionary guards. 'However', he said, 'thanks to the revolution, you have passed an even more difficult test than facing execution or physical torture.' Then he explained the system of the mother organisation. An ordinary member was coded O; OSH was a council member of the organisational *nahad* unit; MN was a *nahad* deputy; MS, a *masoul* or *nahad* representative; and M, executive council member deputy. The highest rank, HE, indicated members of the executive council. K denoted a candidate for membership and S a sympathiser (one rank lower than K: a person who had lived in a base and worked full-time for the Mojahedin). The crucial difference between S and O was that an S had not yet accepted or understood the Mojahedin's ideology. One rank lower still than S was H, an ordinary supporter, who did not live with or take orders from the Mojahedin.

From then on, all present were deemed members of the Mojahedin rather than merely supporters. I was awarded the rank of MN, but I declined membership of the Mojahedin, saying my liberal bourgeois tendencies made me unclean, unworthy of membership in this glorious organisation. Mohadessin looked at me earnestly and said, 'You have had your ideological revolution and it has been accepted. You have no right to call a revolutionary Mojahed "unclean".' My objections thus dismissed, I became a member of the mother organisation. Anna was deemed very close to receiving membership but for the time being was recognised as K. She was also promoted, becoming secretary to Saeideh, the new UK *masoul*.

Now that we had had our revolutions, we had to spread the good news among supporters everywhere. As the organisation's UK deputy, and friendly with most of the supporters, I travelled around the country talking to them. I was very successful, especially in Newcastle and Manchester, where personal ties were strong. Because I liked these people, I wanted to share the joy I had found through the 'revolution' – which, though it might begin with pain, that pain was short-lived, and the joy, permanent. Many opened their hearts to me and told me secrets that had disturbed for years. The official line was that the revolution would be much easier for supporters to achieve than for us. They simply had to see the organisation in a new light and feel that their own existence as dignified human beings and freedom-loving Iranians depended on full commitment to it. They had to jump just one step forward, and many did. Over the next few months we held a series of 'revolutionary meetings' for them, each supervised by a high-ranking member.

My responsibility was to record their revolutions and provide support; most of the time I suffered with them, feeling their pain. The process entailed leaving behind something dear to them. One man had to leave his beloved girlfriend to become a full-time supporter. He put his head on my shoulder and wept, telling me how much he loved her; but with her attitude towards the Mojahedin he could not marry her and support them at the same time. Another had not only to distance himself from his brother, who worked at the Iranian embassy, but even pledge to kill him if necessary. An alcoholic had to swear never to drink again. One young man, struggling between love for his wife and the organisation, described his dilemma in a symbolic form. He looked at a picture of Rajavi and said, 'I see him talking with me, about the sufferings of our people, the hungry, the war dead, the executed, the tortured. What right have I to think about my own happiness? The choice is not between the Mojahedin and my wife, but between living in hell, every day for life, or suffering a minor personal loss but then feeling consciously free and resting easy.' Among those who had their revolutions there were three English women and one English boy. I happily translated their sincere and thoughtful words.

On the political scene there was much activity. Masoud and Maryam met various authority figures, including Jordan's King Hussein. This meeting created a stir, especially among our leftist foes who reminded us that a few years back we condemned King Hussein as a butcher of Palestinians and the Shah's close friend. But their jibes passed us by. The UN General Assembly passed a resolution condemning the violation of human rights in Iran, a move we saw as the fruit of our own efforts. The Mojahedin published a new list of 12,000 martyrs, which demonstrated not only the atrocities of the regime but also our ability to obtain detailed information from Iran and the penetration and strength of the organisation. Photographs were published of a Kurdish march, with heavy weapons, mechanised units and thousands of people on foot, assembling in the hills in formation to spell out the names of Masoud and Maryam, and forming a map of Iran with Rajavi's name at centre. Such events received loads of coverage in the media.

By contrast, other organisations were in disarray. The leaders of Paykar, which had claimed to be replacing the Mojahedin, officially liquidated the organisation. The Fedai'in was now so riven, we joked that each of its members had their own organisation. We joked about the Tudeh Party too – which, after the arrest and public repentance of its leaders in Iran, was in worse shape than ever: 'When it rains in Moscow,' we said, ' Tudeh members open their umbrellas'. Banisadr was, in our view, no more than a 'retired president' writing his memoirs in Paris. The monarchists and nationalists had few supporters and no organisations.

In November 1985, Bazargan (the first post-revolution prime minister) went to Europe for a meeting. Rajavi sent a message asking him not to return to Iran and promising that the Mojahedin would look after his welfare and smuggle his family out. He refused with the words, 'Sorry, I have no young wife to offer you', which signalled to us that he was as dirty-minded as our other enemies. The failing fortunes of all these groups clearly indicated that only the Mojahedin had the means to deliver Iran to freedom and prosperity and underlined, to our satisfaction, how right we had been in our choice of allegiance.

Anna and I rarely had free time. As a kind of reward for our service, the organisation accepted Sarvy at their school in Paris. Reports of her progress suggested she was doing so well that she was on the way to becoming a *masoul*, which made me proud and happy.

This era didn't last long. The UK *masoul* changed again: none other than Sister Tahereh took up the post. She came with news of changes. We were no longer the MSS, but would become part of the mother organisation. New people would come to London to represent different sections, including the financial section. A new secret section was responsible for contacting Mojahedin supporters inside Iran from various countries, including the UK; another, for gathering information. Tahereh asked me to drop whatever I was doing and search for some large new bases to house these sections and their *masouls*. She lectured me on the need to change my attitude in the light of our progress. Part of my task was to visit other bases and talk with their *masouls* to see what needs they had, how we could optimise their conditions, looking at furniture and office equipment and checking to see if our work was as systematic as possible. I began a tour of inspection of the different departments.

Her suspicion was justified. Everywhere, I observed mismanagement and 'petit-bourgeois' attitudes towards work and equipment. Carpets were torn, equipment went to waste, cars needed repairs. Even the publishing department, which was the most modern, resembled a bunch of students using student union facilities. Within a week I produced a list of suggestions. She accepted all the inexpensive ones but rejected improvements that would carry significant costs.

Among the new *masouls* was Fazeleh, whom everybody feared. She was to be my *masoul*. Another sister, Meherafroz, formerly stationed in both Newcastle and Paris, was to share responsibility of our British social section with me. London and the other southern cities were my responsibility, while she was to take charge of the others.

Despite our propaganda and the signatures of world leaders demonstrating their support, the truth was that the Mojahedin were under immense pressure to leave France. The Fedai'in's hostile splinter groups demanded Rajavi's expulsion, accusing the Mojahedin of being worse than the Shah and Khomeini. It was claimed by the Mojahedin that the Fedai'in groups received financial help from the French and Iranian intelligence services. (Perhaps they were just angry at the Mojahedin for helping a defector from their organisation create another Fedai'in group as a new member of the NCR.) These groups organised rallies, distributed hate literature and mounted such protests against the Mojahedin as chaining themselves to the railings of the city council building at Auvers-sur-Oise.

They were active in London too, gathering each week at Speakers' Corner to disseminate propaganda. To neutralise this we had to appear there with placards spelling out their actions.

It was obvious things were coming to a head, that fights would ensue. Fazeleh told me not to involve myself, to remain free to oversee our usual work and arrange the release of anyone detained by police. I have never believed in physical fighting as a solution to anything, and could see no difference between our actions and those of the Hezbollahis in Iran. Besides, I knew some of our adversaries personally, having been responsible for them in the past. At the same time, I felt ashamed for not wanting to defend our 'ideological chastity' (as we were commanded to consider the leadership) from violation. So when Sister Tahereh directed us to physical action, saying that the leadership had to be defended with all our might, I said nothing. But it was a contradiction that remained in my mind for a long time.

In addition to the opposition of the Fedai'in, the new French government demanded Rajavi cease all political activity in France. While in Manchester mobilising our supporters for the 20th June demonstration, I received a call from Tahereh telling me Rajavi had left Paris for Baghdad. He sent a farewell message on video, explaining the circumstances of his departure as a condition for normalising the Mojahedin's relations with France. Our official stance was that he had planned to go to Switzerland, but a conspiracy was revealed to arrest him and hand him over to Iranian authorities there. With no European country left for him to go to, the NCR decided on Iraq. We were later told he had been hoping to go to Iraq for some time, but was mindful of the political consequences.

Mercifully, it was said, *ado shod sabab khair* – good came from evil: the enemy helped instead of hurt us. The regime had worked desperately to force Rajavi out of France, moving him close to their borders organising armed resistance. As usual, what was in fact a failure in our foreign policy was portrayed as another victory for us. In the last part of his speech Rajavi said, 'I am going to make fire among the mountains', a phrase evoking a poem dedicated by a resistance hero to his daughter, and which implied that Rajavi was going further to harass the Iranian regime. Many of our supporters wished he would at least go to Jordan, not to Iraq – with which we were still at war.

In Baghdad Rajavi was welcomed like a head of state. He immediately made a pilgrimage to Imam Hussein's shrine to show he was a 'guest' of Imam Hussein, not of the Iraqis. He made a moving speech paying homage to the Imam, re-pledging himself and the Mojahedin to his teachings and repeating the Imam's plea for help, '*Hal men nasar a yansornie?*' This echo of history was crystal clear: Rajavi was in the same position as Imam Hussein, left alone to fight the enemy. We had promised to help Rajavi overthrow the regime; we could not abandon him.

Shortly afterwards, *Mojahed* was distributed with a note that the paper would cease publication until further notice. The implication was that the French authorities had banned it. This last issue of *Mojahed* contained a photograph of Rajavi meeting Saddam Hussein, as well as a song called 'The Order of Masoud': the first time a living leader had been named in a Mojahedin anthem. Hitherto the organisation had maintained that people were changeable; only it was constant. Now, evidently, the destinies of the Mojahedin and Rajavi were shared. Naturally, the song was full of exhortations to fight for justice with fire.

As members of the Mojahedin, we were expected to know many things supporters did not need to know. To educate ourselves we listened to tapes about the Mojahedin's tactics and strategy. At this stage I began to feel less a stranger, more a Mojahed. But certain things became clear for the first time. It was obvious that lies were told to supporters in the name of 'magnifying' the truth for propaganda purposes. Although this did not square with the organisation's declared belief in 'honesty' to all, I could see how such practices furthered our political aims. I also learned that the Kurdistan we spoke of so frequently was not Iranian Kurdistan, where we had no bases or battalions, but Iraqi Kurdistan.

I was a member of our section's council, dealing with old and new members, but reported to Sister Fazeleh – who had not changed much and, indeed, seemed to have reverted to her former self following her short-lived 'revolution'. In fact, I think it was the same for all of us! We quickly became as before, with barely any detectable difference. Fazeleh remained being bad-tempered, morose and quick to jump to conclusions. Although she rarely showed anger towards me, her temper and behaviour irked me more than before. She was especially unpleasant to the men in my care and to Sister Meherafroz. Every evening, I had to step in as a shield between her and those she accused of 'shortcomings', who got up to all kinds of tricks – like feigning illness – to escape her cross-questioning.

## 24

# Burning the Past

Following Rajavi's departure to Iraq, Tahereh announced a new phase of ideological revolution, known as the 'anti-bourgeois phase'. We who became members of the organisation outside Iran had apparently contaminated the Mojahedin's 'ideological originality', having become lost in a 'bourgeois marshland'. This meant that though for political purposes we would pretend to be liberal bourgeois, we had to keep our anti-bourgeois tendencies alive. As before, we had to examine ourselves for bourgeois tendencies and report them. Everyone began reporting whatever they thought might be so classified, such as the number of shirts and pairs of shoes they owned. All our 'luxuries' were collected and handed in to Sister Tahereh, who soon amassed bags of clothing, shoes, even pens. Nothing was exempt. Food was rationed and everyday items were confiscated.

Anna was even forced to publicly surrender her special facial soap. Tahereh told me Anna and I had a bourgeois relationship inappropriate for a Mojahedin couple. The evidence? Anna had written in her report that she was afraid of developing wrinkles on her face for fear she might lose my love. While Tahereh didn't bring the subject up in a 'revolutionary' meeting, she was undoubtedly looking for an excuse to attack me for 'bourgeois tendencies, leniency and kindness towards various people, including your wife.'

On a videotape of a meeting in Paris, one *masoul* criticised Shari'ati for his views on ownership and accused him of being bourgeois and not anti-exploitation. Tahereh asked me about Shari'ati's class origination. I defended him by saying it was he who had disseminated knowledge about Islam and resurrected it among many of our own supporters. Tahereh was outraged.

'What was his class origination?' she repeated, at the top of her voice.

'Well,' I replied, 'I suppose it was petit-bourgeois.' Others in the meeting unfortunately followed my lead and said the same thing.

Then she shouted, 'He was bourgeois! Can't you understand? There is no such thing as "petit-bourgeois"! Either people are for exploitation or they are against it! There is nothing in between.' Having forced me to repeat with her that he was bourgeois, she then asked why I was unable to recognise him as such. I could easily guess the answer to that one.

'Because I am bourgeois myself.'

Tahereh ordered me to write about my bourgeois tendencies. She then used both my first and family name whenever she addressed me, to remind me of these tendencies and their connection to ex-President Banisadr. Others copied her; in no time, everyone did it. It became a kind of torture I would suffer the whole of my life in the Mojahedin, forced to hate myself through my family name. Furthermore, I had to examine myself and recognise my behaviour – including my 'kindness', 'understanding', 'caring' and 'helpfulness' – as 'bourgeois tricks' to 'fool people and keep them in my trap'. I had to try very hard not to show any affection towards anybody, even to make others dislike or hate me. In one revolutionary meeting, I called myself a 'bourgeois manager' who, with kindness, wanted to 'double-exploit' people for my own advantages. One member formerly under my care stood up and said, 'I always thought "how kind he is", but now I can see how I was duped. He was just trying to fool us into working harder for him.'

One day I received a telephone call from Anna. Strangely, she was not calling from her work base but from our rest base, and crying.

'I'm tired of all this anti-bourgeois talk,' she said. 'I can't carry on. I want to leave the organisation.'

'What do you think I can do for you?' I asked, shocked. 'Talk to Sister Tahereh and see what you can do!'

'I want to talk to you,' she said.

'No', I replied. 'You must decide for yourself. I cannot persuade you to stay; the decision is yours.' The following day my *masoul* informed me that Anna had written a letter and left the organisation. After that our rest base was changed, and we moved to an ordinary house which we shared with another family who were not members but merely supporters.

I was so deep in my own problems that I hardly noticed what was happening to Anna. I thought this was just another phase, that soon she would have a revolution and return to the organisation, criticising me for chaining her within my affection. I had lost trust in my own wife, thinking even she might pour scorn on me to save herself from criticism.

In trying to identify my bourgeois tendencies, I did what others did and wrote about my likes and dislikes, habits and wishes. At a council meeting, Tahereh's reaction to this was, 'Don't write rubbish! Your bourgeois tendencies are more complicated than these simple and obvious things.' Shari'ati exploited the minds of others, she said, stealing the Mojahedin's ideas and passing them off as his own.

During my turn for questioning, she asked for my view on a colleague. I started to speak of his abilities and talent for work, but she interrupted me: 'Do you see your problem? You consider only people's positive attributes, their talents, their ability to solve problems and how much they smile. You completely ignore their class orientation and their attitude towards the organisation and its leadership. You want so much to be loved and cherished by everybody that you are not prepared to challenge anyone. You should have slapped this man instead of praising him.' From then on, I was under observation all the time by my *masoul* and Tahereh, who watched to see how hard and uncompromising I was towards others.

I was expected to reprimand and insult people. It went so entirely against the grain that it was like drinking poison. Once I was ordered to swear at an old colleague who had fallen asleep on a train and been late for work. When I did so, he just laughed and said, 'I know perfectly well these words haven't come from you. Tell your *masoul* this is not the same organisation I joined. I am leaving it.'

'Good', she said when I reported this, 'we don't need people like him anymore.'

My situation was as before, only this time it was even more difficult as I could not remain silent in any 'anti-bourgeois' meeting, but had to attack the bourgeois tendencies of others. My liberal tendencies were more obvious to me than ever. I saw how difficult was for a 'liberal' to become a 'revolutionary'.

I was exhausted. As before, I took refuge in the park to seek inspiration in nature, a solution for my misery. For a few moments I was on the brink of leaving the organisation. This time leaving wouldn't mean losing my family, as Anna had already left. But the moment passed. It was too late to think like that. I could not simply forget about those who were suffering torture and execution in Iran; those who had been killed in the Iran-Iraq war; the man who killed his child because he could not bear to watch him die from hunger and lacked money to buy him powdered milk; the young girls sold in Baluchistan for a few *toman*. I could not forget my friends, killed in battle. I could not forget the gentle smile of Aliraza or Nadir's repeated words ('I sacrifice myself'). I could never forget Ali or Ali Akbar or Mohsen, Anna's cousin, who had been executed as well. The best I could wish for was to be martyred and join them.

Although I had said goodbye to my past many times, I retained links with it. I wanted to say a final goodbye. I went home. Anna asked what I was doing there, and I explained. She said nothing, knowing it do no good. I began tearing up photographs from my childhood up to the time of our marriage, then photos of my parents, as I wanted to deny them – my father, who was perhaps responsible for my bourgeois tendencies, and my mother, from whom I inherited my own 'mild' and 'gentle' nature. Anna looked on, crying quietly. When it came to our wedding album her tears turned to sobs and she begged me to stop. 'Those are not just yours!' she said. But I did not listen, just dumped everything in a rubbish bag and left for the base. There I found everyone worried about me. They thought perhaps I had left the organisation or cracked under the strain and had killed myself. I wrote a long report for Tahereh and sent the rubbish bag to her. She sent back the bag, asked me to burn the contents and welcomed me back to the organisation.

A few weeks later Fazeleh was transferred to Paris, and I replaced her as *masoul*.

Once, before she left, she asked me how we could increase our income from supporters. A few minutes later Tahereh telephoned her and asked the same question. She gave my reply, that we could not ask more from supporters as most of them were refugees living on social security payments. Tahereh berated her, whereupon Fazeleh countered, in self-defence, 'Well, this is what Masoud told me'. This only enraged Tahereh further; she ordered Fazeleh to attack me in the worst possible language, shouting so loudly I could hear every word. Perhaps Fazeleh wanted me to hear, as she neither asked me to leave nor told Tahereh I was within earshot. Fazeleh replaced the receiver and arranged her face into an expression of anger before doing exactly what Tahereh had commanded. It reminded me of the times I had done the same thing to people under my charge. Most of the bitterness my *masoul* displayed, I realised, did not originate with her. She was simply following orders, as I did. The incident shed light on the meaning of organisational obedience, and from then on I ceased to harbour any dislike of my *masouls*.

With Rajavi and the Mojahedin in Iraq, our efforts and propaganda were increasingly directed towards war. In September 1986, our weekly paper resumed publication under the title *MSS*. The first issue contained the full text of the recently released 'anthem of peace', one of the most popular songs of the Mojahedin.

Over the next few weeks the paper carried news of the killing of fourteen Mojahedin in two attacks, not by the Iranians but by a group of Iraqi Kurds. The motive for the killings was, apparently, to get Khomeini's help in the fight against the Iraqi regime. One way of obtaining it was to force the Mojahedin to leave Iraqi Kurdistan. They wanted to show solidarity with the Iranian regime.

The leader of the same group had once written to Rajavi, calling him 'brother' and offering him whatever help the Mojahedin needed in the area. Now, hand in hand with the Iranian regime, they were killing our sisters and brothers. It was an object lesson in the way politics works and how close friends can become bitter enemies in an instant.

We received a video of the burial of the first martyrs, which was viewed by all supporters. Tahereh delivered a speech, which later became known as the 'lecture of honour', in which she said, 'No Iranian may remain in Europe or elsewhere in the West unless ordered to do so by the organisation. We are in the final stages of our struggle. The regime is getting help wherever it can, even from Kurds, whereas we do not even have the benefit of help from our own supporters. This is a time of war. Anyone who can lift a rifle should do so. Whoever does not is not an honourable or dignified Iranian.' She began asking supporters, one by one, what they intended to do. Many people slipped out of the room. I spoke outside to one of them, a lecturer at Leeds University. He explained, 'In the old days, when we wanted to attend your meetings, the only problems pertained to our work or family timetables. Now we must solve the problem "to be or not to be"; and if we don't choose correctly, we are "dishonourable" and "undignified".' He never came to our meetings again. Later, he said, 'Well, she is right, I am a coward. But I love my life and family. Hence I cannot be a Mojahedin supporter any more.'

Following that meeting many supporters and members of both the MSS and the Mojahedin stationed in Europe left for Iraq. Among them were many of my old friends. I wondered if I would ever see them again. Many of them were indeed martyred in battle.

On 17th March 1985 we were summoned to the council room for a meeting. Tahereh asked what I thought about being sent to Kurdistan.

'When can I go?' I asked eagerly.

'Don't you mind about Anna and the children?'

'I am sure if I am martyred they will be proud, and understand that I acted partly for them and their future. The organisation will look after them. Instead of having one father my children will have thousands.'

'You are right,' she said, 'but my question was about something else. When you have a loaded rifle on your shoulder and you think about them and the possibility that you may not see them again, will your hands not shake? Won't you hesitate to fight?'

'It did not do so even before the ideological revolution,' I replied, 'so why should it do so now? No, I believe in the correctness of what I am doing as a Mojahed.'

Tahereh left eventually, and Sister Saeideh returned to become UK *masoul*. I was deputy of the organisation again.

After Rajavi left France, much of the support we had enjoyed among foreign and British leaders and dignitaries seemed to melt away. Although we were invited as guests to the Labour Party conference, unlike previous years there were no resolutions supporting the Mojahedin. The organisation's view of Iranian politicians had been expanded to include non-Iranians, too. We were not prepared to tolerate criticism from anybody. Whoever was not with us was against us. As a result, any of our politician supporters who dared criticise the Mojahedin received a barrage of insulting phone calls from members in the political section. Unsurprisingly, we lost many such supporters for good.

Soon afterwards the 'Irangate' affair burst into the news. While America and Iran pretended to be blood enemies, they were making secret deals. America sold arms to Iran, and Iran sent the proceeds to the Contras in Nicaragua to fight the Sandinista government – ostensibly a close revolutionary friend of Iran!

At the same time the Iran-backed Hezbollahis held American hostages in Lebanon. The deal was that the Iranian regime would help obtain the hostages' release. This affair brought us many political successes. To Iranians, we could show Khomeini as pro-American and pro-Israeli (the weapons passed to Iran via Israel; we could claim to have been right when we alleged, years earlier, that Israel made deals with the regime). For a long time the organisation had tried to prove there were no moderates in Iran, that Iran was behind the hostage-taking; now the world's media backed us up.

During the incident, in America, our enemies exposed the Mojahedin's past activities against the US, turning support there into opposition; now we could claim that those revelations, too, were part of the scheme. The result was that we gained a lot of new supporters – among them 163 members of the House of Representatives and Senate. On another front, the *Washington Post* revealed how much aid the CIA had given to the Iranian opposition, substantiating the Mojahedin claim that many such opponents in fact worked for the Americans. This added to our reputation as credible and trustworthy.

We referred to our bases in Iraq as *mantaghah* ('area'), signifying that this was our part of the world, a place near our home country. Going there became the ultimate goal – a glorious wish. One day Saeideh called and told me I was being sent there for a short time, as leader of a few brothers and sisters going there permanently.

Upon reaching Baghdad, we contacted the airport officials and introduced ourselves. They contacted the Mojahedin, and before we knew it we were being kissed and welcomed by one of our brothers. It was like returning to a free Iran. The Iraqi authorities received us with welcoming smiles instead of vigorous bag searches. The weather was dry with a mild autumn breeze. Palm trees lining the road gave an impression of home. The only thing that reminded us sharply that this was not Iran was the proliferation of huge portraits of President Saddam Hussein in the middle of the road every few kilometres. Beside nearly every hoarding was an inspection stop, normal for a country at war. Nobody bothered to check us, however; seeing our special car registration plate, officials gave us a military salute. At many roundabouts we saw unpleasant symbols of the war and of Iraqi victories over Iran, statues of Saddam depicted symbolically as the victor of Ghadesieh (a war in which the Iranians lost to Muslim Arabs). One displayed the wreckage of an Iranian plane. We could only look away in sorrow.

When we reached the Mojahedin bases at the centre of Baghdad, we parted company, each heading to a different base for a specific purpose. I was taken to the largest, a centre for Mojahedin's political section. I encountered many old friends. Rank and status were forgotten as we talked and laughed together freely. I noted that they ate at tables, not on the floor, without fear of being labelled 'bourgeois' or 'liberal'. Much teasing and practical joking went on. Knowing it was a Mojahedin custom to share a plate with somebody else, someone poured pepper on my side of the plate and everybody laughed uproariously when I coughed and spluttered. Another joker approached me and said, 'Didn't you know that before dinner, a newcomer must go from table to table and kiss his old mates?' I apologised and began doing so, only to find myself the centre of attention and everybody clapping and banging their plates with their spoons.

One day I was summoned to see Sister Soror – or, as she was referred to in *Mojahed* (where she was pictured with the prime ministers of the Netherlands and Ireland) Fatemeh Ramezani – who asked me a few apparently disconnected questions. I discovered later that she had been interviewing me for transfer to the political department, which she directed.

The same day Reza'i called me to say that he was going to be my *masoul* from then on, and I was going to be acting *masoul* for Britain. For my daily work I would report to and receive orders from him. For my organisational work I would have another *masoul*, Hamid Bokaie, who was responsible for diplomacy in several countries including Britain. At the same time I had been moved up from MN (deputy of *nahad*) to the higher rank of MS (*masoul* of *nahad*). As a member of the Mojahedin I now had to watch some videos unavailable in Europe. As my wish was to stay put, these changes didn't impress me much. (By contrast, being demoted meant a lot, ideologically.) My promotion meant that throughout my stay in Baghdad I spent most of the time in a room watching videotapes. As an exception I went one day with a group on a pilgrimage to Imam Hussein's shrine in Karbela.

Did I remember my mother when I was there? Did I remember the time I went there twenty-eight years earlier with my family? Did I remember how my mother cried about getting rid of my father, how the *mullah* insulted her? Strangely, I did not. Perhaps the cold of the grave had obliterated the memories; perhaps I had become a Mojahed without realising it. I was in a kind of limbo. I could not see myself as others saw me, and the title of 'Mojahed', the ranks, seemed unreal and unrelated to me. At the same time I was losing my emotions and memories.

In London, I found Anna more depressed than ever. She was no longer a member but a part-time supporter. Now she said she didn't want to work there anymore. I thought she was depressed because she had to take orders from those for whom she was previously *masoul*. It didn't occur to me that she was simply sick and tired of that life and wanted to return to her normal self and live an ordinary life like other women. With hindsight, I see that her problems started much earlier, just after she left the organisation, when Sarvy was in London for a holiday.

We had quarrelled bitterly about Sarvy's future. Wanting the best for my children, like any father, I naturally wished to see Sarvy become a Mojahed. This was the path that would lead to her becoming a proud, honest and dignified Iranian and human being, the equal of any man in whatever she chose to do. When we sent her to Paris, Anna and I were of the same mind. But our thinking diverged. I could only see that Anna was unable to face the hardship of being with the Mojahedin and adapting herself to its teachings, although I presumed she had not rejected the Mojahedin's philosophy or struggle for national freedom.

But Anna insisted that it was not for selfish reasons but for Sarvy's own sake that she wanted her in London. The more she explained, the angrier and more blinkered I got. She wants Sarvy back, I thought, because she doesn't want to be alone or because she just wants to be with her. As her father I, too, had often wished for her presence but would not jeopardise her future to satisfy my own wishes, as I felt Anna was doing. Aiming her last arrow, Anna said, 'If Sarvy stays in Paris, I know she is not going to be a normal person. She'll develop some kind of complex, maybe even a sexual complex.' This was too much for me. For the first and last time in my life I slapped my wife.

I left the house, went straight to Sister Tahereh and told her I thought my marriage was ending. In the Mojahedin, mothers had all rights over their children, so there wasn't much I could do. Sarvy remained in London with Anna. For a few weeks I refrained from going home, until Tahereh ordered me to see Anna and put the incident behind us.

Our flat had two bedrooms, and we shared it with our friend Shams and his wife. When Anna complained of lack of privacy, the organisation moved them elsewhere. But it didn't solve the problem; whenever I saw her she had a new complaint. One day I heard her yelling at the door of the base. I took her aside to ask what was going on but she only became angrier, swearing and insulting everyone: me, the organisation's members, the leadership. 'People are right to say that you have created a prison and that you yourselves are prisoners and jailers! You are a torturer, you are torturing me, you have chained me in my own house and are torturing me every day! ...' Unable to talk to her anymore, we went to our flat to see what had happened. The ceiling was leaking; there was water everywhere. It was a common enough occurrence for any house during a cold winter when a frozen pipe burst. But for her it was the last straw. In a sense see she was right. What she wanted and had a right to expect was a normal life, with a normal husband a comfortable modern environment ... The Mojahedin no longer provided her with incentive or inspiration to make sacrifices. She had become morose and anxious, and no longer laughed or joked. At the time I understood none of that: to me the problem was a simple leaky ceiling. Instead of comforting and calming her, I laughed.

Our problem was in microcosm the problem of the Iranian people. They were unwilling to answer our call to rise up against Khomeini. They were tired of rallying and shouting, tired of the unremitting onslaught of imprisonments, torture and revolutionary actions; tired of seeing young Mojahedin strutting around claiming to be morally superior and wiser than everybody else. But we were blind and deaf to these realities.

My reaction to Anna's complaint drove her into a fury. She began attacking me, throwing furniture. Sarvy and Hanif were terrified; Hanif wept and Sarvy, not knowing what to say or do, simply froze. Not wanting them to see us like this, I foolishly pretended to be laughing with mirth. I even tried to kiss Anna. Naturally, this only made things worse.

Within a few days we applied for and, with the organisation's help, were allocated a different flat. On the way, I told Sarvy, 'You are very young to understand this, but I am not going to stay with you anymore. Your mother and I want different things; she wants an ordinary life, which I cannot give her as long as Khomeini is in power. Perhaps one day, when we are rid of him, we can return to our home country and lead ordinary lives, but for now we must separate. Each of us must head towards his or her destiny.' She didn't ask details, but instead asked if I was going to see them. 'Yes', I said, 'I will visit you. We will not divorce as long as your mother wants to stay married, but we do not love each other anymore.' I said the same to Anna. She didn't accept it, and tried to kiss me. I turned my head away, and she swallowed her emotions with a choking sound and said nothing. The message sank in.

Hamid was my first male *masoul* since becoming a member of the organisation. Unlike my previous *masouls* he was very mild, understanding and persuasive. Whenever he wanted me to do something he first gave me the reasons and the necessary information. I hardly knew how to respond to this reasonableness and kindness. Those days were the happiest I spent within the organisation. The only problem was that my executive *masoul*, Reza'i – a man with similar qualities to Hamid – was not with us and connected to me only by telephone. As Hamid directed our European diplomacy, he shifted me increasingly towards his area of work at the expense of my usual responsibilities. I was also now the *masoul* for our diplomatic staff in Britain and Hamid expected me to involve myself in their daily activities. I cast around for an excuse to involve myself in anything *but* diplomacy. Not only did I hate the job, but also felt untrained, with serious shortcomings; my English was so poor I could hardly have a proper political conversation. These arguments cut no ice with Hamid, who eventually told me I would be spending all my time in diplomacy while merely supervising other activities. Meherafroz was going to take charge of everything else. He told me to attend some diplomatic meetings with Ramis, *masoul* of diplomacy in Britain, and Farzin, director of media relations. Ramis was a very able and professional person. The more I watched him in action, the less I felt capable of becoming like him. Perhaps it was fear rather than lack of ability that prevented me from liking this work and making the concomitant changes in myself.

In diplomatic meetings we were supposed to act as liberal and bourgeois as possible. These were the very aspects of my character I had tried to shed for the past seven years, so as to become a Mojahed. I had to have a double character, lead a double life. Within the organisation we were straight, simple, honest, humble and dressed modestly. In diplomacy, honesty had no meaning; we weren't to lie, but like other politicians it was clear we had to guard against telling the whole truth on any issue and to magnify that part of the truth to our benefit. We gave out a lot of useless information so as to deter listeners from asking questions, especially questions related to subjects we wanted to avoid. Our language had to be as complex as possible to make it more difficult to find holes in our arguments. We had to behave with pride and not allow anyone to feel superior to us. Our clothes had to be understated but expensive-looking. The first meeting presented me with my first practical problem – not having a suit, white shirt or tie. Any decent clothes I had owned had been disposed of as reminders of my bourgeois leanings. I bought my first suit at Oxfam, a new experience. I wasn't used to spending money on my personal needs.

Ramis announced that we were attending an evening buffet party, invited not as Mojahedin members but as Iranian merchants. Whether we looked like merchants I didn't know. What were we supposed to talk about? Why were we even going? 'To meet people', Ramis said, 'as there will be some Conservative ministers present.' Not only was I clueless about behaving as a diplomat, now I was expected to behave like an Iranian merchant. Clutching our wine glasses (which actually contained Pepsi), we moved around talking to people, mostly about things with which we had not the faintest acquaintance.

One Conservative Party member, fortunately, was more anxious to talk than listen. I asked him about BBC radio's Persian broadcasts and whether they were subject to Party influence, as he said he worked there. He gave me my first lesson in diplomacy. 'Dear chap', he said, 'the BBC is not directed by the interests of the parties but by the interests of the country, as directed by the Foreign Office. Governments of different parties come and go but, as you can see, their direction doesn't change a bit. It changes when our interests change.'

Ramis turned out to be even more able than I had thought. He knew many MPs and their aides by name and had established very friendly relations with some of them. He was even able to work from their offices in the House of Commons and, with their permission, write letters on their behalf and send them to other MPs asking them to support the Mojahedin.

Farzin, for his part, knew the names of many newspaper editors and journalists, and their individual views towards Iran and ourselves. Once, in the offices of the *Financial Times*, I was annoyed to hear an editor referring to Rajavi's 'personality cult'. I took this as an insult to our leadership and started laying into him. As I was superior to Farzin, he didn't say anything, but afterwards he admonished me to be more patient in the diplomatic world, especially in dealing with the media. 'It is their job to make us angry,' he said. 'Only by doing so can they break down our diplomatic front and get to the truth they are anxious to hear.'

My diplomatic training didn't last long. In April 1987, at the start of the Iranian New Year, Hamid announced my transfer to Switzerland to represent the Mojahedin there and in the international organisation. My new *masoul* would be Sister Soror, our head of diplomacy whom I had met in Baghdad. I would become *masoul* of our organisation in Belgium and the Netherlands as well as in Switzerland. When I left I wondered if I would see any of my friends in England again. I did see Ramis for the last time: he later died in battle. I said goodbye to them, to my family and to my memories, and packed my bags.

# 25

# Diplomacy

'You are so lucky,' my new *masoul* said, 'to be entering the diplomatic section at this juncture. We are making progress in so many different directions.'

Our armed resistance against the regime was taking new shape. The Iraqis gave us military bases, where we could train safely under the umbrella of Iraq's anti-aircraft missiles. Our combatants had uniforms similar to the Iranian army's – green for winter, khaki for summer. On Maryam's advice, women dressed the same as the men, only with long shirts hanging over their trousers and scarves instead of berets. Impressive pictures of Sister Tahereh in uniform, handing rifles to new trainees, gave us pride in our new army. We did not wait long to see results. For the first time, we took prisoners of war as well as killing and wounding guards. In March 1987, scores of Khomeini's guards were killed and eleven captured. In April, 111 were killed and 3 captured. We suffered no casualties ourselves. The prisoners provided a lot of new information about the Iranian army. But their most important service to us was to declare in media interviews that they had surrendered voluntarily, tired of the war, suppression and other miseries inflicted by the rule of the *mullahs*. They also remarked on their good treatment by the Mojahedin. Now we could show the world how wise our leader had been to make peace with Iraq, how popular the Mojahedin were among army personnel, how tired Iranians were of their regime and, not least, how strong and effective our new army was.

During that year's 20th June celebrations, Rajavi referred to the new body as the 'National Liberation Army', or NLA, emphasising that, unlike other armies, this one was based on the free will of its combatants; apart from obeying military discipline, they were under no compulsion of any sort. All Mojahedin were members of the new army, but it was not restricted to Mojahedin: anyone of any creed or religion could join. The reality was that NLA soldiers had to conform to rules, such as the wearing of scarves by women and the chanting of Mojahedin anthems each morning, and were rather less free than Rajavi had intimated. It therefore attracted few non-Mojahedin.

Meanwhile, the Iranian regime sank even deeper in international political esteem, thanks to its support for the Hezbollahis in Lebanon; the policy of hostage-taking; the continuing war with Iraq; and later, for attacking oil freighters in the Persian Gulf. Even the Soviets, now under Mikhail Gorbachev, hesitated to support Iran as vehemently as before.

In Iraq I was moved to a Mojahedin military base near Baghdad, which I soon learned was not only Rajavi's residence but also the base for all Mojahedin political sections including diplomacy and broadcast media. Rajavi's heavily guarded quarters were isolated from other parts of the base, so there was no chance to meet him or Maryam as I'd wished. Instead, I was introduced Sister Soror to Rajavi's eldest brother, Dr Kazam Rajavi, whom everyone called 'Doctor'.

As a Mojahedin representative, my responsibilities included pretty well everything, while Doctor – an expert in political work – would be mostly a figurehead, Rajavi's representative in meetings and conferences. I knew by now that the Mojahedin, despite their polite surface, respected or trusted no one, even close family and friends; Rajavi himself was no exception. Still, though it demonstrated ideological weakness, I was not able to ignore these binding ties. From our first meeting I liked Doctor, not only because of his charm, modesty and ability, but also for being

My father Ibrahim Banisadr in army uniform, *circa* 1936.

At the age of eight with my mother Fari Auhei and Ammo Jan (Ato'allah Navidi), during one of my weekly visits.

My siblings and me around the *curcy* in my father's home in Tehran, *circa* 1955. We would fight for a position furthest away from my father's harsh scrutiny. I am second from left; Esau is third from left, followed by my sister Simin, followed by Soria and Saied.

My wedding, September 1974, Tehran. From left: My mother; Anna (seated); Simin; me (seated); my sister Parveen (foreground).

My parents Fari and Ibrahim, before I was born, *circa* 1953. They would divorce about five years later.

Graduation Day, University of Reading (UK), 1978, with my good friend Shams (L). Mahmoud (R) was the one who introduced me to the Mojahedin.

Anna, Sarvy and me, in the idyllic days in Reading (UK), before our involvement with the Mojahedin, *circa* 1978.

Anna in Islamic dress, Hanif (L) and
Sarvy (R), *circa* 1985. We had been
members of the Mojahedin for about five
years.

With Khaled Haj Hassan, Jordanian
Labour Minister and International Labour
Conference chairman, 1987. I was a key
Mojahedin representative at such events.

National Council of Resistance meeting, Baghdad, October 1993, with Masoud Rajavi presiding. I am seated in the first row, far right.

Maryam Rajavi, co-leader of the Mojahedin, *circa* 1995.

Rajavi, *circa* 1991. Note the sun-lion-sword emblem above his head and on the flag, adopted by the NCR on Rajavi's surprise decision.

From the pages of *Mojahed*, October 1991: a show of force by the NLA.

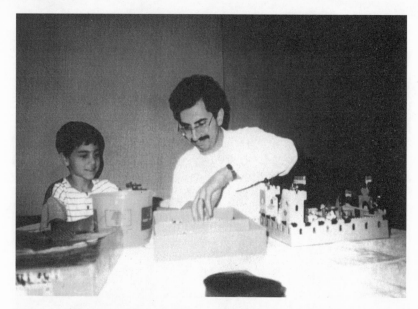

Hanif (L), and me, *circa* 1990. This is possibly the only existing image of me spending time with my son during his childhood; otherwise all my time was devoted to the Mojahedin.

With Hanif (L) and Sarvy (R), in 2001, about five years after leaving the Mojahedin. This occasion marked the first time I had seen my son since his childhood.

Rajavi's brother. When warned several times by my predecessor that working with Doctor was difficult, I was astonished, almost offended. One person even said, ominously, 'If a Mojahed works with Doctor and encounters no problems, I have serious doubts about him as a Mojahed.'

After two or three weeks in Baghdad, during which I read thousands of pages of reports by my predecessors in Switzerland, Belgium and the international organisation, I left for Geneva. I was *masoul* for members in Belgium and two in Geneva: Yasser, a very clever young man fluent in English and German, and Nasser, Doctor's bodyguard. Yasser was responsible for our Swiss diplomacy. He knew much about the country and its media, so I was confident about our prospects there. I worried about the international organisation, which was very important to the Mojahedin, being the main base for all diplomatic activity.

Tall, strong and fit, Nasser lived with us in our modern three-bedroom apartment in central Geneva. A long-standing Mojahedin supporter, he was nicknamed 'Nasser Maximum' for using the word 'maximum' in every sentence, always asking for the maximum of everything. He had been in Tehran in June 1981 and recounted first-hand stories that would never appear in the Mojahedin's papers. He was not from the intelligentsia but from the proletariat, a point of pride within the organisation. He knew too little French to be helpful in diplomatic meetings, hence I could rarely give him other work. I worried about this, as the Mojahedin believed that 'a Mojahed will immediately rot if jobless or useless for one minute.' Here we were, living in a luxury apartment in one of the world's richest cities, separated from other Mojahedin and with my liberal bourgeois self in charge. I had every reason to worry about our ideological health, especially that of Nasser, whose movements I generally could not or did not follow.

In June we attended the annual International Labour Organisation conference where thousands of international representatives of governments, workers, employees and NGOs gathered to discuss labour-related issues. A gang of about fifteen Iranian Hezbollahis followed us, interrupting us and generally disrupting the proceedings. Unkempt and loudly dressed in colourful shirts without ties, they had short hair and thick dark beards. They called Doctor a hypocrite and harassed us to the point where I felt he was unsafe and asked Nasser to take him home.

Having identified me, they then tried to make life difficult. While waiting to meet the president of the Confederation of Belgian Workers' Unions – the late M. Hothuys, who was very influential among international labour unions – some of these louts gathered behind me, speaking in Farsi. Suddenly I was surrounded by them, swearing at me. They followed as I approached M. Hothuys, telling him (in a mixture of English and Farsi): 'Hello, mister. I am a worker. You must not see the hypocrite. He and his kind are enemies of the people and of workers.'

M. Hothuys, astonished, replied, 'Sir, this is a free country and we are free people. You cannot tell me whom I can and cannot meet.'

There followed a lengthy exchange in which the Iranians tried to explain their position, becoming increasingly frustrated at not being understood. M. Hothuys courteously offered them an appointment to meet him formally. Faced with their hostility and intransigence, he grew a bit frightened and said to me, 'Sir, what more can you tell me about the Iranian regime that I didn't see with my own eyes today? When these thugs act so, here in this free country, I can very well see what they might do in their own. Please, can we meet another time, in a more appropriate situation, to see what can I do for you?'

I kept wondering how to shake off these people. Fortunately I knew they were terrified of losing their way in the complicated corridors of the UN building, and missing the bus that ferried them to and from the embassy each day. My solution was to walk fast in corridors when there were lots of people about, and soon I would lose my 'tail'.

Those delegates of the Iranian regime, with their atrocious behaviour, assisted me more than anyone. Symbols of Khomeini's way of thinking, they were living proof of the horrors I wished to describe to potentially supportive delegates. Wherever we were, they were always close by, murmuring insults. Our partners in discussion soon accustomed themselves to this disgraceful accompaniment. The only safe meeting places were bars or restaurants where the serving of alcohol or the absence of *halal* meat kept them away.

The Iranian regime was moved to the International Labour Conference's 'blacklist', joining countries with the worst records of labour-rights violations. The day on which labour representatives were going to decide an Iranian case, the Iranian representative who was to respond to the allegations deliberately didn't arrive until midnight – hoping the meeting would end inconclusively or that most delegates (especially from the West) might have left by then, leaving representatives more sympathetic to Iran. However, the moderator announced that the proceedings would only begin when all delegations were present. Eventually the Iranian representative came. As he began speaking, he was greeted with derisive laughter as it became clear he was representing 'employers', not 'workers' – demonstrating how artificial those distinctions were to the regime and how dishonestly it treated labour unions. The representative's 'defence' consisted mainly of calling the Western delegates representatives of imperialism and Zionism, and insulting America. The result of the voting was as might be guessed.

During the conference, we met labour ministers from many different countries, including the Jordanian minister, who also chaired the conference. I met with the president of the ILO and with the general secretaries of all major labour unions. I quickly learned that the main purpose of attending conferences was propaganda and more propaganda; hence our most important achievement was the number of photographs taken with the key people present. I have to admit it created a personal as well as an organisational incentive: I got quite a buzz from seeing our photographs in Mojahedin publications, although ideologically this was all wrong and forced me to write a long self-critical report for my *masoul*. It was quite a dilemma: we were expected to produce such propaganda vehicles, but not to enjoy doing so. Only the leadership and NCR members were permitted self-esteem. To save our consciences, we made sure those individuals were the 'stars' of meetings and photographs opportunities.

Whatever our difficulties in this respect, the propaganda was used to demonstrate the extent of our support on the international scene and the isolation of the regime. Of course, our leadership knew that our ideological differences meant we would never gain the total support of the West; the main objective of our foreign policy was to neutralise its support for the regime.

Our next task was to gain as much media coverage as possible of the NLA's establishment. In Switzerland, thanks to a high penetration rate of newspapers and Yasser's skill in research and follow-up, this was not a problem. We achieved widespread coverage in papers large and small, which was what our superiors wanted. I made the mistake of telling Yasser I thought we should go for qualitative rather than quantitative coverage, and asked him to make appointments with foreign editors.

The result was a disaster! The editors were better informed than we were and showed us up with a raft of sharp and perceptive questions. When we pointed to our achievements on the battlefront, they asked, 'Where do you get your arms? Where are your bases? Who trains the combatants? What is your relationship with Iraq? What do your people think about your relationship with their enemy?' Not for a moment did they accept our prediction of the regime's imminent collapse. They cited many examples of the regime's popularity and that of Khomeini, which we could not easily deny. German-language editors were particularly interested in gaining information about different factions within the regime. Our stance was that there were no factions, only different faces of Khomeini himself; that nobody else in the regime carried any weight – thus his death would inevitably bring about its collapse. Such assertions merely underlined how immature our analysis of the situation was, and therefore how unreliable our predictions for the future. At this point the editors' silence, a light smile or a word of thanks indicated that we were being asked to leave, and in many cases not to return.

When we went for an interview with the chief editor of the *Journal de Genève*, the most important French-language paper, however, we were welcomed with some ceremony. First they asked if we needed anyone with us. Then we were ushered into a large room clearly prepared for a VIP, whereupon the editor and several assistants entered. Right then both sides, to their great embarrassment, realised their mistake. They were expecting my cousin, the previous Iranian president, not a member of the Mojahedin. Out of politeness, they carried on with the interview. Acting on official instructions, I went on the offensive and asked why they had given us so little coverage in the past in favour of Khomeini's regime. The shape of the interview promptly changed, and the chief editor left me with the Middle East editor, who bombarded me with the usual questions about our army – adding some questions about Rajavi's 'personality cult' and about Banisadr and other former Council members, claiming that the Council was just a political cover for the Mojahedin ...

Meetings like these not only put paid to 'qualitative coverage' but also ensured that we didn't have the quantity either, as Yasser wanted to teach me a lesson and refused to carry on making contacts, doing research and pulling strings ...

In contrast to my abysmal performance in Switzerland, I was fortunately quite successful in Belgium – largely thanks to Simin, a supporter responsible for dealing with the media and politicians. For several years she'd had sole responsibility for our political activities there and was able to brief me extensively about Belgian politics, the tendencies of the various parties, the differences between the French and the Flemish and who was more sympathetic to our cause. I wondered why Simin, with her commitment and background, was still considered a supporter and not a member. I later discovered the reason: attached to her husband and daughter, she had refused a posting in Paris.

Simin was also very media-savvy. Her advice on what to expect during interviews helped me acquit myself pretty well. But most print media ignored pleas to print photographs of Rajavi or Maryam, instead publishing photos of me. I was so embarrassed, I didn't dare forward any to the centre.

In August all the members of the diplomatic section were ordered back to Baghdad, where we had a long lecture from our *masoul* about the 'ideological threat' of our jobs. To counter it, she suggested that when we found ourselves with time we should return to Iraq and undergo military training at one of our bases. Most of us were sent straightaway to a base called Ashraf.

I did not go, as I was due back in Geneva for another conference. While still in Iraq, Sister Soror received a telephone call from Ashraf. It was bad news: our friend Hassan had died of heatstroke. We were dumbstruck, though it was neither the first nor last time we heard about the death of a friend. We were almost used to it, and every day we expected our own deaths. When we travelled we carried cyanide capsules, with which to commit suicide if threatened by a hijacking, kidnapping or other terrorist act. At conferences or demonstrations, we always felt our lives were on the line. In Iraq daily attacks by Iranian fighters over Baghdad put everybody at risk. To be killed by the enemy or while training to confront him was expected, and honourable. But dying of heatstroke …?

Hassan was a British member who had become a supporter almost the same time as I. He was as well-known for his patience and calmness as for his tenacity. He once tracked down an MP on the ski slopes in the Alps just to secure his support for an NCR peace plan. Much impressed, the MP said, 'If you all have this determination, I have no doubt you will win, so I shall be happy to support you!'

Among army personnel we were known as *bachehaie kharaj kashvari* ('foreign boys') – soft liberals unused to the rough conditions of army life. I imagined Hassan would have suffered uncomplainingly from the heat rather than opt out of the programme.

Hassan was given a military burial. It was my first time attending such an event, and also the first time I had seen a corpse, as we were present during the ceremonial washing beforehand. Though his body was stiff and cold, he was so near that I could not accept he was dead, and was offended by the way the mortician moved him about to wash him. We carried him aloft to the shrine of Imam Hussein and then to a nearby cemetery, where I saw the graves of many Mojahedin killed in battles.

We were all deeply saddened by Hassan's death. In his will he had written movingly of his wish to give everything he had to the Mojahedin's fight for a just society.

Attending a month-long conference of the UN Human Rights Subcommittee gave me insight into the contradictory views on human rights violations emanating from different sources. The subcommittee, which numbered about twenty apparently politically independent 'judges' from different countries, was convened to assess violations of human rights in various areas. We drafted a resolution mentioning the Mojahedin and Rajavi. Doctor opposed it, saying, 'I should be very happy to see my family name in an international resolution; I'd like to see the names of my aunts and uncles there too, but it is not right and it is not possible. We're making fools of ourselves by putting it forward.'

He was travelling to Paris and couldn't accompany us to the conference, so without further argument we followed the line handed down from Baghdad. We tried to find a sponsor and co-sponsor for the resolution; the sponsor had to come from a Western country, so we approached them one by one. Eventually the British judge agreed to put forward a resolution similar to the one we had drafted, provided it contained no references to the Mojahedin or Rajavi's name – which were essential features for us, as a first step along the path to international recognition. Rajavi's ultimate aim was to force the UN to hand over Iran's seat in the General Assembly to the Mojahedin.

At the sitting of the Subcommittee, the Iranian representative addressed allegations of human rights violations. Instead of refuting them, he launched into the usual attack on the Americans, British and imperialists. But here he faced individuals, not nations, and had no choice but to attack and insult the person sponsoring the resolution, calling him a 'political liar', a 'puppet of imperialism' who brought 'allegations without any proof'. In response to a challenge to produce evidence, the sponsor agreed to include our documents in the resolution.

The voting was interesting. The Soviet representative, asked to register his vote, neither voted nor abstained but proclaimed loudly, 'Absent!' Immediately the whole room burst out laughing. Some of the judges seemed genuinely sympathetic, but were bound by their governments to vote in favour of the Iranian regime – among them Cuba, a country with a 'revolutionary' leader, and Ethiopia, with a communist government! The Ethiopian judge told us his orders were to vote against; his only way out was to skip the meeting, which he kindly did. The Zambian representative had similar instructions but, strangely, not only voted in favour but also announced his wish to add his name to the resolution's sponsors. He said, 'I have received the documents mentioned in the resolution, and they were so horrific that I was not able to believe them and decided at most to abstain. But when I showed them to the representative of Iran, he did not deny their accuracy, but said something I am ashamed to repeat here but which has persuaded me that these documents are correct.'

Thus, contrary to Doctor's expectations, our resolution passed. So, how to judge the judges? In general, they were 'politicised' and voted according to the interests of their countries. Yet they passed many resolutions concerning human rights in general which could force countries around the globe to comply. Also, whenever human rights were violated in a particularly appalling way, even the votes and influence of the Americans or Soviets could not save the perpetrators from condemnation.

Following this conference, I was instructed to drop everything and attend the annual sitting of the UN General Assembly in New York.

It was my first visit to the US. Everything was strange and different. I had seen and read so much about the Americans' crimes that I didn't want to find them attractive or interesting. Even our members there were different. Meeting our members from different countries had gradually led me to conclude that the national characteristics of the host country influenced us. Our members in Germany were precise, punctual and rule-abiding. Those in France were easygoing, fun-loving, less accurate. We from Britain shared the British traits of politeness, patience and calm. By the same token, American members always struck me with their aggressiveness and occasional arrogance. However, all such attributes were overwritten by and less prominent than our common Mojahedin attitudes and philosophy.

The American members may only have adopted an assertive 'psuedo-left' position for fear of being labelled 'right-wing', as had happened to us a few years earlier. Eshagh, who was nominated to work alongside me for the General Assembly sessions, epitomised this attitude. We missed many appointments simply because he refused to take a car or cab. We always carried two heavy briefcases full of documents, and literally ran from one embassy to the other for meetings. Whenever I asked how far away the next venue was, the answer was always the same: 'Nothing, just a few blocks'. When we arrived late at the meeting, out of breath and sweating, he always explained to our opposite numbers, 'Sorry, we were held up by the rush hour'. We took a packed lunch and ate between meetings. Once, at the Belgian embassy, we pulled some documents from a briefcase and apples and oranges rolled out onto the floor; the ambassador and we ran around chasing them. As always, I was too timid to complain about these practices. Instead of requiring him to follow me as his *masoul*, I followed him. By the end of the

Assembly session we both had back pain from our ridiculous antics.

Our purpose at the General Assembly was clear. We needed to put forward a resolution, with as many sponsors as possible, and have it passed. We also wanted maximum publicity and to that end aimed to hold a press conference at the right time, preferably with some of our tortured brothers and sisters who had escaped Iran. Moreover, it was desirable to have favourable speeches made by representatives of different nations.

The main sponsors of our resolution were known from the start; as usual they were Western European countries, plus the US, Canada and countries from other continents to spread the net as widely as possible. Our relationships with the sponsor countries were clearly based on mutual interest. They needed us to feed them information on the most recent political events and human rights violations in Iran so as to have ammunition for their speeches. We needed their muscle to make the resolution as strong as possible and preferably to mention our documents.

For every sponsor favouring the regime there was another sympathetic towards us. It was a tricky business trying to play them off against each other. At least the Iranian delegates had the same difficulty. That year Austria was the 'bad guy' and Luxembourg the 'good guy', but they, like all the diplomats, served their own national interests. The Germans were blunt and aggressive, having close economic ties with Iran. The Italians behaved likewise, if more diplomatically, and dealt with us more directly. The Scandinavian countries, deeply concerned about human rights, were accordingly friendly and helpful.

In three months we met almost 200 people from governments and non-governmental organisations. We steered clear of the communist countries, as we didn't want to offend our Western friends; besides, we knew nothing could change their minds. Nor did we meet representatives of countries close to the regime, like Libya, Syria and Pakistan, or from Israel and South Africa.

In some cases the standoff originated on the other side. Most Arab countries refused to meet us, perhaps fearful of terrorist activity by the regime, and some African countries were recipients of Iranian financial help.

Although the small countries' decisions were often influenced by the large ones, their votes could be bought easily. Some representatives seemed, without any political reasons and against the tendency of their governments, to be shifting favourably towards the regime. However, others were willing to sell their entrance badges, change their vote from 'no' to 'absent' or to manipulate their votes in our favour, against their orders. On one occasion we sent a car to collect a representative working in another part of New York, to get him to the UN in time for the vote.

There were quid pro quos too: some representatives bluntly told us they couldn't vote in favour of our resolution because Iran and its followers would vote against them. The Indonesian ambassador and Doctor were former classmates and had a long session of fond reminiscences, but when it came to the crunch, not only did he vote against but also co-sponsored a counter-resolution put forward by Pakistan to neutralise ours. Doctor flew into a rage. 'You are all a bunch of criminals!' he shouted at his former friend, in front of a group of diplomats.

It was a different story with the Bangladeshi ambassador. He began our meeting by labelling us mercenaries of the Americans and Iraqis, traitors to our people and to all Muslims, hypocrites … had he continued one second more, I am sure Eshagh would have exploded. I was astonished more than offended. If he was so much against us, I asked, why had he agreed to meet us? At this point he stopped hurling insults and, with a mild smile, said, 'Well, this is what the Iranians called you when I told them I was meeting you. What do you think about that?' He continued: 'From their reaction, I felt you must be a real threat to them, and very interesting people to meet. I thought I must not lose this opportunity.' Our meeting lasted almost two hours, during which he asked not only about our politics but also our ideology. By the end of our discussion he had become a firm friend and told us he was prepared to accept criticism from his government and disobey orders by abstaining from voting. He also offered us the use of the Bangladeshi embassy for relaxation or prayers.

In spite of all our efforts and the promises of support, we obtained only three more votes than the previous year, but the number – 64 – was enough for the resolution to pass comfortably. Our newspapers were jubilant, and we received much personal approbation.

Gradually I developed good working relationships with our men there. Eshagh was the cleverest of them: well-educated and holding considered and independent views on the organisation's policies. Five years later he was transferred to Baghdad, where, as a result of pressures from another phase of the 'ideological revolution', he hanged himself. By committing suicide he had 'betrayed' the leadership and was accordingly buried without ceremony, in an unknown place as an unknown person.

# 26

# Paris

Although the General Assembly session still had a few days to run, I was summoned back to Europe immediately. The French government, in a shameful deal with the Iranian regime to free French hostages in Lebanon, had agreed to expel fourteen members and supporters of the Mojahedin from France to Gabon. To take the political sting out of it they expelled three Turkish Kurds at the same time. Among those deported was Saeid, our head of diplomacy in France, whom I had to replace.

Paris was totally different from the city I had known. It felt like a place under siege. Everywhere there were gendarmes or soldiers, stopping people, searching cars. People with darker skin or hair, or more casual dress, were treated with suspicion and could expect being questioned or arrested in the Métro stations. Siros, my translator, was a handsome man in his early thirties, with blue eyes and fair hair; we were always well-groomed, so never once stopped. The French government claimed at first to have evidence that the people arrested and deported were terrorists or had terrorist connections. Later they changed their story, saying that the mere presence of these people in France attracted terrorist activity, endangering ordinary citizens.

I was supposed to head our diplomatic section. My job included issuing and distributing statements that came to us hourly, monitoring the media for the latest news and faxing the most significant items to Baghdad. I also had to establish relationships with politicians and inform them daily of events. But I soon discovered the real head was Rajavi himself.

Our situation was doubly sensitive. We were at the centre of Mojahedin politics, which was at its most critical point since the departure from Iran. At the same time we were at the centre of French politics, and power struggles. President Mitterand was a Socialist, and Prime Minister Chirac, from the RPR (Gaullists). By freeing the French hostages in Lebanon, Chirac wanted to ensure the victory of his party in the upcoming general election. The Socialists, who could see how hateful this action would appear on the international stage, wanted to make political capital out of it so as to guarantee their own victory. The Americans and the British, who also had hostages in Lebanon, were concerned that concessions towards hostage-takers might encourage the abduction of more hostages and an increase in the demands made for their release. For the Mojahedin, the opportunities for worldwide publicity were boundless.

Immediately after the Gabon expulsions, Rajavi asked all our members and supporters to mount hunger strikes in front of the French embassies in their respective countries. In Paris, supporters went on hunger strikes in front of the offices of the UNHCR; the exiles in Gabon also took part.

This political fight with the French government lasted nearly forty days, and was the Mojahedin's biggest ever political victory. The Socialists came out of it well, winning the election. The strike made headline news almost daily in the French media and in many other countries. The French government was almost universally condemned for its actions. *The Times* reported that 'The British Refugee Council accused the French government yesterday of having violated the international convention on refugees ...', while the *New York Times* said Chirac's government had dishonoured itself. Every day we gathered these reports from around the world and used them to lobby politicians and parliamentarians in different countries. Nearly 1,400 politicians from 16 (mostly Western) countries sent letters and telegrams of condemnation to the French government. In France itself many personalities and former ministers visited the hunger strikers to show solidarity, including Mitterrand's wife.

We who were working behind the scenes were not allowed to join the hunger strike, but nevertheless the stress of the job, coupled with feelings of guilt about the strikers, meant we often went without food and rarely slept more than two or three hours at a time in a proper bed. Every day, Helen, our French assistant, brought along some baguettes, which we ate while working at any time, day or night, whenever we felt sleepy or hungry. The best place to catch up on sleep was on trains going to and from meetings, when there was nothing else to do. One day Siros and I both fell asleep on the last train of the evening and didn't wake up until it reached the terminus. It was past midnight, and we had no change or telephone cards, so in our drowsy state we walked the several kilometres back to our base.

Another time, when we had an important meeting with a government minister from one of the coalition parties, I could stay awake only by talking; whenever I paused for Siros to translate, I nodded off again. To compensate for our lack of alertness, we showed him the booklet detailing coverage of the strike by the various papers, some even from that day. The booklet ran to a few hundred pages and impressed him greatly. So, too, he said, did the weakness of the hunger strikers and the redness of our eyes from sleepless nights. 'But', he went on, 'at the same time I can see your well-documented materials and the strength of your will to defeat your enemies, so I have no doubt that you will win and soon see your friends back in this country.' The next day he announced that he had departed from his fellow government members on this issue.

His prediction was accurate. The French courts announced that no legal basis existed for the expulsions. We received a request from the government for a meeting with our representatives. Abrishamchi and Mohadessin were brought from Baghdad to Paris for this purpose. The result was an accord signed by Minister Robert Pandraud for France and Abrishamchi on the Mojahedin's behalf. It was an unbelievable victory, our first official recognition as sole representatives of the Iranian resistance. The accord was announced simultaneously by the French government and ourselves, after which our friends returned from Gabon to a heroes' welcome, on a plane specially chartered by the French. There was jubilation in our bases around the world. Masoud and Maryam telephoned all the bases, and Maryam announced that the date would henceforth be known as 'the day of "refugees"'. Our struggle, she said, was not intended to serve our present cause only but the rights of refugees the world over.

*Le Monde* greeted the event with the headline 'Volte-face' ['about-face']. 'Paris a cédé' ['Paris concedes'], admitted *Le Point*; the US *Newsweek* acknowledged simply, 'An Iranian hunger strike pays off'.

During those forty days I met many fantastic people on both sides, who were not prepared to tolerate injustice. Ali, a history professor, risked permanently losing his sight if he persisted with the hunger strike. Maryam had ordered that not lose anybody in this action. But it took us a long time to persuade Ali to eat. Our enemies interpreted our sacrifices as madness, claiming we'd been brainwashed. But ordinary French people went out of their way to show support and ease our suffering, bringing coffee, blankets, sometimes flowers, and perhaps sitting with the strikers for a few hours.

The magnitude of the action brought out the best in our supporters. Siros was irrepressibly cheerful and obliging, despite his exhaustion, maintaining a whirlwind schedule monitoring radio broadcasts, translating newspaper reports and racing off to meetings. Annie, the French wife of one of our expelled supporters, was a quiet woman who had led a fairly uneventful life. We asked her to smuggle some equipment, including a fax machine, into the hotel where the exiles were being held as guests of the president of Gabon, but didn't really believe her capable of embracing a '007' role. But she rose to the occasion and accomplished it perfectly. As a result we could communicate with our friends and coordinate their actions with ours. It took some time for the French and Gabonese to figure out how to stop us passing information to each other. By the time they did, it was too late.

That we had, with determination but empty hands, forced the fifth strongest government in the world to surrender, instilled new hope into many disheartened activists. We now saw no reason why we shouldn't defeat Khomeini's backward and unpopular regime.

Our army also scored some impressive victories then, killing over 350 guards and capturing 140 in Ilam, Khozastan and Soreen. Politically, too, the regime was in trouble. Their representative in France was expelled, and internal differences were proving insoluble. They were forced to abolish the only party in the country, the governing Islamic Republic Party. In *Iran Liberation*, the Mojahedin observed: 'Khomeini's dissolution of the party he himself founded signals the regime's extreme weakness. This will boost public morale and escalate resistance, and conversely alienate the regime's forces ... The pack of wolves comprising the regime can only subsist under Khomeini's mediaeval dictatorship, and cannot survive independently of him.' Following the dissolution of the party, an exchange of letters between Khamenei, the president, and Khomeini revealed obvious fundamental differences of opinion and belief.

Encouraged by these inroads into the regime, many hunger strikers obeyed Rajavi's call to join the army to witness the final days of the regime.

A year later Siros was killed in a battle. Annie, who served as a nurse in our final battle with the regime, was captured and died or was killed in captivity.

## 27

# Call to Arms

After this 'victory' we returned to Baghdad to attend ideological meetings, which were called 'old to new' – meaning that we now had to adapt to and play our full part in this new era of the organisation. It was here that I first heard Ali Zarkash, formerly the organisation's second in command, referred to as one who had 'betrayed our leader'. It was explained that while he was commanding our forces, he had failed to provide Rajavi with a full picture of the situation, resulting in the loss of many fighters. He was stripped of his rank and demoted to ordinary membership. Some years earlier, we had been in the habit of giving instructions to supporters in Iran by telephone from abroad, not knowing initially that calls were monitored by the regime. Even when we discovered this, people continued to make contact in the same manner, and many supporters and members were arrested and executed. Somebody clearly had to be blamed for this obvious mistake – perhaps it was poor Zarkash. He was killed in our final battle, and the regime tried to portray his death as the consequence of internal conflict.

After a few weeks in Baghdad, I returned to Geneva to attend the yearly session of the Commission of Human Rights, at the end of which we passed another resolution condemning human rights violations in Iran. Then I was ordered to move my base from Geneva to Rome, and as *masoul* of our Italian organisation continue my responsibilities in international organisations, Switzerland and Belgium.

I had hardly been in Rome a week when I was asked to hurry back to Baghdad. We were about to engage in our first major military battle with the regime's army and Rajavi had ordered that the maximum number of members should take part.

Operation 'Aftab' ('Sun') was to take place in Khozastan, in southern Iran. We shared a base with the Iraqis which we called Saeid Mohsen Quarters after one of the Mojahedin founders. After a year of intense political activity, it was good to be back where we felt we belonged. It is no exaggeration to say that I saw in a single day almost all the friends I had made in the previous seven years. Wherever I turned I encountered a friendly face, and there were endless exchanges of greetings and exhortation. Some already bore ugly battle wounds and scars, which they passed off as mosquito bites. I could only hope those mosquitos would not bite me.

Everywhere we were due to go, the Iraqis had shortly before defeated units of the Iranian army or revolutionary guards. This meant that their defensive lines were open, and we would be able to penetrate to the heart of the unit. When we moved to the fortification we found that the Iraqis (or perhaps retreating Iranians) had already built entrenchments. Our job was to prepare them for our commanding officers. Of course, the supreme commander was Rajavi himself, operating from the base we had left.

Our commander in this operation was my *masoul*, Sister Soror. She explained that I was to command a small group to move prefabricated toilets to the site, dig trenches for burying transmission wires, cover the fortifications with plastic, carpet them and prepare separate areas for men and women ... All this struck me as more cosmetic than useful, but I was in the army and had to obey orders without question. We worked very hard, perhaps twenty hours a day. By the time the commanders arrived, our fortification looked more like one of our bases than a war entrenchment.

Nearing midnight we gathered to hear a message from Maryam exhorting us to 'fire, fire, fire'. We were each issued with a Kalashnikov submachine gun. Throughout the years we were reminded that the first firearm we received from the organisation would be sacred, and we had dreamed of earning this honour. I must admit, however, that when the time came I felt no pride. On the contrary, I felt rather silly with a weapon, as most of us – including myself – didn't know how to carry it, never mind how to load or fire. One combatant at least instructed us in handling it. Then Soror ordered us to keep our guns by our side all the time, and indicated the points we had to guard: to guard against whom or what, she did not make clear.

That night and the following day we kept watch as directed. It was thoroughly boring work, becoming exciting only when our shift came to guard the command entrenchment, where there was always some activity and lots of people talking. Once a comrade woke me in the middle of my two-hour sleep break, on Soror's orders, to look at the sky. 'It is so beautiful,' he said breathlessly, 'full of fire.' I said nothing, so as not to show the wrong reaction, but I didn't understand. Later I did look and, yes, it was full of fire – but I couldn't muster any enthusiasm, unlike most of my comrades, laughing and joking excitedly. These were not fireworks, but ballistic fire raining down on either side to kill people. The operation ended the next day. Soror told me collect all equipment and materials to be returned to base. Some lorries started moving off, loaded with goods and personnel. At this point we discovered someone had taken the keys to one of the Land Rovers. Soror pounced. 'Ok', she said, 'Masoud will stay and guard the car while we get somebody to bring the keys to him.' Suddenly I was left alone with my Kalashnikov.

At first I passed the time walking around the abandoned car, certain someone would soon fetch me. A few hundred metres away was a group of Iraqi soldiers, talking and joking. One of them approached a few hours later and, in a mixture of English, Arabic and Persian, asked why I hadn't gone with the others. In the same *patois*, I explained. He was not surprised, being probably used to military orders of this kind. He left me but returned after an hour to invite me to eat with them. We had been ordered against mixing with Iraqis because of a 'protocol problem' with their officials, so

I thanked him but declined. Then an armoured personnel carrier flying the Mojahedin flag appeared, moving slowly in my direction. I hailed it. They thought I had been left behind like some other combatants and urged me to join them, as they were certain the Iranian army would follow and soon reach that area. I refused, saying that someone would come for me soon, that I could not abandon the car. They left. Another hour passed, then the same Iraqi soldier returned, this time with a message. He said they were leaving the area, as the Iranians were about to bomb it and perhaps approach on foot as well. His commander had told him to recommend I go with them. Again I refused, and within a few minutes they had moved off, leaving me entirely alone in this middle of nowhere. The sun had set and darkness brought with it the cold wind of late March nights. Before leaving, one of the brothers had insisted on lending me his overcoat, but I was still cold. For protection I got into one of the hillside trenches, now empty of the plastics and carpets.

No one was around for tens of kilometres. Perhaps the only living things nearby were snakes, creatures I feared more than anything. Loneliness gripped me by the throat. The previous night I'd been scared of mosquitos; now I had better things to worry about. I heard bombing not far off, which I knew to be a sign of an advancing army. The strategy was to bombard an area with full force, dispersing or destroying the enemy and then advancing. I was not worried about being killed in a bombardment; the thought even crossed my mind briefly that it would teach my *masoul* a good lesson. My worry concerned the enemy's advancing to where I was. I didn't even know how to kill myself, let alone how to kill them. I knew I must not, under any circumstances, let myself be captured, which meant I would have to kill myself – but how? I inspected my rifle for the first time, trying to determine how it worked. While I was still so occupied, squatting on the ground to keep some warmth around me, I was amazed to hear someone calling my name. It was Faried, who had taken the keys by mistake. 'We thought you came back and were somewhere on the base,' he said, 'but by chance we met the guys who had seen you, and they told us you were waiting for us.' Apparently Soror had come in for a lot of criticism from her *masoul* for leaving me behind.

The next day, as restitution, Soror gave me the 'honour' of

preparing a table for the leadership and putting up photographs of martyrs from that operation. Among them was Mehrdad, one of my charges from a few years earlier. He'd been in his mid-twenties, from a rich Tehran family. Mehrdad's trademark was keeping cheerful. Whenever anyone showed cruelty or insensitivity, he would repeat some nonsense words – like '*kara bash bash*' – that would make him smile. His mother had searched long for him, and upon finding him tried very hard without success to persuade him to leave the organisation. I wondered if anybody would tell her about her son. Would she consider him a martyr, worthy of congratulations? Or would she blame the organisation for deceiving Mehrdad, leading him to his death?

The result of this operation was 3,500 enemy dead, 508 captured and many armaments seized, including four British-made Chieftain tanks. Thirty-two of our combatants were killed and 91 injured.

I returned to a hero's welcome in Rome. I didn't think the experience made me more courageous, only perhaps less fearful of change. I was keen to begin teaching my charges, about twenty full-time sympathisers and four members, among them three women – two Italian, one Peruvian. The foreigners wanted an organisation like ours in their country, and it was with pride that we told them the Mojahedin belonged not only to Iranians but to all good people in the world.

Rome was very beautiful and reminded me of Tehran in many ways; the weather was the same, too. Our support in Italy seemed quite strong, with many members of parliament signing our petitions and making donations.

In early July the NLA conducted its most impressive operation ever, capturing the strategic town of Mehran, inflicting 8,000 casualties on Khomeini's forces, taking 1,500 prisoners and seizing two billion dollars' worth of war matériel, including 54 tanks. In this battle we lost 59 combatants.

One of the captured Iranian commanders the enemy had expected an offensive but not at such speed or on such a scale, especially by the NLA. The extent of the operation proved that 'the Khomeini regime had misinformed us about the NLA. Contrary to what they told us, the NLA possesses armoured equipment and logistical fire.' The NLA was, in his view, unbeatable. (It was interesting to note that he had adopted Mojahedin language, like referring to 'the Khomeini regime'.) Other observers were impressed. On 28th July 1988, *The Guardian* reported that

> ... the Mojahedin of Masoud Rajavi is the largest, richest, most active, visible and vociferous of the multifarious opposition forces. Fired by an ideology that proposes to marry Islamic with modern Western (mainly Marxist) thought, they played an important part in the overthrow of the Shah. But they soon fell out with Khomeini and his narrow obscurantist conception of "Islamic government". Ever since 1981, they have been engaged in "armed struggle" against him ... The few outsiders to have visited the NLA tend to come away impressed by its dedication, discipline and general level of education ...

We held a public meeting in Rome to celebrate the victory, under the slogan 'Today Mehran, tomorrow Tehran'. I made a speech which concluded: 'In Operation Sun we captured four tanks and, using them, we took fifty more. Can you be in any doubt that with fifty tanks we can capture 500 – and so defeat the revolutionary guards in Tehran?' I received long applause, during which I turned towards the pictures of Masoud and Maryam and started clapping myself to imply that the applause was for their wise leadership – a gesture I had learned from Abrishamchi.

I was recalled to Baghdad in July. Curious about a crowd gathered around our building's noticeboard, I went over to see what the attraction was. The news was brief but immensely shocking. After almost a year, the regime had been compelled to accept Resolution 598 of the UN Security Council. Consequently, a ceasefire was enacted along the entire Iran-Iraq border. What had seemed unimaginable until a few hours earlier had now suddenly become fact. I could scarcely believe it, so I went to the newsroom, where the air was electric with activity. A bulletin was being rushed out; there could be no doubt about it, although no one ventured to interpret the news. All the high-ranking *masouls* had vanished, apparently to an emergency session in Rajavi's office.

Resolution 598 was the strongest effort made to stop the Iran-Iraq war. Iraq accepted it immediately after ratification, but

Khomeini held off for a year, during which time Iran was subjected to increasing political and economic pressure from the international community, especially the West, as well as Mojahedin and Iraqi advances. After Iraq's destruction of many oilfields and refineries (especially Iran's main oil terminal on Kharg Island) Iran had to import some refined petroleum products and its oil revenue shrunk to a mere fraction of the normal level. The sale of arms to Iran was banned after the Iran-Contra affair came to light; it was unable even to buy spare parts for weaponry. So Iran began threatening oil shipments in the Persian Gulf. The US retaliated, bombing Iranian planes and ships. On 3rd July 1988 the Gulf-based US warship *Vincennes* mistook an Iranian passenger jet for a bomber and shot it down, killing 290 civilians. Meanwhile the advancing Iraqis used poison gas against Iranian civilians, killing 4,000 in one village alone and raising the prospect of similar attacks on larger cities, including Tehran. In April, after a two-day struggle, Iraqi troops recovered the town of Fav at a loss of over 5,300 Iraqis and as many as 120,000 Iranians.

On 2nd June Khomeini appointed Hashemi Rafsanjani head of the armed forces. To serious observers of Iranian politics this was a clear sign of surrender, a move towards pragmatism and ultimately peace. But not for our leader, sunk in wishful thinking and his own interpretation of events, which was diametrically opposed to reality but which we all accepted blindly then. Rajavi issued a statement declaring:

> ... Rafsanjani's nomination implies that Khomeini will never accept peace except in extreme desperation, knowing the immediate outcome of acceptance will be the overthrow of the regime. Also, this nomination will quash any naïve suggestion that acceptance of Resolution 598 is evidence of the regime's moderation. From now on, presenting Rafsanjani as a moderate is a void idea ... By appointing him the top man responsible for continuing the war and suppression, Khomeini has been forced to put an end to this illusion.

Two days after accepting the resolution, Khomeini gave a speech in which he said:

With this announcement we have neutralised the weapon of propaganda of those who would devour the world [imperialists and Americans] ... accepting this was more deadly than any poison for me. But I am pleased when God is pleased, and for his satisfaction I drank this poison ...

By defining this act as 'drinking poison', Khomeini gave us great propaganda. Rajavi seized on it, saying, 'The NLA and the Mojahedin, through their victorious operations, have forced Khomeini to drink the poison ... at any moment his regime will collapse!' Despite his inaccurate predictions and faulty analysis, our leader now had the effrontery to claim he was 'right' and 'victorious'!

Soon afterwards many members and *masouls* from our section, including me, were transferred to the army. We wondered what new adventures awaited. I had additional worries; my physical fitness was near zero. As a result of the accident I had years earlier, I could not even coordinate my movements properly for morning rituals. Our daily routine consisted of sixteen hours' sedentary work. I had gained weight; simply running exhausted me.

We passed through Iraqi controls and saw anti-aircraft missiles stationed around our base. Ashraf was the largest Mojahedin base in Iraq. When the Iraqis first gave it to us, it had a few buildings we called 'the castle'; the rest was desert. The Mojahedin had vastly improved the site, laying asphalt streets, planting trees, installing street lamps and traffic signs. The only reminder that we were in Iraq was the large portrait of Saddam at the end of the main road. We didn't dare remove it, but we directed visiting reporters to other parts of the base where they would not see it.

My commander was Mansur, a gentle and soft-spoken man in his late thirties, the antithesis of the military type. He introduced me to five officers and explained that the commanding council of the brigade would consist of them five and ourselves. Afshin was his deputy, three officers would be battalion commanders, one in charge of ammunition; I was to be logistics commander. He explained that I would head a battalion as well as supervising provisions, medical care, machine servicing, brigade schedules, storage ...

He stopped, seeing my dropped jaw and wide eyes. 'Don't

worry,' he said, 'you don't have much time, but you'll learn what you need to know. Afshin will help you and answer any questions you have. But remember, from now on you are in charge, and you'll have to deal with a constant flow of demands for instant, first-class service at the shortest possible notice, day and night. How smoothly the other battalions work will depend on how well you do your job. You must be as patient and helpful as possible. Unfortunately, we have to allocate all experienced battalions to the front lines; you will usually have the most inexperienced personnel, with special problems of their own.' I saw wry smiles on the other faces, and feared that my own was turning into a mask of death from fear. 'Don't worry', he repeated. 'I am painting the worst possible picture. It won't be as bad as that. 'Well', I said, 'could you please tell me about the easy part of my job too?' Everybody laughed, and he replied, 'There aren't any', which provoked more laughter.

Afshin showed me to my room and introduced me to my four deputies. They were well experienced, but I knew they would not be with me for long before being transferred, so I had little time to learn as much as possible from them. I was in the habit of learning by reading, taking notes and reviewing them calmly in my own time. Here I didn't even have stationery, having to borrow it from a deputy. As soon as I entered the room my phone started ringing and didn't stop until two in the morning. Even when I wasn't in my room, I received demands via wireless. I hadn't driven for some years, but now had an obsolete Iranian-made jeep to drive.

The following day Mansur called a meeting. He said, 'As you know, since the regime accepted Resolution 598, many things have changed suddenly. Perhaps Masoud [he indicated me] can elaborate on the significance of this event later. We had another plan for the final offensive, but events have forced us to act now. Hence we have less than a week to prepare ourselves to free the country. To test our capability, in two days' time we will have our biggest manoeuvre to date.'

I learned a lot in the next few days, including that checklists, which in my Newcastle days had been my miracle solution for everything, were useless in this context. However, preparations went according to plan despite unbelievable haste and pressure; fortunately, unlike poor Hassan who died of heatstroke, I tolerated heat well. During one quieter moment, I approached Afshin and said,

'We are going into battle and I have to command a battalion, and I don't even know how to handle a firearm.'

He laughed and said, 'I thought you had at least fired a bullet in Operation Sun! Well, don't worry. When you need to learn something you do it with unimaginable speed.' He took a Kalashnikov and showed me how to load and shoot it. 'OK,' he said, 'it's your turn.' The noise of that first bullet almost sent me reeling, which made Afshin laugh loudly. I had a few more practice shots and that was it: the sum total of my military training before our final operation. I never fired another shot while in the army, although later it fell to me to learn a lot about firearms.

The next day there was a rally with our leader for all combatants. Our brigade sat close to the stage, as we were going to be the first to cross the border into Iran.

Rajavi gave a rousing speech, interrupted from the floor by the usual slogans – 'Today Mehran, tomorrow Tehran!'; 'With Masoud and Maryam we shall fight to the end!'; and, of course, 'Iran-Rajavi, Rajavi-Iran!' The mood was jubilant, triumphal, manic with energy and anticipation. People jumped up and down, others leapt onto chairs, sang and shouted. God knows how many chairs were broken that night.

Rajavi, still unable to accept that his interpretation was false, was under the impression that an international plot was afoot. In truth, the regime had accepted the resolution of its own accord. But he believed it had acted on the basis of a deal with the West; that Khomeini had been forced to yield power to the 'moderate' faction by choosing Rafsanjani as head of the armed forces; and that the next government to be installed would be similar to Bakhtiar's government at the end of the Shah's era. Perhaps Bazargan might become prime minister again. If these events took place, it meant, quite simply, the end of the Mojahedin, for at least a few years or even for decades to come. He knew that if the Iraqis accepted a ceasefire as the first stage of Resolution 598, the Mojahedin could never cross the border in force; this would be a violation of the ceasefire from the Iraqi side. Rajavi met with Saddam, asking for a few weeks' grace before official acceptance of the ceasefire. He was given only one week to do whatever he could, so this was our last opportunity; if we lost it, we would certainly not get another.

Before any major operation Rajavi usually showed us a map of the area to be attacked; this time the map depicted the whole of Iran. This, he said, was the area we had to invade. These words were greeted with more wild enthusiasm and slogans. We applauded Mojahedin-style, above our heads, stamping our feet to make as much noise as possible.

Then Rajavi came to the battle plan. As the first brigade, our job was to break the defensive line of the regime and invade Kerend. The next brigade would invade Islamabad, then Kermanshah, then Hamedan and eventually Tehran and Jamaran, Khomeini's residence. He warned us to take Khomeini alive, as he would have to be brought to trial in a people's court to answer for his crimes. Rajavi asked if anyone had any comments, objections or questions. Most of us were too overawed to do so, but one sister bravely asked how our small army could expect to take on the revolutionary guards and the Iranian army and win.

'If we leave some of our troops behind in cities on our way to Tehran,' she said, 'there will be no army left to fight when we reach the capital.'

The crowd stirred angrily. Rajavi called for silence and replied, 'We will not be fighting alone; we will have the people on our side. They are tired of this regime, and especially since the ceasefire, they have every incentive to get rid of it forever. We will only have to act as a their shields, protecting them from being easy targets for the guards. Wherever we go there will be masses of citizens joining us, and the prisoners we liberate from jails will help us lead them towards victory. It will be like an avalanche, growing as it progresses. Eventually the avalanche will tear Khomeini's web apart. You don't need to take anything with you. We will be like fish swimming in a sea of people. They will give you whatever you need.'

He concluded, saying, 'This is the most probable outcome. But we are followers of Imam Hussein, so we cannot discount the possibility of another Ashorra where all of you could be killed. Like our ideological leader, we will leave our name and story for the generations that come after us.' He asked if we were ready for either consequence. The question dropped like a bomb into the crowd, and the answer was like an explosion of endorsement.

When the noise died down he turned to the girl who had asked the question and asked if she was satisfied with the answer. She said yes.

She was one of the martyrs of that operation.

My impression was that Iranians were unwilling to get involved in armed action of any kind, and although I wanted to cling to the hope that Rajavi held out, I feared and expected the other alternative, complete wipe-out. So, knowing that this might be our last chance to see friends and loved ones, a group of us from Britain gathered in a corner, laughing and reminiscing about the good old days there. We arranged to meet again, God willing, in Tehran – or if not, at specified points in heaven. Sister Tahereh, who was our *masoul* for several years, saw us and came over, smiling.

'Wherever we leave you British, you start plotting against everyone else. I presume by now you have named where in Tehran where you will meet again? Tell me, on which side of Freedom Square are you going to meet?'

We laughed; someone said, 'On the east side, and we think that after so many years in Britain, you should join us as well.' She turned to go, throwing an amused 'Never!' over her shoulder. Then we kissed each other, knowing perfectly well this would be our last goodbye, that many of us would indeed never meet again.

The next day I spoke with two of our battalion commanders. 'What did you think of our sister's question at that meeting?' they asked.

I replied, 'From what I have seen abroad, Iranians are not prepared to involve themselves in any armed action and will probably never again show any interest in another revolution; but of course, my judgement is based on Iranians abroad. For all I know, the people at home may think quite differently. So I guess they are reserving judgement about what will happen in days to come. Personally, I am going to follow Masoud's advice and prepare for another Ashorra. Anything that is better than that is a bonus, and I shall be happy with the outcome.' They told me I was pessimistic, that Masoud had said we would probably win.

'I hope so,' I said, trying to brush speculation aside, 'but for now we must get ready to move out.'

We worked '48 hours per day by borrowing some time from God'. My phone rang constantly, with endless demands – for food, equipment, flags, vehicles – about which I had been warned. Thanks to the Iraqis we received new equipment daily. We had no clue how any of it worked. Our battalion got some Brazilian tanks for the first time. I studied the manual as we hadn't a clue how to operate them; most of them would be left, empty, on the battlefield. The manual came in handy again when our tankers were stuck in a queue waiting for petrol and oil at a station with a defective main pump. The manual revealed that the tanks had their own pumps. Knowing some English thus saved another few hours' wait.

As we left the base, we passed Masoud and Maryam standing in an open car, waving. It was an emotional farewell. Who could say whether we would see them again?

At the Iran-Iraq Khosravi border a sign reading 'welcome' in Persian had miraculously survived the devastation. Thanks to the Iraqis, who had fought the Iranians before us, the regime's defensive line was opened up to the environs of Kerend, so without any fighting we were able to advance. On the way to Sarpol-Zahab, another ruined city, we passed through Ghasr-Shirin. I remembered this city from my first trip with Anna, sixteen years earlier. Perhaps as young lovers we had chased each other among the city's beautiful trees. Now I wondered if it had really been as beautiful as I remembered, or whether love had lent it a romantic glow and burned it into my memory. It was a scene of total destruction. Not a single palm tree survived; not a single house remained on its foundations. I wondered whether we would recognise our country or our people when we saw them again. Where were the people who once lived there? What were they doing now – that man who sold me a second-hand American cowboy coat, that woman who sold Anna some soap?

We received orders via wireless to stop and rest at Sarpol-Zahab. Immediately, a dreadful smell assailed us 'That', said Afshin, 'is the smell of human corpses. Human physiology is complex; when it rots it has the worst smell of all beings.' I could not bear to sleep with the others in the open air, remaining in the jeep with the windows closed. Who were these dead people, I wondered. What did they look like? Who loved them? But in the middle of a war there was no room for thinking so. After a short break, I woke people for breakfast and came to the horrible realisation that we had forgotten the bread. For all our five-page checklists, for all the different fruit juices, dried foods and containers we had, we had neglected that most essential provision. We had two trucks full of materials and not a single loaf of bread. I had no choice but to send someone to the backing post, before the border, to get bread. Meanwhile, we made do with tea, biscuits and fruit juice.

The Mojahedin had asked all supporters abroad to join the final battle against the regime, and a few hundred came forward. My commander now introduced me to a few new American recruits and asked me to place them in the battalion: they, too, lacked fighting experience. By now I had so many people without experience around me that I began to feel like a professional soldier by comparison. I also had a few new combatants recruited from among POWs, freed by Rajavi. Speaking with them, I saw how much we had changed, how vast was the gap between ordinary Iranians and ourselves. Even our vocabulary was different. We used a lot of French and English words (like 'OK'), and language that meant nothing to them: the word 'service', for example, had several meanings in Mojahedin vocabulary, from requesting a lift to asking for salt at the dinner table, from servicing a car to taking a child to the toilet.

But I never had the chance to get to know these new recruits or even remember their names. Later I heard that all of them had been killed at a petrol station, filling tanks, when an Iranian plane attacked.

I showed a few of those ex-POWs how to fill the tanks of the different carriers and then attended to the bread, which had now arrived, so we could start feeding people. We were all eating when we heard a plane above our heads. We didn't take much notice, thinking it was the same plane we had seen earlier inspecting our area; there was a murmur of '*kabotar*' ('dove'), the code name for an Iraqi plane. Then a voice rose above the rest saying, '*baz, baz!*' ('hawk'), referring to an Iranian plane. At once we heard shelling, some very close to us, near where we had filled our tanks. I looked over to see a pipe from a petrol tank lying on the ground, petrol flowing out everywhere. I ran to it, alarmed, and realised that as the new recruits didn't know how to stop the flow of petrol from the tank, they had simply left the pipe on the ground. God knows how many would have died in the explosions of those tanks if a shell had fallen just a little closer.

We never found out why the plane stopped shelling. We were in an open area and quite defenceless. Some said it was an Iraqi plane aiming at an Iranian patrol nearby, or that it was simply a mistake. Others speculated it was an Iranian plane which had held its fire, thinking we were friendly forces: we had an Iranian flag and wore khaki uniforms like them. Later, Rafsanjani gave an address in which he said, 'We knew they were coming and kept them under surveillance, but we took little action as we wanted them all deep inside the country where we could finish them off. So we let them advance as far as they could.' On Monday 25th July, Maryam's voice came through the wireless with the order to open fire and advance. Everything was very still. It was hot and difficult to stay awake. Suddenly we heard shelling. A few kilometres down the road we saw some Iranian soldiers. They waved, and we waved back. They were among those who had surrendered and been released to go wherever they liked. Then we saw our first ordinary countryman, a shepherd, with his flock. He, too, waved to us. Our dream was coming true. For the first time we could believe in our leader's promise of popular support. My deputy Daryosh and I were deeply moved by these signs of solidarity and, we thought, final victory.

We had strict orders not to stop for any reason, but when we came upon some stationary vehicles with dead or wounded combatants lying in the road, we naturally stopped to help. Just then shelling resumed. Suddenly I felt hot and was thrown aside and lost consciousness, hit by shrapnel. When I came to I found myself beside our jeep. Nobody was around, not even the wounded fighters I had seen before. I had no pain, but there was blood everywhere. My right hand was almost hanging from my arm; my left leg seemed partly immobilised and I could not see properly out of my left eye. I hauled myself into the driver's seat. Fortunately, the vehicle started. I used my left hand for everything. As I felt I might lose consciousness again at any moment, I drove at top speed. After a while, I caught a glimpse of the last vehicle in our convoy, my deputy's. They were astonished to see me alive and took me to an armoured carrier used to transport invalids where I found Daryosh, also injured. He couldn't look me in the eye. 'I thought you had been killed', he apologised. 'We searched for you, but couldn't find you. As soon as those bloody soldiers saw the last vehicle of our battalion pass by, they returned to their positions and started firing at us. They got a proper response from the brigade after us! By then we had moved on.'

We were, disastrously, fatally, taken in by our own propaganda. We blithely believed that all Iranians, even the revolutionary guards, were on our side and fighting for the *mullahs* only out of fear of Khomeini's regime. We assumed anyone who greeted us or mentioned Rajavi was our supporter and a potential combatant. It took me years to recognise this as an illusion. Our enemy knew this weakness of ours and exploited it ruthlessly.

In the vehicle there was another wounded combatant. We chatted and shared our happiness at being inside Iran. After a minute or two, he stopped talking. I lost consciousness again, and when I awoke I found him dead beside me. It was an instant in which the meaning of death changed for me utterly. Hitherto I had been afraid of touching a dead body; now I instinctively touched him and said, 'Goodbye, unknown friend, perhaps we shall meet again in a few hours' time.' Was this the meaning of martyrdom? According to our teaching, martyrs are not dead but alive. They are clean; after touching them one does not need to perform the ritual of religious washing. Suddenly this made sense to me. I could not see this man as a corpse. He was alive, perhaps even more alive than other people. I felt no sadness or pity for him. I was sure he was where he hoped to be. What higher honour could one wish for than martyrdom, with a relatively painless death, in the final operation between good and evil, in our own country, on the edge of victory?

I was taken to the 'hospital' in Kerend, really an empty building with a few beds. I had no pain, perhaps because of an injection, and was overjoyed to speak with a few of my countrymen from Kerend who carried me in and kept me company. Our television crew there even filmed me and wanted an interview. 'Tell me the questions and answers first,' I joked, referring to the Mojahedin's habit of dictating answers to interviewees beforehand. Behrang, our brigade doctor, explained that I would be moved back to Iraq. He told me he couldn't stop the bleeding, which came from the shoulder; even amputating my arm wouldn't save me. He said, 'I am pretty sure we are going to lose you within a few hours, at most in a day.' I sensed he was wrong and said so, reminding him that I was still his commander, that he had to report to me and await my decisions.

When I next awoke, he handed me the wireless and said, 'Mansur [my commander] wants to talk to you.' Mansur said, 'Congratulations! We took Kerend without many casualties, and captured Islamabad too. We are on our way to Kermanshah.' Then he continued, 'I am afraid we must move you and some other injured fighters behind the lines.' I started to remonstrate with him, but he dismissed my arguments. 'Let me be frank with you. In your condition you are no use to us. You occupy a bed that we will need for wounded men. You are taking up the time and energy of our doctor, of which we need every second. And what can you do here, even if you live? You can't walk properly and you'll have only one hand, as the other one will most probably require amputation. Anyway, this is an order. You will be moved back. See you in Tehran.'

So, ten other badly injured men and I were returned by truck behind the lines. On the road we saw corpses lying by the roadside, the same soldiers who had waved to us, and the old shepherd in a pool of blood, along with his dead sheep and goats. Iranian jets flew overhead, bombarding the area. Another truck carrying the bodies of combatants was hit and burst into flames. To avoid being hit, our driver deliberately drove erratically, sometimes leaving the road completely. The swerving movements caused us intense pain. One young boy – I guessed, from his attitude and speech, a POW – shouted and swore at the driver, not understanding the situation. His left leg hung by a few nerves and blood vessels from his body. As the truck lurched into the air the boy yelled again, louder. I think he must have lost his leg altogether at that point. Most of the time we were barely conscious because of the pain.

Eventually we were airlifted by helicopter to the nearest hospital, where some of the wounded stayed while the worst cases, including myself, were moved to another hospital in central Baghdad. I was operated on immediately. When I came to I was in a very large hall, with perhaps thirty people in adjacent beds. I asked the person to my right the date and time, and when he told me I said, 'By now, according to plan, our forces should be somewhere close to Hamedan. We should already have taken Kermanshah.'

'I think not', he said. 'If that were the case, the mood here wouldn't be so calm: even the dead would be dancing!'

There was a needle in my arm and a bag connected to it for collecting blood and other liquids. I was told my leg and eye injuries were not serious, but the vein in my shoulder was still bleeding and I might need another operation if it did not stop. A few Iraqi nurses looked after us, but were too busy most of the time to dole out painkillers or help us go to the toilet. Fortunately, morale was high among the patients, and they helped each other as much as possible. My bleeding worsened, and I was returned to the operating theatre. During the operation, I somehow regained consciousness, perhaps because of a weak dose of anaesthetic. At first glance I saw no one beside me, but then I looked around. The scene was more slaughterhouse than operating theatre. Naked boys and girls lay in adjacent beds. In one bed they were amputating the leg of a girl, in another, someone's arm. There was blood everywhere; doctors moved swiftly from one bed to another to minister to the worst cases first. I couldn't believe what I was seeing It was a nightmare. Someone must have realised from my reactions that I was not unconscious, and gave me another injection to knock me out.

When I awoke, some of my comrades were around me. A radio and a television set in the room broadcasted Mojahedin channels. It was obvious that the programmes had been pre-recorded. None of the Mojahedin present was prepared to talk about current events, saying only that everything was going according to plan. But how could that be? According to plan we would then have been in Tehran. Even if we took only Kermanshah, I knew many things would change: the establishment of a free-Iranian government on Iranian soil would be announced, followed by its recognition by Iraq, a treaty signed between ourselves and Iraq and perhaps recognition by some other countries, including friendly Arab ones, then an inflow of financial and military aid. If we held Kermanshah, we could mount another struggle against the regime, this time from within our own country. This would cause the regime serious problems on the international scene as well. I concluded that we had not been able to reach Kermanshah, which might mean we had lost the war and most if not all of our fighters.

Everybody seemed think the same. The high morale and optimism had gone. Most of the time we were sunk deep in thought. One *masoul* visited me and said, 'I presume you have guessed by now what has happened. We have lost many people, and many more are in hospitals or held captive by the regime, although fortunately the majority have returned safely. We must keep morale high and help others to face the situation. Once they know what it is, the wounded are going to feel even sorrier for themselves. The Iraqis are doing what little they can, but essentially it is up to us to help everybody.'

For the first time real sadness set in. I envied the dead. I had prepared myself for another Ashorra and here I was, alive, facing an unknown and unpromising future. I felt betrayed by our leader – not because of our failure, but because he had promised either victory or another Ashorra, and now we were in a hellish, desperate situation. The regime could now make peace with the Iraqis on better terms than before. Even if they did not bury their differences, at least neither would take offensive action against the other. So we were to be band of refugees for the rest of our lives, wandering without a home, without a goal.

Still, I tried to put on a brave, happy face and cheer people up. I visited another ward housing patients with appalling injuries, far worse than ours – perhaps because they'd been less prepared for battle. One woman who had featured on the cover of our magazine had lost an eye, a leg and an arm. Hers was not a rare case: everywhere I looked I saw people without limbs or eyes. One patient told me his story. 'When we were attacked, we abandoned the tank as we didn't know how to use it and were afraid it would became our coffin. We found out that everybody did the same thing.' Then he brightened unaccountably. 'Well, there was fire everywhere, suddenly I saw my leg on fire, I had no choice but to cut it off and leave it behind and get out of there.' When he saw my shock and puzzlement, he laughed. 'You know, it was an artificial one. I lost my leg in another operation, and what could I do with a half-burned artificial leg? So I left it behind.'

One of the Mojahedin who was helping us in hospital was an old friend from London. When he saw me he said, 'Oh God, I am so happy to see you. Your name was on my list of the fallen!'

'Sorry to destroy your faith in the list. Yes, I am alive. But tell me about the others. Who is alive and who is martyred?'

Many from England were martyred: Mohsen, my deputy during the time of the Sadatti Society and afterwards, perhaps the kindest person I ever met in the Mojahedin; Allah-yar, one of my charges in London, who was transferred after I left England; Ali and his wife from Pakistan, who told us how to benefit from the British tradition of sponsorship;. Behnam, who had banged his head in frustration during the ideological revolution; Sharif, who made us all laugh; Hamid, the best of my old *masouls*; Siros, my Paris assistant; Morad and Azita, who had met in the organisation and married; Hamzeh, torn between his girlfriend and the organisation, who eventually chose the latter; Aliraza from Belgium; and too many more besides. The list grew longer daily; with each loss I called them to mind one by one, crying and laughing over the memories I had of them.

Amidst all the sadness, there was jubilation and congratulations in the media about the accomplishments of the NLA in what we now called 'Operation *Forogh Javidan*' ('Eternal Light'). Islamabad and Kerend had been liberated. The NLA had penetrated 150km inside Iran. Tens of thousands of Khomeini's guards had been killed or wounded. But there was no mention of the number of our casualties. The regime first announced a figure of 4,800, but later discovered this was far too close to the number of our troops, estimated at 7,000, and therefore false. About ten years later, when the organisation published names and photographs of martyrs from that operation for the first time, the number of martyred was announced as 1,304. Our other losses were officially 1,100 injured, of whom 11 subsequently died; 612 vehicles, 21 cannons, 72 tanks ...

Those of us who didn't need urgent or intensive hospital treatment were discharged to free up beds and staff time. Although my bleeding had stopped, the nurses didn't have time to do anything about broken bones. Not until a few weeks later did they realise my bones were broken in seven places and put my shoulder and right arm in plaster.

On my return to the base, I found that as our brigade had been stationed in Kerend we had sustained fewer casualties than others. Some brigades had been completely annihilated. One of the battalion commanders explained that, 'in the last days of the fighting, rules and order broke down. Many of our combatants lost the white sleeves that differentiated them from the enemy. The enemy had got hold of some, anyway, and tricked us by wearing them too. We had code names, but it was often impossible for the commander to transmit them to all his combatants. Many units became separated and we ended up fighting each other, although it was the same for the regime's guards. Once we encountered some fighters and asked who they were. They said they were NLA. We asked them the password but they didn't know, so I ordered them to retreat. They said, "If we do that we will reach the enemy lines and we'll all be killed." They started to approach, so I had no choice but to order my men to open fire. Even now I am not sure if they were ours or enemy soldiers, but what else could we do?'

Mansur asked me to lead the morning ceremony every day, as my being 'heroically' injured would restore morale. He suggested showing some funny films, organising celebrations, serving better food and arranging sporting matches between brigades.

Soon we were summoned to a general meeting with the leadership. Naturally the mood was more sombre than before. We recited all the usual slogans but without our previous fervour.

As one of the commanders, I was privileged to sit in the front row. Abrishamchi came up to me and lightly asked, 'Are you a wounded commander?'

'Yes', I said with a laugh.

'Ok', he said, 'go and sit in the back row with the other wounded men. We don't want to portray our army as injured and broken, do we?' Then he added, 'And while you are sitting there make sure you fulfil your responsibility to keep up morale.' He was right. This was a demonstration that we were alive and ready for further action, that we had not sustained many losses and that our morale remained high. Slogans were recited as before, if not as profusely as before, and in a more controlled way. Inevitably Rajavi called the operation another victory for the Mojahedin, the most important one to date and 'a severe, strategic blow to Khomeini's remaining forces of suppression, coming at a time when his regime is on the verge of complete disintegration.' The resistance had got the upper hand, he added, and the consequences would shortly be seen in various political, military and social domains.

The next day I was reluctantly transferred back to the diplomacy section in Paris, as deputy *masoul*.

# 28

# Love, Loss and Logic

Apart from political duties, my main job was to head the NCR's secretariat. My new *masoul* was Ahmad, a man well-suited to dealing with a range of people with different expectations. I believe our Paris office was the only branch of the organisation outside of Iraq receiving money, instead of giving it; having lost so many members and supporters in battle, we were short of cash. Hence one of my main tasks was to reduce our budget. This was a theme common to all the posts I held thereafter.

Ahmad filled me in regarding the mood of the NCR members and others around us after Operation Forogh. Emotionally they were in very bad shape, he said. They thought it was a total failure, not a political mistake but a wrong decision taken by Rajavi based on poor judgement. Many had died, others lost children. They were saddened, upset and *talakbar* (a Mojahedin word meaning they felt the leadership owed them something; it was a most insulting term). 'The main reason you are here,' he said, 'is to neutralise these feelings. You participated in the operation and were injured, you can tell them first-hand what you saw. They cannot deny your courage and sacrifices. They will listen to you.'

Ahmad gave me the files of my colleagues and charges. Reading them gave me insight into the Mojahedin's ranking system. Whenever we were promoted we were told it was an award, but reminded that 'rank' was a token of more responsibility not a reward. By contrast, only in the most dire cases were we told about demotion. We would be left to guess our status when asked not to attend certain meetings. In public my brief was to respect as a person anyone under my supervision, as he or she was a member of the NCR and supposedly a Mojahedin coalition partner. In work and in private, I dealt with them according to their rank and did my best to help them rise to a higher level of sacrifice and thus rank. I was expected to be even more contradictory and two-faced in this behaviour than in diplomacy. At least in diplomacy we were only actors playing roles *vis-à-vis* foreigners, who understood the nature of the play and were acting in it themselves. But we used the same artifice in relation to our own people.

Our council base was a very large house named after one of the most respected Marxists executed by Khomeini, Shokrollah Paknajad, or 'Shokrie' for short. It was near a forest and had an extensive garden with many old trees. Most of the residents had their own rooms in the main building or adjoining bungalows. Everyone's job consisted of writing – for Mojahedin publications or other organisations that were members of the council, and primarily for *Shora*, a periodical edited by Dr Hezarkhani, one of the foremost intellectuals of the Shah's era and a council member. Publishing that booklet was our principal preoccupation. My deputy was a former football player who had played for the national team during the Shah's time. He and his wife were our housekeepers and general administrators. I divided my time between Shokrie, where I dealt with issues concerning council members, and the other Mojahedin base, nicknamed 'Oeuvre', short for 'Oeuvre-sur-Oise', where I was concerned with our political activities.

I was at Shokrie during the day and also one night a week, when members of the council and many 'personalities' vaguely designated 'supportive of the organisation' gathered for discussions. We were to be as charming and hospitable as possible on these occasions, just to sit and listen. My reports on the discussions went straight to Baghdad, to Rajavi himself. It was fascinating to meet these diverse characters with their different agendas. There was a poet, apparently full of fine sentiments who hesitated to say anything except relate stories from his youth. Behind his back, Ahmad whispered to me, 'Damn poet. With all our hardships, we have to pay him extortion money every month just to stop him writing anything against us.' There were a few old Marxist 'revolutionaries', talking to each other about recent events in the USSR and their comrades in other Marxist organisations.

Strangely, the Mojahedin tolerated people with different ideologies much more readily than they tolerated non-Mojahedin Muslims – presumably because it was unacceptable for an Iranian to call himself a Muslim and share our political goals without subscribing to Rajavi's 'ideological leadership'. After all, who would such a person's Imam be? There was a deserter from the Iranian navy, who was still in mourning his young daughter, killed in Operation Forogh. He could scarcely disguise his bitterness. 'We criticise Khomeini for sending young children into minefields,' he said once, 'yet we did exactly the same, sending untrained, inexperienced young people to fight against revolutionary guards and inevitably to be killed.'

While I was studying them to see who was genuine, perhaps they scrutinised me too. Certainly it made me question myself. I seemed to have been trying to deny my own character in deference to the dictated by the organisation. I saw in the non-Mojahedin members of the council a humanity and frankness, an ability to care for and relate to others that had long since vanished in the Mojahedin. Of course, Mojahedin did not deny such character traits in ourselves, but feelings for individuals were regarded as superficial and peripheral. The exception was Rajavi, through whom our love could be transmitted to all humanity. Other personal relationships were 'like very small lakes, which can vanish in the hot summer sun', whereas our love for Rajavi was 'like a sea growing ever larger with tides rising ever higher'. Anyway, after a while I allowed myself to accept these people as they really were and show affection for them. Whether they felt the same I do not know; perhaps they thought me just another accomplished actor. The only time I put on an act was when my *masoul* required me to reproach someone for not showing Rajavi enough respect.

A few months later Rajavi decreed that high-ranking members

who had lost spouses remarry to restore morale. A host of such
enforced marriages took place, in Paris and elsewhere. One young
man came to Paris to marry a woman who had lost a leg and was
still in hospital having treatment. The edict was not restricted only
to those whose spouses had died, as I discovered when our section
head asked to see me while I was in Iraq. He asked, very bluntly,
'What is going on between you and your wife?' I was taken aback,
and paused before replying, wondering what the 'correct' answer
was.

'Well, we have not seen each other for almost two years.'

'What does that mean? Are you divorced, or what?'

I said, 'I realised I couldn't respond to her demands and those
of the organisation at the same time. So I told her we would have
to separate for as long as Khomeini is in power. I also reminded her
that it is her right to divorce me and remarry at any time she
wishes.'

'What about you?' he asked. 'Do you want to divorce and
remarry?'

'No. I don't want to think about divorce or marriage, I want to
do my job.'

'I don't think so. As one of our *masouls* you can't stay in this
situation. You must decide; either ask your wife to come and stay
with you or divorce her and marry somebody the organisation
introduces you to.' He asked me to think about what he had said
and give him my reply the next day.

This was a painful time for me. I was still very much in love with
Anna and devoted to my children; I didn't want to leave them as
long as they hadn't left me. I thought the decision to part for the
duration of the war was right for all of us. Anna and the children
could lead ordinary lives in London, without all the upheavals my
commitment imposed on them. It was not an unusual situation in
wartime: millions of families in Iran had done likewise, even
families in Britain during the recent Falklands war. I did not see
why, when separated for reasons beyond our control, our love
should die or our family ties be destroyed. Now I was forced into
this terrible dilemma. I could not ask them to join me when my life
and prospects were completely unpredictable. They would only
reproach me for uprooting them. But nor was I able to discard my
beloved wife and family and marry somebody for whom I had no
feelings, just to obey orders.

Ahmad was in Baghdad too, and asked my decision. I explained that I was not prepared to accept either alternative. 'Don't be a fool,' he said, 'if you still like your wife, the organisation will arrange to bring her to Paris to reunite.' He overruled any further objections, assuring me he would arrange everything.

A week later, back in Paris, I was called to his office. I was amazed to see Anna there. Apparently she had expressed her readiness to move to Paris. Ahmad sent us to one of the houses we owned, and for the first time in years I played the whole day and night with my children. But I was not convinced this was the right decision. The following day I went to Ahmad and said, 'This can't work. I demand they return to London. I know that in a few days' time they will want more of me, and I won't be able to give them that, and the old problems will arise again. Or I might be posted somewhere else, and their lives will be ruined.' He said, 'Don't be so pessimistic. Sister Tahereh spoke to Anna and believes she has changed greatly. She wants to be with you more than ever and is ready to pay the price. Apparently she regrets her past behaviour. She even wants to work with us again, and we will give her some responsibility at Shokrie, where you can be together more often.' Evidently I had not persuaded him. Perhaps, deep down, I had not persuaded myself.

Whatever the military outcome of Operation Forogh, politically the regime's hardliners were the main winners. The regime had been failing, politically and militarily, over the previous months, and with the lessening of the hardliners' influence the moderates, under Rafsanjani's leadership, had gained the upper hand. The defeat in battle of the Mojahedin and the creation of many new martyrs on the Iranian side – 11,000, according to them, about 55,000, according to us – gave the hardliners new spirit. Perhaps the Mojahedin captured during the operation had divulged, under the appalling torture practised in Iranian prisons, Rajavi's promise that Iranian prisoners would come to our aid. This was enough reason for the hardliners to demand the execution of all political prisoners.

President Khamenei, a hardliner himself, said on 6th December 1988, 'Have we abolished the death penalty here in the Islamic Republic? No ... When a prisoner has contacts with the *monafaghin* [hypocrites, i.e. Mojahedin] from inside prison, what do you think we should do with him? If his contacts with that network are established, what do you think we should do with him? He will be sentenced to death, and we will execute him ... Execution is a means of carrying out a divine verdict ... Do you think we should give sweets to those who have links from inside prison with the *monafaghin*?'

Hossein Ali Montazeri, Khomeini's designated successor, was a moderate who opposed executions. He wrote three famous letters to Khomeini revealing what was going on in the prisons, the result of which he lost his position and was put under house arrest. In one of his letters he mentioned the case of a prisoner being cross-examined by a prosecutor: 'Are you prepared to go to the front to fight against Iraq?' the prisoner was asked.

He said, 'Yes'.

'Are you prepared to walk on a mine?'

The prisoner balked. 'You should not expect so much from a new convert to Islam,' he said. This answer 'proved' to the prosecutor that the prisoner still adhered to his anti-regime position and the prisoner was, in Montazeri's words, 'subsequently subjected to the fate of such a person'.

In another letter addressed to the religious judge, prosecutor, and intelligence representative at Evin prison, Montazeri wrote that he had more reason than most to pursue revenge against the Mojahedin, who had murdered his son. Nevertheless: 'I take into consideration the judgement that will be passed by posterity. Such massacres without trial, especially of prisoners and captives, will certainly benefit them in the long run. The world will condemn us, and they will be more encouraged to wage armed struggle.' He cited wise and pious judges who testified to excesses and executions carried out arbitrarily. 'In the end,' he wrote, 'the Mojahedin are not individuals. Theirs is a way of thinking and an interpretation, a type of logic. Wrong logic must be answered with right logic. Murder will not solve it, it will spread it.'

The failure of Forogh and the number of our people killed or injured in that operation had ceased to be an issue. The only legitimate discussion concerned those executions – to condemn and stop them. The Mojahedin, in every statement, took care not to mention the operation, lest anyone link it with the wave of political executions. Their official line was that the executions were connected with the Iran-Iraq ceasefire. The number of executions rose inexorably, until they totalled around 12,000, according to Rajavi. He announced a new, unlimited hunger strike protest and urged Mojahedin everywhere to take part. The response was tremendous in Europe and America. Even those of us who had to work and could not demonstrate in the streets had to respect the hunger strike, so we did not eat anything for almost two weeks.

The executions produced a huge wave of outrage around the world. Within a short time we had received almost 1,800 signatures of support from Western politicians. The European Parliament passed a resolution of condemnation, as did many other international organisations. The UN Human Rights Commission passed its strongest ever resolution against the Iranian regime.

For years we had no dealings with Amnesty International, deemed tools of the British government, but now I opened a dialogue with them and started passing on news as I received it from Iran. In response they issued a series of daily 'Urgent Action' statements protesting the executions.

Many foreign politicians who supported the regime lost confidence in the so-called 'moderate' faction, while those inside Iran who saw their own positions endangered, like Rafsanjani, now adopted a more radical stance to save their skins. Rafsanjani even made a speech condoning the killing of Europeans and Americans by Palestinians. To keep the hardliners happy and boost the morale of the revolutionary guards, Khomeini stepped up his proclamations of the leadership of the Islamic world and reconfirmed the *fatwa* against Salman Rushdie and the publishers and sellers of his book *The Satanic Verses*.

Rajavi said the *fatwa* was 'due to the extreme desperation of the regime and the effect of drinking the "poison" of the ceasefire. Khomeini himself is the worst enemy of Islam … ' Rajavi and we who followed him were quite happy about the *fatwa*, which was a propaganda gift to us: Rajavi called it 'our political Forogh' and urged us to mobilise all our efforts to capitalise on it.

Around then Reza'i, my previous *masoul*, was transferred to Paris, replacing Ahmad, to coordinate our political effort in Europe. I was made his deputy in dealing with our council's and the Mojahedin's representatives in Europe. My job consisted of taking calls from representatives, giving them instructions and providing information for their interviews or press conferences. One of my main problems was resolving disputes between Mojahedin and council members, largely arising from different perceptions about who the supreme representatives of the resistance were who had ultimate responsibility.

Years earlier I had faced a similar problem. Doctor represented the council but, though he was our leader's brother, was not a Mojahed and was not trusted to act on behalf of the organisation or to speak for it. As the Mojahedin representative, I conducted delicate meetings without him. To avoid giving offence, we kept details of these meetings from him. Once, however, in my absence, my deputy showed him our agenda, on which was entered a meeting with Americans that I had denied was taking place. From then on he changed completely, calling me a liar and an egotist for not wanting him to participate in that important meeting. That day he insisted on giving us a lift to our base; when we got there he jumped out of the car to open the door for us like a 'chauffeur'. I thought I would melt like ice in the sun from shame. Later I called my *masoul* and demanded she find a solution. I assume they talked to him but I don't think he ever forgave me, nor did I get the opportunity to explain my conduct.

Meanwhile, many more on the international scene were coming round to our side. The rules of the European Parliament precluded us ever being allowed to pass a resolution through normal debate, but if we persuaded a majority of its members then a declaration could be converted into a resolution. So we mobilised all our people around Europe to get support for our declaration. We obtained around 300 signatures, a majority of parliament members, and the resolution was announced in Parliament as representing the position of the parliament towards us. Inevitably it angered not only the regime but as also many Iranians outside Iran who objected to recognising the Mojahedin as the true representatives of the Iranian people. We emerged as winners, though the European Parliament changed its procedures thereafter and made it more difficult for anybody else to repeat our action.

This success, and Rajavi's unremitting claim that 'we are the victors of Forogh', eventually persuaded us that Forogh had indeed been pure gain, perhaps even our biggest victory ever. It was another lesson in the magical efficacy of drip-fed propaganda.

Anna had changed too. She did not object to my scarcity around our new flat in Paris or to my frequent travels but even volunteered, in spring 1989, to go to Baghdad for a short military training course. Rajavi had persuaded us that war was imminent. Having learned their lesson from Forogh, the army organised training in combat and the use of armaments.

While Anna was away, I had the excuse I needed to spend more time with Hanif and Sarvy. The realisation of the depth of my love for my family now overwhelmed me. Every night, reading Hanif a bedtime story, I watched him with the whole of my being. Working beside him while he slept, I continued to watch him, thinking of his past and future. I missed Anna, and reproached myself for lacking sympathy and understanding when a colleague had lost his wife. I was horrified to recall how I had judged him 'less of a Mojahed' than I was.

On her return, Anna was less happy with her work in Paris. She regretted having gone to Iraq for training, where conditions were hard and over-militarised. A few weeks later she decided to take the children back to London to live with her mother, who had recently moved there. 'It is better for them,' she said, 'and after all we can visit you any time we want.' Again, I was to be separated from my children. I tried to dissuade her, but she was right and I knew it.

Between 3rd and 4th June 1989, we spent 24 hours straight on the phone. Khomeini's death was reported from several sources and eventually announced on Iran radio. This was the moment we had been waiting for. It was time, Rajavi said, to prepare for the final offensive. The organisation announced full mobilisation, and many members and supporters were ordered to leave for Baghdad. Within days the number of people in our bases shrank to a new low.

We saved time and energy by moving our people from Oeuvre to Shokrie. To that end we had to convert a stable, but as we lacked permission we had to do it ourselves. While moving a very heavy block into a well, I felt a severe pain in my back; for the next few days I could not move. I was hospitalised for a month. Once, when Anna came to visit me, I was overcome with emotion and begged her, for the first time, not to leave me. She said, 'The children are waiting for me, I must go.' When she left I recognised that I was on the verge of leaving the organisation. My feelings for my family were so strong, but I could see no end to our struggle, no prospect soon for reunion. If Anna had been less understanding and more selfish, if she had been less accepting of my way of thinking, or asked me to go with her, I probably would have. But she didn't and I was left with the dread of confessing to my *masoul* that I was on the edge of slipping into the 'hell' of an ordinary man with ordinary love.

When I was discharged I watched a video of Khomeini's funeral, followed by another that showed Rajavi rejoicing in the death of the 'bloodthirsty murderer'. A man was dead whom we had loved immeasurably ten years earlier as hero, leader, guru, and for whom our love had turned to implacable hatred. In his will he appealed to the Mojahedin:

> Wherever you are, if you have not committed any crime, you can return to your country and to Islam. You can repent and God will forgive you, and, God willing, the people and the Islamic Republic will forgive you too. If you have committed a crime, your penalty is known. If you are courageous enough, you can return and accept your punishment to secure your place in heaven ... Why waste your youth serving foreign powers, those who would devour the world? What wrong have your people done to you? You have been deceived ... Accept your mistake ... If we were to die at the hands of the murderous Americans or Soviets, we could meet our God with honour. Better than to live in wealth under the flag of the Red Army of the East or the black flag of the West ...

Khomeini married once and was reputedly reluctant even to harm a fly, preferring to whisk it away. He wrote and published poems. Who was he? Rajavi said: 'We wished he would steal our money as the Shah did, but kill our people less. We wished he would end the war sooner and avoid the killing of one million Iranians. We wished he had married 100 times and had not pushed our women into hiding and their worst conditions in history.' Who was he? Was he the absolute essence of evil as we depicted him? Or should we admit that no living creature is pure black or white?

The organisation predicted that Khomeini would nominate his son as his successor, that his regime could not last without him as, like the Shah, he had made everything dependent on him. On the day Khomeini died, Khamenei was elected the new leader and Rafsanjani was later elected president. A long and bitter fight between different factions of the new regime lay ahead.

It was the end of summer. Because of my injury, part of my body was in plaster. When the organisation summoned me back to Baghdad, I was ecstatic I had been rescued from the contradiction that was making my life hell.

# 29

# Throwing Stones at Satan

All the way from Paris to Baghdad, I worried about writing my report. How could I express my feelings? My faith in the organisation was ebbing fast. My belief in God and Islam was no stronger than it had been before I became a Mojahedin supporter; in fact, I was now losing any sense of morality or faith in anything, including the principle that 'one should not lie or deceive others for one's own objectives'. Emotionally I was on the edge of collapse. I was on the point of surrendering to love for my family and forgetting my oath to my people, my country and my God.

'We will achieve the downfall of the regime in a short time,' Abrishamchi had said. 'It didn't happen. So the Mojahedin extended the meaning of "a short time". And if "a short time" turns out to mean "as long as it takes" – a year, 100 years – what is the alternative? What else can we do? Live under Khomeini's regime?'

Operation Forogh dashed our political hopes. Worse, it signified the end of ideology, of moral belief and expectation – for me and, as I soon discovered, many others. Our basic values no longer had any meaning and ceased to sustain us. We had all become actors playing to each other, encouraged by each other. This lie reached its intolerable climax when our 'ideological leader' failed to admit his predictions and judgement had been wrong. The lie was prolonged not only in our propaganda, which would be an understandable political strategy, but among ourselves. Even in high-ranking meetings we had to praise Rajavi for winning victories no one could have brought to fruition.

Once, we had been told that belief in the Mojahedin was based on two premises: the sacrifices they were willing to make and their honesty. After Forogh the well of honesty completely dried up, and from then on the organisation rested on only one foundation: 'sacrifice' and more 'sacrifice'. To strengthen our belief in the organisation, we had to sacrifice more and accept that Rajavi had sacrificed more than anyone else.

Perhaps if we made ever greater and deeper sacrifices we could polish up our rusty beliefs and be moved to go forward. But were we able to gain the support of the people as before? We called Khomeini '*dajal*', the ultimate deceiver. We did not call him a thief, sex monster or mercenary in the pay of foreigners. Nor could we deny the sacrifices his supporters had made for him. So the main difference between them and us was truthfulness. People believed Khomeini when he promised them democracy and respect for individual rights, and were subjected instead to a new dictatorship. We, too, made promises, and before we even attained power we were making plain the contrast between our actions and words. Paralysed by selfishness, we were unable to acknowledge mistakes and criticise ourselves. How could we expect the people to trust us and support us against the regime?

The plane neared Baghdad, and I was nearing desperation. I was supposed to file a report, but I had no idea what to write. On the Hajj we throw stones at an effigy of Satan, representing the stones Abraham threw when Satan was about to deceive him. Did I have to throw stones at my own devil? I did. I wrote a detailed report criticising myself for the weakness I demonstrated when I went back to my family, the weakness that made me doubt the organisation, the leadership, my beliefs and my path towards God and the people.

The first thing I was required to do in Baghdad was watch a videotape of an ideological meeting for 'executive and high-ranking members'. The meeting, called 'Imam Zaman', started with a simple question: 'To whom do we owe all our achievements and everything that we have?' Among the answers proffered were 'God', 'the people' and 'the leadership'. All these answers were wrong, Rajavi said, 'Before I tell you the answer, I must emphasise that what I am going to say is the final word in our ideology. Anyone who thinks he is unable to stay in the organisation and fight to the end should leave the room now; only those who are prepared to sacrifice everything can and should stay and listen to me.' As I watched I found myself trembling with a mixture of fear, anxiety and curiosity. I switched off the tape and started pacing up and down the room, thinking, 'Am I worthy of seeing this tape? Am I prepared to stay with this 'Imam Hussein' of our time to the very end?' Apparently I answered 'yes' to that question. I switched the tape back on. It was a disappointment: Rajavi did not claim, as I thought he might, to be the Imam of our time, but merely said we owed everything to Imam Zaman.

However hard the leadership tried to make us believe that Operation Forogh was a victory, they were not able to change the fact that we wanted to be to Tehran and here we were in Baghdad. In our internal meetings, especially those for high-ranking members, the commanders were expected to act as Rajavi's scapegoats and shoulder the blame themselves. The object was to show that we could reach Tehran if we were more united with our leader, as he was with Imam Zaman and God. He was ready to sacrifice everything he had (which in fact meant all of us!) for God, asserting that the only thing on his mind was doing the will of God – like Abraham, who was prepared to sacrifice his only son upon God's request.

In the discussion about Imam Zaman, we were expected to draw the conclusion that no 'buffer' existed between Rajavi and Imam Zaman; yet there was a buffer between ourselves and him – and certainly Imam Zaman and God – which prevented us from seeing him clearly. This 'buffer' was our weakness. If we could recognise that, we would see why and how we had failed in Operation Forogh and elsewhere. Masoud and Maryam had no doubt that the buffer was in all our cases our existing spouse.

Apart from this, to overcome the loss of morale after Forogh, the organisation set about finding suitable spouses for almost all high-ranking members, especially those who had lost one. This resulted in a complete change of atmosphere: we had endless excuses for parties, festivals and celebrations. Anyone who had any talent as a folk-dancer, singer or actor could occupy his time rehearsing and practising for performances. These were relayed on television, sending a message to Iran that, contrary to the regime's propaganda, we were happy, prepared and ready for action. Every Thursday was family day, when we gathered for recreation and had dinner together. Friday was sport day, when we went along to support our department or battalion teams in sporting matches. The organisation even spent money importing food and luxuries from abroad to enhance the atmosphere. We tried hard to create parks and green areas around the battalion bases. The organisation became more like a large happy family, instead of an army gearing up for war.

Although the spate of marriages had revived the morale of the relevant members, it also created a difficulty for a great many of the men who were unable to find wives, as there were three men for every woman in the organisation. Thus, the leadership had to get rid of the issue of family and sex once and for all.

In October 1989 we were called to a special meeting of the 'central committee'. This was the first I knew of any such committee or of my membership in it. It took place on our base, close to Rajavi's residence. As usual, when he wanted to shock us, he asked us to stand and then read a handwritten speech. Unlike his usual sermons, this one was short and clear. As 'ideological leader' of the Mojahedin and leader of the new Iranian revolution, he announced that 'Sister Maryam Rajavi' was to be the *masoul aval* (chief executive) of the Mojahedin. It was the duty of all Mojahedin to pledge 'revolutionary submission' to her as *masoul aval* and deputy commander of the NLA. The new ideological revolution arising from Maryam's new position was reaching its zenith and would be the source of great benefit and blessings for the Mojahedin and their loved ones. Rajavi concluded with the wish to be pardoned for his failures and wrongdoings during the years he was *masoul aval*, for which he accepted all responsibility. After reading the declaration, he gave the paper to Maryam, who pressed it to her face. We all applauded and many wept.

The speech left us puzzled, however. Some got the impression from his last sentences that he was admitting his failures as a preliminary to resigning. I wished this was true, but from the first sentence of the message I saw that his action in fact advanced his position – not just by one step, but perhaps by 1,000. The supposed act of contrition was merely part of his transformation from political leader to sole ideological leader, above everyone and everything else.

Maryam then spoke, saying that 'the only thing that lets me accept this great responsibility is the presence of Masoud as my ideological leader.' Then Rajavi opened a dialogue with us. He asked one of the sisters to come up onstage and asked whether she could see him or if not what stopped her. Obviously she was unable to give the right answer, so Rajavi then asked her husband to come up and stand between her and him. Again Rajavi asked her what prevented her from seeing him; still she could not see the answer, although everyone else understood it clearly and even began laughing at the poor, astonished woman. She could simply not imagine that her husband was the 'buffer' that stood between her and her ideological leader. Rajavi repeated the scene with one of the brothers. What we did not realise was that the dilemma he was identifying was the fate of all of us, not just of those few.

In the next meeting for our department, I was asked to identify my own buffer: by now we knew we all had one, that it was only a matter of finding it. I had thought about the matter long and hard, and concluded that my buffer was selfishness. My statement was greeted with laughter, scorn and even insults. I was bewildered. Surely my buffer was worse than anyone else's? Others whose spouse was the buffer could divorce them. But what could I do? How could I divorce myself?

For the next few days I was retired from my responsibilities in order to consider further. the more I thought, the less I could find the answer. While others mentioned their spouses, I was not able to name Anna. After all, I had overcome the temptation of my family and returned to the organisation. Then I read the reports of two of my charges who had indicated their spouses as their buffers and accordingly asked for a divorce. It seemed to me the easiest way out to write the same.

Before I did so my *masoul* summoned me and asked me to represent the NCR in Venezuela at a conference. As my body was still in plaster restricting my mobility, I asked if they could send someone in my place. He declined, saying I was the right person. Knowing I would have to stop in London to obtain a visa, I asked what I ought to do there; Anna would surely learn I was there, and I would have to see her and the children.

'All right', he said, 'be with them for a day or two. What's wrong with that?'

I felt he was testing me, so I replied, 'What about the "ideological revolution"?' He seemed to feel I had at last recognised my buffer, and asked me to wait while he went to Mohadessin for an answer. Mohadessin called me in. How had I reached that conclusion, he asked. I couldn't lie. I said it came from reading other reports. He said, 'You should have reached the conclusion by yourself, but nevertheless it is good that you have come to it. Congratulations.' Then he asked me to give him my wedding ring and instructed me, while in London, to avoid seeing Anna. Instead of going to our house or the organisation base, I would stay at a hotel.

Mohadessin's congratulations signified acceptance of my 'revolution' and gave me confidence and self-assurance. I got rid of the plaster and prepared the necessary documents for Venezuela. In Caracas my colleague and I made significant strides. We met the chairman and other members of the parliament, and at the conference of the main trade unions from around the world we succeeded in passing a very strong resolution supporting our resistance, paving the way to gaining material support from European trade unions as well. On our way back to Baghdad we were asked to stop in Paris and talk to people there about our new ideological revolutions. It was an honour for me, especially as we were still tasting its sweetness and as yet had no inkling of the bitterness to come. Shortly afterwards we went to Malta to represent the movement at a conference of European Christian-Democrat parties, where we were equally successful in garnering support.

We felt we had achieved a good deal in Venezuela and Malta. We had been told that one should be demonstrably 100 times more effective after one's 'revolution'. We believed our success was the fruit of the new stage of the ideological revolution. But, contrary to all our expectations, nobody in Baghdad was remotely interested. The atmosphere on the base was completely different. Nobody spoke or smiled, nobody did any political work. Questions and reports from our people in Europe and America lay unanswered. The daily news bulletin had shrunken to almost nothing. People avoided conversation and locked themselves in their rooms for hours. The mood was one of unremitting misery. What on earth was going on?

It seemed everyone was in the process of the new phase of the 'ideological revolution'. The only legitimate discussion was about the revolution and the exchange of relevant experiences. Apart from that nothing was important; there was no outside world.

We were astonished. Why, we wondered, couldn't they have their revolution and set themselves free from all that pain? We did not know yet that recognising the 'buffer' was but the first stage of a long process. The next stage was the 'ideological divorce' from the buffer, which everyone now knew meant their spouse. Even poor single people were required to divorce their buffers, having no idea whom that meant; apparently the answer was to divorce all women or men for whom they harboured any feelings of love.

One day we were asked to take our personal belongings and move to Ashraf to attend ideological meetings with the leadership. At that stage I could still not see any reason for the misery. I saw that in my own case divorce was the only solution. It would save Anna and the children from their present difficult state. She was young and could marry again and have the sort of life she desired, and the children could have more stability. Only later did I realise the organisation demanded not only a legal divorce but also an emotional or 'ideological' divorce. I would have to divorce Anna in my heart. Indeed, I would have to learn to hate her as the buffer standing between our leader and myself.

Rajavi announced at the meeting that as our 'ideological leader' he had ordered mass divorce from our spouses. He asked everyone to hand over our rings if we had not already done so. That meeting was the strangest and most repugnant I had ever attended. It went on for almost a week, but we had lost all sense of space and time, and for all I knew it could have been months. From the very first, it was different from any other meeting. Although there were a few hundred members present, one rarely heard any noise except when people spoke with Rajavi or when he or Maryam were giving a speech. Every now and then, we were startled by a loud cry as somebody arrived at her or his revolution, following which the leaders would talk with the person amid sobs and tears. Tea break provided the only respite from this grim intensity.

On the board behind Maryam were written all our names. Those in red were in the process of revolution, those in green had had theirs. At first it was up to any individual to volunteer for revolution, but by the end of the meeting it became compulsory to do so. Maryam read out the names, five at a time, of those who were in the final stages of revolution and called them up to have their revolution there. Those who did had to stand up and say what they had learned about themselves. At that point everyone else was free to ask them questions, accuse, criticise or even insult them any way they wished. Here rank was unimportant; there were only two classes of people, those whose names were written in green and therefore now real Mojahedin, and all the others.

Until this stage of the revolution, the leaders said, the organisation had had no real 'ideological members' except Maryam, as only she could recognise the true 'ideological position' of Masoud. She was the only one who'd paid a price to be a Mojahed. The rest of us were receivers who had not had to pay any ideologically valuable price to be members. During the first stage of the revolution we had been mere observers, whereas Masoud and Maryam had been the victims of all accusations and undergone all suffering. We had watched, and others had even praised us, considering us to be the victims of their selfish whims. Now it was our turn to pay the price of being and remaining Mojahedin.

To understand the Mojahedin's 'monotheistic [towhidi] ideology', we had to realise that only two different ideologies existed in the world. One was based on exploitation and discrimination among people according to class, race, religion or gender. The other distinguished between people only in terms of their willingness to sacrifice more for God and people. As discrimination on the basis of class, race or belief had been abolished in many cultures, the 'anti-monotheistic' ideology at this juncture manifested itself in a most fundamental and indeed primitive form, in the shape of discrimination based on gender. This anti-God, anti-people, anti-evolution ideology – the antithesis of the *towhidi* ideology – should therefore rightly be called the 'ideology of sexuality' (sometimes also called 'Khomeini's ideology').

Each of us individually had to accept that we were not yet believers in Mojahedin ideology and were thus, like others everywhere in the world, deeply mired in the 'ideology of sexuality'. The cure was to distance ourselves from our sexuality. The first step was to forget sex for the rest of our lives. Hence we had not only to divorce but learn to hate our spouses, as love was based on sex and delivered us up to the ideology of sexuality at the same time as holding us back from embracing the Mojahedin's ideology.

This was the basic premise. At one stage Maryam drew a table comparing and contrasting the values of the two ideologies. For example, 'sin' in Khomeini's ideology was always related to sex. Such transgressions as adultery or sodomy attracted the harshest punishments – death by stoning and eternal damnation. In the Mojahedin ideology, the greatest sin was to lose faith in God's mercy. There were seven great and unforgivable sins in this ideology:

> 'dualism', or blasphemy;
> running away from *jihad* (holy war);
> killing someone who had done no wrong;
> sorcery, defined as the ultimate form of deception;
> usury or exploitation;
> stealing from an orphan, which equated to 'stealing from the treasury of a nation';
> and accusing a pure and innocent woman of adultery.

Apart from these deadly sins, the two ideologies differed in many ways – for example in the status of women. In our organisation women could rise to the highest position as *masoul aval*. In Khomeini's ideology they were denied basic rights. The God of Khomeini was a god of hatred and hell; ours, of mercy and compassion. They were motivated by hate; we, by love. Their emotions and affections were for their immediate family only; ours encompassed all humanity. They gained from receiving; we, by giving. Their character was made up of complexes; ours, of beliefs. They lived in their graves, thinking ceaselessly about death and how to avoid going to hell; we thought of life and what we could do for others.

Our fight with Khomeini's regime, unlike our effort to topple the Shah, was not only political but ideological. It was a clash of ideologies to match any of the classic struggles in history. To be able to fight against it, we had first to purify ourselves of it. For that we needed help from Rajavi. The trouble was, we were unable to see him as he was or reach him where he was. Here, Maryam's intervention was vital. She would help us understand Rajavi – but only if we accepted her as *masoul aval* and understood why she filled that position. If we could answer this question correctly, we had reached the point where we could benefit from her help in understanding Rajavi: understanding his love for God and the people, and his hate for Khomeini and his regime, and understanding Rajavi's stamina, resolve and courage which we too would need to exercise with every last drop of our blood. Rajavi spoke:

> To be able to see and understand, one has to sacrifice something. To understand more, one has to sacrifice more. To understand an ideological concept, one has to sacrifice the most valuable things one has. Abraham, to reach understanding of God, had to be willing to sacrifice his son, his most precious thing. Mary sacrificed her chastity. What is more valuable to you than anything else? It cannot be your wealth; you gave it to the organisation long ago. Is it your life and your health? Again the answer is no. At Forogh you proved capable of sacrificing your life and health. So what is most valuable to you at this juncture?
>
> Yes, it is your love for your spouse, alive or dead, seen or unseen. Even if you are not married, still you have somebody in your mind and heart. You have to give up that love. But how? By understanding why Maryam is *masoul aval* ... To understand Maryam you must divorce your spouse ideologically. But in order to do that, you must first understand Maryam. This is a conundrum, a dilemma, is it not? Which comes first? The answer is, neither. You cannot solve this problem by mental logic but through the understanding of your heart. After all, was it logic that

persuaded Abraham to sacrifice his beloved son? Or Mary to trust an unknown person as an angel of God?

To understand Maryam and remain a freedom fighter, you must prepare to give up everything. Our slogan from now on will be "all or nothing". Give up everything you have. The alternative is to leave the struggle and give nothing. Either you will have your "ideological revolution" or you will leave the organisation and become a simple supporter. You must leave that deadly grave of your sexuality and be reborn, this time not from your biological mother but from your ideological mother, Maryam. Then you can fly with her ...

Then it was Maryam's turn to give a sermon. She said that none of us yet truly understood Rajavi or accepted him ideologically as leader. She drew attention to the fact that women normally operated on an emotional level and men on a logical one, but that ideological understanding was different from either. Women, she went on, were natural givers, but they instinctively gave to their husbands, not to the organisation. It was now necessary for all of us to become givers to the organisation.

She lectured us at length on the subject she called 'signature for sins'. The era of sinless leaders had passed. In the present era people had to choose their leader from among themselves. Having accepted all Rajavi's sins, we had to give him the 'signature of sin', which meant that we no longer doubted him, that we assigned to him the power to make decisions on our behalf in all matters, even our own private lives.

From then on our relationships with everyone and everything would not be bipartite but tripartite, Rajavi being the third corner in every triangle. We were free to love anyone except those who opposed him, whom we had to hate. Departing from this triangle of love and hate was like killing or selling our leader. Our new ideology, later called 'the ideology of Maryam', would provide us with a protective shield.

To help us break free of the old ideology and its protective shield, there were many willing to help, there and at subsequent private meetings. Teasing, insulting, abusing and dishonouring, euphemistically known as 'offering a helping hand', were the methods used to propel people into their revolution. Rajavi teased me by calling me 'yoghurt', as I had no revolutionary roughness and was soft and yielding. Others chose to call me not by my first name, which was the same as Rajavi's, but by my family name, to remind me of my tie with ex-President Banisadr.

Sitting in meetings daily with Masoud and Maryam for an average of twelve hours, we had further five- or six-hour meetings with the head of our section, Mohadessin; we scarcely had time to eat or sleep, or for private reflection. I suffered immense physical distress, too. The premature removal of my cast plus a high level of activity in Venezuela and Malta left my back worse than ever. Sitting every day up to seventeen hours without proper rest added to the pain, which had now spread to my legs and feet. I could barely walk. Even the strongest painkillers did not help. Fortunately the mental agony blotted out most of the physical pain.

Against all advice not to think but to feel, I approached my dilemma intellectually. The more I thought, however, the further away any result seemed. Sometimes I tried to cheat by using other people's expressions to describe my feelings. But often it was impossible. Some members called their spouse a 'monster' or 'demon' and vowed that to return to them would be like eating vomit or sleeping with a corpse. It was their petty, material love for their spouse that had for such a long time separated them from the love of our dear leader. However hard I tried, I could not see Anna as the root of my 'ideological separation' from the leadership. What could I do to avoid being put to the test? I tried to hide, to sit where I would not be seen or called upon or teased, especially by Rajavi.

One day I simply lost my fear. I focused not on what others were saying or doing but on Maryam herself. I started thinking about love. I recalled that when I had first heard of the marriage of Maryam and Masoud I had privately judged Maryam and found her wanting in understanding love. How else could she have left her family? But what *was* the meaning of love? Did I love anybody?

My mother came to mind. What was the nature of her love for me? How could I define it? She was always giving; was this be the definition of love I sought? I believed so. Thinking about my mother unleashed a flood of tears, tears I had always stemmed for fear of being labelled 'attached to mother'. Now I was free to cry, do or say anything. I was not afraid of losing anything anymore.

Rajavi's voice broke into my reverie. He was talking about Fahieme'a, a sister who'd replaced me in my department. The first thing I remembered about her was her smile. Then I recalled that once in Switzerland, she came to our base and, although she was very busy with the people in her charge and with her work, she found time to cook for those of us due to attend a conference the following day. We were bowled over by her kindness. Now Rajavi was asking if anyone had anything to say against her. Nobody did. I didn't know it at the time, but her revolution had been recognised first among all; as a result she had been named deputy *masoul aval*. For once I raised my hand to talk. I had no intention of saying anything against her; instead, I wanted speak of my thoughts when she succeeded me in my job. Rajavi saw my hand and said, 'Silence, silence. A very dead man, from deep down in his grave, wants to talk.' (In their eyes, anyone who had not yet had his or her revolution was living in a grave.) I explained what went through my mind when I heard she had replaced me, knowing she had neither the experience nor the education equal to the task. Unexpectedly, I began crying. I remembered her kind face, her smile, her care for others, and my distress grew recalling how she had been required not to divorce her husband legally, as he was not in the organisation, but to divorce him ideologically. 'How could she?' I wondered aloud. 'How painful must that have been for her? To be with somebody as his wife but not to be permitted to love him.' Such a situation was more like prostitution than marriage. Moreover, she had a child, whom she was not permitted to leave but had to stop loving!

There was silence in the hall. Nobody had expected to see me crying, especially for someone else. Then Rajavi asked me about my revolution.

'I didn't want to talk about my revolution,' I said. 'I am still in conflict with Maryam.'

'How so?' he asked.

I said, 'I accused her of not knowing the meaning of love – love for her child and husband, of sacrificing her emotions for the organisation. Later, I came to believe no woman is capable of real love. A long time ago, my own wife left me, quite easily, though she had claimed to love only me. [I referred to the time when Anna became engaged to another man after our road accident.] So I say that men are more capable of long-lasting love than women.'

'How do you define love?' Rajavi wanted to know.

I said, 'I think love is giving.' I began weeping again and when he asked me why I said, 'I have not given anything to anyone. In my whole life, I cannot point to a single instance where I gave anything. Yet when I think of Maryam or Fahieme'a, I can see they are "giving". Then everything changes. I see that women are more capable of love than men; I see my mother and other women around me who were always giving, while we men were always receiving. Then I feel, "Who am I to judge them?".'

I talked on – and on. A few hours earlier I had been unable to speak for a few seconds before all those people. Now I felt I could hold forth for hours. I had found a source of energy. I could feed on love, get my incentives from love.

'Wait', Masoud interrupted me. 'Wait, is this the same "yoghurt Masoud" we knew? Is this the person lying in his grave? It seems he has changed into a philosopher, giving us a lecture and a new definition of love! I think he has had his revolution.' He turned to Maryam questioningly. Now it was her turn to talk to me. What did I think about Masoud's sins, she asked.

'I forgive all his sins,' I replied instantly. At this they both jumped from their chairs.

'Forgive?!' they echoed. It was not for us to forgive, but for them or for God.

Quickly, I corrected my error. 'I meant that if he has any sins,' I said, 'I accept them as if they were my own. Before I became a member of the organisation, I considered all Mojahedin as "sinless" – not only Masoud but all of them. Compared to me they were and are the purest and cleanest people in the world! Yes, I accept his sins as mine. He is the purest person I know.' Although Maryam still had some doubts about my revolution and my 'signature for sin', Rajavi simply wrote my name in green on the board and asked Maryam to congratulate me, which she did. I was lucky. Without claiming anything or being attacked by anyone, I had had my revolution.

I could not attend the nightly meetings anymore; my back condition was deteriorating rapidly. Soon I was not able to walk, and was moved to another base where the doctors asked the organisation to send me abroad immediately for an operation.

# 30

# Freedom Fighters

By the time I reached Paris, I had lost almost all feeling in my legs, and lost it totally when doctors attached a tube to help me to pass urine. I now had no feeling at all from the waist down. Surgery was scheduled for that night.

On regaining consciousness I saw Dr Saleh Rajavi, a very capable physician and another of Masoud's brothers. 'You must be very dear to Masoud and Maryam,' he smiled. 'They personally called me several times and asked me to do everything to help you make a complete recovery.' But how, he wondered, had I borne the pain until that late stage? Why had I left having an operation so late?

I replied, 'To be honest, most of the time I could not feel the pain. I was in heaven with angels.' Oblivious to my situation or the presence of others, I started talking about Maryam and what I had seen in her.

Under normal circumstances I would indeed never have been able to bear such pain for so long. Yet the only time I had been conscious of pain was while walking from the meeting hall to the dining room or my room. It seemed I was likely to be paralysed, but that prospect held little importance for me. I felt I had gained something that would serve me many times more productively than my feet or legs. Even after the operation, although my legs and feet were still partly paralysed and I could not control urination, I was unconcerned. My mind was in the meeting room, and I was with Maryam.

I had found something lost to me for years: a new reason, a new incentive, a new direction, not only for political resistance but even for living itself. Love had pushed me into politics and forced me to forget everything else. But for years, it was submerged under waves of hate. I focused exclusively on the regime's actions, on ever finding new reasons to hate them. As a result, I had no time to think about myself and what I might want. I was attracted to the Mojahedin not because of their hatred of the Shah or Khomeini, but because of love of their words and promises for the future; because of love for the people, the wish to see them happy, healthy and free of hunger, to see an end to injustice, exploitation and misery.

Now Maryam had a new message for me: 'love'. Even hatred had acquired a new meaning: hatred not for its own sake, but arising out of love. We did not hate the regime because we had suffered or been tortured because we had lost families and friends and normal lives. We hated the regime because it stood against our love for the people, because it had betrayed them, made and broken and denied and subverted promises; because of the rise of injustice, the increase in number of the poor, of children bought and sold in Iranian cities as their families could not support them; because of the women and men sentenced to public stoning on charges of adultery or sodomy; because the regime had returned our country to the Middle Ages, implementing the most barbaric of ancient Arab traditions.

During this time, Maryam's smile and use of the word 'love' soothed and comforted me in a way no painkiller could. What I had found was not new. Years before, taking LSD for the first and the last time, I saw how forgetting oneself and thinking of others could make one forget one's own pain and misery. Narcotic effects, however, lasted only so long. Maryam had given me the same experience for life. I felt that as long as I held Maryam and her ideology in my heart, I could continue to enjoy that experience, to live in a 'pain-free zone'. Every word she said in the meeting lived on in me, sharp and clear. I could see how miserable I had been as long as I was thinking about myself and how I had been blessed with happiness and freedom as soon as I forgot my own concerns. Now that I had found the answer, I was filled with zeal to pass on this magic medicine to everyone and save them from misery. If only this medicine could be administered to all Iranians, a miracle might happen. I could scarcely contain my happiness. I don't know what the other patients in the hospital thought of me, watching me smile and even laugh out loud to myself.

I received a phone call, nearly jumping from bed for joy when I heard Rajavi's voice. He asked how I was, whether I needed anything. Then he passed the phone to Maryam.

She said, 'You must concentrate on recovering so that you can return. We have a lot of work to do.'

'Just hearing your first word has cured me,' I said. 'What should I do? Tell me to move the earth and I shall do it.'

She laughed and said, 'We don't want to move the earth, but to free our people. Look, you have had your revolution and understandably you cannot feel the pain and problems you are facing at the moment, but you are more useful to us walking on your feet rather than being pushed in a wheelchair. So from now on your duty is to regain your health as soon as possible.' I was in hospital for a month. Exercise and treatment restored me to a semblance of health and I asked to return to Baghdad.

For almost eight years the UN had asked the Iranian regime to allow its special representative, Reynaldo Galindo Pohl, to visit Iran and report on the human rights situation there. To improve relations with the West, the regime finally consented. The main concern of many Western countries at the time was the issue of hostages and achieving success in this regard in order to help win elections. Meanwhile, lacking excuses after the war's end for the plight of the people, Iran needed to repair its devastated economy, rebuild ruined cities and villages and find jobs for millions of demobilised revolutionary guards and soldiers. Solving these problems required help from the West, to which the main obstacle was the world's attitude on human rights. At the time, human rights violations in Iran rang alarm bells for merchants, capitalists and bankers, implying that the regime was not stable and hence their capital might not be safe. Iran was therefore prepared to help the West and exchange hostages taken by Hezbollah in Lebanon in return for a good report from the UN representative.

Our supporters staged another hunger strike to draw attention to the dangers of accepting the regime at face value. At the same time our political department mobilised to do everything it could to stop the publication of reports favourable to the regime. Several documents containing accounts of mass graves and hidden prisons in Iran, names and particulars of prisoners and details of torturers were handed to the representative. For the first time, we even named some of our political prisoners – those we were sure would not betray us – and asked him to see them when he there. We also asked our supporters to send requests to him to supply details of loved ones killed or imprisoned in Iran. In this way we made sure Pohl received not only official documentation but also thousands of individual letters, which could not be easily ignored.

Back in Baghdad, there was no time for talking about the ideological revolution or personal feelings. Even a report I had sent Maryam as a gift while convalescing, resuming an old project of mine in search of a formula to express the connection between thought and feeling, had been unwelcome and considered 'showing off'. In this revolution, I was told, we had to realise we were empty-handed without the leadership, and rely on them for everything – not on personal ability or talent. The expression was, 'we must walk on their feet, not ours'.

Back in the real world, the imperative was pursuing the issue of human rights, the only way we could legitimise resistance against the regime. Without it, we would be labelled just another 'terrorist organisation'. We monitored Pohl's activities daily. Eventually, after his return from Iran, we received a copy of his report. Rajavi phoned and asked my opinion of it. I thought it overwhelmingly favoured the regime; even the parts referring to human rights abuses did not mention us. He asked me to write a statement, which could be issued when the report came out officially.

Luckily, I found a few obvious contradictions in the report along with some misinformation and errors. So I wrote a statement showing clearly that it had no value and was written intentionally to help the regime. Our statement was published at the same time as the report. Rajavi called it a 'shameful report intended to whitewash the bloody record of the *mullahs*', adding that it was part of 'a dirty new deal with the regime'. Our evidence was so strong that Pohl had to admit to some mistakes in the report, though he strongly denied the existence of any deal. At a press conference he responded angrily to reporters' questions: 'My report has nothing to do with hostages; this is absolutely wrong and a lie.'

I was then transferred to a newly established department called the secretariat, reporting to Mohadessin, our 'shadow foreign minister and spokesman', and instructed by Rajavi himself to write a book in response to Pohl's report.

In his report, Pohl pursued several paths that could be read optimistically as intended to secure permission for him to revisit Iran and help improve human rights conditions gradually. In our eyes, this was part of the alleged deal. First, he wanted to show that the violations dated from the past, a result of the up and downs of the first few post-revolutionary years and owing frequently to the wrongdoings of junior officials. Second, documentary evidence of violations, produced mainly by the Mojahedin, contained many mistakes and was thus of little value. Third, most importantly, he claimed that the Mojahedin was a terrorist organisation and had killed and tortured many people, including its own members. If any of them had been executed, therefore, it was because of these terrorist activities, punishable in any country. I was able to counter the first and second arguments readily, as there were enough documents indicating that all officials of the regime had approved all the crimes of which they were accused, and some were personally involved in executions and torture. In attempting to prove our documents unreliable, the regime picked a few cases which their own media, including Iran radio, had announced executed. Then the regime demonstrated that the 'deceased' were alive and well, making it look as though we were mistaken. It proved, however, just another trick.

The problem was the allegation that we were guilty of terrorism. I did not see eye-to-eye with Mohadessin on this issue, as I wanted to concentrate on it while he wanted a brief book that would discredit the representative. In the end I wrote a few chapters on this subject. I argued first that it was not part of the representative's mandate to investigate this question, but that if he had come to a view on it he had to listen to our response. Second, none of the facts mentioned in the report were proven acts of terrorism. Third and most importantly, 'our fight with the regime is on the basis of the laws and conditions of normal warfare, which fortunately is admitted by the regime as well'. I went on to ask what Pohl had done to save prisoners of war (many of our combatants poisoned in Iran could be classified as POWs according to the Geneva Convention) claimed by the regime. I wrote:

> The Special Representative could also have realised that the Geneva Convention of 12th August 1949 applies to the Mojahedin's military forces ... He could have cited these internationally recognised rules to save the lives of numerous POWs from certain death ...'

Then I added another chapter to show why we had no choice but armed resistance. If, therefore, one wished to call us terrorists, then American freedom fighters in their revolution, plus those who resisted the Fascists in Italy and the Nazis in Germany, should be called terrorists too.

# 31

# From Assassination to Crucifixion

One day we learned to our horror that Doctor had been killed near his house in Geneva. Though his help to us and improvement of our image on the international scene had never been acknowledged, after death he was universally praised; Maryam even called him a 'Mojahed', as had, I think, been his wish.

Doctor, his sister Monyra'h and her husband Asghar, who lived in Newcastle during the Iranian revolution, were all killed by the regime. None of them, even according to the norms of the regime's 'justice', had done anything punishable by death. Perhaps this was why their deaths hurt so deeply. Death for us activists was accepted and expected, but they had been eliminated simply because of their ties to Rajavi.

After Doctor's assassination, I added another chapter to the book about the aftermath of the report, specifically the blank cheque that it gave to the regime to continue its atrocities. Rajavi agreed that the book be named after Doctor, who had been my main source of knowledge on these matters. I think the assassination and perhaps the book's logic made an impact on Pohl, as his next report took a completely opposite line to the previous one and was mostly in our favour. When I met him a year later, he kissed me and said, 'Shall we forget the past? The past is past, yes?'

I said, 'Yes, but we paid the highest price with the blood of one of our dearest.'

'You are right,' he sighed, 'but what can one do?' It was then announced by Swiss authorities that thirteen people with Iranian diplomatic passports had been responsible for the murder. From then on all Pohl's reports had a section dedicated to the case of Doctor's assassination and the regime's likely involvement.

Our main responsibilities in the secretariat included advising political departments (including diplomacy and media) with proper research and analysis. After my ideological revolution, I felt braver and more inclined to object openly to things I felt were wrong. I soon learned my limits, however. Once I was summoned by Rajavi, who showed me a letter of condolences from the UN Deputy Secretary-General and asked how I thought we should reply. I gave him my view. Then he asked me to write it as he dictated. Whenever something in his text jarred or seemed inappropriate I stopped and told him so. He said nothing, pretending not to have heard me; after a few seconds' silence, he resumed dictating along the same lines as before. With shame I learned that in the presence of Rajavi one spoke when asked to and not otherwise. (The letter, though obviously private, was – despite my opposition – published, and inflicted some damage on our relationship with the UN office in Geneva.) I learned that the same limitations applied in all the political departments, whose aims and directions were dictated by Rajavi. A personal view that parallelled the official line, favouring or suggesting a means of facilitating it, was acceptable; opposition was not.

Apart from Mohadessin and me, everyone in the secretariat came from the media department, all old members of the organisation and close associates of Rajavi. I felt I had much to learn from them; nevertheless I found fatal flaws in their analysis of events. They habitually drew 'tableaux' of different alternatives, rejecting the impossible scenarios one by one and ending up with 'the most probable one'. There were two flaws in this kind of logic. First, the alternatives were always limited and often neglected to take into account possibilities that were actually the most likely.

Second, complexity was banished from all analysis, allowing favourite conclusions to be reached. Iranian politics was likened to a 'magnetic field' with two poles. All Iranian politicians were either at the negative pole, with the regime, or at the positive pole, with us. As a result we lost many friends who perhaps had some reservations about offering us total support, or who perhaps could not see the regime as darkly as we were projecting it.

While I was still in love with Maryam's messages, I could see some destructive effects on people around me. Mehdi, one of our top army commanders then retired in our section, had not achieved his ideological revolution and was a lost soul. Scarcely anyone spoke to him, and he spent most of the time alone, always with a sad face. He was on the edge of losing his mind, or perhaps had already lost it. Others were in similar situations.

Among the married couples some suffered more than others. The organisation ruled that couples in which one partner had had a revolution and the other had not must continue to live together; but those who had been successful could not show or feel any affection for their spouses. People who had not revolted were often sent to different departments to avoid embarrassment, but were soon recognised and treated like lepers. Nobody spoke to them or showed any sympathy. These people had two alternatives: to leave the organisation, which for some high-ranking members like Mehdi was impossible, or assert that they had had their revolution or were trying to do so. The husband of one of the sisters in my charge did quit, and after a long struggle the family was transferred to France. I heard later that she killed herself.

In the beginning only high-ranking members had to have their revolutions. Later, it was decided that all members should go through a revolution, and later still that all army combatants had to do likewise, or they would be unable to fight when the time came. Daily, compulsory meetings in the presence of Masoud and Maryam took place at Ashraf. Every other activity was secondary. For those of us who had had our revolution attendance was optional, though we were strongly advised to come on the grounds that revolution is never-ending, that there was always the danger we might revert to our pre-revolutionary state. I was rarely able to attend because of my back. Although my revolution had been approved, I knew deep down that it had been only partial. I had understood and accepted the 'Maryam side' of the revolution, but had not understood or accepted Rajavi as ideological leader; nor did I think I ever would. It meant putting him first in my mind and soul, giving him precedence over my conscience, logic, beliefs, principles. I did my best to become what they expected me to be. But I couldn't, and perhaps this is the main reason why I write these words today.

Contrary to the good I felt had come from the ideological revolution, now and then I could see the dark side. Once, a member originally from the US explained his revolution, claiming he had understood Rajavi's position in 1985 and accepted his ideological leadership then. To me there was nothing wrong with this claim – but it aroused the most vicious anger among his listeners. For the first time, I saw Rajavi angry. At last I realised that the speaker's claim to have understood Rajavi's position raised him to the same plane as Maryam; yet until 1989 and the new stage of the revolution, the leadership maintained that no one but Maryam had understood. Only those who accepted Maryam's position could request her help in understanding Rajavi. The poor guy lost his rank and for several months had no responsibilities – the worst punishment in the organisation – then was sent abroad to work as a sympathiser.

During those days many sisters were asked if they were prepared to love and marry the ugliest and most unpleasant man on earth if the organisation asked them to. To answer 'yes' was to prove they had divorced their husbands emotionally and ideologically, that there was no longer any bond between them. Men were not asked this question. It was presumed that their love for their wives amounted only to sex, that men could 'love' any woman, however ugly or bad-tempered, provided they were sexually available. One poor man, hoping prove his credibility, misguidedly claimed he was prepared to marry anyone the organisation asked him to. Amid the laughter this provoked, he went further and asserted that the true proof of his revolution would be to marry Maryam. This declaration, tantamount to committing suicide publicly, caused an uproar. Rajavi was enraged; only Maryam's intervention restrained him from attacking the man. Other brothers wanted to beat or even kill him. It seemed that people who had personal difficulty with their own revolutions often turned their frustration into aggression against others. The organisation encouraged such attacks, which furthered the anxiety and misery that culminated in some suicide attempts among the victims.

High-ranking members unable to have their revolution were not allowed to leave the organisation but at the same time, while living among us, were forbidden to do any work, even menial jobs in the kitchen. To an outsider this punishment might hardly appear harsh, but work was our entire *raison d'être*. Not to feel useful was worse than being dead. For such people – including an army commander who killed himself with a shaving blade and a colleague of mine in New York who hanged himself – suicide was often the only answer. A few managed to escape the organisation's grip by defecting. Suicide, in Rajavi's view, was worse than murder: 'with suicide you are killing our ideology'. Suicides were buried apart from our martyrs. The official line, as expressed by Maryam, was that anyone who did not want a revolution was free to leave the organisation, but that we could not overthrow the regime without it. The reality, however, was far removed from that sentiment.

On 2nd August 1990 we heard news of the invasion of Kuwait by Iraq. It was too awful to elicit sadness, so our anger transformed into humour. 'Look', said one of our *masouls*, 'in the whole world we have one friend, and he is a madman.' Iraq's action had a significant effect on all our activities, military and political. The day after the invasion Rajavi met with Iraqi officials and announced the shutdown of our radio and television and a stop to all our political work. He assumed the Iraqis would wish it so, as they wanted to improve relations with Iran and not have the Mojahedin stand in their way. He told them, 'If ever we are not welcome here anymore, please let us know and we will leave your country immediately, taking nothing but our rifles. Our only request would be for you to allow us free passage across the border.'

The UN embargo on Iraq made life increasingly difficult by the day. By November we suffered shortages of everything. Our food was reduced to half or perhaps a third of the usual quantity, and quality declined in equal measure. We rarely had meat. Cleaning materials were scarce and rationed. Later it became impossible to find proper bread; dates and bread were our staples when we could not get enough of other foodstuffs. With news of an impending attack by the allied forces, we were ordered to prepare for the worst. We dug trenches near all major buildings. I learned how to handle and use various weapons. Every now and then we were ordered to move from one building or even one base to another; each move meant much packing and carrying.

Everyone's most visible reaction to the situation was keen interest in the news, which was somehow interpreted as anxiety about the future, until eventually Rajavi decided to act. At what was later called 'the crucifixion meeting', he passed on the news and as usual presented various scenarios, beginning with the worst case: a peace treaty between Iran and Iraq, united against the West, the precondition being our surrender to the regime. 'You all have to prepare for this,' he said, 'the crucifixion of us all, from here to Tehran, like the slaves who revolted under Spartacus. My only wish is to be the last person crucified beside the gates of Tehran, to suffer more than all of you by witnessing your deaths.' He asked us either to leave the room – and hence Iraq – or stay and prepare to fight to the finish. 'It is going to be a confusing war, as we don't know whom are we will face: America, Iran or Iraq.'

I wished he would genuinely let us decide. I was sure none of us would leave that room, as nobody was afraid of death or torture any more. We hungered after frankness and trust. But it seemed he was not so sure of us. Before waiting to see our proper reaction after we heard a few speeches by other speakers, he painted the more optimistic scenario which entailed our freedom to move back to Iran. A war between Iraq and America, might open the border between Iran and Iraq. After presenting a welter of facts he concluded by reminding us to prepare for the final offensive. That meeting fired us with eagerness to fight, and from then on the mood at all the bases became much more positive and even jubilant.

In January 1991 I was sent to Geneva to represent the organisation at a session of the Human Rights Commission. The atmosphere there was quite different. Hitherto the Western countries, Iraqis and we were all united against Khomeini's fundamentalist, terrorist regime. We remained opposed to the regime, while the Iraqis and the West wanted to establish good relations with it. We had to maintain friendly relations with Iraq, as all our bases were situated there, but at the same time we wanted to align ourselves with the West, against the regime.

Apart from this political confusion, I was very angry to find that whatever friendly connections we had made during our years of working at the UN had disappeared. Our 'international organisation files' were also gone, and nobody knew where they were, so I had no record of what had gone on during the time I was not in charge of that section. We had lost most of our contacts and friends at the UN office and in many NGOs, not because of the changed political situation but because of the Mojahedin's narrow-minded insistence that they were going to overthrow the regime next month or next year, and thus didn't require long-term plans – and had to squeeze the last drop of advantage out of any facilities we had access to. What had taken years had been dispersed in a matter of months. Scarcely any of our former allies at the UN office were prepared to see us.

Finally one of them agreed to see me in my role as an old friend, not as a Mojahedin representative. She said, 'Sometimes I cannot understand you. We helped you here a lot, but your friends were prepared to risk everything for some petty benefits like using their badges to get into one of our offices and making "free" photocopies. When they were seen by an Iranian who complained to the deputy Secretary-General, we all got into trouble and were warned strongly against helping you in any way in the future.' Our former NGO friends were also wary of us, mostly because they were reluctant to do anything to jeopardise their relations with Western governments; but I believe our own actions intensified their attitude. Some of these old friendships were restored thanks to a lunch held in memory of Doctor, attended by many representatives, including those from Western countries, who had held him in high regard.

Despite all our speculation, we were shocked when we heard that the allied attack on Iraq had begun, and extremely frightened. All our hopes and desires were tied up in a compact area near an Iraqi military base, which could easily be an allied target. It would take just one missile to kill all our dreams along with our loved ones living there. These missiles were capable of destroying heavy concrete shelters; how safe could our people possibly be in our hand-built trenches? Our fears extended, to be honest, to ourselves as well. What kind of future would we have after everything had been destroyed? Our training had inculcated in us the idea that 'even if only one Mojahed survives, he or she must hold out, against all the odds; the survivor must recruit and start the struggle from the beginning again.' In our minds there was no room for notions of surrender, but thoughts of the difficulties we were going to face inevitably crowded in.

Perhaps for the first time, I wondered about the value of having a single unquestionable, undeniable leader, accepted by all. If we were to lose him, what would we do? There was nobody with either the self-confidence or capability to replace him. Western-style democracy had no place in the internal business of the organisation – though we sometimes pretended otherwise for propaganda purposes – so there was no possibility of electing a leader democratically. *Masouls* were imposed on us, and we accepted their authority. They enjoyed their position not by virtue of expertise, but because of 'ideological rank'. The whole hierarchy rested on passionate devotion to our leader. It was drummed into us that 'our most valuable capital was our organisational relations', without which we were 'a bunch of individuals, incapable of doing anything'.

I was deep in these thoughts when a sister, Badrie, called from Germany and said that as long as we had no contact with the Baghdad office, she was in charge. If we needed anything, we were to ask her. Although I knew the allies were well aware of our Iraqi bases and would avoid bombing them, I drew enormous comfort from knowing Badrie provided that safety valve.

Our association with Iraq isolated us at that time. The Western countries and even the Arab and developing countries were united for the first time in condemning Iraq, and at the same time showed less animosity towards Iran. Iraq's foolish threats of terror and revenge against the West – despite its unwillingness or inability to carry them out – put us in a difficult position. Many nations viewed us as Iraq's close allies and perhaps the only organisation capable of perpetrating any terrorist activity on its behalf. Our telephone lines were bugged, and diplomats hesitated to meet us at their embassies or, if they did, mounted high-security operations.

That year, we managed to get a resolution passed condemning human rights violations in Iran. This, together with our history of regular meetings with Western ambassadors, helped establish an image for us independent of the Iraqis.

# 32

# Love and Right on Trial

A year earlier, while I was still in Iraq, Rajavi had told me he would name me Doctor's replacement as his representative in international organisations and Switzerland. In this case I was to have two faces, one as a Mojahed representative with the relevant organisational responsibilities, the other as a representative of the NCR, which had nothing to do with the Mojahedin. He told me that as my wife was not a member of Mojahedin, I could not officially divorce her as long as she had not asked for it. So we would be able to live in Geneva as an ordinary married couple, which was very desirable for the organisation. I looked at him in astonishment, wondering whether he was serious or just teasing and testing me. When I saw the earnest look on his face, I stammered, 'But I am divorced. I gave my wedding ring to my *masoul*. How can I live with my wife?'

Rajavi looked at Maryam, who was present, and asked if this was true. 'Yes', she replied, 'but we were going to talk to him and return his ring to him ... You see,' she said, turning to me, 'the revolution for people like you is harder than for others. You must divorce your wife ideologically and emotionally, not legally.' A few days later Mohadessin elaborated. I was to see my family and show them kindness and consideration, but no real love or affection towards Anna. I was not able to do this, nor would I be able to lie to my family about anything, and I said so. He arranged for me to meet some men in my situation and hear how they were trying to solve this dilemma. What they said only strengthened my resolve to disobey the order. From then on my *masouls*, whoever they were, would occasionally argue with me at length about this subject. I was never able to figure out their intentions. Did they want to test my revolutionary commitment? Did they have a political objective? I think their chief worry was that Anna might start asking about me, which could create a political dilemma. News of divorces within the organisation had not yet leaked out, and the Mojahedin were afraid that if it became public knowledge it might redound to the benefit of regime. Once my *masoul* insisted I phone Anna, as she was worried about my health. He said this was Maryam's order and had to be obeyed. I did as told but was very guarded. I knew the organisation well enough by then not to let its irrational and short-lived decisions jeopardise my family's lives.

Now, after a few months, my new *masoul* Badrie urged me to go to London and see the family. She even pressed £100 on me to buy presents for them. I was reluctant to accept, as the organisation had so often stressed that we should spend no money for personal interests. But the big issue was how to approach Anna, treat her with care and affection and yet not love her, as all my love had to be reserved for our leader. It was almost a year since I had last seen my family, and I could not prevent myself from loving them with all my heart. Thanks to unremitting and repeated emphasis of this point by the Mojahedin, I now felt guilty about loving my family. Hence on my return to Germany I wrote a long report criticising myself for my feelings. The response was that next time I should be more careful not to give my emotions free rein, to control them better.

Soon afterwards I was told that Rajavi had chosen me to represent him and the NCR in America. I was therefore ordered back to London to get a US visa. In London, Anna had to leave the children with me as she wanted to go to Germany. Although all couples in the organisation were separated, they retained all rights to their children, had almost equal access to them and were not forbidden to show affection towards them.

Thanks to their mother, Sarvy and Hanif were happy and comfortable. I was resolved not to disrupt their lives. My stay with them was the happiest time I'd had in ages, but it lasted only a few days before I had to leave for America. That was the last time I saw or heard from them for many years to come.

I hated being transferred to America. I had bad memories of the place, but had no alternative but to put on a brave face. My *masoul* there was my old London colleague Meherafroz. She told me I was to be in charge of diplomacy, and had to start learning the ropes immediately.

Our diplomacy there was much more complicated than in Europe: more quantitative than qualitative. Unlike in Europe, we rarely had any relations with members of Congress, but were instead fobbed off onto their aides as they were almost all totally ignorant about the situation in Iran; all they knew was that the Iranians were 'bad guys'. The aides knew as little as their bosses. In political terms it was virgin territory, which we could cultivate. But, like everything in that country, politics was on a grand scale and so was our work in this field. We had to have some sort of relationship with almost 200 aides to members of the House of Representatives and senators. In addition we had a section called 'Personalities', responsible for dealings with politicians and political researchers outside Congress: people in research institutes, public servants, members of the National Security Council, the Pentagon or Voice of America, and later some people from the FBI. Our media section was highly active, and had many contacts with columnists, reporters and editors. Our principal strategy was lobbying individuals. We found that representatives were generally amenable to approaches from their constituents, as long as there was no strong objection from anywhere else. Since our aim was maximum propaganda, we usually needed to issue declarations with as many signatures as possible We could get those signatures with a few phone calls. Instead of having to build a strong base of support, we needed only access to two representatives from opposing parties who were prepared to sponsor our declarations.

The first real test of our diplomacy came when Mohadessin visited America for the first time. We managed to arrange only a handful of meetings for him with members of Congress or senators, and at a luncheon in his honour only two congressmen showed up. It was a lesson in the fragility of our diplomacy there. Our propaganda machine could fool almost everybody, not only our opponents (especially the regime and monarchists) but also our supporters, members of NCR and members of European parliaments, especially those who could be easily impressed by America. But we were fooling ourselves more than anybody. The organisation was playing a numbers game: more declarations, more signatures, more column inches in the newspapers were the measures of success in its eyes. The optimism of old had turned to naiveté. Soon I discovered that neither Meherafroz nor Rajavi himself shared my concerns about our real diplomatic achievements to any degree. Next year we would be in Iran, they argued, and then we could operate from a strong position. So I took the onus on myself to find more members in both houses of Congress to become our real supporters. The objective I set was to find at least ten sponsors for our next letter of support in the House of Representatives, where hitherto we'd had only one solid supporter; and two sponsors in the Senate, where we had none.

Of course, one never knows what is round the corner. I had just started work on this endeavour when I was summoned first to Paris and then immediately sent on to Geneva. Apparently we were on the brink of a new huge political mobilisation. In September 1990 the Iranian regime filed a complaint against a reporter of *La Suisse* newspaper for accusing Rafsanjani, its president, of masterminding Doctor's assassination. The regime wanted to use Swiss law to prevent any reporter from revealing the facts of the case. Confident of winning, they aimed to broaden the case into a trial of the Mojahedin's claims in every sphere. Our objective was twofold: defensive, to win the case; and offensive, to provide proof of the regime's terrorist activities everywhere, including in Switzerland. The difficulty was that it was not our case, and all the evidence had to come from the reporter and her lawyers – and they were reluctant to surrender to our propaganda machine. I was nominated to deal with them, to persuade them to take advantage of our help and later to call various people we would introduce as their witnesses and follow the line we requested. The lawyers' initial goal was simply to clear their client and prove that her allegations were no more and no less than claimed by Rajavi's family at their press conference. Thanks to the research I had done for my book, I found it reasonably easy to persuade the lawyers to follow our lead. I had the documents to demonstrate the regime's will and tenacity in killing Mojahedin members everywhere around the world. It did not take us long to prepare two huge briefcases of relevant documents that would overturn the prosecution's claims. As time was too short for the defence to absorb all these documents, I had to sit beside them in the courtroom ready to find documents they wished to cite.

Long and moving speeches by Doctor's widow and brother paved the way to victory for the defence. The regime's side, seeing they were going to lose the case, attempted a few manoeuvres, including requesting that the following sessions be postponed for a month, and then offered to withdraw the case. It was a very delicate situation. If the defence accepted their offer, the reporter could return to normal and put the matter behind her. But we were on the edge of a major victory. I had to persuade her lawyers not to accept the regime's offer, explaining how our victory would benefit her as well as ourselves. At the next stage of the trial, we brought out the big guns. Almost fifty high-ranking members of our organisation, including Mohadessin and many NCR members, were there, along with many supporters from Germany and Switzerland, all demonstrating against the regime. We were prepared for anything. Many of our members who had been tortured were also present, to testify against witnesses for the regime. We even had members of the British and Canadian parliaments testify.

At that point any differences between the defence and us simply evaporated: we had the identical objective of inflicting a crushing defeat on the regime and deriving maximum publicity from international media coverage. Unlike us, the regime had no official representative there, and their witnesses were weak and quite unprepared for the questions we asked them. When one of our members gave evidence that she had been tortured by one of the regime's witnesses, that witness was thrown off balance and said things that in fact undermined his case and favoured ours.

The judgement of the court was inevitable. The Geneva newspaper *Le Matin* headlined the decision: '*L'Iran attaque une journaliste: c'est lui que le tribunal condamne!*'['Iran accuses a journalist: it is Iran that the court finds guilty!']

Rajavi called this victory our 'political Morvarid', a reference to the regime's attacks in the Morvarid mountains, when they had tried to destroy us but lost many of their guards and had been forced to retreat. There was jubilation everywhere at this victory, even in the streets of the Geneva. But now that it was over I returned to my job in America.

Even after twelve years with the Mojahedin, I was still able to relate to people outside the organisation. For a long time we hated American politicians for their crimes in our country and other developing countries. Now I lived among them, in the country responsible for many of our miseries. Still, I found many Americans kind, sensitive, humble and humane, and was able to befriend aides and even representatives. I was as honest as I could be about our past. Our presence in Iraq and our policy of armed struggle made us vulnerable to attack and criticism. I developed a pre-emptive strategy of reciting whatever they were going to hear about us from our enemies, adding our justifications. That way, they got no surprises when they received a State Department letter or were lobbied by the Iranian regime or a remnant of the Shah's. It was also a more effective than just using lobby muscle. I called this policy 'vaccination' – inoculating people against the poisonous claims of our enemies. At first my fellow diplomacy department members were doubtful about this method, but eventually they accepted it and let me carry on. By this means I managed to gain the trust of many, who allowed me to write letters on their behalf or use their offices for our work. In addition, they always informed us about the activities of our enemies in Congress, so that we could prepare a response. The experience taught me that Americans are human beings with fine qualities, not the evil automatons we liked to believe. My monochrome vision was beginning to fragment at that stage...

By the end of the summer a majority of representatives supported us, in spite of the State Department's opposition. On Mohadessin's next visit our standing had improved to the extent that we could quite easily organise a well-attended luncheon and meetings for him.

Rightly or wrongly, I truly believed in our ability to establish genuine good relations with America based on mutual respect and self-interest. Perhaps it was naïve of me to think we could have equal relations with the world's only superpower, but the Israelis had set the example by maintaining their independence and good relations with America through a strong lobby and their understanding of the American political system. If they could do it, why couldn't we? Two million Iranian-Americans lived there, many of them rich and educated. It was my hope to achieve a similarly strong lobby and close links with members of both houses of Congress, although here I differed with our department and the organisation. It was not until much later that I realised why mine was an impossible goal: not because of US superiority but because of Mojahedin duality.

Mohadessin, too, was a liability and an embarrassment. His method was opportunistic and good for propaganda only. In fact, he was merely toeing the official line, being a 'good Mojahed', repeating like a tape recorder whatever he was told to say. It was not a recipe for good diplomacy. Having found my feet in the House, I was about to start work in earnest on the Senate, when I was called back to Iraq.

# 33

# Further Articles of the Revolution

In Iraq I was required to watch some videos about a new stage of the ideological revolution called 'Article J' ['J' for *jensieat*, or sexuality]. We were to learn how to look at the opposite sex as equals, not sex objects. In an introduction, Rajavi said:

> Male sexuality is aggressive; it should be called 'savage male sexuality'. Men see women as objects of sexuality; they judge them first as sex objects and only then perhaps as human. After the last stage of our revolution, your sexuality is responsible for losing the ground we gained, and you see everything as a sex object. Men among us are even more aggressive than before. Now is the time to push your sexuality into retreat.

In a set of separate meetings for men and women – the only woman present at the male sessions was Maryam, now considered our 'ideological mother' – we were instructed that men's sexuality was on the increase, while women were accused of trying to flaunt their femininity and attract men more than before.

To get through this stage, we had to report all our sexual urges and thoughts to our *masoul* (a male substitute if our *masoul* was a woman). Even the tiniest loss of control had to be reported. Everyone was to write a weekly report of his or her 'lost moments'. Then we had to watch more videos in which various brothers talked about their sexual thoughts and feelings. I was shocked when, after watching one of them, Rajavi strode into the meeting room and asked, in front of Maryam, who had masturbated in the past few months. Those who raised their hands kept their eyes lowered so as not to have to look Maryam or Rajavi in the eye. Each individual then had to talk about his sexuality, his feelings and the way he looked at women around him. In another meeting Abrishamchi described sex as 'the physical contact between two pieces of meat': was this worth sacrificing all our ideological goals for?

I had been mystified by the change in behaviour of brothers and sisters towards each other since I had left; they looked at each other like bitter enemies, if at all. Now I understood why. It was no longer all right to exchange smiles and friendly gestures with members of the opposite sex, which might be interpreted as sexual signals. Men and women sat apart during meetings and at mealtimes, leaving an empty no-man's-land between their segregated areas.

We had to report not only on ourselves but also about any perceived misbehaviour by others. God knows what might have been reported about us from abroad! Sometimes I could not believe my ears: a brother who sat on a seat previously occupied by a sister was accused of wanting to touch a seat already touched by a woman; another condemned himself because of a dream he'd had. People went to astonishing lengths to protect themselves from accusation. A man would not pass anything to a woman, even a pencil or a book, but instead would leave it on a desk so she could pick it up without touching him. If a sister fell over in front of a brother, he would not come to her aid.

This lunatic policy inevitably led to disaster. A young man who had fallen in love with a girl wished to tell her of his feelings. One evening she did not come to the communal gathering, feeling unwell and resting in the sisters' hall. He went there but she, shocked to see a man in the dormitory, started shouting for help. Horrified of what might happen, the boy tried to silence her and in

the struggle accidentally killed her. The tragedy was compounded
by the fact that some young men guarding the area heard her cry
for help, but as it came from the girls' hall they didn't dare enter
and instead went in search of a sister who could go see what had
happened. By then the poor girl was already dead. Apparently she
had choked to death; there was no sign of rape.

The obsession with sex was, of course, entirely counterproductive and only increased our awareness of sexuality. In my
childhood home we had many drawings of beautiful women and
men, mostly nude, hanging in our house, and I had grown up
thinking it quite natural to admire human beauty without thoughts
of sex. Similarly, in our family we would shake hands with and even
kiss the members of the opposite sex to show courtesy and
friendship, without any hint of sexual affection coming into play.
Now, however, any look or word could be defined in sexual terms.
I found tendencies in myself that somehow shocked me –
demonstrating, of course, the 'rightness' of the ideological
revolution. Once I even felt drawn to one of the sisters; it was an
unpleasant revelation to me, as I had always thought that it was my
wife alone who attracted me. Needless to say, I felt obliged to write
a full report on my inappropriate thoughts. Equally, though, there
were times when I had no 'moment' of transgression to 'capture'
and ended up inventing something just to keep the authorities
happy. Others did the same, I learned later, thinking it better to
accuse ourselves of something imaginary than be accused of hiding
our urges. In fact, we were often praised for these self-accusations,
which were taken as signs of our honesty and confirmation of the
leader's integrity.

While in this sexual cesspit my *masoul* suggested I write to
Rajavi as the president of the NCR and ask for membership. I'd
had enough problems being a representative of the NCR, and
didn't want further complications. I imagined having to write a
report about my feelings every time I shook hands with a female
politician. No, indeed, this was the last thing I wanted to be drawn
into: to become like those members and supporters who had to
pretend they were not Mojahedin but NCR members.

'No', I said, distraught, 'please, not that.'

She was a bit taken aback and said, 'OK, OK, let me see what
can I do. Forget about it for the time being.'

When I next saw her she said it would be different from what I imagined. It was going to be 'an NCR resolution', according to which all representatives and the secretary had to become members of the NCR and as a result had to resign from the organisation they belonged to. That meant that Reza'i, my previous *masoul* and British NCR representative and I had to 'resign' from the Mojahedin and become NCR members. What did these resignations mean? Nothing for us or the Mojahedin. I think the purpose was only to prove that the NCR was growing and acquiring more 'non-Mojahedin' members. That night Rajavi elaborated on the advantages of this resolution. 'We cannot accept requests from just anyone who wants to become a member of the NCR, as new members will bring new complications and expectations with them. On the other hand, with the limited number of members we have at the moment, anybody in the NCR is "somebody", and we can be blackmailed easily as we are worried to lose any of them. If anyone resigns or is expelled it may not be significant to them but it is a catastrophic blow for us. Our enemies will portray it as another split in the NCR ... Our solution proposes increasing the number of NCR members by adding some of our own members and trusted supporters as individual, independent members. We can even accept a few people introduced by other members of the NCR. The eventual plan is to increase the number of members to 600, one member representing 100,000 Iranians.' (Thus, in 1991–93, the number of NCR members rose from 21 to 235, and on it went.)

That same week, again to demonstrate our democratic practices to the outside world, the organisation called an election to the post of deputy *masoul aval* and to the committee. Everything in this meeting, which was entirely for propaganda purposes, went through on the nod, except for one person's ludicrous attempt to nominate another sister to the post of deputy *masoul* in place of Fahieme'a. But not everyone was happy with the outcome of the elections, notably older members from the Shah's era who wanted their contemporaries posted. It was decreed immediately after the election that from then on we should not display Rajavi's picture but only pictures of Maryam and Fahieme'a. This was supposed to be a sign of his 'modesty', but the rule stopped short at desks and didn't extend to walls, placards, posters and publicity materials, which were always plastered with his photographs.

The next show we held was our biggest and most impressive military parade ever. Most of our American and European supporters and members came to help organise it, and all combatants had prepared for the parade for months beforehand. Everything that moved was painted; new flags and emblems were made; roads were rebuilt and trees uprooted and planted around the parade route. The media were invited and plied with imported luxury food and drink, which occasioned some teasing, as there was generally a shortage of everything in Iraq. For almost five hours vehicles, tanks, guns and uniformed combatants paraded in front of our leaders. For years afterwards people asked embarrassing questions about this: why had the big three (Rajavi, Maryam and Fahieme'a) arrived in a luxury car and sat in an 'imperial pavilion'? Why did Abrishamchi bow to them? Why had we spent so much money on the event? It was, admittedly, uncomfortably reminiscent of the Shah and his wife showcasing their wealth. At the time our main feeling was pride. We saw nothing in common with the Shah and his entourage; the whole extravaganza was necessary to show the world that we were not a small guerrilla organisation but a force to be reckoned with and to quash any rumours about internal conflict and Rajavi's position.

We published a record of the parade, in full colour and in many languages, and of our central committee meeting where our 'democratic' election process was plainly on view. The aim was to demonstrate our strength and independence but also the extent of our international support, including in America, Iraq's number-one enemy.

Returning to America, I found renewed opposition to us from senators. On one occasion I met with the administrative aide to a leading Republican senator on the Foreign Relations Committee. She recited the usual accusations against us, producing documents proving that we had been responsible for the killing of Americans during the Shah's time and had supported hostage-taking in Iran. 'Well', I said, 'our response to all these accusations will be published soon in the congressional record. But let me say that whatever our people did during the Shah's time, they did as patriotic Iranians, and if you were Iranian perhaps you would have done the same. You acted similarly against the British when you fought for your independence. You supported the Shah during a time when he executed and murdered large numbers of our people. But just because you were once at war with the British doesn't mean you have to remain enemies to the end of history. It is the same in our case. We are the sole democratic opposition to the regime. There is no other alternative, and it is evident that you cannot live with that regime either. Good relations between us will be beneficial to both sides. Islamic fundamentalism is the next threat to international peace and we are the only counter to it. Do not repeat your mistake at the beginning of the Iranian revolution. Do not imprison yourselves in the past; listen instead to genuine Iranian voices.' I don't know how persuaded she was, but at the end of the meeting she promised to support neither any action for or against us.

The aforementioned response to the accusations was published in 1992, and we sent copies to the offices of various senators. A State Department statement published at the same time included some arguments in our favour, including the recognition that we were not a communist organisation but a Muslim one. It also accepted in part our assertion about the assassination of Americans during the Shah's time; our leader had been in jail then, and later there was a coup in the organisation, so the current leadership and almost all the central committee, who were not then even members of the Mojahedin, could not have been responsible for those acts. These reports paved the way for the re-establishment of normal relations with many offices.

I concluded that the State Department was wary of us not because of our past or our Iraqi bases, but because we could not demonstrate a commitment to democracy. The US had no special interest in promoting a democratic regime in Iran, but knew this was the only way to guarantee stability in the modern world as well as their own interests around the globe. They also knew that unless we could present a democratic face to the Iranian people we would be unable to attract the support of the majority. Unfortunately we were unable to prove that commitment. Our so-called elections fooled some people but certainly not the State Department, nor those politicians who were themselves past masters of such trickery. We claimed that the NCR had many non-Mojahedin members, but were very hesitant to let even NCR members like Dr Matin-Daftary, one of the genuine non-Mojahedin council members, have any meetings with Americans for fear that he would defect. When he visited the US, I had orders to take him anywhere from Disneyland in California to sightseeing in Washington, but not to meet with any American politician. As Bazargan had said a few years earlier, we were as monopolist as the regime itself; even as an opposition we were unprepared to share anything with anybody not fully committed to our cause and our leader.

Rajavi always characterised the Mojahedin as the only real alternative to the regime because of its organised structure, whereas, he said, other so-called 'alternatives' had none. However, the real question for the Iranian people was how to achieve democracy in Iran. The Mojahedin manipulated this yearning, framing it before the intelligentsia as a question of choosing between a faction of the regime or the Mojahedin; those who chose neither sunk into passivity. I believe the Mojahedin fell into this self-created trap. Rather than try to prove they were democratic and devise solutions for achieving democracy in Iran, they relied instead on proving the might of their armed forces to bolster their claims of being 'organised' and powerful enough to overcome the regime. Thus they further alienated Iranians for whom such demonstrations of power were only too familiar.

I was in an ambivalent position, being introduced in American politics as a non-Mojahed and representative of the council but at the same time being in fact a Mojahed. Having wrestled with this dilemma long enough, I eventually complained that I was not the right person for the job and recommended that a real non-Mojahedin council member represent us there. Appointing such a person would show that not all of us were from the Mojahedin, that we really believed in a pluralistic society, a clear sign of democracy. The suggestion was always brushed aside; instead of a response I was asked for more propaganda materials.

The regime's answer to our parade was to attack our bases in Iraq. In late March 1992, Iranian planes attacked Ashraf, killing one combatant and damaging some buildings – although we shot down one plane and captured two pilots, so the gain was largely ours. The attack raised many unanswered questions. How could they fly from a 'no-fly zone' set by allied forces at the end of the Gulf War, without American blessing? Why had they stopped short at this moderate level of damage, when their planes were capable of destroying the whole fort and killing all its inhabitants? The Iranian regime claimed this operation was in retaliation against our destruction of an Iranian village on the border and the deaths of several people there. This was untrue as we had not yet started our guerrilla attacks in Iran, a claim the UN inspection team substantiated.

Immediately, all our branches around the world received an order from central command to launch retaliatory strikes against Iranian embassies. In a single day our supporters in thirteen cities – in Europe, Australia, Canada and America – attacked Iranian embassies and took some of their staff captive. In some cases they burned the buildings to the ground.

The exercise was a fiasco, and we were the main losers. During this time I was in New York, trying to persuade members of the UN Security Council to pass a resolution condemning the Iranian regime for its action. For the first time, even the Chinese were willing to meet us, partly from curiosity; before we launched our attack, they had not known our strength. When the regime showed itself prepared to violate international norms to attack us, they became more intrigued still. Their view about the mildness of the Iranian attack was either that we were well prepared thanks to our intelligence, or that the pilots held back because of our popularity among army personnel. All the member countries welcomed us, even Russia, which had always favoured the Iranian regime. Until then our chances of securing that resolution had been high, but our attack on the embassies shattered that hope and the final declaration of the UN not only condemned the attack but even shifted the balance of favour towards the regime. In many countries, such as Canada, we lost ground totally to Iran and our poor representative in that country suddenly found himself isolated. In Sweden, our *masoul* was expelled to France. In terms of real diplomacy, the episode put us back several years. In many countries our bases were put under constant surveillance and our activities circumscribed.

Worst of all was the human suffering we had inflicted on ourselves. Many of our supporters were imprisoned. When a member of the NCR asked if this action had been a wise one, he received the reply that the regime had wanted to kill Rajavi. To preserve his life we had to pay any price, and we also had to teach the regime the cost of any action against him.

But this was not the final assault on our bases in Iraq. On a few occasions the regime attacked with planes and on many others they used agents in Baghdad, resulting in the deaths of a handful of members.

By the beginning of summer we were undergoing yet another phase of ideological revolution, and we were recalled to Iraq. This new revolution was called 'Article D' and its subject was the superiority of women over men in organisational relations and activities.

# 34

# Articles of Faith

'Article D' specified that women had more revolutionary potential than men and were therefore ideologically superior. Having suffered from 'double exploitation' throughout history, women were like coiled springs, capable of more energy when released. This was why they had 'leapt' to higher positions than men in our organisation.

Another explanation for the rise of women within the organisation, propagated by the leadership, was that our commitment to the revolution had exponentially multiplied our energy and capacity. Previously we'd had to rely on our own capabilities; now we drew strength from Maryam and Masoud. The slogan was, 'we must forget our own feet and walk with Maryam's feet. Then instead of walking we can fly.' It was argued that men had traditionally relied on themselves, whereas women were dependent creatures with no resources of their own. Thus it was easier for a woman to switch from dependence on a man to dependence on Maryam than it was for a man to reduce to 'zero' and then 'rise to infinity'.

The organisational consequence of this phase was that from

then on, no man could be the ideological or organisational *masoul* of any woman, although in executive work, when having expertise was essential, a woman could for a short period tactically be under the responsibility of a man. Moreover, it was ruled that every man within the organisation had to have an 'ideological woman *masoul*'.

About the same time they changed the ranking system of the organisation, creating two parallel systems for men and women. Rankings had not hitherto been a major issue for the majority of members – we were all light years away from Masoud and Maryam anyway. Previously I ranked 'HE' (executive committee member), the highest rank then available to members. Attaining it was no different from being first told I had been accepted as a member of the organisation. In this new phase, all men became deputies of a *masoul* who had to be a woman, so our rank was 'M' (*maven*, or deputy). I was elevated to 'MO', the highest among the 'M's. (I never learned what the 'O' stood for, nor did I bother to ask.)

In one meeting for all the HE members, the first thing Rajavi said was, 'I have heard from the doctor that your urine has bubbles in it. Strangely, according to him, HE members' urine has bubbles in it while ordinary members' urine doesn't.' We sat there dumb with astonishment. 'Don't look at me with surprise, as if you don't know what that means! It means that, even years after the ideological revolution, you have not been able to neutralise your sexual desires, and still have ejaculations, which create bubbles in your urine! Yet the people under your charge have cured themselves of this problem!' As usual, a few brothers who followed Rajavi slavishly rushed to reinforce his statement by piling on exaggerations. One of them said, 'We are not HE, we are "hee-haw"!' – and imitated the braying of a donkey. The implication that we were animals unable to control our natural urges was obvious. For a time after that meeting we were without rank, which of course meant nothing, as our responsibilities were the same as before. But whenever we met we jokingly greeted each other with 'hee-haw' – and we were careful not to leave bubbles behind when we urinated. Then the new ranking system was brought in, and our individuals ranks made known to us.

After watching almost thirty hours of videotapes, I was required to write a report on what I had learned. The long flight from the US to Jordan followed by a long drive from there to Iraq, then sitting for days watching those tapes, had left me with severe back pain and I needed some time out. It was a blessing. To be alone was itself a luxury, as we were normally with other people all the time, sharing work, meals, rest times and even feelings. We were sad or happy when everybody else was, according to the news of the day. We were proud of having shed our individuality and moulded ourselves into some kind of super-organism. Outsiders (or, as we called them, 'enemies', 'anti-revolutionaries' or 'traitors') said simply that we had been 'brainwashed' and changed from human beings into cogs in a big machine, so that Rajavi could gain power. Essentially there was no difference between our perspectives and theirs, but we considered that our self-abnegation was a privilege undergone for a greater good. Forgetting ourselves allowed us to become one with our leaders.

For a day or two I wracked my brain. We had to explain our objection to the issue of female superiority raised in 'Article D'. But the more I thought about it, the fewer objections I could find. I knew perfectly well I could not ask to be considered a special case, as according to the organisation there was no such thing: all men were alike, with 'savage male sexuality' – an aggressive attitude that looked at everything from a sexual viewpoint.

Long before joining the organisation, I had read in a book that Hassan Saba'h, an Iranian revolutionary leader with his own cult who fought against kings and Mongols, demanded that his male disciples rid themselves of their sexuality through castration. I couldn't help feeling now that castration would be the easier option, involving one surgical procedure, some physical pain and perhaps a soothing convalescence, whereas being required to castrate ourselves mentally inevitably meant gradually and slowly, with tremendous suffering dragged on for years.

Apart from writing about 'Article D', I had also to take a position on another issue: that of *borida-ha*. The terms '*borida*' (singular) and '*borida-ha*' (plural) in Mojahedin vocabulary had connotations of 'surrender', 'failure', 'fatigue' and 'loser', and were applied to people who, for whatever reason, had reached a point of being unable to work with the Mojahedin any more and were on the verge of leaving the organisation.

Until a few years earlier, perhaps until Operation Forogh, this had not been an issue of concern. It was a term mostly used for prisoners who had capitulated under torture and confessed or repented. Such people were not condemned, as we knew how terrible torture could be; indeed, many were welcomed back into the organisation and some resumed normal lives. However, we'd made it known to potential recruits that 'our exit doors are wide open, but our entrance doors are shut to all but the most tenacious.' In earlier days it was easy for anyone unable to stand the pace to leave the organisation with no disrepute attached to them. Now, however, after the start of the new phase of the ideological revolution in 1989-90 (with the issue of divorce), there was more ill will directed towards those who wanted to leave, especially old members.

As defectors usually lived apart from others, some found segregation without responsibility so painful they preferred refugee camps in Iraq. After the Gulf War, however, the number of people leaving the organisation as a result of both the ideological revolution and the war increased sharply, and the situation in the refugee camps worsened. Most of the inmates had lost their refugee status and had no passports, so they remained stuck in the camps in harsh conditions for a long time. The Mojahedin had no objection to ordinary members or supporters leaving the organisation; in fact, those who had not had an ideological revolution were not welcome in any department. The situation was different for high-ranking and long-standing members. The organisation made no effort to help them to return to Europe, and in many cases they were surely forcibly restrained. Although the official line remained that anyone who wanted to could leave, we knew perfectly well that the credo had been reversed for good: entering the organisation was easier than ever, but leaving – especially for high-ranking members in Iraq – was almost impossible.

During the ideological revolution, to call someone 'ordinary' or *borida* was the worst possible insult. As we considered ourselves the most revolutionary, sophisticated and purest human beings, to be ordinary was to be as different from us as it was possible to be. The word acquired the connotations of being a savage, an animal with crude and 'dirty' needs. To become an ordinary man or woman was just one step short of becoming a *borida*, as those needs would force the person to leave the organisation. *Borida* had an ideological meaning too; it connoted forgetting the oath made to our leader, betraying or abandoning him as Imam Hussein was abandoned in his final battle.

In one videotape, during a discussion about this issue, our *masouls* in Europe reported on their activities, saying how hard they were working to change the Mojahedin's image among Iranians and even foreigners. In almost all Iranian media outside and inside the country there were testimonies from former members about alleged torture and imprisonment by the organisation and about the ideological revolution, the forced divorces and the separation of children from parents. There was a memorable meeting in which one of our sisters cried out that those who left were traitors and should be executed instead of being set free to work against the organisation. Her feelings were echoed by speaker after speaker until Zari, who was from Britain, stood and reminded everyone of the slogan about our wide-open exit doors. Uproar greeted her, and one sister called her an 'ordinary woman' while another chimed, 'No, she is not ordinary, she is *borida*! This is why she is defending them!' Another sister demanded she be ejected from the meeting. Then Rajavi rose as the angel of mercy and compassion, showing his 'kindness' and 'understanding'.

'Zari is right,' he said. 'We cannot execute everybody who wants to leave. We must give such people the facilities, money, everything, to go wherever they wish.' He was not allowed to finish, nor did he wish to; he had already dropped the poison in the cup. We all knew the organisation was short of money for its own activities and could not obtain passports even for our own people who needed to travel abroad. By his words he saved face; yet the sarcasm contained beneath them merely plunged Zari and those of like mind further into the mire.

One very high-ranking sister said, facing Rajavi, 'You, with your compassion and mercy, have every right to dictate what you think is right, and we are sure you would never let us do things we feel are right to punish those traitors. But we must take a position against them. If we do not sharpen our boundaries by condemning them, we'll always have our own bridges back to the past and to ordinary life, which means we could end up in the same situation. I think all Mojahedin must have a clear position on this issue.' The silence that followed her remarks was a sure sign that her view would prevail. Naturally, everyone had to write a report after the meeting to clarify his or her position on the matter.

I admired Zari's courage in speaking out in defence of the objects of our hatred. Courage, however, was not what the organisation valued most; the crucial thing was not to maintain any links with the past or with people outside the organisation. I knew, too, that the admiration I felt for Zari arose from my own weakness and 'liberal tendencies'. I had long known that a revolutionary must hate as much as love. We were to hate the enemies of our leaders as enemies of our people, indeed, of humanity itself. But being able to hate was not one of my virtues and I had always been ashamed of it. I had every reason to hate those people, not only as a member but even personally, as it was I who, on behalf of the organisation, had to counter their reports against us within diplomatic circles. During the previous few years, they had inflicted more damage on the Mojahedin than had all the activities of the 'anti-revolutionaries' since 1979.

I had been told repeatedly that love and hate are two sides of the same coin: one cannot love someone without hating his enemies, and one cannot hate without love. When I was entirely alone, I saw that, deep down, I didn't even hate the revolutionary guards. I was able to fight them if required to, but I was not sure I could kill them. The more I thought about my inability to hate, the more I questioned my ability to love. After all the coin does not exist that has only one side! I began to doubt my love for Maryam, for our people, for humanity and justice. Did I love them with my whole heart? If I did, why couldn't I hate their enemies? If not, what was I doing there? What had I been doing during the past fifteen years? Why had I left everything, including those dearest to me, my own family? Had I sacrificed anything? If so, for whom? If not, then what was the meaning of sacrifice? Did I love only myself? But if that was the case, then why I was putting myself through that amount of suffering?

By then there was a question mark over everything in my mind and heart. I wrote a report mentioning all these questions and asking for help from my *masoul*. She said it was good that I was honest and criticised myself, but that there were certain things I had no right to question. 'You are a member of the Mojahedin,' she said, 'and this membership has an ideological meaning. Masoud has approved your ideological revolution and you have no right to put a question mark over it. Yes, you have your weaknesses, your liberal tendencies. You have not destroyed all bridges to your past, and this is why you feel sympathy towards *borida-ha*. Your responsibility is to find those bridges and destroy them. That is all you have to do; nothing less, nothing more.' She told me to forget about that issue for the time being and concentrate instead on 'Article D', which was perhaps where my difficulty lay.

However much I considered 'Article D', I could find no problem with it. During my life within the organisation, most of my *masouls* had been women; on the whole they had been very hard on me, sometimes misjudging me, insulting me and even wrongly punishing me, but I felt no resentment towards them. On the contrary, I liked and admired them. As a matter of fact, the only *masoul* I did not much approve of was a man, Mohadessin. He was the only one who never criticised, teased or insulted me, who worried more about my health than I did myself, who insisted I take care of my back. But for all his kindness, I doubted he cared enough for the organisation. My disagreement with him related to our policy in America and also in our international organisations section, where it seemed to me that most of our achievements, especially those of Doctor, were going to be lost and nobody cared. I wrote many reports about this, accusing Mohadessin of wasting our achievements and of turning our diplomacy into a sham, whereupon I was accused in turn of trying to safeguard my personal stake and not the gains made by the organisation. Finally Badrie, *masoul* to both Mohadessin and me, ordered me bluntly not to write any further reports against Mohadessin. I think she took my criticisms as personal, whereas in fact I had no personal grievance against Mohadessin. I now realise that the organisation didn't care at all about personal relationships among us; in fact, they wanted to destroy them completely, even fomenting hatred, as this was the only way they could neutralise division within the organisation at grassroots level. It was the age-old policy of 'divide and rule'. So, they were angry about my views on our diplomacy, not on Mohadessin, who was Rajavi's favourite to conduct our diplomacy as he had no personal designs and unfailingly followed Rajavi's orders without question or hesitation.

I could still not produce any substantial objections to 'Article D', so eventually I dredged up some old stories about myself and exaggerated them in the hope that my new *masoul* would be convinced I had looked deep into my unworthy soul. Apparently I went a bit further than necessary, as my report went straight to Rajavi and he called me in.

It was about five or six in the evening. He was alone and was eating lunch. He usually worked until midday, then slept until five or six in the afternoon, after which he carried on with meetings and work right through the night until the following day around noon. Had I had my lunch, he asked, but didn't wait for my answer, smiling. 'Oh, I forgot, you are one of those normal people who have lunch around the time when I have tea before going to bed!' Then, still without letting me speak, he continued. 'What is this rubbish you have written in your report? Do you know what your problem is?'

I said, 'Well, I have no problem with sisters acting as my *masouls*, but according to the revolution I know I cannot be a special case and must be like the others and have problems too. Maybe something is wrong with me ...'

'Rubbish!' he broke in. 'You are not opposed to anybody because you are "yoghurt". You are unable to oppose anybody, because you are a liberal. You want to love everybody and be loved by everybody. But that is not your problem. Your real problem is Anna. You have not divorced her permanently, and you are still hoping to return to her.' I had difficulty suppressing a smile; he had, of course, hit the nail on the head. I nodded. He laughed loudly and said, 'So, if you know what your problem is, why are you playing with us and your poor *masoul*?' He asked after my marital situation. 'Well', I answered, 'we have not officially divorced, but I presume she knows all about the ideological revolution.'

'Good', said Rajavi. 'You know we could not agree to your divorce for political reasons, but as everybody now knows about them, and we have not denied them, that problem has been resolved. There is no longer any obstacle to your divorce. But you must give us the right to announce it to Anna whenever we feel it is fitting. You should write her, asking for a divorce; give the letter to your *masoul* and forget about her.'

The meeting concluded with smiles on both sides. He was right. Against the rule of the ideological revolution, I had not divorced my wife ideologically and was, deep down, still in love with her and hoping to resume our life together after our victorious return to Iran. But the struggle looked set to continue undiminished. I could imagine how miserable Anna felt, not knowing where she stood or what the future held for us, and I was not prepared to let her suffer any more. Divorcing her would be an act of loving kindness, which I wholeheartedly wanted to do.

I duly wrote my report and my letter to Anna announcing our divorce, and handed them to my *masoul*. The letter was never passed on to her. Accordingly, my situation didn't change in the slightest.

# 35

# Steel

We had heard about the new elites of the NLA, responsible for guerrilla operations inside Iran, and a few of us asked to see them in training in Iraq. They were trained to survive for days in the desert and marshes without food or supplies, relying only on the water they found there and eating whatever animals, frogs or insects they found. They were made to stand for hours under a lamp without moving, all the while subject to attacks from every kind of insect ...

When we were there, their commander staged a night raid on them. The surprise caught some of them unawares, but within a few minutes they were all up, ready for action. This included running barefoot over stones and brambles, crawling through mud, walking on their hands and rolling on the ground. At a given signal they climbed the nearest tree or lamppost and stayed there as long as their commanders wanted. The physical training – which made even observers feel completely out of breath – was supplemented by psychological training. The commander might, for example, order them to bring back the largest stone they could find, promising that 'the last person to return and the one with the smallest stone will be punished'. When they returned, he did the exact opposite: all except the last and the finder of the smallest stone would receive a punishment in the form of fifty pushups. The lesson was to expect the unexpected, and to respond logically to the illogical. Other exercises were designed to teach the men that they would suffer mostly not because of their own wrongdoings but because of the wrongdoings of others. Though we were tired and frustrated, they seemed fresh as daisies and full of heroic songs and chants. Whenever their commanders asked if they were tired or wanted to return to camp, their answer was, 'Steel, steel' – which was the new slogan of the organisation, not just for them but for everybody. 'Steel' represented hardness, inflexibility and endurance, desirable characteristics for all members.

To keep morale up, manoeuvres were conducted occasionally, always hyperbolically described as 'the last and biggest manoeuvre before the final operation' but hardly a substitute for the real thing. It was almost three years since the new training regime had been introduced, based on the rejection of methods dating from the Shah's time and drawing on things learned in Palestinian camps in the 1960s and 1970s. Those methods had failed during Operation Forogh, when many combatants preferred to leave their tanks and use guerrilla tactics. After the second stage of the ideological revolution, older commanders were retired from active service and combatants were told to forget everything they had learned in the past and start again from scratch. An 'army university' was established, staffed by Iraqi trainers and instructors in the art and armaments of classical warfare.

Maryam believed women learned much faster because of their swift progress to ideological revolution and because they had 'blank slates'. Gradually, therefore, they replaced men as commanding officers at every level, especially after the implementation of 'Article D'. This 'positive discrimination' was not a great success, as many older members resented being commanded by a woman much younger than they who lacked the necessary experience or ability.

A few months later, elite troops exploded three bombs at Khomeini's tomb on the instructions of Rajavi, who had exhorted them to destroy it completely – having first removed its gold contents, which belonged to the people. As far as I was concerned, this was self-defeating, counterproductive in moral and military terms and sacrilegious. Using the same argument about removing the symbols of previous authorities, we could justify destroying all the ancient and historical buildings of Iran – something we accused the regime of doing. Rajavi congratulated the perpetrators on providing the 'response to the massacre of political prisoners and the recent attack on Ashraf base'.

Further action followed in the name of our recent martyrs, including the destruction of many military bases and matériel and the killing of revolutionary guards and 'mercenaries of the regime', which could include anybody. For the first time economic targets were hit such as oil wells, refineries and pipelines. After such operations the regime took revenge by attacking our Iraqi bases or carrying out terrorist activities against members in Europe, especially Turkey – among them the assassination of Naghdi, the NCR's representative in Italy. However just or unjust our retaliations, our people were the losers in terms of wealth and freedom. Even we in the political section suffered. The US State Department, replying to a letter from one of our supporters in Congress, wrote,

> ... Just as we vigorously oppose the Iranian government's support for terrorism, we cannot in turn condone the continuing use of terror by the Mojahedin or any opposition group. Recent violence has included simultaneous attacks on thirteen Iranian diplomatic missions around the world, including the Iranian UN mission in New York. In October 1992, the Mojahedin claimed to have exploded a bomb at Khomeini's mausoleum, visited by hundreds of civilians each day. As recently as March 1994, the Mojahedin continued to claim responsibility for bomb blasts in the streets of Iranian towns. These activities are supported by their military wing, the National Liberation Army ...

Needless to say, the violence raised questions we could not answer and, far from bringing us closer to overthrowing the regime, actually distanced us from our goal. Perhaps the only advantage of the actions was that they postponed any chance of moderation within the Iranian regime, which could seriously jeopardise our victory. As Maryam had said, our main objective was no longer to install democracy in Iran but to guarantee Rajavi's right to lead. At the same time, it was obvious that the regime had infiltrated our elite section right from the start. The first evidence came when one of the members of the section, on an operation inside Iran, killed five or six fellow members of the section. This incident, embarrassing for the organisation, was hushed up. Although ex-members of the Mojahedin who showed any opposition towards us were described as 'the regime's agents' and 'members of the secret police', real agents managed to live among us happily without any problem. The regime was more successful at infiltration than we were. Despite infighting between different factions of the regime, which worked to our advantage, their sophisticated methods gave them the upper hand. All they had to do was 'admire our leadership' and perhaps shed a tear or two to show how much Maryam's message and the ideological revolution had moved them.

We learned of the regime's spies within the organisation from their own confessions. One, named Tabandeh, claimed to have been one of the most cruel torturers of the regime, and published his experiences in a 100-page book. The confessions of another came to me when I was the Mojahedin's representative in human rights and international organisations, and I was asked to decide if they should be published. For several weeks I tried to read it, but could not bring myself to contemplate the horrifying sexual tortures described, such as dripping acid or forcing broken bottles into vaginas or anuses. I simply could not decide what to do about those memoirs one way or the other.

I was certainly not a newcomer at bearing witness to such disturbing material. It was part of my job to interview ex-prisoners to see if they should meet representatives of human rights organisations or attend international meetings, and I eventually became accustomed to the most traumatic descriptions. According to the ex-prisoners' testimony, sexual torture was common in Iranian jails. Most of those interviewed had been raped in prison, several times by different men. Even those who had resisted other forms of torture often cracked after being raped a few times. Once, two young men who had been raped came to Geneva to meet Galindo Pohl. While we were with Pohl we noticed that Doctor, who was translating their testimony, hesitated to translate everything they said, as it was too horrific. One of the boys then asked me for drawing materials and began illustrating their experiences. He was a skilled artist, and it was obvious that his images depicted real events. These two boys were among the finest people I ever met; tragically, they were killed in Operation Forogh. Despite my familiarity with such stories, I nevertheless vetoed the publication of Tabandeh's memoirs from fear that people would find them exaggerated or entirely unbelievable.

Back in America I began to grasp the full implications of 'Article D'. Few people doubted the potential of women or had reservations about elevating them to high positions, but there remained a gap between the principle and the reality which had to be filled to some extent with positive discrimination. Of course, the gap could not be fully closed; moreover, our prime objective was the overthrow of the regime, not the establishment of an egalitarian society! On the other hand, when our leader wanted something, that was the end of the argument. Our response had to be: 'We can and we must'.

Most of the sisters joined the organisation when they were less than fifteen years old, some even as young as ten. Not only had they had no chance of university or even secondary education, but they also had largely missed out on all the up and downs of normal lives. We recognised that we had to accept orders from them even if they were illogical or unreasonable, as most of our logic and reason were inherited from our old way of life and class orientation, which had to be denied. Outside in the male-dominated real world, things were tougher for the women, especially when dealing with non-Iranians. They had to work much harder to achieve the same status or respect as men.

It was our responsibility to transmit our knowledge and experience to them as quickly as possible, to prepare them for real action. The difficulty was getting them to accept us as their tutors. The more ideological they were, the less faith they had in us. We relied, after all, on 'savage male' logic, yet at the same time we were weak and passive. On top of that, it was Rajavi's view that we were reluctant to concede our jobs to women and educate them to replace us. The women were under immense pressure to confront and criticise us any way they could, to show us up for our wrongdoings and demonstrate their superior capability and sophistication. They had not only to achieve everything we had achieved but more, to prove the correctness of the leader's analysis.

Having a woman *masoul* caused new problems. When we entered any Congress building, as Muslim female dress evoked fundamentalism (and therefore terrorism) amongst Americans, we had to go through security double-checks. Instead of greeting people I knew in a friendly way, I had to guard against giving what could be interpreted as a 'sexual look'. Our women were our 'ideological defence', and were very punctilious in identifying our 'wrongdoings'. Not only did they scrutinise us, but they were expected to encourage the men to confront each other, too. For example, my *masoul* once pointed out our spokesman, standing with one foot on a step higher than the other, and said, 'Shame on you! You see him standing like that, advertising his sexuality, and you don't confront him!'

In America I was the highest-ranking among our brothers and thus had some responsibility towards them. To me this meant helping them with personal problems, which perhaps they could not share with a woman. Far from it: I was expected to watch their behaviour when there was no sister *masoul* present and remind them of the danger of sexual wrongdoing or reproach them for transgressions. In most cases what they were supposed to have done wrong was completely beyond me. The rationale for all this nonsense was that the women had to prove their 'revolution' by discarding their defensive position towards men and adopting an offensive one. They, too, reported weekly about themselves.

In our political meetings the main concern was no longer political but sexual. Our women were not permitted to shake hands with men, and we had to warn those whom we met to save embarrassment. There were other complications. As the NCR representative, obviously I was head of the delegation and the spokesperson at any meeting. But the rule was that we had to let women play an equal part. This caused endless confusion and irritation. Besides, there was usually no need for two people to be present at all. Especially in the early days, our sisters did nothing but repeat what they had learned from public meetings and articles in our papers, much of it completely contrary to what we wanted to say in diplomatic settings. They were not able or permitted to have normal friendly conversations and could rarely answer nonstandard questions. Whenever they spoke, they tended to preface every statement with an elucidation of Rajavi's teachings, starting with the story of Adam and Eve. Before they even got to the matter at hand, the people they were addressing often become so bored they excused themselves. Fortunately, our old supporters in politics knew us well enough by then not to be offended by changes within our organisation and tolerated the annoyances this caused. Thus, our reports could continue to show how successful our meetings had been and how true the vision of our leaders.

It was important for us men to toe a careful line between being passive and being perceived as over-keen on our own positions. I saw little hope for improving our political achievements. The organisation got what it wanted, but only because its concern was not for the quantity and genuineness of our achievements but the extent to which our activities could be advertised as shows of our political strength, especially to Iraqis and our members and supporters. For example, the American custom of holding fundraising luncheons or dinner parties with personalities and politicians, with tickets costing 1,000 dollars or more, was turned to our advantage. Mohadessin managed to secure an invitation to a dinner party with President Bill Clinton present. Photographs of the party were printed in our papers, described as the official meeting of our representative with the president, who even sent regards to Maryam. The usual courtesies of American politicians were portrayed as something special, like personal letters of congratulation or messages of support for the organisation. It was sometimes amusing to see how the papers generated this false impression, especially among our supporters, but more often it was depressing.

I joined the Mojahedin with a purpose and stayed with them mainly for the same reason. But I was frustrated by our lack of real progress. It was clear to me that we could not go forward in the US without a strong lobby, like the Israelis did. We had all the means to set up such a lobby which, even after the revolution, was the only guarantee of our independence. With our supporters' help we could establish such an organised lobby, and that was where I directed my efforts. There were obstacles here, too. Our women *masouls* were generally unsympathetic towards ordinary supporters and habitually belittled any complaints or worries they had by comparing them with the suffering of people in Iran. This reasoning was thought to be enough to win over these people, but in fact our inconsiderate attitudes drove them away by the day.

Money was the ever-intractable, ever-nagging problem. We criticised the regime for not being able to solve the financial problems of the country, but over fifteen years we had not been able to solve even a fraction of our own. The official justification of our situation was that no government in the world was helping us and that we had to find the solution ourselves. But in that case, we wondered, did we have to dissipate all our energies earning money? There were many merchants with good business acumen among our old supporters, who, with the right encouragement, could probably have been persuaded to part with some capital and help us start up businesses that would generate income. But our leader's short-sightedness left us with the problem forever. These former merchants were employed as drivers or sent to buy provisions for the bases, a catastrophic waste of their talents.

Our leader's answer to our financial or any other problems was to put more pressure on his followers. Rajavi's main talent was finding words, ways and tricks to force his disciples to work harder physically. After each stage of the ideological revolution the instruction came from on high to multiply our energy and achievements tenfold or even hundredfold. Our sisters, obliged to demonstrate their ability and commitment, then transferred at least part of the pressure to the members and supporters in their charge. As a result, many of these – some as old as sixty and ailing, others as young as ten – had to stand in the streets for ten to fifteen hours per day asking people for money. Their suffering, which we branded the 'price of our independence', was in reality the price of our incompetence and naïveté.

The American states were now divided between several *masouls*, each of whom had to raise a certain amount of money from supporters within her geographical boundary. The target amounts were always unattainably high and rose with every new phase of the ideological revolution, with every piece of 'glorious news' such as 'the meeting of Mohadessin with President Clinton' or 'the letter from Bill Clinton to Masoud [Rajavi]!'. I had no allotted geographical area and nobody under my charge to help me, so I had to travel from state to state calling meetings with supporters and other sympathetic Iranians, explaining the situation, answering their questions and asking for financial help.

A difficult issue arose at a meeting in Lexington, Kentucky. Somebody asked about the virtues that suited Fahieme'a to the position of Maryam's deputy. I answered in a way that I believed myself.

'Whatever she has is from Maryam. Her main quality is her ability to minimise her individuality and become united with Maryam. Her incentives come not from personal achievements but from the achievements of the organisation. Hence she can think, learn and act faster and more effectively than any of us.'

My questioner interrupted me. 'What is wrong with individuality?' he demanded. 'I am an individual. I am married and have my own children. This is our individual home [where the meeting took place]. I love my wife and children more than anything else in the world. I like certain foods and colours. I like to be successful and see my talents and achievements bring a happier and more comfortable life for my family, and of course that enables me to help others as well, including the Mojahedin. I even might join you in fighting against the regime as I think of Iran as "my country" and want to see it free and happy. So my individuality helps me not only to achieve a better life for myself and my family but also to be a useful member of the local community and citizen and, of course, able to help your organisation. Now tell me, why should I put all that aside and get my incentives from somebody else, even someone as pure and noble as Maryam?!'

Frankly I didn't know what to say. I had become used to accepting without question the principles promulgated by the leadership. But now, after many years, I was back on earth, facing real people and real questions. 'Well', I said eventually, 'nothing is wrong with you, but you have chosen not to be a Mojahed, whereas we have. Individualism and monotheism are contradictory ways of thinking and living. One person might believe in the former, another in the latter. It is a matter of belief and conviction, not of logic or scientific proof, and I don't think we would ever be able to persuade each other of the correctness of our own positions. But what is important is that we have a common interest in our country and our people, and a common enemy. These are enough, I think, to unite us for life.'

In another meeting in San Jose, California, I spoke about the Forogh operation and boasted of our political achievements which had made that operation worthwhile and justified the deaths of so many. I made it plain that the peak achievement was to stifle any possibility of *estehalle* (the regime's shift towards moderation). One listener argued that *estehalle* could be a desirable thing. I was taken aback, because nobody had questioned the rightness of our position in this respect for a long time. Whenever anyone questioned something we considered as fact, rather than examine our views we dismissed the issue by calling the questioner an anti-revolutionary. We were implacably opposed to any regime in Iran except a revolutionary one, which obviously could not be anything but the rule of the NCR, which meant the Mojahedin. My questioner persisted. What was our position *vis-à-vis* Bazargan? Surely he displayed courage by continuing to live in Iran, but at the same time openly and constantly expressing his opposition to the regime's totalitarianism? Why had Rajavi recently condemned Bazargan?

I was familiar with the issue. A few years earlier Bazargan, in one of his open letters to Khomeini, wrote: 'In the Iranian situation, one either has to stand up and resist the regime or lead some kind of petty and treacherous life …' This statement became famous and was quoted endlessly in articles against Bazargan. He had also opposed the UN's condemnation of human rights violations in Iran, calling it an excuse for foreign countries to become involved in Iranian politics and a threat to Iran's independence. Rajavi, in response, accused Bazargan of cynically positioning himself to secure the nomination for the forthcoming presidential election. In fact, the opposite was true: Bazargan believed the election was illegal and should be boycotted. My own view was that, right or wrong, Bazargan was an honest man who meant what he said. So again, I had no proper answer for my questioner. Fortunately, at that point in the meeting, arguments broke out between close supporters and others and he himself was accused of being a 'supporter of Bazargan' and an 'anti-revolutionary'. This gave me a little time to think, and I was able to show that we were democratic enough to tolerate opposition by rescuing him from his accusers.

That night I realised how distant we were from the Mojahedin's original position at the beginning of the revolution. They had accused the same Bazargan (when prime minster) of not caring about our independence, and had issued an almost identical statement to the condemnation of human rights violations.

Not only were we not the same Mojahedin of old, but we were unable to understand the needs and hopes of ordinary Iranians or give satisfactory answers to a supporter's questions. On the other hand, I recalled the misery of our people, the murders of our members, the recent assassination of Naghdi and the torture and murder of our political representative in Turkey. I recognised the sacrifices and hard work of our people. I thought about those questions, of course, but without conviction, hence my thinking did not crystallise from feeling into understanding and believing. I was also intensely conscious of having changed myself. I could not speak heart-to-heart with people as I used to. But I blamed everything on my own personal weaknesses and my mental resistance to the new article of the ideological revolution. After all, Maryam had warned us many times to beware of the personal devil that would reject and undermine our new characters. We had to forget our individual selves, our personal desires, and melt into the leadership, become steel ...

# 36

# Finance and Fitness

'Article D', intended to elevate and promote women, was a mixed blessing. In order to show their superiority compared with men, women had to work much harder. Many of them, in their efforts to obtain support, resorted to tactics that were morally and ethically wrong. We all told 'white lies', saying, for example, that we needed money to buy tanks or helicopters. Many of our supporters found these excuses laughable, as they knew perfectly well that with the kind of money they were giving us we could not buy a rifle, never mind heavy armaments. The organisation announced a few months later that our total earnings from all activities had been 6 billion *toman* over four years or, at then current rate of exchange, around $7 million on average annually. As far as I know, it never went higher. Our demonstrations in America alone cost between $500,000 and $1 million per year. On top of that, we had to meet expenses incurred by personnel outside Iraq and in Iraq itself, where the embargo required many goods to be imported from Europe. It was well-known that we received our armaments from Iraq.

Our sisters, finding deaf ears to pleas for money, resorted

increasingly to emotional tactics, but even these had a limited shelf life and worked once or twice at most. To reach the level of earnings we required, they had no choice but to ask for loans. This was another disaster that had repercussions for years to come. Everywhere and almost every day, as representative of the NCR, I faced complaints that the organisation was long overdue in settling debts. When our *masouls* found rich close supporters dedicated enough to accept their excuses, they did not hesitate to use any trick to get help from them. In Washington, our main base was a house on which not even a third of the mortgage was paid off. I think we sold that house to supporters more than once, each time after being confronted with banks wanting to confiscate the house because of overdue mortgage instalments. Supporters would agree to 'buy' the house on condition that we pay the remaining instalments. But after some time, faced with our non-payment, they would be more than happy sell it back to us for nothing, just in order to save their names. One was even prepared to pay the bank instalments himself, as long as the *masouls* told him in advance, but said, 'they simply don't know what credit is and what it means in this country to have a good or a bad credit record.'

He was right; our *masouls* knew nothing about such things, nor anything about ordinary life and its problems. Worse still, they understood nothing about promises, except for the one they had made to Maryam and Masoud. It was left to me, far too often, to sort out problems they left in their wake. They made assurances and promises, breaking them immediately afterwards until the next time, when the cycle was renewed. I was not as 'ideological' as my *masouls*, and still respected my personal promises and tried hard to honour them. But how could I, when I was forever having to duck and dive in financial matters?

Women *masouls* had their hands tied by orders from Baghdad: they could not spend a dollar from their earnings and had to get their budgets from the main office, which came with no mention of debt repayment. I realised the extent of the pressure on them when I encountered a special case.

My *masoul* asked me to go to Los Angeles to sort out a problem. One of our full-time supporters had allegedly stolen about $20,000 of our money instead of transferring it to our account in Europe. I was expected to arrange some kind of trial for him in front of our supporters and force him to repay. I was acquainted with the supporter in question and his wife, whom I knew to be fine, honest people. When I asked the finance department to show me the evidence against him, I saw immediately that all the receipts were poorly executed fakes. Even putting aside my personal judgement of the man, I could not accept the work as his. So I told my *masoul* that, if she wanted me to solve the problem I first needed to conduct my own investigation. 'It is not up to you to find the truth,' she said. 'It has already been established who stole the money.' I was positive that our supporter was innocent and could not bring myself to do as asked.

Someone else took the case over. I never forgave myself for leaving the supporter in the lurch just to keep my own hands clean. A year later I learned the truth: our *masoul* in California was always under pressure to raise funds, and in the end, having exhausted every other source she could think of, found no choice but to pretend she had transferred the amount in question. In fact, the money never existed. She knew how our financial system worked – or didn't work, thanks to irrational and erratic decisions – and hoped nobody would discover what she had done. But eventually the scam was revealed, and she admitted to it – too late for our poor supporter, whose reputation had been ruined; the organisation never felt as obliged to clear his name as blacken it in the first place.

My main hope for improving our parlous financial state was to approach Iranians who were not among our usual supporters. I had some success in this area, but some notable failures as well, thanks to the intervention of my *masoul*. Badrie, one of the organisation's highest-ranking members, had been transferred to America because of its enormous political importance. I had great respect for her and was grateful for the way she had handled my depression and confusion during the Gulf War. However, when an Iranian I met in Los Angeles eventually consented after much persuasion to give us around $20,000, Badrie's reaction was to insist on nothing less than $50,000. I could not change her mind and eventually had to go back to our would-be donor to ask him to increase his offer. Understandably, he was so annoyed by the request that he not only withdrew his original offer but also declined to have anything more to do with us.

Though by now I was at least half-Mojahed and had lost almost all feeling for anything and anyone not beneficial to the organisation's objectives, still I had the capacity to feel affection. When I fortuitously discovered where a cousin of mine was living, I hesitated to visit him from fear that this would reopen the door to family relationships, which I knew I couldn't follow through. Somehow my *masoul* discovered he was a rich man and an old friend of Doctor, and she urged me to contact him and ask for financial help. I balked at the suggestion that I should ask for money on my first visit, when I hadn't seen him for twenty-five years; but she insisted, and I went. At first we had a pleasant time exchanging family memories, but as soon as I mentioned the organisation the atmosphere cooled. He was bitterly opposed to our policies and practices, especially the ideological revolution of 1985 and the marriage of Masoud and Maryam, which he said was an embarrassment to all Iranians. 'I never expected to see Rajavi do such a shameful thing,' he said. 'To steal his friend's wife!' When I tried to explain, he refused to discuss the matter. This was hardly the moment to ask for funds for the organisation, and I knew I would have to lie to my *masoul* about my failure to secure any. I changed the subject and started talking about the NCR, hoping he might show some sympathy towards me as the NCR representative in America and as a relative. 'If you were asking anything for yourself,' he responded, 'I would not hesitate to give it to you. But I am not prepared to give anything to the Mojahedin.'

The situation was a disaster for me, whichever way I looked at it. I was ashamed of myself for giving my cousin the feeling that my only reason for visiting was to raise money for the organisation, especially as he and his family had shown me great respect and kindness. On the other hand, from the Mojahedin's point of view, I was ashamed of my weakness in valuing the outside world's morality, feeling bad about breaching it and, in short, considering anything other than the needs of the organisation.

From my cousin I learned about my brothers and sister, living in California. My visit to my brother put me in precisely the same cleft stick, and he was justifiably angry with me for apparently approaching him only for money. Of course, the organisation was also angry with me, as I had succumbed to the personal happiness of meeting my relatives for the first time in many years. Although I wrote a self-critical report about my feelings, to my lasting regret I never found the opportunity to apologise to my family.

Badrie's arrival should have heralded a new, more successful era but in fact she merely magnified all the ills she had inherited.

I was so tired of everything. There was the continuing pressure of the ideological revolution, especially 'Article D'. Every night there were long, boring, useless meetings where our *masoul* set out various plans and promises which I knew would be no more durable than a piece of ice in summer. Every day we had to see supporters with questions and problems I had not the slightest clue how to answer. I repeatedly asked to be replaced, suggesting that the NCR representative in America be either a non-Mojahed and real member of the NCR, which could benefit us in our political activities, or the head of our organisation there, namely, Badrie, who was capable of answering our supporters' questions. Every time I brought this up, the reply was the same: 'You don't understand, you are the best choice for this job and you should solve your problem.'

In spring 1993 it was decided we should have one of our largest demonstrations in Washington DC, with the aim of forcing the new administration to take us more seriously and perhaps persuading them to establish official relations with us. Preparations lasted one month. We had to persuade people to paticipate, arrange for their overnight stay in Washington, see to their food and so on, as well as making banners and flags. The trouble was that we prepared not for the expected actual numbers, but for the number Rajavi decreed we should have. Thus, at many of our demonstrations, people could be seen sporting more than one banner or flag each.

That was not the worst of it. We chartered planes to take people to Washington and grossly over-catered for the supposed numbers, with the result that for months afterwards we had to use up leftover frozen food, find some use for spare plane tickets and store superfluous flags and banners (although the colours and slogans changed every time, so we could never reuse them anyway). My biggest headache was how to find a way of repaying the loans that had propped up all these activities.

I was beginning to have some success in establishing the hoped-for lobby, with representatives in almost every state and many

major cities, proper points of contact in many places and a
monthly paper in the pipeline. It looked good, and we wanted to
use the network to obtain maximum advantage from the
demonstration. In practice this was complicated, as many from our
lobby group didn't know who the congressmen were or what to say
if they met them. As they were in Washington for just one day, time
was short. While I did my best to achieve some semblance of order
and purpose, dealing with perhaps 100 people almost
simultaneously, my *masoul* suddenly remembered I was the
representative of the NCR and supposedly the host of the
demonstration, and had therefore to give a welcoming speech. This
while being everywhere at once, trying to spend a few minutes with
each of the politicians I knew while directing other people's
activities and sorting out technicalities! It hit me forcibly then how
phony and superficial everything in the organisation was. I felt like
a puppet dancing to whatever tune they played. I don't know what
I said in the speech, but for days afterwards my mind was sorely
troubled.

One day, while returning from the Senate to our base, I paused
at Union Station to observe a homeless man lying in the street. I
was reminded of the slogan of the ideological revolution, 'We must
change to zero in order to reach infinity'. Perhaps that man was at
zero, I mused. He had nothing to worry about, nobody to care for
and nothing to lose. He ate whatever he found and slept wherever
he wished. Above all, he was himself, he had his individuality. Then
I asked myself, 'Who am I?' The answer came with a rush: I was
nobody. In a way, I was lucky: wherever I went, in any city or
country, there was a base or a supporter's house where I could feel
at home. There were people, scattered far and wide, who I knew
and cared for me and for whom I also cared. But who was it they
cared for? A Mojahed! Often, they complained to me about our
*masouls*, and it was only their respect for me that prevented them
from fully venting their fury. Yet, according to the definition of the
ideological revolution, they were more Mojahed than I. So, did
people like me for my individual self, or was I just some useful
figurehead or spokesperson? What was left of me, and what would
I become? I felt I was on the edge of a breakdown. I asked my
*masoul* again if somebody could replace me as NCR
representative. I said I thought I would be more useful shorn of a

particular role or title. She evidently sensed my urgency and agreed it was time I returned to Baghdad for a few weeks.

A day or two after I arrived, Fahieme'a called me. She was her usual smiling, welcoming self and she asked me how things were back in America. She put me so much at ease that I didn't hesitate to tell her everything, including all the things I thought were not right: our political policies; our unfair and inappropriate treatment of supporters; our propaganda, which mainly blazoned our strength, with the copious use of film footage about our army and political achievements. 'Iranians there don't have much doubt about our strength, and it is not their main concern. What they want to know is how democratic we are and how free they will be in a future Iran. We cannot prove our democracy just by announcing it. They have to see and feel it; they need proper answers to their questions and doubts. Whenever they watch our television programmes, they see either men talking or women wearing scarves – and then we criticise the regime for being male-dominated and not giving women the freedom to wear what they choose.'

I continued: 'We interview people and arrange round-table discussions, and they are all meaningless because the people involved share the same views and only echo each other in different or even the same words.' While speaking, I watched her closely to see how much further I could go. I risked raising another issue. 'The way we portray our leader makes him look, to an ordinary Iranian, like a cross between the Shah and Khomeini. On the one hand, he and his entourage enjoy luxuries and behave like the Shah; and on the other hand he maintains disciples and promotes fanaticism and radicalism like Khomeini.' No doubt I actually expressed myself more mildly, but I still felt the need to apologise several times for my outspokenness and emphasise how difficult it was for me to say these things. I did not want to stir up any ideological anger. In fact, she said nothing. Perhaps she felt it was not her responsibility to answer, but rather that of Rajavi, who directed our political and propaganda policies in both principle and detail.

At her request I worked in her office during my stay. Masoud and Maryam lived and worked in the same building. She asked me also to watch some videos, mostly of Maryam's sermons. The gist of them was much the same: the essential qualities of the Mojahedin, namely, commitment to honesty and openness, refusal to deceive people and willingness to defend their beliefs to with their own lives and even those of their children. Her words made me wonder. How much were we really bound to our promises and words? I knew that Rajavi's sermons were thinly disguised politicking, but Maryam's speeches were different, based on genuine ideological principles and spoken in good faith. If I tried to judge our crimes and misdemeanours against her words, I never found myself doubting her honesty or integrity but rather how she was being informed about what was going on in the real world outside those walls in Iraq.

My job was to read bulletins and reports of our political activities and select the most important ones for the leadership to read. Many items, then and later, were about women. There was news such as the arrest of 13,000 women within a year on charges of not respecting the regime's dress code, and of many who had committed suicide or set fire to themselves to escape from their misery.

Normally Maryam responded to reports of the suppression of women in Iran with a message of protest, which was taken up by various bodies such as the European and national parliaments, in the form of letters of support or resolutions swiftly followed by media coverage. Rajavi's analysis seemed to be that eventually women, as the most oppressed and exploited people in Iranian society, would rise against the *mullahs* and lead the revolution. Maryam substantiated this view, using language like 'reactionary sexual ideology' and 'double exploitation of women'. I never quite understood what made them believe ordinary men, who were clearly implicated in the exploitation of women, could be readily mobilised to fight alongside or under the command of women. After all, many of the crimes perpetrated against women in Iran and neighbouring countries were committed not by governments but by ordinary men according to old traditions. In fact, compared with Afghanistan, Pakistan and some Middle Eastern countries, the situation of women in Iran was more tolerable. To make this the primary issue of the revolution was a gamble. Most supporters now realised that to become a Mojahed or align themselves closely with the organisation they had no alternative but to separate from their spouses, there being no way to stop the exploitation of women other than by physically separating the sexes and enforcing positive discrimination. So if they wanted to keep their families, they had to maintain their distance from us.

Naturally I took pride in the elevation of women, but there was a contradiction in the leadership's aspirations. They always said we could not fight on two different fronts at the same time: the regime was to be dislodged first, then we would come to grips with our other historical enemies. Yet here we were, postponing our struggle against imperialism and capitalism to some unknown time in the future while trying to resolve the tensions between women and men that had deeper roots in the history of society than did those political systems. It was easy for Masoud and Maryam to boast about the number of women we had in key positions, but in reality the existing contradictions were not solved but buried under orders and slogans. Women occupied these posts simply because they were amenable to accepting orders and believed in Rajavi – the real decision-maker – more than men did.

After I had been in Baghdad a few days, Rajavi sent for me. 'What is this nonsense you are always talking about, "not being fit for the job of representative of the NCR"?' he demanded. 'I know what is going on in your heart,' he added, 'and I know that you want that job badly, so stop repeating this rubbish. You are fit for it and should carry on doing it, as it is and exactly as we have defined it.' He then changed the subject and asked if I had read a recent article by Banisadr published in his paper. In the article Banisadr repeated allegations made by an American senator who was helping the regime. As our US representative, Rajavi said, I should be the one to issue a reply, to be published in *Mojahed*.

The last time I had been asked to write something against Banisadr was in 1985, after the first stage of the ideological revolution. It was never published, as in the organisation's view it was not sufficiently hard-hitting. But I knew Rajavi must have had a particular reason for asking. Perhaps the idea was to kill any residual sympathy I might have towards my cousin, or vice versa.

I researched thoroughly to be sure that I had proof of any claims I made. I handed the resulting long article to Towhidi, editor of *Mojahed*, and he thanked me without comment. A few days later he told me the article was too long and could not be published as it was.

'May I reduce it?' I asked.

'Well, unfortunately, there is too little time and I have had to do it for you,' he said, handing me a few pages of the shortened article. I could not believe my eyes. Of course, the issues and the quotes from Banisadr's papers and speeches were there, but the language of my argument had been completely changed. In place of my moderation were the kind of repulsive, vitriolic insults regularly used in *Mojahed*, to the disgust of all Iranians, including many of our supporters. I could never understand how Towhidi had become editor when everyone detested his writing. Now his words were going to be published under my name. I protested, barely able to conceal my fury. He explained that the only way to shorten the article was to rewrite sections of it completely. Seeing that I was not satisfied, he offered, 'Let me ask Masoud what we should do.' The next day he told me that Rajavi had sanctioned its publication as it was, in view of the shortness of time.

In 1981 Rajavi had written in *Mojahed* that 'a revolutionary has every right to say what he thinks is right with the strongest and most poisonous words ...' Now I realised what he had meant. My guess was that he felt my article was too mild, not 'revolutionary' enough. All the while I had been objecting to Towhidi's writing style; in reality, I was opposing Rajavi's. In ideological terms, this had obviously been a mistake on my part. If I disagreed with Rajavi, I must be wrong. Publicly I had to defend the published article against critics who found it as offensive as I did myself. I never had the chance to ask my cousin's forgiveness. Perhaps the chance will still come one day to apologise not only to him but to all Iranians for contaminating their culture and literature with so-called 'revolutionary language'.

# 37

# Sun-dried Flowers

In June we made preparations for the celebration on the 20th, with shows of force on many fronts. The regime was, unfortunately, doing likewise, and more effectively in the political arena at least. They managed to ban us from entering UN buildings, establish normal diplomatic relations with nearly every European country and, in the US, broadcast free on one of the national television channels – securing several hours' airtime per week in many states, obviously much more than we could afford. What was the key to their success? They were better listeners than we were. They had learned what Iranians abroad wanted to hear. It was depressingly ironic to note how 'the most reactionary regime in the world', which was completely oblivious to the nature of the modern world and its demands, could make strikingly attractive television programmes that were far beyond what we, 'the most progressive force in the universe' could do. When I pointed this out to various *masouls*, the response was to offer a weekly half-hour question-and-answer programme, which was a showcase for Rajavi to mouth all the old answers to the old questions. Nobody dared tell him that this did us no good and that we should learn from the regime not to show their leaders, even in the news. Instead, we had to praise the programme and say how magical his speech and answers were.

On the military front too, the regime trumped us. Their planes attacked our bases in Iraq as a show of force. Either the Iraqis or the Americans, who were guarding the 'no-fly zone', were powerless to stop these repeated violations of Iraqi sovereignty, or they turned a blind eye. At least the affair allowed us to feed our addiction to 'coverage' in the media. Even when Iran complained to the UN about our incursion onto Iranian soil, we were pleased to acknowledge it as an admission of our strength and power. It was more food for our propaganda machine which, as ever, focused on military might and not democracy.

After this exchange of operations it was decreed that, as we were very close to the final battle, all efforts should henceforth be concentrated on drafting supporters into the army. Fundraising was deemed irrelevant; only taking up arms carried any dignity. Thus, staying abroad was not an option. Of course, some long-standing supporters were outraged that the financial support they had given for years was cavalierly dismissed as valueless. Others could not or would not join the army and bitterly resented being labelled dishonourable. As so often in the past, a sudden change of tack had consequences that we would bear for years to come. Many *masouls* responded to the call-up, leaving behind all debts and obligations on the assumption that when we gained power in Iran, nobody would question debts of a few thousand dollars to this or that person or unpaid instalments for equipment and rent for our bases. Complementary orders also allowed them to escape obligations. For example, all money and useful equipment was needed back in Iraq and therefore we were not to pay even for food. Whatever we needed had to come from supporters, not from the organisation's resources. Those of us who remained suddenly became so destitute as to ask our supporters to cook meals and bring them to us. Those bound for Iraq were the lucky ones. I was among those who had to remain. Badrie left, replaced by a junior *masoul*.

Two months passed and still there was no 'final operation', nor even a minor assault by our army that would at least save face and give our supporters hope. On August 1993, we were called to our *masoul's* office. Usually sweets and tea on her desk were a symbol of 'good news', but we were not fooled by sweets anymore. 'Good news' in organisational language meant nothing but another phase or article of the ideological revolution. We were used to such gambits any time the overthrow of the regime had been wrongly predicted.

We were right. Maryam had announced that twelve of our sisters had been appointed to our 'leadership council', and another twelve to 'replacement or deputy leadership council'. These terms were both brand new in the organisation, and we didn't know what they meant. We watched on video the announcement and the ceremony in which the 24 new appointees were unanimously 'endorsed' by the audience, which in this case included Rajavi sitting in the crowd as an ordinary member. Maryam spoke passionately about the debt we owed to Rajavi's ideological leadership, without which we would all have remained weak, fragile beings susceptible to reactionary exploitation. She spoke, too, about the 'qualitative distance' between Rajavi and the rest of us. Hitherto she had always worried what would become of us, of the revolution and of future generations when he was gone. But now she realised that the Mojahedin had collectively reached a sufficient level of understanding and intelligence to be able to carry the revolutionary banner to victory, even without a leader of his calibre. At the same time she urged us to take full advantage of our good fortune in having Rajavi as leader, as any time lost would never come again.

By now, as had been promised during 'Article D', all men had a woman *masoul*. The ruling had given rise to some ludicrous cases; one older member was placed under the responsibility of his daughter; Mohadessin was supervised by a junior female member of his department; and Abrishamchi's niece had become his *masoul*. Questioned by Rajavi, Abrishamchi vowed that he accepted this situation, saying, 'Our measure of the merit of a person has always been ideological. The days are gone when we derived our motivation from position or rank, job, individuality, ego or gender. If I, having held all those positions and ranks, am not now able to reject them all, I will become a corrupt sponger and extortioner.'

Turning then to the sisters who had been elected to the leadership council, Rajavi asked the meaning of their rank. With one voice they replied, 'Maidservant in the second degree', which apparently meant they were servants of the servants of the leadership, answerable to all supporters and the Iranian people.

This development was called 'Article SH' of the ideological revolution, and as usual we had to write our feelings and thoughts about it, as well as holding a celebration to welcome it. Celebrations, lasting a day or two, inevitably followed any such event, such as the announcement of Maryam as *masoul aval* and Fahieme'a as her deputy. One form these took were a kind of Mojahedin Olympics, when our boys competed in various sports; others performed folk dances and staged plays. We made monumental representations of Maryam's face or name, decorated with lights and flowers. No man, of whatever age or condition, was excused from dancing as a display of his happiness and approval with the changes in the organisation. A few short years earlier all these things had been regarded as cultural symbols of the West or the Shah, and were vehemently repudiated; but now they were considered revolutionary, and even old members of the NCR, when they were in Iraq, were encouraged to join in revolutionary dances. Funnily enough, for all our fighting talk about equality of the sexes, women did not take part in these active pursuits, being restricted to singing or playing musical instruments – which even the regime permitted them to do freely. It was remarkable even to us that in plays performed then, men took women's roles to avoid the possibility of physical contact between the sexes.

The same day as the announcement about the 'leadership council', our *masoul* told us we were to announce it to all our supporters and that celebrations in the bases would be more enthusiastic than ever. Turning to me, she said, 'This time you have to forget about your back. People will be looking at you to see your reaction. I want you to dance all night.' She was right; that night I was the centre of attention and the butt of many questions. If two-thirds of our members were male, among them all the older Mojahedin, how was it that not one of them had sufficient merit to become a member of that council? What was the council for and what authority would it have? Back pain notwithstanding, I much preferred doing the 'revolutionary dances' that night to answering such questions.

'Article D' and its consequences had not become known outside the organisation, and therefore were not subjected to public scrutiny. This new development was a different matter. The questions that now arose related not so much to the elevation of women or equality of the sexes as to the apparent denigration and demotion of men, who were being filtered out of the organisation's decision-making bodies and whose skills and experience were being discounted. In response, we either had to admit that our men had not been able to achieve anything in the past and were therefore without merit or to announce that ideological issues were more important than the overthrow of the regime; otherwise our policy made no sense.

On the ground our situation was dire. Nobody was joining the organisation and long-time supporters drifted away day by day. In Iran we now had no more than a few hundred supporters whom we had not been able to relocate to Iraq. In Iraq itself, what we liked to call the 'most effective and educated army of the Middle East' was paralysed by its inability to cross the borders, and apart from a few guerrilla incursions per year was did nothing but hold revolutionary dances and conduct the occasional manoeuvre for show. Our political activities were a sham and our propaganda activities a disaster, which I wished we could stop altogether. My feeling was that we required radical change to our modes of operation or we would say goodbye to our dreams forever.

Rajavi wanted to swell the NCR membership to his magic number of 600. The immediate target was 250. It would have been easy enough to reach the target by making all Mojahedin into NCR members overnight, but he wanted people with special qualities – famous personalities, people with higher educational degrees, people from ethnic and religious minorities – to prove that the NCR was an inclusive coalition. We had to look beyond the Mojahedin to our supporters, especially those in the US. The problem was that they were not as predictable as members. All my nominations had to be approved by at least three *masouls* who knew them and could attest to their good characters and that they would not create problems. Once approved, they had to be persuaded to write applications for membership. Most were surprised to be approached, perhaps because they expected things to be the other way round; genuine requests were more often than not refused.

NCR meetings were the most tedious of all organisational

procedures, consisting of long, boring sermons. Still, they meant a few days out of the daily grind. It was a pleasant surprise to see the new building in the centre of Baghdad purpose-built for NCR meetings. Like the old parliament building in Tehran, it was called Baharastan, and the two symbolic stone lions by the entrance harked back to Iran of old. Inside was a large portrait of Mossadegh, another symbol of nationalism, and the conference hall again was modelled on the parliament chamber. It seemed that if we could not get back to Iran, Rajavi would bring Iran to us. At Ashraf there were already miniature replicas of famous Tehran monuments, and the Tehran bazaar with all its traditional shops was often reproduced as a backdrop to ceremonies.

This was the biggest-ever meeting of the NCR, but that didn't make it any more gripping or enlightening. Photographs taken inside the conference hall all show one or more members of the audience fully or half-asleep. After the opening speeches and reports of our 'successes', Dr Matin-Daftary got up and spoke out strongly against our propaganda policies. What he said exactly reflected everything I thought. But his outspokenness did not go down well with Rajavi, who laid into him angrily. It was the first time I saw him reacting so harshly towards one of the few remaining non-Mojahed council members. His usual calm and moderation had evaporated. Here was the 'revolutionary' lambasting a 'representative of the bourgeoisie' within the council. The essence of his argument was that 'our policies for dealing with Iranians, our diplomacy, our radio and television broadcasts are our business, decided on by Mojahedin and run with Mojahedin money and personnel. If you want a different kind of propaganda, you should finance your own broadcasts and run them yourself.' Poor Matin-Daftary was silenced by this outburst, although it was obvious that no one had the wherewithal to run a parallel propaganda operation. Apart from that, Rajavi was wrong on two counts: supporters and members outside Iraq vehemently opposed Mojahedin propaganda tactics and suffered greatly as a result; also, although most activities outside Iraq were financed by the Mojahedin, most were done in the name of the NCR; hence it was every member's right to ask questions and take part in making decisions.

The following day, perhaps out of contrition for his attack on

Matin-Daftary or because he had it in mind to ask him for support, Rajavi made a totally unexpected suggestion: that the sun and the lion, the symbols of old Iran, be chosen as the NCR's emblem. Immediately, the whole meeting burst into spontaneous applause. The sun-and-lion dated back several thousand years and lasted until the revolution, when the regime adopted a new symbol. It was our profound wish to see the old emblem restored, although we held little hope, as it seemed contradictory to Rajavi's Islamic beliefs and values. The sun symbolised Meher, an ancient Persian religion predating even Zoroastrianism, and the lion was Meher's protector. During the Qajar era, the sword, representing the sword of Imam Ali, was added to the emblem and later was approved by the only real parliaments we ever had. Members congratulated Rajavi for suggesting its adoption, but he modestly deflected the adulation, saying it was originally the idea of Matin-Daftary, who had hesitated to say it himself.

The next major item in the proceedings was a proposal to elect a future Iranian president. Banisadr, our previous nominee, had long since been removed from contention. Who better to replace him, asked Rajavi, than Maryam? I had felt for some time that it was vitally important for us to have a new political device to stand up to the Iranian regime, and that Maryam as president was the very device we needed, so I wholeheartedly endorsed this proposal. Being a woman, she represented the humane and progressive alternative to the fundamentalism of the regime, whose so-called 'Islamic law' could not countenance a female president. Although she was a modest Muslim, she was beautiful and educated and embodied a modern social and political philosophy. I was still enthralled by her message of love, which I believed was the cure for strife among Iranians with different views. Above all, with Maryam as president, we could step out of our organisational cupboard and, in concert with real people, undertake real action with their support, perhaps heading towards final victory.

It was obvious from Maryam's demeanour that she was torn by this nomination. She was reluctant to accept a position that would elevate her above Rajavi, her ideological leader. When offered the post, she said she had always done whatever Rajavi asked of her, and she deeply regretted departing from such compliance. At most she could see herself as *masoul aval*. But she would defer to Rajavi and the council's greater vision and understanding, provided she did not have to make the decision herself. Rajavi did his best to persuade her, with the result that when it came to the vote, the council endorsed the nomination and she accepted it, kissing the Iranian flag and swearing to fulfil the role as best she could. Then she spoke again in praise of Rajavi and what he had done for the Mojahedin, the NCR and ultimately the heroic Iranian people. Rajavi was the living continuation of the way first forged by the great Mossadegh. This was a message we had to take to the people.

Had the whole scene be pre-planned? If it had been, then I have to say that Masoud and Maryam were the most capable actors I have ever seen. With her humility and compassion, Maryam moved her listeners to tears. That night we celebrated extravagantly, with much dancing that signalled genuine elation.

At the same meeting Rajavi nominated eighteen people, mostly non-Mojahedin, to head various committees and be our future ministers. Now he had both his president and cabinet.

After the sweetness came the pain. Rajavi called about a dozen of us to see him immediately after the end of the session of the NCR. He was patently very angry to begin with, though I never found out why. He wanted to say something bitter, but as usual he preferred to let us speak so he could wind up with a conclusion. Had we any self-criticisms to offer arising from the past few days? he asked. I spoke first, saying how happy I had been when I heard about the adoption of the emblem and also of Matin-Daftary's views, which echoed my own; so that when Rajavi attacked him, I felt great pity for him and was offended by the outburst. I said I felt I had more in common with non-Mojahedin members of the council than with Mojahedin.

This was, I think, the most uninhibited and shocking self-criticism I ever uttered. After all, who in his right mind dared say that ordinary people were more correct or more honourable than Rajavi, who was closer to God than to us? Who dared say that Rajavi's words offended him? I knew I could expect the most horrible consequences, only I didn't know how or when. After that, other people made confessions. Usually at these sessions we had to criticise each other, breaking the ties of comradeship in the interests of defending our 'dear leader'. The fact that nobody did so made Rajavi angrier. I assume he felt unable to attack me, as it would be too personal, so he turned his attention to the others, beginning with our German representative. His 'crime' was that, because of terrorist acts perpetrated by the regime in Germany, he'd had police protection for a time. Rajavi's voice rose to a violent crescendo, using the most brutal words I'd ever heard from him. We shuddered with the force of his emotion and from the frightening cold of the atmosphere. The German representative was reduced to sobs and could scarcely breathe. It was almost as terrible for us to witness as it was for him to suffer. I wondered what would happen when my turn came. This poor man might, if he became accustomed to the 'luxury' of police protection, lose his ideological faith and become a bourgeois; whereas it had already happened to me, and I had admitted having more empathy with liberal council members and ordinary people than with the Mojahedin and our leader.

Rajavi's comments on my contribution referred only to the seal of the sun and lion. He accused me of having become a representative of our enemies, but he stopped short of venting all his venom on me. He knew the others would take up the challenge to teach me a lesson. He said, 'When I suggested adopting the lion and sun, I meant the lion representing "the lion of Imam Ali", the sword as his sword and the sun representing, as always, the shining sun that is Maryam, the sun that lights our darkness. I didn't choose it for its associations with that worthless Meher religion or old "Iranian beliefs".'

Suddenly Abrishamchi bore down on me, standing above my head and saying, 'Nobody has said anything about this dirty rat, this noxious creature. He pretends he is an intellectual and criticises himself mildly, gently! And for what? For opposing our propaganda policies, he says. What rubbish! This so-called "philosophical self-criticism" is just a cloak to hide somebody called Anna.'

At this, Rajavi laughed out loud and others joined in. Abrishamchi had cleverly chosen the best way to attack me. This way neither he nor Rajavi needed to refer in any way to the content of what I had said, yet they could still condemn me in the harshest possible terms for not being able to meet the most elementary objectives of the ideological revolution, which the simplest and least intellectual of our members had been able to accomplish years earlier. When Abrishamchi finished insulting me, others took their cue and continued the assault. Among them was Nadir, whom I knew personally well. I was tired of his passivity, and this meeting was a good opportunity for him to prove his ideological merit. As Abrishamchi had already exhausted the usual organisational vocabulary of insults, he had to dig deeper into the barrel of abuse, swear words and vile language.

Afterwards my *masoul* advised me to go to a bungalow and think. I had become a *bangalli*, which meant being put in solitary confinement, ordered to do nothing but think and write. It was an extreme kind of mental torture, and there were members who preferred to kill themselves than to suffer it. When opponents of the Mojahedin referred to imprisonment by the organisation, it was this abominable punishment they meant. Clearly, though on the face of it our German representative had taken the brunt of the 'beating' from Rajavi, in the end it would be I who felt the pain most.

I don't know if it was part of my punishment or a chance for Abrishamchi to prove himself, as his popularity had slipped, but he was delegated to deal with me instead of the usual sister. During our first 'consultation' he told me my job had corrupted me, and ruined me as Rajavi's representative of in America. If I wanted to save my soul, I would have to beg to be transferred from there to the army. 'This is what I have been doing for nearly two years now,' I said, 'especially in the past few months. But nobody has accepted it, not even Rajavi himself.' He promised to investigate and arrange for my transfer. But I was, of course, required to think deeply and write a report. A few days went by, and still I could not produce anything new, so in the end I had no alternative but to confess what they wanted to hear from me – that my real problem had nothing to do with Mojahedin policies or principles but was love for my wife. Having read it, Abrishamchi instructed me to write another letter to Anna and divorce her. I told him I had already done so several times, but that nobody had delivered the letter to her. He promised he would arrange delivery.

For the next few days I was on a rollercoaster. Sometimes he was mild, even praising my renewed belief in the ideological revolution; more often, he was rough. I had the feeling he was acting on orders in using these different approaches. No doubt the intention was to destroy my morale. It worked; I was frustrated and miserable. I didn't know what more I could say or write, yet every time I produced what I thought they wanted, he said it wasn't good enough. Apparently they wanted more – but what *was* more, and how was I to provide it?

Suddenly the logjam burst. Perhaps it was because, as Maryam was going to America, they realised they needed me there, or perhaps my desperation warned them I was on the edge of breakdown. Whatever the reason, Abrishamchi came to me one day and said, kindly, that all was well. He kissed me and congratulated me on having understood where my problem lay and turning to the correct path. Then he told me to prepare to return to America as soon as possible. Now it was my turn to remind him about his promise to transfer me to the army. He did not reply directly, but showed me the latest issue of *Mojahed* with a photo of Rajavi and Maryam with the emblem. 'Photos like this matter more than anything else, even our organisation', he said. 'They are your safeguard. As long as you carry them in your heart you are safe everywhere, even in Iran among personnel of the Iranian regime – or among American capitalists.'

I still believed in Maryam, and with recent changes in the organisational structure there was still a chance of doing something real for our people, so I had to do whatever I could to fulfil my pledge to the cause. A general meeting was called for all Mojahedin members, in which Maryam's election as president-designate was announced, and at which she 'resigned' as a Mojahed. Fahieme'a was nominated the new *masoul aval*, with five sisters as her deputies. As always, a show of hands was called for to approve the nominations. Combatants then threw flowers in Maryam's direction, and she picked them up and threw them back. People felt it was lucky and an honour if she had touched their flowers, so everybody scrambled to get one. I was among the luckiest, as Maryam herself gave me a few. I dried them and for a long time carried them wherever I went, treasuring them as my dearest possessions.

# 38

# Doubts and Dollars

The plan was that Maryam should move, via Paris, to America and carry out her future activities there. The US was tremendously important not only because it was a political giant but also because it was home to more Iranians than any other country except Iran itself. Her impending arrival was not announced publicly for fear it might jeopardise her chances of obtaining a visa. Usually that was a matter of simply asking one of our friends in Congress to write a letter of invitation. Hundreds of such letters had already been written and served their purpose. But in Maryam's case the request had to come from higher up. Mohadessin took on this task, with help from me, as representative of the NCR in America, Mojahedin spokesman and a member of the NCR foreign relations committee.

The aide to the congressman we approached became suspicious: why had the big guns been lined up to secure a simple letter of invitation? Instead of writing the letter, she called the Iran desk of the US State Department to check whether they had any objection. This was like asking someone to invite an enemy to come live in his house! Needless to say, the visa application was refused and the incident ushered in an unfortunate new state of affairs, in which all future applications from our friends in Paris were vetted by the Iran desk. We spent the next week collecting signatures from many members of Congress for a petition asking the State Department to overturn its decision – to no avail. Eventually we gave up, and the organisation had no choice but to announce Maryam's trip to France. The news stirred up trouble. A bomb exploded by the door of the French embassy in Iran. There were articles in the regime's papers and petitions protesting the presence of Maryam in France. We, however, were upbeat about the significance of her trip. Just as Khomeini's visit to France had signalled the overthrow of the previous regime, so we expected that hers would augur a new era in Iran, with Maryam as president.

We were summoned to Paris to explain why we had failed the simple task of getting a visa. This time it was Mohadessin's turn to suffer: he was accused of misinforming the organisation by oversimplifying the job. In fact, the failure stemmed from the organisation's habit of rushing and magnifying out of proportion everything that had anything to do with Maryam.

Maryam, now based in Paris, asked me to build on my ties with Iranians and sympathisers, directing all my efforts towards informing them about the new phase of our resistance and gaining their support. Thus on my return to America, I moved to Los Angeles, where about a million Iranians live.

My *masoul* adopted a hands-off approach to me, probably on Maryam's orders, so I was quietly excused from routine work. Somehow I felt that, despite having lived among the Mojahedin in almost total isolation from ordinary life, I was still able to understand most ordinary people and communicate with them. Perhaps, therefore, I might be able to build a bridge between the Mojahedin and our countrymen there. Also, I knew in my heart that Maryam and her message were extraordinary. If she was capable of attracting me as a Mojahed and an Iranian, surely she would, with her appeal, shorn of demagoguery and fanaticism, speak to other Iranians too. Then she might really become the saviour we waited for.

My encounters with Iranians in California now showed a new tendency. These people's eyes would glaze over when I spoke about our cause, and when I passed the baton of conversation to them they bombarded me with questions couched in blunt and offensive terms. Why did we help Khomeini gain power? Why did we approve the executions of people at the beginning of the revolution? Why were we on enemy soil, working with Iraqis, killing our own countrymen? Plus, of course, why did we approve of the marriage of Masoud and Maryam? They also launched into diatribes against the Mojahedin. At first I found this kind of interrogation embarrassing and disturbing, until I realised that we had faced exactly the same thing from our supporters over the last fifteen or twenty years. It was our fault that questions were expressed aggressively. We had distanced ourselves from ordinary people on the grounds that our sacrifices and ideology made us superior to them. But, as one of them pointed out, 'Sacrifice by itself doesn't bring legitimacy for a cause and doesn't whitewash your mistakes and wrongdoings, just as it didn't bring legitimacy for Khomeini.'

I found that the way to turn these encounters round and win people over was to approach them from the standpoint of my own personal feelings towards them and our beloved country. Instead of answering their questions, I started from what we all had in common: being Iranian, caring for our country and people, their freedom and prosperity, taking pride in their success. Added to that was a certain acceptance and contrition for the errors we had made.

Once someone challenged me about the Shah's son, saying we ought to be prepared to talk to him. When I said we wouldn't, he said, 'What do you have against him? He hasn't done anything.'

'Precisely', I answered. 'If we want to restore a monarchy, let's at least have someone who has done something! The only thing he is proud of is having a criminal for a father!'

It did not take long for Maryam's message of love to filter through, create a new attitude towards our nationalism and forge new links with many Iranians whom we had previously branded monarchists and remnants of the Shah's regime. The Iranian papers in California tempered their language towards us and seemed prepared to wait and see how things proceeded. We had clearly changed and accepted things that had previously been unthinkable. Choosing the Iranian seal as our emblem and a woman for president was itself an unmistakable sign of how far we had come in terms of tolerance and modernisation.

I was now able to make many friends among Iranians, to learn their needs and wants, to speak their language. In addition, I met many celebrities, including writers, poets, theatre directors, filmmakers, musicians and singers, and through genuine respect for their artistry had gained their trust, too. Often they asked me questions, knowing I would not take offence and would answer honestly, admitting our previous mistakes and accepting their advice. Not only did I form good relationships with such people, but from an organisational point of view they were clearly our most valuable assets.

I discovered that my reports about dealings with US Iranians were read by Maryam herself, so I began to include more detail and something of my own feelings, which I had not been able to express as a Mojahed. She was understanding, and gave me a free hand to act as I thought fit. I even got permission for my own half-hour weekly television question-and-answer programme. It differed from what we had done before in two important ways. First, the person who fronted the programme was the wife of one of the NCR members, who didn't wear Mojahedin or Islamic dress. Second, the questions to which we then provided answers replicated, in tone and content, those we normally got from ordinary people, even those on the side of the enemy. Feedback from viewers indicated that the programme was popular. But a few weeks after the programme went live, it was pulled on orders from the propaganda office in Baghdad. They took exception to the way the presenter dressed and, probably moreso, to the free and relaxed way in which questions and answers were put. (In the past, whenever I had been interviewed by Mojahedin media, I dispensed with the clichés and slogans I was directed to use and instead expressed myself my own way. These bits were always cut.) I wasn't surprised, although I concluded that our propaganda machine was beyond saving, set in stone like the old Soviet media. I would have to find other means for promoting the true face of our resistance.

Every month or two I went to Paris and reported to Maryam. Once I mentioned the wrongs I believed we had committed, especially against our own supporters. Her response was, 'Where were you when those things were happening?' I had no answer for her, any more than I did for my own conscience. I could only promise her and myself never again to be silent when I saw wrong being done. She asked me to create a series of democratic associations among our supporters in America, who would be a force for good and a strong voice in the future Iran.

And so I crisscrossed the US, from Washington to Los Angeles and between. Armed with Maryam's assurances and a newfound self-confidence, I was able to promise repayment of the organisation's debts to our supporters. Such repayments were indeed made to supporters who still wanted them. I also answered questions and fielded criticism, including about our bases in Iraq and the ill treatment the organisation had meted out to members who wanted to leave. One longtime supporter was troubled by a lot of issues he had heard about, including segregation of the sexes, hardships imposed on members, restrictions on people's normal lives and much else besides. To him I said, 'A few years ago in Britain, I was forced to do things I had never done before: I had to carry people on my back or lie down nearly naked on a cold hard floor while people ran on my stomach. I was beaten, too; in simple terms, I was tortured. But it was my own decision, and it was not actually torture but a karate class I had joined to learn self-defence. All of us who joined the Mojahedin or NLA accepted the hardship entailed in learning to defend ourselves, not only against external enemies but against personal temptations too.'

Commitment and willingness to serve, I explained, made hardship acceptable, even welcome. It was only when loyalty vanished and one no longer subscribed to the movement's principles that everything became torture, even eating, sleeping and breathing, and the base became a prison. Then, in my view, people ought to be allowed to exercise their free will and leave if they so wished, without penalty. But I admitted that the organisation had not always acted accordingly, perhaps because the defectors had sensitive information that it did not want leaked or because their passage out of Iraq could not be arranged – or, indeed, because the organisation simply made mistakes or behaved with ill will.

Most of the people I spoke with had been attracted to the Mojahedin in the first place because of its values and aspirations. Many had lost heart. But usually all they needed was to feel that humanity, honesty and the humility to admit to misdeeds were still embodied therein. I knew that I did not have all the answers to their problems, but if I didn't then certainly Maryam did – so there was nothing to fear.

I genuinely believed that the past had gone for good, and a renaissance in our work and relationship with the outside world had begun. Not everybody shared my view. There were those who simply could not trust us, who had fallen for our propaganda too often before and been constantly let down. The associations Maryam had asked me to set up had to be democratic, able to grow without our involvement and become capable of concentrating around different areas of expertise addressing the real needs of Iran. We even appealed through our newspaper for volunteers who were not Mojahedin to work with the heads of NCR committees, our putative future ministers, in their own areas of expertise. The latter were themselves at first extremely sceptical, and it took some persuasion to get them to agree to work with these newcomers. I had my work cut out too, next time I was in Paris, to get my view to prevail. A constitution had been drafted, along with guidelines on management, by some of our older members addicted to dictatorial procedures. It was a patent contradiction in terms to create 'democratic' bodies and then impose rules on them.

The political situation also changed to our advantage. Maryam had many meetings and interviews with politicians from various countries. The late Lord Ennals of the UK was so impressed by her that he issued a press release about their talks. The head of the British Parliamentary Human Rights Group, after meeting her, was inspired to publish a book titled *The Tehran Murder Machine: An Account of Terrorist Assassinations by Iranian Agents*. Some journalists called her 'the Iranian Joan of Arc'. Apart from the PR gains, for the first time we enjoyed some successes of substance too. An Iranian diplomat was expelled from Norway, and Sweden ejected a group charged with spying on Iranian refugees, thanks to the vigilance of the Swedish police who uncovered the regime's spies at the Mojahedin's central base. The French government freed two Iranians implicated in Doctor's assassination, but at the same time gave Maryam total freedom to carry on her political activities, and full police protection. The French media had also shifted in our direction. When the suspects were returned to Iran, *Le Monde* headlined the story: 'Dr Rajavi has been killed again!', and French national television aired a twenty-minute programme about our army, which provided independent confirmation of its strength.

Every month or so a reception was organised in Paris for

Maryam to meet supporters and other Iranians from all over the world. It gave me great joy to see our supporters' faces when they met Maryam for the first time and succumbed to her charm, modesty and understanding. At one meeting guests were keen to pose questions and bring accusations directly to her. She answered patiently, and with practical advice. For example, someone complained about our television and radio programmes in America. Maryam said our people could only do as well as they knew how, but that if others thought they could do better, then they had a right to try. To a complaint about the situation of children sent from Iraq to the US, Maryam replied by acknowledging their misery and suggesting that her questioner take responsibility for solving that problem, asking me to assist her in any way possible.

After the reception I came down to earth with a bump. In her office with her close associates, Maryam was angry. Why had those people been brought to see her, she demanded. It was the first time I had ever seen her lose her temper. It distressed me, because she was my teacher, who loved and respected even our opponents, as long as they opposed the regime too. But after a while, doubtless realising that showing anger against people who were absent was neither right nor useful, she vented it against those who had done wrong in the past and left a legacy of problems.

The newly established associations had to pass their first test by holding seminars with NCR committee heads as their guest speakers. They were also in charge of the planned New Year celebrations, although it fell to me to arrange programmes and book Iranian artists to perform – including individuals whom until recently we had labelled anti-revolutionaries and monarchists. Compared with previous years, these events were a fantastic success. It seemed the new associations were working exactly as they should. They showed they could organise things we had previously thought only the Mojahedin could.

The challenge was not only to organise a concert for a few artists and singers. Every day there were complications and rumours: 'There is going to be a bomb at the venue' … 'The Iranian regime is going to take photographs of everyone in attendance and not allow them to return home' … and so on. Most of the problems arose in Los Angeles, where the media reverted to their previous hostility towards us, resentful at our success recruiting celebrity performers. In the past, we invited people to our shows almost free of charge and even paid the airfare for supporters to come and fill the hall; now tickets had to be sold to cover the costs of staging the event.

Throughout this time I think I was working even in my sleep – not that I had much time for sleeping or even eating, though strangely enough I never felt stressed or tired, perhaps because it was such a thrill to see ordinary Iranians mingling with our members and supporters, happily enjoying our entertainment. Every week I shuttled once or twice between Los Angeles and Washington, sometimes with a stopover elsewhere, just to see representatives of our newly established associations and coordinate their activities. My hope was to see an umbrella association established, a national council that would harmonise and direct their activities. This dream was coming true, and I could foresee the day when all our people would be united in victory under our national flag.

I got almost all my orders and guidance straight from Maryam. Not only were my *masouls* not opposed to what I was doing, they were actually helpful in many ways. For the first time in years, I was free to direct my full energy as I wished, no longer forced to attend long, useless organisational meetings or waste time on initiatives that would be here today, gone tomorrow.

The first major problem hit when Reza'i called asking me to arrange a trip to Paris for some celebrities. There were famous singers who had agreed to work with us but tasted the bitter fruits of that collaboration when they became the butt of offensive articles and interviews in the Iranian media. Others had doubts about our credibility and were reluctant to be seen in our company, among them a famous director and a musician. I knew that, with time, some of these issues would resolve themselves. They were not like the singers who had met Maryam several times and treated her with courtesy and dignity; they would ride roughshod over these niceties and put their questions and criticisms in the most blunt and blatant manner. In Paris this kind of behaviour would be interpreted as animosity. However, I tried to buy some time to work on the celebrities.

I couldn't persuade Reza'i and others who wanted to see them in Paris to change their minds. They were convinced that just one look or word from Maryam would win over any doubters. In Reza'i's eyes, I was an obstacle blocking out the effects of Maryam's magic, like a black cloud standing in front of the sun. Although Maryam had great charisma which worked its spell over those who were prepared to accept her as the leader or future president of Iran, there were others for whom she was still tarred with the brush of our history. Having too much work to do, I couldn't travel with them to what I knew was going to be a disaster. Afterwards I was reproached for my judgement. How could I call those 'anti-revolutionaries' our potential friends? Apart from our *masouls* in Paris, the disappointed celebrities themselves were giving me a headache, with their new and never-ending stream of questions.

Financial difficulties were intensifying as well. Maryam's activities needed extra money, as did her promises to repay our huge debts to supporters. In addition, we ran various television and radio programmes, which were at best useless and at worst damaging, but they all needed to be paid for. The money earned from our normal sponsorship work, which only the members were doing, was not enough; we had no choice but to seek help from our supporters. But by then most supporters had joined the new associations, and believed all their financial commitment should be to those associations. They were prepared to help pay our debts or perhaps support Maryam's activities, but in no way were they prepared to pay for our propaganda programmes, which they hoped would end as soon as possible. Abrishamchi was sent to America to help us over our difficulties, one of which was that we were not permitted to name Maryam in our appeals for money; with his arrival, the clock started moving backwards.

Abrishamchi had once been a capable negotiator and administrator, but by now he was completely out of touch with ordinary people. In the past, he had used the blunt but effective instrument of organisational language to force people to conform and pledge allegiance, but our present supporters were not prepared to follow like sheep, and had their own ideas and expectations, including that we behave in a way that would attract rather than repel. Abrishamchi's meetings with supporters were a disaster: the new ones couldn't understand him and came away with more questions than answers, and the old ones were unhappy to see how far he – and the organisation, if he truly represented it – had deviated from its former principles. When I protested, Abrishamchi brushed me aside with, 'That was the past. Now we have new rules.' Among those who fell away in disgust was a man who had previously donated a huge portion of his salary every month, almost $10,000 dollars.

Gradually, the tensions and contradictions between the organisation and the newly established associations increased. Most of our activities – political, organisational and financial – were done through our supporters, who were mainly involved in the associations. The organisation should have made a choice either to abolish the associations and revert to central control or accept them as useful instruments. I was personally caught in this web of contradiction. On the one hand I received new orders and demands daily from Paris and sometimes from Baghdad, which I was expected to fulfil and which could only be done by asking the associations to oblige. On the other hand, the associations were supposedly democratic, so it was up to their councils or even their whole membership to decide whether to commit the extra energy and money carrying out orders required. Usually the organisation wanted everything done quickly and efficiently, whereas the associations took their time and sometimes even refused to do as demanded. As messenger and mediator I was blamed from both sides. The organisation accused me of not understanding the issues from the point of view of my *masoul*, and the associations branded me undemocratic for wanting to impose the Mojahedin's wishes on them. While I was in Los Angeles trying to push through the latest orders, our *masouls* in other cities and states were operating in their set ways and as a result causing tension with the associations to flare up; I had to rush often to the scene to extinguish the fire. At the same time many of Maryam's promises remained unfulfilled.

Our propaganda machine worked exactly as before, even dominating the newly published weekly *Iran-Zamin*, which was supposed to be independent of the Mojahedin and supportive only of the resistance. In the first and second issues the editor, Dr Hezarkhani, emphasised that *Iran-Zamin* was not a propaganda paper and was dedicated not to any particular person or group, but to a wide range of Iranians who lived outside the Iran, loved their homeland and wanted to see its people free from the dark dictatorship of the *mullahs*. He welcomed any criticism of their adherence to these goals within this framework. Unfortunately, while he clearly tried his best to fulfil his promise and gain the trust of Iranians abroad, as the paper was financed by the Mojahedin and its staff were all Mojahedin members and supporters, there was not much he could do. The paper failed to appeal to its intended new readership and disappointed existing supporters, as it was neither of the standard of *Mojahed* with its usual organisational news and comment, nor free, informative and independent, to be trusted for unbiased news. Hezarkhani lasted a few years before finding some pretext to resign. Towhidi replaced him, and not long afterwards *Iran-Zamin* folded altogether.

In addition to these familiar problems, new ones emerged as many things that had previously been hidden within the organisation were now coming to light – for example, the issue of children sent abroad. Whenever we had read anything about this in Iranian papers, we had put it down to enemy propaganda. I met one of those children, a boy of ten, and asked about his parents.

'Which ones?' he asked. I could not imagine what that meant.

He said, 'Well, my real father was killed in Iran, so I was transferred with my mother to Iraq. Then my mother remarried and I had a new father, but after a while my mother was killed in a battle. After that, my second father remarried and I had another mother. I lost both of them in Forogh and got new ones afterwards. During the Gulf War, lots of children, including me, were separated from their parents and transferred here to live with supporters. I hear from my third mother sometimes, but not so often ...' His story made me weep with pity for this poor boy's suffering. Most of us have the misfortune to lose a parent during our lifetime, but this child had lost three pairs. While I was trying to hold back tears, he let the floodgates open and cried his heart out, hugging me all the while.

Those who cared for such children told me about their situations. Many of them had been born and grown up within the organisation, knowing nothing about the traditions and customs of the outside world, sometimes not even being able to understand its language, as the Mojahedin had its own jargon. The concepts of money and ownership were unknown to them. On the bases they felt free to take whatever they wanted, but then did the same thing in the outside world with unfortunate consequences. Within the organisation, partly to keep their parents happy and fill the long gaps between their weekly visits, the children were given almost total freedom to do whatever they liked. It then became very difficult for them to adapt to the real world. Their adopted parents could not understand them and sometimes wrote them off as difficult or even bad. As a result some of the children were deeply disturbed, and mistreatment by their adopted families was all too common. As these stories emerged, our friends and supporters began to have new doubts about the the Mojahedin's behaviour and philosophy.

When the *masouls* saw that the associations were not working as had been envisaged, and that Articles 'D' and 'SH' of the ideological revolution were being disregarded in this context, they concluded that it would be better to revert to the old form of organisation. Obviously this could not be done in a day, so they decided first to break up the associations into smaller ones, then nominated a sister to be responsible for each one.

# 39

# The Last Arrow

In June 1994, it was announced that 21st July, the day of the uprising in support of Mossadegh, would henceforth be Iranian National Day. At the same time, our customary celebration to mark 20th June would continue, though this year they were, rather to everyone's relief, to be small and modest and therefore no great drain on our time and money. Instead, we concentrated on preparing for the next demonstration, which was going to be our biggest ever.

I was as happy as could be, and dedicated with mind, heart and soul to the success of that demonstration, which I saw as a way to tie all Iranians from all walks of life together. So committed was I that I didn't need to be told what to do. Every day for a month, for fifteen to twenty hours, I worked towards this goal, mostly trying to raise much-needed funds from supporters and other Iranians. For two demonstrations alone in the US, one in Washington, DC and another in Los Angeles, we needed around $1 million. During that month I spoke with more than 300 people in different states. At the same time, I was responsible for persuading the associations to comply with the organisation's requests.

As usual, instead of matching our preparations to the predicted numbers of people attending, we operated according to numbers that Maryam or Rajavi demanded. This time they asked for 10,000 demonstrators; supporters told us we should be very pleased if one-fifth of that number showed up. It was not a simple rally where a wrong estimate had little impact, but a ten-hour celebration, with an extensive programme including a rally and party. From banners and flags to food and temporary toilets, everything had to be hired or bought, and although we were penniless – every single dollar had to be begged or borrowed – we spent five times as much as necessary because of the edict from Paris specifying the desired number.

Another bone of contention was the slogans to be used. The associations, which this time were officially the organisers of the rallies, argued that as the celebration was a national one, no Mojahedin slogans should be used, especially the famous 'Iran-Rajavi, Rajavi-Iran'. The argument was most bitter in California, where some association council members threatened to withdraw participation in the demonstration if that slogan were used. To keep the peace, it was decided by Paris that the slogan be excluded in Los Angeles only.

Another of my responsibilities was to engage musicians and singers to perform at the rallies; most of them lived in Los Angeles. As soon as they consented to appear, they came under attack from all directions, notably from monarchists. As a result they lost not only earnings (apart what we paid them), but also many friends. They were constantly quizzed on the Mojahedin's history, about which they knew almost nothing; it was my job to brief them so they could respond to queries from the media or friends. As the day of the rallies drew closer, our enemies stepped up their attacks. Every day there was a new rumour and a new challenge – posters torn down, our people insulted in the streets. Of course, having a foolish foe can be a boon. In the end, they managed, with their excessive hostility and boasting in the media, to portray us as a democratic and oppressed organisation, which generated more sympathy and support for us, even among former opponents.

Eventually the day of the first rally dawned. I went to Washington to welcome the crowd and the invited members of Congress and Iranian celebrities. Immediately after the rally, I flew

back to Los Angeles, where the next one was to be held the
following day and where we expected disturbances. We were asked
by Maryam to make that rally as glorious as possible without
counting costs, because whatever we did was noble and
worthwhile. In fact we managed to reduce costs immensely thanks
to help in kind from new supporters. An Iranian floral artist did the
flower arrangements for the whole area. A famous Iranian
photographer was in charge of documenting the day, and an award-
winning cinematographer did the filming. In addition to singers
and musicians we hired a marching band to play the national
anthem. The area was covered with Iranian flags, flowers and sun-
and-lion emblems. Three huge balloons carried Iranian flags and
huge portraits of Maryam, Rajavi and Mossadegh, and slogans
were hung above the rally area. There were numerous food and
souvenir vendors. On top of all this we had hired huge, expensive
equipment to show a film of Maryam addressing expatriate
Iranians in Paris.

The disturbances materialised in the form of a dozen or so
people carrying portraits of the Shah's son and chanting anti-
Mojahedin slogans. Their numbers, compared to ours, were so
pitiful that they merely showed up our strength in Los Angeles,
previously considered the capital of Iranian monarchists abroad.
Their presence also drew coverage from Iranian and American
media, which worked to our benefit. They had also hired a plane to
trail a portrait of the Shah's son above the rally area. By luck, we
had hired a plane too, to carry a portrait of Maryam and create the
Iranian flag from coloured vapour trails. When our plane appeared
everyone thought we had reacted to their challenge, although the
speed of our response seemed unimaginably fast. For some time the
two planes circled above the area, but theirs left, along with the
monarchists on the ground, when our rally started, handing us a
propaganda victory widely reported in the media.

The rally had gone well and was well-attended – though not by
the overwhelming numbers the leadership demanded – and I was
satisfied – until I heard a message from Maryam passed on by my
*masoul*. She congratulated us on the demonstration but then said
something that had a lasting impact on me, and ultimately changed
the course of my future. '*Beh koorie chashem X, Y, Z*', it read, an
expression translating roughly as, 'May the eyes of those who

cannot see the success of others, X, Y and Z, be blinded'. X, Y and Z were the names of three of our older supporters, who had, as a matter of fact, helped us greatly. What crime had they committed to be cursed by the 'kindest', most 'merciful' woman on earth? It appeared that their 'crime' was to resist and reject our slogans, especially 'Iran-Rajavi, Rajavi-Iran'. Yet they had not even objected on their own accounts, but on behalf of people invited to a 'national' rally with promises that slogans for or against any organisation would be prohibited.

I was very tired and had severe backaches as the result of a month's relentless work, but until then I was oblivious to both. Suddenly, all my energy and happiness, all my eagerness to carry on, drained away and I was overwhelmed with physical pain and fatigue. I left for my office. My *masoul* jokingly likened me to Arash, a mythical archer, who used up all his energy shooting his last arrow and fell down dead. I had indeed used up all my energy, not by shooting my last arrow, but – although I didn't fully realise it yet – by losing my last bit of faith.

For some time I'd had a separate office in Los Angeles as NCR representative in America. From early morning until late at night, the office was until then buzzing with people, all wanting to keep up to date with our latest programmes and plans. Most of the time I was so busy, I ate and slept there and sometimes even washed in the small shared lavatory cubicle. Now I lay in the office, staring at the ceiling and thinking about nothing. Once or twice my *masoul* called to ask how I was and suggested I go to our main office so they could look after me. I asked her to let me to stay where I was, on the pretext that any movement only made my back pain worse. A day passed, and still I could not bring myself to think about Maryam's message; the pain was supremely comforting, because it freed me from thinking about anything else.

However, gradually my mind started up again, and that message was the only thing I could focus on. I could not imagine my *masoul* lying to me on behalf of Maryam. She was one of the five highest-ranking members of the organisation and ostensibly a 'servant of the people and the supporters', so it seemed beyond the bounds of likelihood that those words could have come from her. Even less credible was the thought that she had put those words in Maryam's mouth, for nobody dared speak on behalf of Maryam or

Masoud unless instructed to do so. But I could not imagine Maryam saying those words, this woman I still regarded as an angel of kindness and mercy. Was I dreaming? Was I a wishful thinker, who saw only what suited him?

I was not able to deny Maryam. If I did, it would be the end of everything for me, the end of my work with the organisation, the end of all my hopes, the end of my aspirations to see my homeland free and happy. If I rejected her, I could not imagine ever smiling again; it was too difficult for me to discard everything I had done, all my sacrifices, and accept the bitter reality. The easy way out of the dilemma was to persuade myself that various *masouls* must have given inaccurate reports about the three supporters to Maryam, and I had not been strong enough to defend them. This line of thought was reassuring enough to give me the energy to get off the sofa and return to work. But there was a dark stain on my heart which could not be rubbed away.

All the celebrities who worked with us suffered grievously. Everyone, especially the Iranian media abroad, assumed they were new recruits to the organisation and accordingly their other jobs completely dried up. Their only source of income became the Mojahedin, but their association with us brought them insults and vilification from monarchists, pro-regime elements and the media. Day after day I received complaints demanding that we defend them. We considered giving interviews and statements to put the record straight, but our feeling was that the media were essentially monarchist and would not represent us fairly.

Eventually the organisation came to grips with the artists' dissatisfaction. I was summoned to Paris to discuss the matter or, rather, to hear the already-formed view of the leadership. To them it was nothing more than a question of money, which could be resolved by paying the artists a monthly salary in return for which they would be expected to perform at our functions. Money was a part of the problem, I conceded, but certainly not the whole story. Besides, the amount on offer was derisory. I knew the performers would reject it, and we would lose their services altogether. Abrishamchi, who had been given the task of dealing with this issue, insisted that the organisation couldn't afford a penny more, and there we left it. Afterwards all 'our' celebrities were invited to Paris for individual discussions, which culminated in our making them the offer. As I'd guessed, none of them accepted it. Even when we raised it a notch or two higher, two still declined, as the money would not support their standard of living. One, an old and highly respected singer, was forced to go on Iranian radio, where he was humiliated. A few days later Rajavi himself called to ask why I hadn't stopped him from consenting to that interview. He said I was to find him immediately and offer whatever salary he wanted, but it was too late: nothing would induce him to return. Even those celebrities who stayed aboard were unhappy, complaining that Los Angeles's Iranian media still maligned them. Eventually I persuaded Maryam that the only way out of the situation was to end our ban on those media that did not fully support us. (Hitherto the organisation had taken the view that anyone who did not support us was a supporter of the Iranian regime, a monarchist or an agent of the CIA or MI6.) From then on, however, I would be allowed to talk to any of the Los Angeles Iranian media.

This was quite a victory for me, and led to my having the first-ever appearance by an Iranian activist or politician on a live question-and-answer television show. My *masoul* and I, along with our supporters and friends, were simultaneously very excited and worried about this show. The producer, too, was extremely committed to its success. Originally we planned for a single broadcast, but as it was greeted with much enthusiasm it expanded to three shows, broadcast over three consecutive weeks. Each time, one of the celebrities and a few of our close supporters accompanied me.

Our anxiety was understandable. The Iranian media, and many Iranians living in Los Angeles, had long been considered our first-degree foes abroad. Since the revolution and even during the Shah's era, these people – mostly upper-class Iranians – had been subjected to the harshest anti-Mojahedin propaganda, which we had done nothing to counter; on the contrary, we had compounded the damage with unwise propaganda. One man told me about the number of times he was insulted by our people selling papers in the streets, just for asking the same questions as the media.

I asked our supporters not to call the programme so as to leave the lines free for our opponents and ordinary Iranians. The lines were accordingly jammed with calls from people lobbying for the regime and monarchists. In the second show I gave out my personal phone number and was deluged with calls throughout the night and for days afterwards. I doubt whether there was a single issue connected with the Mojahedin that was not raised during that series. In addition to answering questions, we hoped to project a new image. For many ordinary Iranians this was the first time they had seen a live Mojahed, and it showed we were not all guerrilla types with thick moustaches dressed in military fatigues. The other side of the coin was that hardly anyone watched our own one-hour weekly television programme, full of news and films about our army and leader!

The programmes made a big splash; no one was more pleased than our supporters. One of them presented me with a suit to wear on the next show; others brought flowers, sweets, cologne. Until now we had lived surrounded by our opponents, and for many the only friends had been other supporters. The series presented the Mojahedin in a different light and succeeded in winning over or at least enlightening a whole swathe of people who had been beyond our reach. The whole atmosphere changed. Iranian shopkeepers, out of respect, refused to accept money from me or offered sweets. In one Iranian restaurant, the owner asked to have his photo taken with me. People had been thirsty for democracy, it seemed, and we'd offered them a draught.

Strange to say, whereas reaction from nearly every quarter was voluble and positive, it was virtually nil from our own organisation, which apparently didn't know what stand to take. My *masoul* was complimentary about the first programme, but thereafter said not a word. By then I had learned that personal success was the most dangerous thing for anybody in the organisation. I had seen what had happened to those who had achieved some personal success – how soon they lost their ranks and jobs. Once, an independent NCR member told me, 'We don't dare to say anything good about any man. If we do he will be removed and replaced immediately by somebody completely inexperienced.' Our ideological explanation was that personal success corrupts, and makes one ideologically vulnerable. In order to steer clear of this trap, I always maintained that what I was doing could have been done by any of our members and supporters, if not better than myself then certainly no worse. The only one who deserved praise, I said, was Maryam, who had let me have these interviews. I genuinely believed this, but my worry was that the organisation might think otherwise and put a stop to the good work that had been initiated.

My worry grew when I received phone calls praising me for my endeavours and asking why I was not going to replace the wrong-thinking Rajavi. Later, the person the órganisation rated Enemy Number One in the media praised me on a television programme, and on the radio a presenter answered a question from a listener who asked what was wrong with my speech by saying, 'Nothing was wrong with it. As matter of fact, I wish everybody in the Mojahedin was like him, but the problem is Mr Rajavi is not anything like him, but the complete opposite of Mr Banisadr.' I could do nothing to prevent the organisation from hearing this and taking action, so I refused to continue the programme after three editions and stopped talking with other television and radio stations for the time being, to see and feel the organisation's reaction first. But the only criticism I received was from a brother in America, who took me to task for my answer to the question, 'Why do the Mojahedin hate the Hezbollahis?': I had referred to atrocities such as cutting women's lips for wearing lipstick, not to the atrocities committed in prisons. I argued that torture of ordinary people was worse than that of fighters who have knowingly chosen a path that could lead to martyrdom and torture, because such a crime infringes upon the freedom of the whole nation. He had nothing to say to this; clearly his criticism came from our *masoul*. What puzzled me was that she hadn't criticised me herself. Not until a year later did I discover why.

# 40

# Seeing Reality

In August we made two announcements, both of which received a lot of coverage in the Iranian and even international media. The first one was described by Rajavi as the 'organisation's sacrifice'. From then on, all our offices abroad became offices of the representatives of Maryam as future president of Iran; they would belong not to the Mojahedin alone, but to all Iranians. Furthermore, if he felt it was in the interests of the revolution and people, he was prepared to abolish the Mojahedin. In truth, the organisation had long since become little more than a machine for churning out Rajavi replicas. Many of our opponents interpreted this news as evidence of internal conflict within the Mojahedin. The second announcement had more substance. The Associated Press ran a photograph with the following caption:

> (AP) *23rd August 1994 – Auvers-sur-Oise. Marzieh, once the grande dame of Iranian music during the Shah's reign, poses with Iranian resistance president-elect Maryam Rajavi at her residence in Auvers-sur-Oise, north of Paris. Marzieh, 69, vowed Tuesday never to return to the homeland she left*

*three weeks ago until the hardline clerics who rule it are overthrown.*

I knew about Marzieh's intention to join us several months earlier, when she was introduced to Maryam by Mrs Matin-Daftary, an independent NCR member. Like many Iranians, I loved her voice and even before joining the organisation I had a near-complete collection of her songs. I later destroyed the records, as was anathema to the Mojahedin, having been a 'singer in the court of the Shah'.

One of the other celebrities in our circle cleverly suggested that Marzieh announce her support for the organisation not in a meeting with Maryam but at a huge concert abroad, perhaps in Los Angeles, where her first concert after the overthrow of the Shah would probably attract tens of thousands of people. I was very taken with this idea, but the organisation thought otherwise. I realised that my attitude towards celebrities was different from the organisation's or, more accurately, from that of Abrishamchi, who was in charge of this enterprise. My view was that they should serve as bridges to ordinary people. The organisation, on the other hand, wanted to turn them into new Mojahedin and admirers of the Rajavis.

It won the day when Marzieh was persuaded to give her first concert after years of silence, not for ordinary people but for Rajavi and the Mojahedin in Iraq. Later she performed in military uniform, standing on a tank and singing the Mojahedin anthem. These live shows and videos, instead of bringing us closer to ordinary people, gave the impression Marzieh was singing for the new 'Shah', simply transferring allegiance from one ruler to another. Her old fans, who loved her renditions of traditional love songs, felt betrayed when she switched to the Mojahedin military anthem instead. Many of them fell away, leaving her with a fraction of her original following and us with a huge bill for staging her concerts and filling the seats with our supporters. Soon she was persuaded to become an NCR member as Maryam's adviser on 'art'.

The regime tried to use her children to force her back to Iran. She resisted, pledging that even if the regime killed them she would continue to support the Mojahedin. One more time, the hatred between the Mojahedin and the regime resulted in separation and even hatred among close relatives – the same tragic story that had been repeated thousands of times in the past fifteen years. In the eyes of the public Marzieh, once the adored diva of the Iranian people, changed into another Mojahed without any will of her own or common feeling with ordinary Iranians, prepared to say whatever she was told.

Encouraged by Marzieh's activities and speeches in praise of Maryam, the Mojahedin decided to monopolise all the celebrities associated with us. Our work with them was, in my view, a sorry tale in the end. Instead of getting them to introduce us to people as a democratic alternative to the Iranian regime, they were merely drafted as new 'members' of the NCR, like any others, good for nothing much except praising our leaders unreservedly.

I maintained good relations with many in the media, and even arranged to be interviewed on one of the best-known Iranian television programmes. Meetings were held and the questions sent to me in advance, at the request of our Paris office. As the day drew near I received not encouragement but an order from Paris to withdraw from the agreement: the interviewer bore the stamp of 'enemy'. There was nothing I could say or do to change their minds. As I learned later, when a decision was made that nobody, not even Maryam, could overturn, one could be sure it came from Rajavi himself. Soon after that I was asked to go to Paris where, with Abrishamchi, Jabarzadeh, Towhidi and Mohadessin – some of the oldest members of the organisation – I argued (or, rather, listened to their robotic sloganeering) about the withdrawal. I wasted a lot of time and breath, not realising then that the only thing motivating them was blind support of Rajavi's position. If he decided something, they would strain every muscle finding the 'logic' to support it.

On a more positive note, Maryam asked me to produce a plan for establishing a 24-hour Persian radio station for America. 'As we want to have the widest possible audience', she said, 'this station should be recognised as politically impartial, except insofar as its position is anti-regime.' I immediately began drawing up a plan, and when it was ready I took it to Maryam. She asked me what I needed to get the station going. 'Your blessing and nothing else', I said, 'except I need to devote myself to this full-time and be able to call on the part-time help of supporters who are not helping the organisation in other fields.' How would I finance the project? she asked. 'If we keep our promise that the station is to be politically impartial, I will have no problem in financing it. Almost all our supporters and many other Iranians have been dreaming of the establishment of a radio station like that, and we can count on them.' With that, Maryam approved my plan and asked my *masoul* to clear my slate so I could dedicate all my time to this project; but she asked me to continue being responsible for our celebrity partners.

Helped by two part-timers, I set about the task with gusto. There were many challenges. We had to find entertainers and technicians willing to be involved, and we needed seed money. We also had to find a radio station we could hire and a means of broadcasting in many states. But my main worry was the Mojahedin. By now I had lost faith in the organisation. I saw how easily promises made even by Maryam could later be broken simply with a phone call or a one-page fax. I was therefore very hesitant to sign any contracts or make promises. I wanted more assurances, especially with respect to the station's impartiality. To solve the financial problem we printed $1,000 bonds in the name of 'Iran Zamin Radio'. For few weeks I travelled around the country persuading people to buy these bonds, and managed to raise about $100,000 – enough to get the project off the ground. Many supporters were suspicious of the enterprise, viewing the bonds as yet another trick on the part of the organisation. Still, I hoped that once we started broadcasting advertisers might make the project self-financing.

At the same time as keeping in touch with our existing panel of performers, I tried to engage new ones. We were so successful that we soon had more than enough celebrities lined up. In every report to the organisation I emphasised that our co-workers would participate only if they had full independence; they even asked that the director of the radio station be elected by them, not nominated by us. The response was always positive, although the Paris office questioned the advisability of including this or that opposition spokesperson. After a few weeks we found a suitable radio station, but before signing a contract, as I was still wary about getting final approval from Paris, I asked for a free one-month trial to explore its domain and efficiency. As a technical test, we broadcast music twenty-four hours a day. Throughout this time, I resisted pressure from Paris to announce the opening of the station or ask our designated collaborators to resign from their present posts. Even when the establishment of the station was announced in an Iranian paper, we kept silent.

Soon I was to learn how right I had been to doubt the organisation's good faith. My resistance to signing contracts, renting huge buildings, buying equipment or entering into other commitments was entirely vindicated. In November 1994, after a year of political activity on both sides of the divide, the State Department published a new report about the Mojahedin. According to this report, as in a previous one, they were recognised as a 'terrorist' organisation. The Mojahedin had, in the meantime, striven to show itself as a moderate, democratic force through a variety of measures, including the cessation of guerrilla activity inside Iran. Rajavi even followed a suggestion made indirectly by the CIA through back channels that the Mojahedin meet with members of the Kurdish resistance (then the great enemy of Saddam Hussein, our benefactor) as well as with special Israeli representatives (though at the time Labour held power in Israel, and a solution to the conflict with the Palestinians seemed inevitable).

But it was all to no avail. The State Department refused once more to have any dealings with us. Their choice was not based on our terrorist activities of the previous year, but of the prior year. They didn't 'buy' our moderation as a sign of our tendency towards democracy, as they saw no change in our attitude towards other political groups. Changing names and faces in the organisation, even electing Maryam as future president, didn't help us whitewash our history as long as Rajavi was the sole ideological leader of the organisation and 'resistance'.

The report was a great blow to the Mojahedin. For years the organisation tried to prove we had the full support of America in the fight against the Iranian regime. We had adduced hundreds of signatures of support from members of Congress, a 'letter' from President Clinton, a photograph of him taken with our 'foreign minister', but to no avail. That report signalled an end to our hope that the Iraqis would allow us to cross the border into Iran with all our armaments. Any failure of such an operation, as in 1988, would be interpreted as a new incursion by 'Iraqis' against Iran and would probably not only precipitate a war between strong, internationally supported Iran and weak, isolated Iraq but also bring the wrath of the Americans and British down on Iraqi heads, validating an invasion and the imposition of a change of government.

Of course, American support could significantly change everything for us, and this was why Rajavi was so keen to have it. To achieve it he sent Maryam to the West, along with many other Mojahedin. But the goal eluded him, and to make things worse the organisation was, perhaps for the first time, facing serious internal problems.

On the one hand it tried to prove how honest, genuine, democratic and liberal Maryam was. On the other, they confined members within the iron bars of the organisation's old beliefs, and encouraged them to be hard and unyielding, with no emotional connection whatever to the outside world. Perhaps if they had been honest enough to admit that Maryam's message of 'love' and freedom was just a political device for furthering our goals, they could saved us much confusion and soul-searching, although they would always run the risk of losing some who had joined the Mojahedin and stayed loyal to them at great personal cost expressly for their honesty and probity.

The organisation had no solution to this dilemma. They tried to separate members from everybody else, including supporters, ultimately by asking supporters to leave our bases and find alternative accommodation. When this didn't work they organised weekly self-criticism sessions to help us withstand the impact of the outside world.

Perhaps the unbridgeable gulf between Maryam's words and their effect on members of the organisation was the main reason why Rajavi's decisions came thick and fast in the following months. Once my *masoul* handed me a small package, saying it was a present for me from Rajavi. This was the second present he had given me, apart from portraits of Maryam given to us every New Year. His first had been one of his undershirts, which at the time was very valuable to me. When I opened this new package, I found a small *mohr*, a piece of holy clay for prayers, and with it a small note from Rajavi: 'Never forget your morning prayers!'

On the day of commemoration of Ashorra I entered our base in Los Angeles – then called the 'office of the representative of the president', stripped of all signs and references to the Mojahedin and supposedly open to all Iranians – and found, to my surprise, that the place done up in black flags, with black writing adorning the walls. Obviously everything had been prepared for the observance of Ashorra according to Shi'ite custom. I went straight to our *masoul* and demanded to know what was going on. It was not a Mojahedin base anymore, and in previous years we had never decked out the office that way. An order from Rajavi, she said: we were to observe the ceremony to the letter. So we did, beating ourselves, putting pages of the Qur'an on our heads, turning off the lights and staying motionless for hours and so on.

Self-beating, whether with hands, chains or even swords, as a reminder of Imam Hussein's fate 1,400 years ago, was condemned by many Muslim and even Shi'i intellectuals including Shari'ati, as an export of mediaeval European Christians to Iran and completely contradictory to Islamic beliefs, according to which martyrdom is a happy event, not a sorrowful one. Among the Mojahedin we considered such ceremonies the acts of fanatics, contrived to deceive ordinary people. I suppose by forcing 'Islamic' observation on us, Rajavi was attempting to check our tendencies towards 'liberalism' and 'moderation' and to neutralise the effects of the rise of 'nationalism' among members and supporters. Subsequently other changes were made, including playing a record of *Azan* at top volume in the morning and at noon at all bases to remind members to prepare for prayers. The idea may have been to show that there was no contradiction between the new policies of the Mojahedin and full observation of 'Islamic traditions'.

In October 1994 Iranian revolutionary guards attacked Ashraf base in Iraq with mortar shells, and in November hit another of our military bases with three Squad B missiles. Rajavi interpreted both incidents as consequences of the American report against the Mojahedin. Our loss of support in America and France, where the government even cancelled Marzieh's concert because of its political nature, caused a shift in Rajavi's thinking. He could see no further purpose for Mojahedin outside our bases in Iraq, and was afraid of further defections; so, using those attacks as an excuse and the prospect of a final assault on the regime as an incentive, he recalled to Iraq nearly all members and supporters who could fight. Many members left our bases in Europe and America for Iraq. Activities outside Iraq were downgraded and curtailed, and publication of *Mojahed* ceased.

I was one of the few instructed to remain active in the West, and shortly I returned to Paris to receive new directions for my work in America. While there I discovered that many of our recent 'liberal' policies towards other Iranians had totally changed; Maryam's attitude towards the radio station I was establishing had undergone a complete reversal. She now declared that it could not maintain a neutral policy towards opponents of the regime, but had to be introduced as an organ supporting the NCR. In that case, I replied, there will be no radio station, as independence was the prerequisite for both our collaborators and financial backers. Involved in the argument were Maryam's advisers: Jabarzadeh (policy towards other Iranian groups); Mohadessin (diplomatic and foreign policies); Towhidi (publications and propaganda); and Abrishamchi (almost any matter). I had come to believe this 'Gang of Four' was responsible for our ruinous propaganda, sham diplomacy and policy towards Iranians, performers and other Iranian organisations.

The accusation against me was of wanting to establish a station beneficial only to monarchists and 'political leeches' (the organisation's name for other Iranian political organisations and personalities). I countered by saying that giving free access to the airwaves to all was the best way of neutralising poisonous propaganda against us and showing democracy in action. Their argument was that we could not 'leave sheep alone with wolves'. I never understood this logic, as I could neither see our people as sheep nor our political opponents as wolves. Besides, we were hardly going to leave them alone together, but would be there ourselves, expressing our own point of view and refuting invalid charges. But there was nothing to be done: these four lived in the past, in the Shah's era, and simply could not see that monarchists were harmless and, indeed, might respond to our democratic, nationalist agenda.

During my last meeting with Maryam on the subject, she said, 'Apparently we cannot have the radio station, so return the money to the donors and apologise; tell them the project has been abandoned, as we are preparing for the final battle with the regime.'

I smiled. 'I am afraid there is no money to return,' I said. 'My *masoul* gave it all away to settle our debts to the people who lent us money for our previous demonstration.'

She looked astonished. 'Why did she do that?' she demanded. 'How are we going to return the money now? We shall lose all our prestige and respect!'

'Well, if she hadn't repaid those debts,' I replied, 'we would have lost all our respect and prestige anyway.'

She laughed and said, 'You are right.' Then she asked if I had any suggestions for sorting out our financial predicament in America.

I had already given this matter some thought and replied, 'I see no alternative but to establish some commercial companies, with the help of our supporters, which will bring in a regular monthly income.' She asked me to write a business plan, which I did, and as none of the enterprises required any input of money or personnel, it was immediately accepted and I was told to return and put all my efforts into setting it up.

I spent most of my time upon my return travelling the country in search of funding that would help pay off our existing debts. By then I had lost all hope for the organisation. It was quite clear in my mind that as long as the 'Gang of Four' remained advisers to Maryam, there was no hope for the establishment of proper relations between us and ordinary Iranians – which in my view was the only way we could rescue our finances, reconnect with our people inside Iran and resolve our differences with America.

I believed the State Department's antagonism towards us had nothing to do with our past (our anti-American activity during the Shah's era or our policy towards the hostages in Iran) but was based on our present policies and activities. The US's main concern was that we lacked support even from a fraction of Iranians, let alone a majority. It was no good shifting supporters from one city to another to ensure an impressive-looking turnout at demonstrations: the government had all the facts, and in some cases even knew the participants' names and addresses. But our old-fashioned policies were our downfall.

While it was still my job to work with Iranian celebrities and maintain contact with the Iranian media, my main concern was honouring the personal pledges I had made to donors (who did not trust the organisation's pledges) and finding enough money to pay back our debts, or else asking them to consider them as donations.

One day, just as I was about to pay back the last of the organisation's debts incurred in establishing the radio station, my *masoul* intervened and told me not to. Whenever the organisation planned something new, it turned its back on previous commitments. At this time they were refurbishing Maryam's home in Paris to make it more appropriate for the future president of Iran. Some time earlier my *masoul* had told me that they'd had a small fire in the house and had to repair the damage. I was asked to contact our supporters and, without mentioning all the facts, ask for help. At the time I was very upset about the fire and called whoever I could; I even became annoyed with some who were very close to me and didn't help as much as we wanted. But gradually the suspicion began to grow that this was another trick, that they were playing on our feelings for Maryam and trying to dupe us into soliciting money. Their orders were for all branches in all countries to stop spending money or paying off debts until further notice. I knew that if I didn't repay that debt then, I would not be able to pay it in the near future; for the first time in my organisational life, I defied my *masoul* and, convulsed with desperation and anger, insisted that I would not accept the order unless it came straight from Maryam herself, as she had ordered me to repay all the debts. Obviously quite taken aback, my *masoul* asked me to go to my office and await instructions. Before I left, I told her that I had made an appointment with the man to whom we owed money, and if by then I had not received any instruction, I was going to pay him.

As the time of the appointment approached, I called my *masoul* several times to ask if she had had any response from Paris. Hours went by, and in that time I realised I was losing all my remaining faith in the organisation. I was alone in the office. I did some dusting, swept all three rooms and watered the plants. Apart from answering a few phone calls, I was incapable of doing anything. My emotions were in turmoil and my heart pounded noisily. By way of distraction, I switched on the television and found myself watching a film called *Hercules and the Amazon Women*, a story about Amazon women exploiting and sometimes killing men in a neighbouring village. It caused me a flicker of ironic amusement to identify with those poor men who, like me, had to deal with the illogical behaviour of their women superiors. The end of the film coincided with my deadline and, as I hadn't received any instructions from Paris, I had to make up my mind: I paid the money. Then I called my *masoul* and informed her what I had done. Her anger was surpassed only by her astonishment, as she had never expected me to behave like that. She said nothing, except that she would await further instructions from Paris.

The reprimand I inevitably received for disobeying my *masoul* was quite mild. After all, I was following Maryam's orders. Though the incident passed and was soon forgotten by everyone, for me it marked a turning point in my relations with the organisation. From that day on I gradually distanced myself. I had little to do, apart from liaising with our performers, paying their salaries and occasionally meeting them socially. Even then I could see no use in what I was doing, as the attitude of the organisation remained fixed.

As my faith and trust ebbed steadily away along with my hopes for the future freedom and prosperity of Iran, I sat alone in my office, day after day, silent, inert, unable to think, my glazed eyes sometimes fixed on a corner of the room. I had a reputation for working at my own initiative, and on the whole my *masoul*s never needed to instruct me. So my *masoul* left me alone. Now and then orders came through from Paris; I ignored most of them, knowing they would either change or forget about them. I began to feel like a stranger among my colleagues, though when I did have contact with them we shared news, information, even a few jokes and laughs; but my heart was not with them anymore. Moreover, in my emotionally fragile state, my mind magnified every problem and solutions came hard. One of our celebrity colleagues, an award-winning filmmaker, echoed my feelings when he complained that one of the sisters had tried to tell him how to film a demonstration and refused to listen to his advice. 'You have so little money', he said, 'yet, through lack of coordination and common sense, you waste whatever you have.'

The only visitors to my office were people bringing complaints. For every one they had, I knew many more similar cases. While in the past I had been able to find excuses for the organisation's wrongdoings or accept the blame myself as NCR representative, now I had no answers and nothing to offer them. Consequently they stopped turning to me to solve problems but came merely because no one else would listen.

My only interest was to fulfil my small duties with the minimum of fuss and hassle. To smooth things I prepaid the salaries of our employees, so that when the organisation was late in paying, as it invariably was, I was the only person who knew about it.

My orders were to forge relations with younger performers who could link us to the younger generation. By then I had enough experience to know that I could not make promises on behalf of the organisation because they would be broken. I duly made the contacts, only to be directed a mere matter of weeks later to stop doing so as the organisation's moral code prevented it from working with this younger generation of artists. It was laughable but wholly predictable that the Mojahedin could not stomach the way young people dressed, sang or danced, at the same time as criticising the regime for precisely the same attitudes.

I felt useless. But compared with many in the organisation, I carried some important and sensitive responsibilities, and was considered busy and successful. This was mainly because others struggled to fill holes they themselves had dug, on orders from above while I ignored all orders, saving myself and the organisation a lot of time, energy and money, doing nothing.

I tried not to think about my family. I never stopped loving them, against the organisation's dictates. Every time they crept into my mind, I felt their suffering and then immediately felt guilty because of the millions of people whose lives were far more pitiable. As a father and an Iranian I had always justified my decision to leave them and deprive them of a normal life by arguing that my first responsibility was to put an end to the suffering of our people and to free our homeland for them. That argument now rang hollow. I was wasting my time and could see no improvement or progress coming from anything that we did.

I felt I had to do something to turn things around. At that time I still believed the root of the problem was the 'Gang of Four', Maryam's malign advisers. I knew that while I was fully involved in the organisation, restricted by its rules, I would not be able to stand up for what I thought right, so I decided to leave it for a month and, once free, think freely and write Maryam a long and fully documented report. If she reacted favourably or proved me wrong, I would return and accept the consequences. But if I received no response, I would take that as proof that the leadership was corrupt or inadequate and leave the organisation for good. After all, I had promised Maryam and myself not to keep silent when I saw things that were amiss.

A year earlier, by a stroke of luck, I had found that my closest friend from high school, Farzad, lived alone in northern California. Whenever I was there, I called on him. At first it was difficult for him and his family to accept me in my new guise, but we soon re-established our old relationship and he developed an interest in the Mojahedin's activities. I thought of staying with him while thinking and writing my report. For some time one of our supporters, a physician, had been urging the organisation to send me for a medical checkup, but as this was very expensive in America, I kept postponing it. This gave me the excuse to say I was going to see my brother, who was a physician and would examine me for free. The organisation welcomed this, as it would save money, adding of course that I should persuade my brother to consider helping the organisation as well.

I took everything with me that was precious and reminded me of the good old days in the organisation, and set off for Farzad's house. But almost as soon as I got in the car and headed north, I realised how emotionally attached I still was to the organisation, especially to Maryam herself. Though it was clearly impossible for me to carry on as before, lying to the organisation I had loved so much and for which I had jettisoned everything was not easy. I said nothing to Farzad about my intentions, nor did he guess anything was amiss. He asked about my work and about Marzieh, whose voice we had both loved when young. Over the next day or two, the certainty gradually grew in me that I was not yet ready to leave the organisation and that, even if I found it to be in error, I had no alternative but to try to bring about change from within. I had to find enough courage to stand up to the people I identified as obstacles to progress and talk to Maryam or even Rajavi himself. I headed back for Los Angeles, where I was happy to find that I was expected in Paris the following day.

I stayed in Paris for almost a week. We held the usual meetings, with discussions about the performers working with us and plans for future concerts in various countries. Several times I asked to see Maryam, but each time was told she was too busy with political meetings. Then a group of members who had gone to Iraq came to Paris, and I was asked to see Reza'i to receive the latest information and advice from Rajavi. The key point, in Rajavi's interpretation, was that whatever we did, we could not attract any more people in Iran and certainly not in America or Europe. Nobody, he acknowledged, was prepared to go through another revolution for at least another fifty years; hence the only tool we had against the regime, was the NLA. The final battle would be between the NLA and the revolutionary guards. Responding to the demands of those who wanted to continue to recruit Iranians abroad, Rajavi said, 'Forget about gaining the support of tens of thousands of Iranians abroad. If you can prove that you can gain the support of only a few thousand more, I am prepared to send you half of the NLA staff and budget.'

With these words suddenly everything became crystal clear to me. Instantly I understood things that had hitherto been a mystery, things I had interpreted in a way completely opposite to reality. First and foremost, I realised that I had for years pursued the wrong objective, which had nothing to do with our leader's objectives. It seemed gaining new support among Iranians had never been one of his aims. Perhaps that was the main reason he did not worry about losing public support after the 'ideological revolution' of 1985, or moving to Iraq, or about many other decisions and ventures likely to be unpopular among Iranians, such as the thrust of our propaganda. The intention had been to show our strength, mostly to rally and retain supporters but also to our foes, to prevent them forging any kind of alliance against us and forming new political alternatives (the prevention of which was Rajavi's ever-present obsession).

How wrong I had been to blame Maryam's advisers, when all they did was prevent her from countering Rajavi's wishes. For Rajavi, only the NLA itself was real. The supporters abroad were a means to an end, a way of raising money and gaining the superficial backing of Western politicians. He knew very well we would never seriously bring Americans and Europeans alongside if we did not become more open and democratic. But their real support was never, in fact, his aim. It was the *appearance* of Western support he sought, because that brought in its train Iraqi permission for the incursion of the NLA into Iran, which was essential if we were to maintain any hope for the future.

All my confusion evaporated. There was no problem to be solved, and I had nothing to prove. Maryam was scheduled to see me the night before I left Paris. I didn't sleep that night, waiting for her to call me, but in the morning I was told again that she could not spare any time. I had no regrets about not seeing her as I had nothing left to say, except perhaps to apologise for the way I had acted the previous few months. I headed back to America with many things to reflect upon. Maryam and Masoud were still my leaders. My 'reality' was their reality – what they did, what they said – while everything else was deceit. To become more of a Mojahed and more like Rajavi, I saw that I had to destroy another part of my own individuality, get rid of my way of understanding and thinking. Yet something happened on the flight back that undermined my new resolve.

On the plane I fell asleep immediately, as I hadn't slept for almost two days. When I woke up, an elderly African-American woman in the next seat offered me some food and drink. 'I kept everything that was brought for you because I knew you would be very hungry when you woke up,' she said, adding, 'I felt it was not only sleep you needed.' I was so moved I wanted to hug her and weep my heart out. It had been so long since I had received an ordinary kindness from anyone. For us everything was black and white: we in the organisation were white; those outside, black. Yet here was a 'black' person with a heart of purest white. Inevitably I had to write a report about this in which I censured myself for showing so much weakness in response to a kind gesture: a clear sign that I was turning from a Mojahed into an ordinary human being with ordinary needs and desires.

# 41

# Boiled in the Pot

I no longer knew what was right or wrong, real or fake. I couldn't think or act or smile. The only thing I could do right was keep silent and shed tears when alone. Not until later did I learn that almost everyone in the organisation, except those at the very top, was as confused and desperate as I was. To put everyone on the 'right' track, the organisation announced that it needed another ideological revolution, one much deeper, harsher, harder, longer and with more misery than any other had been. It had already begun in Paris among our members and in March 1995, at the beginning of the new Iranian year, I was recalled there to attend the ideological revolution meetings.

A newly refurbished old house was the base for the potential ideological revolutionaries. At any one time there were twenty to thirty people living there. It was obvious the moment one entered that those residents would be there for weeks, months, even years. The depressing atmosphere was totally unrelieved by chat or cheer or laughter. People barely spoke, and none dared to share his misery and hardship with others. In each of a series of rooms, videos of Maryam's sermons at various ideological meetings were being screened. They were classified; one had to progress from the first room to the next, in the right order. Another, larger room was set aside for people who wanted to write their ideological reports, and another for brothers to rest; sisters went to a nearby house at night. There were two brothers always hanging around the rest room in a permanent state of silent, sleepy gloom. I discovered that they had finished seeing the videos, but were not prepared to go through the revolution. In other words, they were *borida* and were waiting for their destiny to be decided.

The theme of this stage of the ideological revolution was the war on *fardiat*. *Fardiat* is a term that can be understood fully only within the context of Eastern philosophy. It has a full spectrum of meanings, from individualism and egoism to self-sufficiency and self-esteem. Someone who has *fardiat* can be aggressive or arrogant, while another, at the other end of the spectrum, may be modest, peaceful and humane. A modest person may have more *fardiat* than an arrogant one. But the essence is 'self', in all its good and bad degrees.

Mojahedin ideology required one to banish this sense of self and replace it with love for 'God' through the leadership. One was to receive all confidence and esteem from the leader, depend on only him, love only him. A Mojahed had to love the leadership with total and unwavering devotion, defending them, fighting for their rights, being kind to their friends and implacable to their foes. In short, a Mojahed had first to divorce himself from his family, friends and normal life and then go through the final stage of divorcing himself, repudiating all self-love. This stage was called *tallagh khood* ('self-divorce').

According to Maryam's sermon, the sole objective of all previous stages of the ideological revolution was to enable us to get to this one. Articles 'A', 'B' and 'J' served to rid us of our sexuality (*jensieat*) and prepared us for the next phases; 'Article D' related to the ideological superiority of women over men. 'SH' entailed the ideological acceptance of a leadership council consisting exclusively of women; and 'R' proposed the ideological acceptance of Maryam as the sole future president of Iran. These later articles were supposed to prepare the ground for 'Article F' (for *fardiat*). She said that although we had accepted 'D', 'SH' and 'R' as organisational orders, we had not gone through them ideologically.

None of us, she claimed, had honoured our commitment to 'Article A', according to which we had to be united with her throughout every second of our lives (i.e., to confess and self-criticise weekly, even daily or hourly, to her for our mistakes, wrongdoings, non-ideological thinking, emotions, wishes and personal and sexual desires). Thus, of the first three articles, only 'J' had been achieved. We might have conquered our sexuality, but without advancing to the next stage of the ideological revolution, the fight against our *fardiat*, our ideological evolution would eventually reverse until we changed into 'ordinary' men and women, became *borida* and eventually descended from right to wrong, from Rajavi to Khomeini, and became enemies of the leadership, the organisation and therefore God.

How were we to save ourselves? First, she said, we had to realise our situation and be appalled. Next, we had to understand that the distance between 'being' and 'not being' was the mere 'thickness of an onion skin'. Third, we had to decide to change. Finally, we had to pay the price by writing a full report about our situation, divulging things we had never before written or said, and revealing ourselves in front of others during the revolutionary meetings.

These revolutionary meetings were called *dig* ('the pot'), meaning that the experience was as painful as sitting in a 'pot of boiling oil'. At first we couldn't take this concept seriously, but our levity turned to nausea when we saw non-Mojahedin NCR members making fools of themselves by joking about it in front of Maryam.

According to Maryam's sermon, all members and supporters, even perhaps ordinary Iranians, fell into two different categories: '*talabkar*' and '*bedehkar*'. *Talabkar* means 'creditor', and was applied to those who felt that the leadership and the organisation owed them something; *bedehkar* means 'debtor' and referred to those who felt they owed something to the leadership and the organisation. In simple terms, creditors were bad and debtors good. She listed forty conditions or adjectives describing creditors and debtors so that we could identify the ones that applied to ourselves. The descriptors included the following:

> Creditors thought the organisation and the leadership needed them to survive and function properly. Debtors

believed they needed the leadership for their survival and humanity, to evolve and reach up to God.

Creditors sought reward or enhancements for good deeds. Debtors felt they could have done more; they sought out extra tasks so as to pay their dues to the leadership, who gave them the opportunity to fight against injustice. They shunned higher rank and position.

Creditors used any opportunity to elevate themselves, even at the expense of the organisation. Debtors believed all positions belong to the leadership, and any position they themselves occupied were held in trust. They blamed themselves for all the organisation's failures and attributed all its victories to the leadership.

Creditors shrunk from the enemy and lied to the organisation about their bravery. Debtors were bold, obedient and modest.

Creditors placed no great value on the organisation's principles and retained all their 'bridges' to the past and personal relationships; debtors took all their relations with others from the leadership, whom they would defend with their lives.

We were now at the stage when each of us had to recognise ourselves as 'creditors', acknowledge the sin and ugliness of our feelings towards the leadership and work towards becoming debtors. This was a prerequisite for the final struggle. There was no person or organisation fighting Khomeini's regime except the Mojahedin and the Mojahedin could not survive or fight without the leader and without total faith in his ideological leadership. We had been 'the beneficiaries of the leadership and the organisation, parasites, leeches feeding from their blood ...' *Fardiat* was the real Satan, Maryam said, and the struggle to rid ourselves of it would never end as long as we lived; therefore we had to be vigilant and obdurate. We could not worship God so long as we worshipped ourselves, or, in other words, worshipped the Satan within. Our salvation was to make ourselves *ro-sieah* (black- or dirty-faced), instead of defending ourselves and presenting ourselves in the best light. From then on it had to be our ambition not to be loved and respected by others but to be hated, especially by those opposed to the organisation. We had to love only the leadership, and only the leadership would love us. They were the channel through which all love passed.

I was still absorbing the content of the videos when I was called to an ideological meeting with Maryam. It was a small meeting limited to about forty high-ranking members. The depression I had suffered for so long lifted with the realisation that others suffered in the same way. Moreover, we had got used to the idea that all problems and failures stemmed from our ideological weaknesses, and all we had to do to remedy the fault was write a few self-damning reports and perhaps criticise ourselves in front of others. God forbid we should find the organisation at fault! They encouraged us, gave us everything we needed, had a long history, martyrs, principles ... To oppose it meant opposing the struggle against the regime and against injustice, forgetting our love for our people, our country and even God; and denying our own sacrifices and our own ability to understand, to choose and to separate right from wrong. Far easier and more bearable than 'losing everything in life and the afterlife all together' (an expression beloved of Rajavi) was to confess oneself happily to be a sinner. I was therefore impatiently looking forward to criticising myself as harshly as possible and making myself more 'black-faced' than anybody else.

From the very start of the meeting, I had my right hand raised to signal my wish to speak. Maryam ignored it long enough to allow me to listen to others and pick up clues on what to say. Far from learning from others' experiences, I didn't even benefit from my own. I should have known by then that the art of self-criticism was to do it stage by stage, to show an ever-deepening understanding. Otherwise you would continue to be asked for more and more self-revelations and by then you would have nothing significant left to offer. I had the unwise habit of tearing into myself all at once and without reservation, with every self-criticism I could think of.

Maryam called on me but before allowing me to speak she asked if anybody had anything against me. I assumed this was done to help me, as I was the most inexperienced person there. Others who had spoken had been interrupted and heckled from all sides, with worse criticism than the speaker himself was offering. Strangely, when it came to me, although almost all my previous *masoul*s and brothers with whom I had worked were there, nobody made any major allegation against me. One brother said, 'To be honest, I have worked with Masoud for several years, but when I think carefully I find I have not got much to say against him; as matter of fact, I can say many good things about him. Unlike many brothers in America, he was usually very accurate, calm, punctual, patient, hard-working He always wore a smile and he seemed actively to welcome new difficulties and challenges. None of us ever had any conflict with him ...'

As he spoke I watched Maryam's face, which bore a meaningful smile, though I wasn't able to interpret it. Suddenly she broke in. 'What you are saying is that he was the perfect brother, kind and understanding, never harming or bothering anyone ... He wanted to be loved by everybody, to be *"everyone's representative"*.' Her last words were accompanied by a sarcastic laugh. What did she mean? 'Representative' or 'your representative' or 'representative of the people' were designations that President Banisadr liked to apply to himself. This was her way of giving me a clue about the direction my self-criticism should take. By now my crimes were clear to everybody in the room except myself. Unusually, I was not accused of not working properly or disobeying orders, not for being obstinate or bad-tempered, not for bullying or making life difficult for others. On the contrary, my crime, which I had to recognise and elaborate upon by giving more facts, was that I was keener on working and seeing progress than even my *masoul*s; that I was kind to everybody around me, that people enjoyed working with me; that so many supporters, celebrities and ordinary Iranians wanted to share their ideas and complaints with me; that I was more optimistic about our work than my *masoul*s and always full of ideas and new projects ... I was astonished. How could these things be crimes? I could imagine being criticised for anything except doing my job! Perhaps these qualities were thought to be examples of 'positive' *fardiat*, that is, a strong sense of self couched in positive virtues – viewed in many cases as worse than 'negative' *fardiat*.

I simply didn't understand. I thought Maryam was teasing me and that her remarks were sarcastic references to things I had not

done, orders I had not obeyed in the past few months. Immediately
as I started talking, people grew impatient and wanted to cut me
short as I wasn't following the line suggested by Maryam. My
*fardiat* manifested itself in my wanting to be loved by everybody,
including the organisation and my *masoul*s, and all my actions
were motivated by this desire, not by obedience to the leadership or
dedication to the organisation's work and aims. Unlike most, I
wasn't expected to cite my shortcomings and faults; I had to
explain why there had not been a single report against me by my
*masoul*s or others. (Obviously even those occasions when I had
flouted the wishes of my *masoul*s, which loomed so important in
my mind, had meant little for them and had perhaps never been
reported.)

But I didn't know any of this. Misreading all the signals once
again, I thought people grew impatient because I was not being
sufficiently ruthless in censuring my own misdeeds. So I spoke
faster to mention all my worst points, using the harshest words I
could think of. For example, in explaining how I had put money
aside to pay bills that the organisation postponed or rejected, I
said, 'I *stole* that money to pay the bills, which the organisation had
*forbidden* me to paid'. I cited all the times when I hadn't obeyed
orders or complied with directions issued by Paris or my *masoul*s.
I described all the times when I retreated into a passive state and did
hardly any work.

Throughout, people were murmuring and indicating that they
wanted to interrupt me, until I started explaining my decision to
leave the organisation temporarily to write a report about those I
held responsible for our failures and shortcomings. Suddenly
everybody fell silent and started listening. The moment I finished,
a forest of hands shot up, but without waiting for permission to
speak, everybody started talking at once and the babble rose to a
crescendo as those who were most passionate shouted out their
comments above all the rest.

Maryam laughed to see how everyone had sprung to the defence
of the leadership. I was confused. What had I said to change the
mood? Why did everyone suddenly have so much to say? Suddenly
Towhidi, his voice rising above the din, shouted, 'He is a *borida* and
he must admit it!' After that, all I could hear from all sides was the
word '*borida*'. Until then I had been calm, but now my equilibrium

cracked and I broke down and wept pathetically. Nowhere in that sea of faces could I find one whose expression could give me comfort. If there had been anyone who sympathised, they would not have dared to say so; defending a *borida* was a crime second only to being one. The voices grew louder, some saying, 'He is a *borida* and has no right to be here!' and 'He should be thrown out of the room!' My *masoul* apologised to Maryam for not recognising me as a *borida* and started criticising herself. Another *masoul* apologised for letting me stand in front of Maryam and talk to her. A third said I had sullied and shamed the meeting. In desperation I looked into Maryam's eyes to see if she was inclined to rescue me. At that point she called the meeting to order and when everybody was silent she asked me if I thought they were right or not.

I had no doubt in my mind that I was not a *borida*. My worry was only to discover why the organisation was not succeeding in its aims and who was responsible for suppressing Maryam's words. Nor did I harbour the slightest doubt of my love for Maryam and Masoud. Nothing – certainly nothing material, not even my love for my wife and children – had ever, even for second, distracted, diverted or deflected me away from the organisation and the ideals to which I was committed. By what stretch of the imagination, therefore, could I call myself a *borida*, a person who wanted to abandon the struggle and return to normal life without any concern for others?

I knew that my answer would breach one of the principles set for that stage of the ideological revolution, namely 'not to oppose, reject or resist whatever people in revolutionary meetings saying about you, but to listen, accept and later find reasons for proving those accusations against yourself'.

I looked Maryam in the eye and said: 'No.'

Immediately another wave of attacks broke out. Towhidi demanded to know why I was refusing to accept the designation *borida*. 'I was a *borida* too for a while', he said, 'but I realised it and confessed to the organisation. Yes, I lost my rank and position, I had to start again from the beginning, and now I am very happy I lost everything except my honesty towards the organisation. You, too, must realise it and confess. You may lose many things, but not the most important thing, which is your relation with the organisation and the leadership.' He seemed to be showing me a way out of my miserable situation. He spoke more kindly than before, in the tone of a friend offering wise and understanding advice. Grasping at the straw he held out to me, I said, 'Yes, I think I was a *borida*.'

Again, the atmosphere shifted and more questions rained on me. Towhidi asked me to give more facts about my situation and prove I was a *borida*. He said I should explain my reasons for wanting to leave the organisation and admit that everything I had said earlier was 'lies' and 'rubbish'. All I could think of was to repeat some of the things I had already said, only perhaps in stronger and more personal terms. Every word was greeted with derision. Again Towhidi stepped in. He said, 'You have been with the organisation for the past seventeen years or so, so by now you should know the meaning of *borida* and be familiar with the facts that bear witness to a *borida*. You have to tell us about them yourself, as obviously nobody has monitored you closely enough to be able to testify to the facts.' Perhaps his words were intended to be helpful, but I had by now completely lost my nerve and all my senses had become dulled and distorted. I had but a single intention: to extricate myself from this situation.

I looked over at Maryam. She was smiling, but her smile lacked its usual kindness. It was like the smile of a gloating conqueror, sarcastic, humiliating. There was a long pause. Then she said, 'OK, let him go away and think and write what he has to say.' With that, the meeting concluded. All I had to do was to think and write – but I had nothing to write. Like a fool, I had already spilled out every self-criticism I could find at the first meeting, leaving myself nothing to bring up in the many later meetings I would have to attend.

Over the next few days I struggled to unearth even the simplest and slightest of my mistakes (while even inventing a few) and wrote about them with a most brutal censure. I wished I had committed more wrongs or 'saved up' confessions for later.

Members from different countries came to watch the videotapes and attend revolutionary meetings. High-ranking sisters were free to attend brothers' meetings, but not the other way around (men being the inferior gender). This gave them an insight into the way we were being treated, which somehow made the process even more painful.

By mid-April 1995 over 100 members had assembled to attend one of the 'pot' meetings, too many to fit into the original house. Accordingly, we were moved to an office building far from the centre of Paris, called the 'Hundred', reflecting the number of rooms. Part of the ground floor, which was separated from the rest of building, was designated for non-Mojahedin members of the NCR who lived in Paris. At first I didn't mind talking to them, but gradually they asked more and more questions about what I was doing there when I was supposed to be representing them in the US. It was embarrassing not to have a satisfactory answer, so I began avoiding them as much as possible.

All who had come for the 'revolution' were divided into three groups under the direction of three high-ranking sisters, all of them among my previous *masoul*s. The political section formed the first group, members from other countries the second and people from other sections of the organisation working in Paris formed the third. For some time I was confused about which group I belonged to: I came from abroad, I was in the political section and also a member of the 'artists' section' responsible for Paris-based celebrities. It did not take me long to realise that my unique situation meant I was to endure a triple dose of misery. If, for example, people from the political section were under attack for dressing showily or adopting bourgeois behaviour, the first accusations would be hurled at me. When people working with artists were condemned for becoming 'ordinary', like the celebrities themselves, again I was on the front line. And when it came to laying charges at the door of people who worked alone or had strong individuality, mine was the first door called on.

For the next two months, almost daily from two in the afternoon until two to four in the morning, we had to attend the *dig* meetings. None was as frightful as that first one I experienced in front of Maryam, but these subsequent sessions brought a different kind of intense pain. To prove my revolution, I had to show my readiness to defend the leadership by attacking others who were going through theirs. Of course such attacks, in Mojahedin thinking, did not come under the heading of animosity but were seen as acts of kindness: we were helping the poor victim to fight his internal Satan, or *hamzad* ('devil twin'), in Maryam's parlance.

During those meetings we had to 'read our past history'. This no longer meant what it used to. Maryam had turned the tables on us. Our sexual weaknesses, our disobedience, our laziness or lack of enterprise were no longer at issue. To confess these was to be accused of wanting to run away from one's real crimes. According to Maryam, our downfall – our loss of faith in the organisation or the leadership – would not be brought about by our weaknesses but by our strengths. Our experience or good nature, our ability to solve problems or artistic talent, our good voices or good looks: anything we might regard as positive qualities we could be proud of was the source of anti-ideological, anti-revolutionary behaviour. They were 'the slippery points on which, if we were not careful, we could slide from the heaven of being a Mojahed into the hell of becoming an ordinary person and later working with the regime.' They were what changed us from 'debtors' into a 'creditors'. Thus, in 'reading our past', we had to expose the very qualities about which we felt most positive and excoriate ourselves for them, because every time one of those attributes came into play, we would rejoice not for the achievements of our leader but for our own.

The upshot of this ghastly procedure in my case was about 100 written pages about my good points and how they had corrupted me and separated me from the leadership. Others fared still worse. Former political prisoners, victims of torture in Khomeini's or the Shah's prisons – heroes to us – had to come forward and castigate themselves for being proud of resisting their jailers or suffering torture. They had to say they'd betrayed the organisation and the leadership, been traitors responsible for many deaths and arrests. They had to say that the only hero among prisoners and victims of torture is the dead one. Equally, people whose relatives had been martyrs had to come forward and insult them. Martyrs died for the sake of the leadership, and only the leadership could take pride in them.

The main objective of these meetings was to destroy any values we had except loving our leaders, being honest with them and 'becoming from head to toe an ear' for obeying their orders. By attacking others we were destroying any relationship that existed between ourselves; all relations had to pass from the leadership.

The more I thought, the less reason I could find to continue living that miserable life. I felt I was not a Mojahed any more, however much I still loved the leadership and embraced the goals of the organisation. In one of the meetings I said so to Maryam. She laughed, saying I was going from one extreme to the other, from worshipping myself to denying myself. 'You should not deny your ideological revolution or the part of yourself that is Mojahed,' she went on. 'That is like surrendering yourself to your Satan. You are a Mojahed, perhaps not a very good one, but a Mojahed all the same, and you must remain one.' After that, many who knew me and had worked with me, including my previous and present *masoul*s, spoke up to prove to me I was a Mojahed.

At that meeting I realised how wrong I had been to believe that people like Abrishamchi were the real decision-makers. Abrishamchi, who had recently returned from Iraq and had obviously had his ideological revolution under the direction of Rajavi himself, talked for a few minutes about himself. Like the rest of us, he called himself as a traitor to the organisation and the leadership and accused himself of destroying or neglecting all manner of things that were his responsibility. Clearly, we were all in the same boat, oceans away from our leader.

# 42

# Asses' Ears

We now had to absorb and follow a new set of 'values and principles'. While many of them were not new, Maryam's emphasis made them somehow more extreme and absolute. The Mojahedin had always been opposed to class society, the bourgeoisie and their values. Rank, position and profession were not important for a Mojahed. Mojahedin had to live and die simply. All Mojahedin, both women and men, were to wear Islamic dress all times. There were to be no physical contact, private meetings or joking and laughing between brothers and sisters, which could engender mutual attraction. Work harder, sleep less, eat less were the instructions. Behind any comfort there lurked the potential for exploitation. We were to avoid doing or even thinking of things we liked.

Maryam warned that anybody whose values differed from these, anyone who was 'ordinary', should not remain in the organisation. 'You must all decide,' she said, 'either to become 100 per cent Mojahed or to leave the organisation.'

The list of things we had to think and talk about grew daily. The next to arrive on the scene was *korsii*, another invented word which at its simplest meant 'position' – although in Maryam's mind it meant positions real and imaginary, materialistic and idealistic, past and present, originating from within or imposed from without. Each of us had many *korsii* of our own but we also expected to receive *korsii* from the leadership; if we didn't, we first became passive, then changed into ordinary people, eventually became *borida* and finally changed into an enemy of the leadership and the organisation. Hence our responsibility was to rid ourselves of those *korsii* we considered we had as our right, in order to save our souls from corruption. Confused and feeling less like a Mojahed than ever, I couldn't bear to sit in on those ideological meetings, mainly because I felt unable to criticise others. I neither remembered nor wanted to remember their wrongdoings. So, having excused myself on the grounds of back pain (which was real), I wandered up and down outside the door listening to the proceedings, which were painful in the extreme both to the participants and to me.

One day we were told that all three groups were to have a joint final session under the direction of Sister Nasrin, whom everybody knew as the third-most important person in the organisation after Masoud and Maryam. Most of us knew or had guessed that Fahieme'a had fallen from favour and lost her position, although the matter was not referred to. In that joint meeting, I sensed I would be under closer scrutiny than others and suffer more than anybody else. I guessed it would be a rough time, although I could never have imagined to what degree.

By then Maryam had apparently decided that that stage of the ideological revolution be brought to a conclusion, as for months almost nobody in the organisation had done any real work. Already it had been decided that we would have our largest-ever meeting in Germany, where Maryam was supposed to make her first official speech, in front of a large crowd of Iranians. Therefore the aim of the meeting was to force those who had not concluded their revolution to do so and get back to work.

It was more than two months since I had entered the process of revolution. I had attended more than a dozen difficult 'pot' sessions and written reams of reports about my past, magnifying hundredfold all my wrongdoings and discrediting anything good about myself. The only thing left to criticise was being born, and my parents for bringing me into the world. Nevertheless, the organisation was not satisfied. They never told me what was wrong or what they expected to hear. I supposed they had a dilemma. They had long been puzzled by my hard-working and caring attitude, i.e. my ideological status, which in their eyes surpassed that of my *masoul*. This contradicted their 'ideological hypothesis', which stated that no Mojahed man could be as caring as any Mojahed woman, let alone the fifth-highest ranking among them (my *masoul*). At the same time I made known my intention to leave the organisation, a decision that, in the Mojahedin lexicon, could have no other meaning than that I was a *borida*.

The puzzle was that I was a *borida*, but not passive. I had every opportunity to leave and return to my family, yet not only did I stay, but I also continued to work as hard as before and welcome the new stages of the ideological revolution. I tried to change myself, to follow their advice, to do whatever they wanted. But they simply could not understand or accept that anyone might love his country and his people enough to tolerate the hardship of working within the organisation. According to their theory, anyone who did not embrace the ideological leadership with total and unswerving love could not and would not go to the lengths that I did, to strive and persevere. They could not see that for me – as perhaps for many other members and supporters – the Mojahedin was the only organisation that offered a chance to achieve our goals, a chance that could not be missed. Nor did they accept that my love for Maryam was not related to the sacrifices she had made for Rajavi, but to her message of unconditional love for all.

None of this made sense to them. So they diagnosed me as having 'an unspoken hidden contradiction'. According to their revolutionary theory, such a contradiction invariably and completely destroyed a person's ability to revolt. He might continue to work, be happy and remain a member of the organisation for a long time, but all these signs, which appear to be signs of good character, are completely contradictory and in fact signify a *borida*. So where did my contradiction lie?

I never found out for sure; all I had to go on were their sarcastic remarks; but perhaps their theory was that I had had a relationship with a female supporter in Los Angeles. My love for that imaginary woman would have given me incentive enough not to leave the organisation and return to my family and energy enough to work as enthusiastically as I did; at the same time it would explain my situation as a *borida*.

While others in the joint meeting spoke of their 'contradictions', Nasrin took pleasure in teasing me whenever she could. She watched me out of the corner of her eye, monitoring my reaction to others' confessions. Eventually she decided to talk about me. I was clearly a special case. Only one of my previous *masouls* was permitted to talk about me; I was barred from saying anything at all.

She started by putting her hands erect on her head to represent the long ears of an ass. She said, 'When you were in your first *dig*, none of us knew that you were a *borida*, otherwise I would never have dared let you see Maryam or speak in front of her. We thought that you were obsessed with the desire to be admired, and this was what we expected to hear from you. Yet instead, you censured yourself for the worst possible things in the most savage and vulgar terms. You thought you would make asses of us all. Nobody could say anything worse than what you had already said about yourself. So as easily as that, you could have your ideological revolution and, perhaps with a new title and rank, you could return to your beloved America and carry on doing whatever you were doing there in the past. You thought nobody would realise that you were hiding a huge contradiction behind those words. But suddenly you were confronted with hostility from all sides, when they called you *borida*. When you discovered you were on the verge of losing everything – your position, your rank and your job in America – you went pale. You started shaking, you forgot how to speak.'

Again she put her hands on her head. 'Yes', she continued, 'instead of making asses of us, you yourself changed into an ass, stupid and mute.' She smiled sarcastically. 'Now tell us, after more than two months, what you were hiding behind all those accusations against yourself. Tell us why you were more caring and enthusiastic about the organisation's work and aims than your *masouls*. Tell us how you always developed new ideas and projects and never needed guidance or instruction from anyone else. Tell us where you got your incentives and energy from. Tell us what you have hidden in America ... perhaps in Los Angeles.' At this point one of my previous *masouls* said, 'Yes, tell us about your relationship with the female supporters there and why it was always you they wanted to talk to and share their problems with!'

I had expected any kind of wild or vicious accusation except this. It was so outrageous I could barely hear or see any more. My head spun and I felt feverish. Truly I was being boiled in the 'pot'. Without waiting for permission to sit, I fell back into my seat.

Well, said Nasrin, did I have anything to say? I didn't answer, just sat looking at her, numb with anguish. She said no more, just gave me another sarcastic smile to flaunt her victory. Her arrow had found its aim. She had discovered my real contradiction and forced me to admit it with my silence. Instead of speaking, she made the asses' ears on her head again and laughed loudly to signal to others to laugh too, which they did.

For the rest of that session, I sat motionless, like a corpse, unable to respond to anything. At break time I went up to Nasrin and begged her to tell me what to do. As far as I could see, I had three options. I could leave the organisation and forget all about my aims and ideals. I could kill myself and be free of all this misery. Or I could stay in the organisation and gradually lose my mind. She smiled again and said, 'Do none of these. Instead talk about your contradiction.'

'And when I have nothing left to say?' She turned and walked away.

I was not sad any more, just angry. I felt betrayed. If they had so little trust in me, how could I possibly have total trust in them? I remembered Mahmud, our old supporter in Los Angeles, who years before was accused of stealing money. When Mahmud called to ask for help, I assured him that if he was innocent, he had nothing to fear, that he should trust the organisation to resolve the matter fairly. Now I realised how wrong I was. Perhaps there are things one never understands until faced personally. Trust, after all, is a two-way street.

Nasrin now changed tack and announced to the gathering the organisation's programme for the next 20th June festivities in Germany and America. How many people could we expect to have at the demonstration in America? she asked Various numbers were called out, ranging from 2,000 to 5,000. Then she looked at me and, perhaps as a conciliatory gesture, said, 'Masoud, you are the NCR representative there and know the situation better than anyone. What do you think?'

'Ten thousand.'

The meeting erupted with protests and exclamations of surprise.

'He is joking,' someone said. 'I demand he back that figure up.'

I spoke very calmly but sarcastically, fuelled by anger. Instead of citing the evidence, I decided to use the logic and language of the organisation and the ideological revolution. I discovered how easy it was to talk the kind of nonsense they did, picking figures out of the air and making wild claims that could not be substantiated. The organisation never used to reveal the true number of participants in any demonstration or gathering, even to its own members. But for the previous demonstration they had claimed 5,000.

'Ok', I said. 'At our previous demonstration we had 5,000 people, didn't we?' I knew nobody in that room agreed with that number but nobody dared to say 'no', as it would have meant that the organisation lied to us. I let the silence hang in the air for a moment, then continued, 'That was before this stage of the revolution, when we were all *borida* or in danger of being so.' (It had become a convention by then, even a fashion, to call oneself *borida*.) I continued: 'Now that we have passed this stage, our energy will have been magnified 100 times, so we can surely expect twice the previous number. In fact, I should criticise myself for being so pessimistic and not saying 20,000, in the light of present circumstances.' My logic was perfect and nobody, not even Nasrin, dared reject it. She just mentioned that Sima, then the *masoul* for America, had estimated an attendance of 5,000, and asked how I responded to that.

'Well, I believe Sister Sima has not been here in the last few months, so she doesn't know what the effect is of the new stage of the ideological revolution. She doesn't know what kind of people she is going to have under her command very soon, and how they will improve our prospects. The number she gives is based on her previous knowledge, so it seems reasonable to multiply her number by at least two.'

'All right', said Nasrin, smiling stiffly to conceal her anger, 'let us conclude this discussion and say that you should have at least 5,000 people there.'

Afterwards, the man who had questioned my seriousness

approached me and said, 'Tell me the truth. You were trying to make fools of us, weren't you?'

'Well', I said, giving nothing away, 'I gave my reasons. If you thought them wrong you could have stood up and opposed them.'

The next day my *masoul* called and asked if I had anything to bring forward as my 'contradiction'. I told her, 'My answer is still "no", and I have nothing more to say.' I said if they had heard anything that could be held against me it would be better if they told me.

'No', she replied, 'but we know what your contradiction is and Nasrin tried to give you a helping hand to find it. Like many other brothers, your problem is *korsii* [loving my position and struggling to keep it].' If this hadn't been sad it would have been funny: after all the virulent accusations, suddenly it appeared that Nasrin had meant to tell me only that I was guilty of *korsii* – just like everybody else in the meeting directed by Maryam. The 'contradiction' business was a red herring, a distraction. All they really wanted to prove was that I loved my job and was doing all I could to keep it. I had only to write my report along those lines and they could close that file with a victory. As always with the Mojahedin, they just wanted to say they were right and had won. Certainly they were right on one score: I did love my job and had worked at it harder than ever during the past year. If that was my crime, I was more than happy to confess. I wrote a very short report admitting not only that I loved my position, but adding also that I loved the climate in Los Angeles, which suited me much better than the cold. I admitted that I loved to be loved and respected by others; I admitted that I hated to see anybody unhappy about anything I said or did; I admitted that I loved to be useful and hated to be useless. Whatever their intention and whatever their judgement about me, they at least pretended to have accepted my revolution and asked me to return to my job. When my *masoul* put the proposal to me, I refused, saying, 'How can you send me back when you know that circumstances there pushed me to the edge of leaving the organisation?' Eventually she accepted that I should not actually live in America but go there whenever necessary. In the first instance I should go for a week or two, to talk to celebrities and invite them to attend our rally in Germany.

Shortly before I was due to leave Paris for Los Angeles, I was stopped by one of my *masouls*, Badrie, who was head of our political section. 'Anna has legally asked for a divorce,' she said. 'You should reply as soon as possible.' I guess Badrie had been chosen to give me that news because she knew the full story of my relationship with Anna. It was she who had forced me to go see her for the last time, to be with her without loving her, to see my children without becoming attached to them. It was to her that I complained time after time that it was wrong not to let Anna to know my situation and equally wrong to expect me to be a revolutionary Mojahed and withhold love from her and the children.

I did not allow Badrie to see any reaction from me. 'Thank you,' I said. 'I will do it.'

I read the letter several times. The content, though expected, was still a hammer blow. I didn't cry; I hardly knew how to anymore. But my heart was beating very fast, filled with the pain of love mixed with sadness. It was news I had been hoping to receive for years, knowing it would set her free and at the same time give me the freedom to see my children. But now that I had it, I didn't want it. Deep down, I wanted her to wait for me to return to her, perhaps after we had all returned victorious to Iran, though I knew I had no right to ask that of her. She was still young enough to make a new start and enjoy the rest of her life. Painful though it was, I knew I should be happy for the person I had loved most for almost twenty-five years. I signed the petition and posted it on my way back to America.

I first met Anna sometime in June 1971. At the end of June 1995 our marriage ended, and a few months later I received notice of the decree absolute. I never let the organisation know what I felt. In any case, their focus had moved on; nowadays the only kind of self-confession they were interested in was on the subject of *fardiat*.

I went back to America a changed man, devoid of hope and motivation, an automaton working without initiative or imagination, empty and unfeeling. I decided that to protect myself from further interrogation and condemnation, I would have no unnecessary contact with anyone. The suffering I experienced I likened to the torture inflicted on inmates of Khomeini's jails, and I'd had enough. Unfortunately, at this time the regime's agents assassinated two of our sisters in Iraq and we had to mount a small protest demonstration in Los Angeles. This meant that I had to

encounter many of our supporters, including new ones I'd
recruited. Some were curious about where I had been, so I made up
a story to explain my absence. But if in conversation they showed
concern for me or paid me a compliment, I rejected it angrily. I
recognised in myself the same change as had happened a few years
earlier to Abrishamchi. He had been a favourite among supporters
and members for a time, and had been treated with love and
respect. But suddenly he changed and acted as though he wanted to
create resentment or even animosity towards himself. People
thought fame and fortune had withered his good nature. But now I
saw what had happened to him: he, too, had had to fend off
kindness for fear of being criticised for 'stealing' people's love for
the leadership.

Some curious and amusing situations arose out of the
conflicting demands of the ideological revolution. In Los Angeles I
was introduced as a non-Mojahed member of the organisation and
Maryam told me I could, accordingly, shake hands with women at
political meetings. According to the new principles of the
revolution, however, I was not supposed to shake hands with
women under any circumstances. In order not to infringe upon any
rules, I had to get a ruling from Paris on this weighty subject. I
suggested I should pretend to have a cold and excuse myself from
shaking hands on that account, and this solution was accepted.
The results were often embarrassing. 'How come,' asked a man I
met once, 'you don't want to give your cold to Mrs ... by shaking
hands with her, but you don't care if I catch cold from shaking your
hand and kissing you?'

On another occasion, a supporter gave a lift in his car to one of
our sisters and two brothers. Somehow this situation had to be
squared with the ideological ruling that no man should sit beside a
woman. 'I was already sitting in the driver's seat, and they were still
out on the pavement hesitating to get in,' he said. 'Eventually the
sister told me to sit in the back seat beside the two brothers while
she drove the car. I was surprised and annoyed, and reminded her
that she didn't know the city or the directions to our destination,
had no American licence or insurance and any accident it would be
considered a criminal act. But she would have none of it and
wouldn't even allow me to sit in the front passenger seat to give her
directions; she sat alone in the front, and we three in the back.'

Another set of contradictory principles was that no brother and sister could be alone together, and that a brother should always be accompanied by a sister at a political meeting so as to allow the sister to learn and ultimately fulfil that job herself. The upshot was that many of our political meetings became jokes: a simple one-man job now required the attendance of three people, often all with titles. To make up the numbers and balance the sexes, we often needed a *nafar ham-rah*, or 'company person' (a term invented for the purpose), a kind of chaperone who had no role except to meet that principle. It was a terrific waste of that person's time. Nevertheless, *masouls* were forever calling each other to see if they had a free 'company person' to spare. They even kept a count of the number of hours a 'company person' had put in and used their time as a rate of exchange. 'I'll lend you my *nafar ham-rah*,' one might bargain, 'if you can lend me your car or your computer.'

I finished my work in Los Angeles, anxious to return to Paris to get away from all these ludicrous issues, but was asked to go to Germany instead. Preparations were underway for our largest political meeting outside of Iran. Here we hoped to get Maryam in front of a large crowd, something we had failed to do in the US and France. Posters were plastered all over Germany announcing Maryam's appearance. Gradually, however, we became aware that the Iranian regime, with its economic and political influence on Germany's government, was applying pressure to prevent Maryam attending the meeting. The political section had to work at full pitch to neutralise that pressure. We approached politicians and journalists, intellectuals and humanitarian organisations, putting it to them that in the interests of democracy Maryam must be allowed to appear, but failed to convince the government. Instead, we hired a satellite company to broadcast the meeting live, including in Iraq to NLA combatants. We recruited supporters from everywhere to swell the numbers at the meeting. Marzieh and other celebrities agreed to perform, a major attraction for the estimated 100,000 Iranians living in Germany. Maryam, as future president of Iran, would deliver an address based on adherence to Islam and Mojahedin values and allegiance to the ideological leadership, namely Rajavi.

# 43

# Changing Roles

I was nominated host to our foreign guests, my most important and sensitive job after the new phase of the revolution. I was determined to follow orders precisely without using any initiative, making any suggestions or asking unnecessary questions. For some unknown reason, I was given no details of my role until two days before the meeting. In that time I had to hire a few cars and find a hotel as near as possible to our base; then, newly armed with a list of guests and their arrival data, meet them at airports in Frankfurt, Düsseldorf, Dortmund and Cologne, and at railway stations. Our hotel was in Bonn and the meeting and receptions were taking place in Dortmund. Although I had three brothers as assistants, I had to do all the meeting and greeting and ended up being driver, host, porter, adviser, guide, escort and lunch and dinner companion. After the meeting, when they all had to be taken back to airports, most of my assistants had collapsed, exhausted on the floor; only one other and myself managed to keep our eyes open long enough to drive a car.

It was quite an experience for me, simply to obey, to be a good member and 'from head to toe just an ear'. At the end of it all, I was very pleased that none of our guests had been killed as a result of our sleep-deprived driving in a country we didn't know, always in rush to reach to the next appointment. Later a member wrote a report criticising me for borrowing money from his budget to buy a return ticket for one of the journalists who needed to bring his flight time forward. My *masoul* showed me the report and asked my comments. I laughed. 'Either he was very ignorant or he was being kind to me, because borrowing money was the least of my wrongdoings! I borrowed and took chances with everything, including everyone's lives, to get the job done as I was supposed to!'

Immediately afterwards I returned to America for our demonstration. There, the elderly woman widow of a famous Iranian singer and close friend of my mother and aunt approached me. She kissed me in front of everyone, and it felt strangely as though I were seeing my mother again. She smelled of my country, my mother and my family. Somehow she gave me the sense of being human and an individual again. It was a pleasant feeling but short-lived, as I then returned to Paris and stayed there the whole summer except for a few short business trips. Seeing that woman and remembering my past life again made me feel I had no more connection with the organisation, no role in it, and that it was doing nothing but make noise. Nevertheless I continued in harness, and even managed to secure one or two improvements in the operation of the political section. This may have been why I was invited to accompany a delegation led by Nasrin to Norway to evaluate the possibility that Maryam might be allowed to visit the country or even live there. At that time she was enduring more and more restrictions placed on her by the French authorities and could not get a visa to travel anywhere else. Later I even played host to a few members of the British House of Lords who came to Paris and promised to try to persuade the British government to allow Maryam to reside in the UK.

Although the revolutionary meetings for lower-ranking members concluded, for older, higher-ranking members from the Shah's time the torment continued with weekly or twice-weekly meetings under the direction of Nasrin or Maryam. These new meetings were much crueller, and the things being admitting to were stranger and harder to believe. They called themselves and each other thief, murderer, traitor, bloodthirsty beast, enemy of the leadership. No mercy was shown. It was like a gladiatorial contest, where one fighter had to crush or kill another to save his own life. As I didn't know most of the participants I had a good excuse not to get involved. Strangely, Nasrin rarely called on me to speak, and seemed to have lost interest in me. Perhaps she had bigger fish to fry or she had simply given up hope of changing me into a 'good member'. It was pitiful to see the decline in others – past heroes reduced to empty wrecks with nothing to do except wait to die. To help these people work in the new atmosphere, people were employed to teach them a foreign language, a venture that was stopped as soon as it was realised that a foreign language was a passport to a job outside the organisation – which many of the students were on the verge of leaving. By then, as far as I heard, at least five or six long-time members had already left and at every meeting more were admitting their intention to do so. Although I noticed the change in others, I could hardly detect what was happening to me. I said nothing more about the times I had been tempted to leave for good. Every now and then, as a defensive exercise, I produced some minor confession, but always in a calculated way, careful not to repeat my old mistakes. For me, as for everyone else, survival was at the top of the agenda. Thanks to my back problem, I could usually sit by the door and slip out whenever I sensed Nasrin was about to pounce on me and insist I comment on somebody else. If I got caught out, I just repeated what others had said, in different words.

Once when Nasrin observed that a particular speaker's case was similar to my first experience and asked me to comment, I did something I thought amusing and that offered me a free escape route. Instead of saying anything I made the 'asses' ears' with my hands on top of my head, just as she had done. She nodded her head approvingly and laughed, and soon everybody joined in. Here was a real change in myself: in order to save my own skin, I now betrayed and humiliated a friend.

Another incident compounded my self-disgust. I was walking with a colleague from the political section, and he said, 'We must be merciful towards sister Maryam and this stage of the revolution. God knows what would happen to us otherwise. Sometimes I feel that if there had been no revolution, and we had left the Mojahedin, we would have had miserable lives. Apart from losing our hopes and desires, what could we do outside the organisation? We have lost our youth, and perhaps part of our health, our families and friends. What can we do after living here for fifteen years or more? One day we will think back and dream of the food and the comfortable beds we had here.' The next day he repeated these sentiments at the ideological meeting and I asked him if he stayed in the organisation because of his beliefs or because he had nowhere else to go. He acknowledged that I had a point, and admitted that the latter was perhaps the stronger reason. Afterwards I was furious with myself. This was something I had never believed I could do: take a friend's confidences and expose them publicly for the sole purpose of saving myself from the accusation that I never attacked anyone in meetings. I was changing into the kind of person I had always hated. I stopped talking in those meetings altogether, either to criticise myself or to condemn someone else. But before anybody noticed my new policy or the silent protest that lay behind it, I was whisked off to America again to solve problems relating to a concert Marzieh was due to give in Los Angeles.

On my return to Paris, I was transferred from the political section to the NCR secretariat. For the next two months almost everyone, including even members of the leadership council, were consigned to sponsorship work to try to raise the money we needed to pay debts arising from the rally in Germany and the concert in Los Angeles.

I think by then Nasrin realised I had no intention of advancing through the ideological revolution. I was told about the 'pot' meetings, to which I wasn't invited, and about colleagues who'd had a 'very good revolution'. Perhaps the idea was to make me envy others' success and re-motivate me; but since no such effect resulted, they eventually decided I should retire, except insofar as I still had clerical work to do in the NCR secretariat. I retained my title as the NCR representative in America, however, and nearly everyone continued to think I was still in charge: articles and letters were published under my name in US papers and I was still treated as spokesman for the NCR and as the key contact for celebrities, despite the fact that I had not the slightest clue what was going on there.

Working in the secretariat gave me a chance to see whether I could live as a retired person within the organisation, without the daily struggle against the internal and external enemy and without the pressure to conform, to obey and to innovate. Yes, compared with becoming a *borida*, being called a traitor and espousing Khomeini's ideology (the 'fate' of someone who left the organisation), it was better to become a retired person within it. Maryam had said that in order to change, we had to work harder, accept greater challenges, sleep less, eat less. The office building had a capacity of several hundred, but now there were only about twenty-five people working there full-time. But the building and its huge yard had to be cleaned at least weekly. Thus, while there was little clerical work for me to do in the secretariat, there were still plenty of jobs that needed doing. So I now became a kind of servant, including to members of the NCR who had previously been in my charge.

Because of my back and the old injury to my right arm, physical work was neither very easy nor suitable for me, but I insisted on doing as much of it as possible. I might sweep the whole yard one day and be unable to move the next, but it gave me some sort of satisfaction and helped me to forget other things. It made me feel useful and alive, and gave me back some individuality and capacity to love. There was no need to fear that I might inspire affection, as nobody now could accuse me of doing things for personal gain. And I noticed the change I could make in our surroundings. Day by day I worked harder at becoming close to the ideal of a real Mojahed, not only in my own view but also in the eyes of my *masouls*, who liked to cite my case as an example of Maryam's correct judgement and advice. My colleagues' main concern was my health. Sometimes, when even doctors' orders didn't immobilise me, they forcibly restrained me so that I had to rest. People were unforgettably kind, bringing food, taking me to the hospital, running errands

By the beginning of 1996 I was almost paralysed, as sitting and walking were agony. My health had been compromised, but I had no regrets: I had come back to life, my soul had been saved and I was a Mojahed again. The organisation wanted to send me back to America, but I refused to go on account of my back. Then Maryam came to me with a different proposition: to write a book about the problem of *borida-ha* that afflicted the organisation, a factual, fully documented book that could be translated into various different languages and serve as a political tool.

Apparently the few members who had left the organisation in Europe or America did not present any problem, but defectors in Iraq turned into enemies of the organisation and sought to undermine and denigrate it, using politicians, the international media and even the UN. I now understood, better than ever, what they meant by calling the Mojahedin's bases 'prisons' where the inmates were 'tortured'. When I was under pressure to write about my own animosity towards the organisation, I wrote a report for Maryam, saying: 'Sometimes I sympathise with the *borida-ha*. I feel they are right to call our base a prison. As a matter of fact, I think they are not going far enough; the Mojahedin prison is the worst in history. In prisons from the Middle Ages up to the present people have been restrained by walls, water, steel or even fire and electric shocks. Here there is no visible wall or steel or electric shock to prevent us from escaping. But there is something worse. Not only our bodies but our minds are in chains, and the jailers and torturers are ourselves. We are controlled physically and mentally, and everything we do or think or even dream is constantly monitored – by us, our own jailers, and punished in the most viciously agonising way. The organisation has spies who can report everything back to them. Who are these spies? Why, we are! Who better to spy on us than ourselves?'

The worst of it was that there was no sympathy, no comfort, no protection to be had outside or inside the organisation. We were accused of not having any love or feelings for anybody, of being selfish and cold. Once when Abrishamchi met Sarvy, he told her she looked like me. 'Good', replied Sarvy sarcastically, 'then tell my father whenever he misses me he can look in the mirror.' Yes, indeed, we suffered infinitely more than any ordinary prisoner. But as soon as one was prepared to surrender himself and change into a 'good Mojahed', a 'good soldier for the leadership', one could feel free. Whether the Mojahedin had any right to impose this kind of regime on us, to act as God and use their divine right to mould us into their desired form, is another question. But imprisonment and freedom are perhaps matters of interpretation. Some would say that Khomeini's torturers were right to call their prisons 'universities' and to tell their victims, 'You should thank us. This small degree of suffering you bear now will save you from everlasting suffering in Hell.'

The organisation wanted me to prove that those acting against us were the regime's spies or members of its secret police, fed and financed by it, and that consequently whatever they said about us was void. As evidence they gave me files of 'documents' about each of them, mostly their own reports and self-criticisms when they lived as Mojahedin, and clips from various Iranian newspapers with stories about them. Jabarzadeh briefed me on how to use these 'documents' to prove our claim. I knew from experience how this 'proof' worked. In simple terms, it was based on the idea that 'the friend of my enemy is my enemy'. Any newspaper that published a pro-regime item would be branded as anti-Mojahedin, and anybody subsequently associated with the paper, whether as contributor, interviewee or subject of a story would be tarred with the same brush. It didn't end there, for if such a person then wrote for or gave an interview to another paper, that paper would also fall into the pro-regime category. Using this kind of 'logic', the Mojahedin 'proved' that almost all Iranian media inside and outside the country were either financed by or in the service of the regime, the monarchists or, in a few cases, the CIA and foreign governments. Thus talking with them made one an agent of those bodies too.

In this way, they had amassed so much 'proof' that they felt they did not need anything else and it would be quite feasible for me to finish the book within a month. I didn't want to use their logic, however, or depend on the Mojahedin-standard allegations and criticisms, which were exaggerated or even fake. Instead of proving that our foes were collaborators with the regime and traitors to the revolution and hence the country, I wanted to show that their arguments against the Mojahedin were baseless, and that our 'armed struggle', our peace treaty with Iraq and our stay in that country were just and right. To do all this occasioned a lot of research, not only into the regional and organisational background but also into world history, so I could produce meaningful comparisons and examples for foreign readers. Luckily I was sent to Los Angeles on another mission and while there, with the help of a very good friend, I found many relevant documents in a library. Unsurprisingly, the research alone took me several months. During the whole of that time I was under pressure to finish the book as soon as possible. I had a few changes of *masoul*, and had to persuade each one in turn that what I was doing was necessary and took time. When I eventually received the go-ahead from Nasrin and later from Maryam to write the book my own way, I relaxed a little and felt free to follow my own instincts. Rather than being purely defensive, the book would now become a history of the Mojahedin aimed at showing that it had right on its side, something I wanted to prove more than anybody else, especially perhaps to myself. I hoped to finish the work in time to present it to Maryam as a gift for the Iranian new year, but when the time came and she gave me a tie and a photograph of Rajavi as a present, I had nothing to offer except an apology for not having completed the book.

It took me almost six months to finish writing the book, which numbered over 400 pages and cited thousands of documents. When it was done, Nasrin sent copies of it to various *masouls* to read and comment on before publication. None of them found the time or incentive to read it and as a result it was never published, which, as it turned out, was fortunate. A few months after I left the organisation it struck me how wrong and biased I had been when writing the book, so when the organisation asked if they might publish it under my name, I answered, 'No. I no longer accept many of the arguments in it. Obviously when I wrote it, I was a Mojahed and thinking as a Mojahed. I saw only the facts and events that cast the Mojahedin in a good light and dispensed with everything else. If I were to write it again, I would take a much broader view, and the result might not accrue to your favour.'

# 44

# Back in Britain

My back condition had so deteriorated with the physical stress of sitting and typing that I was forced to return to England for further surgery. On reaching London, my first thought was to see my children. For the first time in many years, I was not under the restriction of 'unresolved marriage status', hence I was entirely free to see them.

So many critical articles had appeared by then in Iranian papers about our children and their relationship – or lack of it – with their parents that the organisation now welcomed reunions between members and their children and was even spending money and time to ensure that these happened. Many of the children were now reaching adulthood, and as a group they tended to be rebellious and totally opposed to the Mojahedin cause – especially those who had been separated from their parents during the Gulf War. The organisation could not brook a fifth column, so it was essential to get those children back onside, and Maryam personally facilitated reunions and even sent children presents to mark the occasions.

The last time I had seen Sarvy was on 20th April 1991, exactly five years earlier. She was fourteen years old then, still a child, and

I had bought her a gift of pens and pencils. Now she was a nineteen-year-old woman, in the first year of medical school. What could I get for her now? I pondered extensively, and in the end I bought her a pocket organiser like the one a supporter had presented to me a few years before.

I was on the second floor of our base, where the *masoul* had lent us her private room for the meeting. I expected Sarvy to arrive at any moment, so with every ring of the doorbell, I jumped out of my seat and over to the window to see who was there. Eventually she came. I didn't believe my eyes: could this beautiful young lady really be my own little daughter? I almost didn't dare embrace and kiss her. I don't remember what either of us said or did; I only know that I didn't cry: tears were for the ideological revolution, and I was far beyond that now. When I gave her the organiser, she said she already had one and didn't need it. Later we agreed she would pass it on to Hanif. Meanwhile, I gave her my cherished fountain pen and my wedding ring, the only valuable things I had.

I sat opposite her, taking her hands in mine, not wanting to speak, just happy to watch her for as long as I could. Out of habit I think I recited some organisational jargon, but then she started asking me the real questions. Why hadn't I called or tried to see them, even when I had been in London during those five years? I could not tell her that the ideological revolution required me not to love them, as 'our first and deepest love' had to be given to our leader. I didn't want to provoke her opposition to the Mojahedin's way of thinking. Instead I told her part of the truth. 'Because of the ideological revolution I had to divorce your mother, but for political reasons I was not permitted to do it legally, so I didn't know what to do or to say to her.' She seemed to accept this and said no more about it. She told me Anna had decided it would be better for Hanif not to see me, as he would be very depressed when I left again. Later she told me it was Hanif's decision, too. Even she had been so angry with me that she hadn't wanted to meet me, but my old friend Shams had persuaded her. I was sad that Anna would not allow me to see Hanif, but I understood her decision. After all, I myself had suffered greatly as a child with constant partings from my mother. I was familiar with that pain.

Sarvy and I met for a few hours several times after that. She even took me to her university and with her help I found some books and documents about the role of women in the new political era after the end of the Cold War, which was valuable to my latest research for the organisation.

Back in Paris Maryam had made the revolutionary decision to use the Internet to communicate with members and supporters. There being no woman the organisation could draft to do the job, I was asked to be in charge. They introduced me to two brothers who would work with me in designing the appropriate systems. It turned out they were much more capable than I was; I felt totally useless. All I had to do was listen to these two experts, then each evening convey their ideas to my *masoul* and ask permission to do what they recommended. I was nothing but a messenger boy, and an inadequate one at that, because I often couldn't grasp things well enough to be able to pass the message on accurately. I could not understand why one of them had not been put in charge. My guess is that they were not 'ideologically fit' to be under the responsibility of my *masoul*. I was in post for only two weeks but during that time truly felt the misery of our sisters' situation for the first time. They had to do exactly what I was doing, acting as messengers between brothers with expertise and higher-ranking sister *masouls*, not for two weeks but for their whole organisational lives. I admired the ideological stamina that prevented them from feeling like parasites.

Fortunately it had already been decided that Maryam would go to London to hold her largest audience ever. I returned to join scores of members who were arriving every day to prepare for her arrival.

It took me less than a day to become aware how much the situation in the UK had changed since I had worked there a few years earlier. Many of our supporters had fallen away and not been replaced by new ones. Those who remained were unwilling to come to any meeting, even when we put it to them that this was an international concert to demonstrate solidarity with oppressed women. By way of inducement to Iranians and to local Arabs and Latin Americans – whose appearance allowed us to pass them off as Iranians! – we invited not only Marzieh but also some dancers and singers from Egypt, Lebanon and Bolivia. Still they hesitated, fearing that the organisation would interpret their attendance as proof of support among Iranians in Britain, which was not the message they wanted to convey. In Newcastle, one of our old supporters and an old friend of mine welcomed us to his house warmly but declined the invitation, saying he felt deceived and betrayed by the organisation. In Edinburgh a woman who had been as close to me as a real sister refused to see me. Another supporter wondered why I still worked with the Mojahedin when all the clever people he knew had left. Another friend sent me a message saying he would be very pleased to see me as long as I came alone and promised not to talk about the Mojahedin. The story repeated itself in Manchester and many other cities, and it was clear we had lost our bases there for good. Even those who, out of politeness or friendship towards me had promised to attend the concert, failed to show up.

After a fruitless seventeen-hour day trying to persuade old friends and hearing nothing but complaints and accusations, I reported these disturbing findings to my *masoul*. That night I could not sleep. I was much troubled by the fact that I was no longer able wholeheartedly to defend the Mojahedin. I sounded like a tape recording, reciting the lines like a robot. This is the way people like Mohadessin and Abrishamchi used to talk, and I'd hated it until I realised that these poor chaps had no say at all in what we did. Now I was talking a lot, but my words came only from my mouth and were patently not as effective or persuasive as before.

The next day I accompanied my *masoul* to see Maryam, who had arrived in London. It was a meeting of women *masouls* responsible for recruiting an audience in various countries; I was the only man present. When Maryam asked how many I guessed would be there, I told her about my experience with the old supporters. 'What do you think is their problem?' she asked.

'I think it is due to our failings, mainly in communication and in management.' I mentioned various points I had heard but didn't dare to say that their real problem was that they had lost trust in the organisation, and that trust was the only tie that connected us.

'What', she pursued, 'do you think is the source of their problem?' I hesitated, but then made a veiled reference to trust. 'You are wrong,' she said brusquely. 'The main reason for their dissatisfaction is that all of them are *talabkar* [creditors].' Then she asked, 'And who do you think has made them *talabkar*, and why didn't you realise this obvious fact?'

At this point a tearful Nasrin broke in. 'We members have made them *talabkar*, and all the blame rests on us. We have made them *talabkar* as we were *talabkar* too.' Then Nasrin turned to face me and challenged me. 'What about you? Why didn't you realise their problem?'

I said, 'Because I was *talabkar* too?'

'Yes,' she said, 'because you were *talabkar* too. But of what? What did you want from the organisation and the leadership?'

I wondered how to answer her when Maryam interrupted and said, 'This is not an ideological meeting. Let's forget about this matter and see what are we going to do.' She asked each *masoul* to say how many people they had recruited to attend the concert.

Even when our supporters heard Maryam was going to speak, it didn't persuade them to work harder or recruit more. Nor did the advertised meeting between Maryam and Yasser Arafat, who was in London at the time, or a long article in the *Sunday Times Magazine* illustrated with an enormous and beautiful photo of Maryam. But word spread, and the celebrities drew their following from among people of different nationalities, so for the meeting Earls Court was crowded enough for Rajavi to claim it as a vote of confidence by the Iranian people in Maryam's presidency.

The gathering served as good propaganda for some time, but it could not fool any foreign government into believing that we actually had the support of a majority of Iranians. It was not possible to reconcile this claim with events on the ground in Iran, where a bloody demonstration against the regime, in support of a junior *mullah*, had been well attended; but no one showed any sign of willingness to challenge the revolutionary guards at the behest of their 'beloved future president'. Maryam could not reside in Britain and was unable to be as active as before in Paris, so a few months later she returned to Baghdad. Of course the intention had been that she should return in triumph to Tehran. Rajavi put a fine gloss on it by announcing her departure for Iraq as a victorious day for the Mojahedin and a clear portent of her early return home. He vehemently denied that pressure from the French authorities had forced her departure.

I thought a lot about what Maryam had said in that meeting with the *masouls*, and decided she was right: our supporters were *talabkar*. But not only them. We too, plus members, supporters,

Iranians, foreign dignitaries and politicians, journalists who'd had contact with us. Yes, everybody was *talabkar*, a creditor of the organisation. Therefore should we invite them all to go through the ideological revolution with us? Or should we ask what credit they gave us, and what it was we owed them that they wanted returned to them? It could all be summed up in a simple word: 'trust'. Iranians and non-Iranians alike had all given us their trust and in doing so had sacrificed something. Some had helped in small ways, signing a petition or making a donation in the street. Others had given up their families, laid down their lives. And their 'reward'? Gradually, probably without realising it, they came to feel betrayed, lied to, cheated. They had given the Mojahedin their most precious commodity, 'trust', and it had been squandered, held cheap, discarded or sold in exchange for propaganda.

Two days before the Earls Court concert, I had to play host to our celebrity guests and performers. As I couldn't be with everyone, a colleague came from Newcastle to help. By now it was a struggle for me to put on a happy face. I had come to the end of the road with the Mojahedin, and I knew it. I had not finally made up my mind to leave, yet I was hanging on by a thread. I tried to be a charming host but kept drifting off into my private thoughts and having to jolt myself back to reality. Who are we, I kept wondering. I remembered Rajavi had once called members and supporters of the organisation 'diamonds' – the hardest and most precious of elements – because we had left behind all bourgeois temptations and seductions and were pure, bare and ready for use. For the first time I understood the imagery. We were honed to perform the most difficult tasks, but that was all we were – stonecutters, instruments, not human beings.

Several incidents around this time alienated me further. I wanted my colleague from Newcastle to join me in the front row of the concert, where I thought he had every right to sit, having helped not only to host visitors but also coordinate events. But my *masoul* refused, with mockery besides.

In a meeting for supporters, a man famous as the father of several Mojahedin martyrs in the time of the Shah sat on the floor in a corner of a corridor. When I asked him what was wrong, he said he had chest pain, perhaps because of his heart. Much worried, I rushed to tell my *masoul*, who merely said, 'This is not your job. Your responsibility is to be a host to your guest. Let him die; I hope he dies soon.' After a few seconds' silence she relented a little and said, 'OK, go find his son and tell him. He knows what to do.' This father of martyrs, the 'crown of the organisation' as Rajavi once called him, had outlived his usefulness by holding meetings with old friends now considered foes by the Mojahedin; all his credit lost, he was 'better off dead'.

When I was told to accompany a guest to a banquet in Maryam's honour, I asked my *masoul* about the friend who was helping me. 'I have introduced him to our guests as their host,' I said, 'and they expect to see him there too.'

Her reply was, 'He is a supporter, and this celebration is not for supporters.' I was astonished, as previously supporters were welcomed as publicity fodder, and our magazine had carried photos of them with Maryam.

'In that case', I replied, 'I think it will be better if I stay with him, as it is not right to leave him alone.'

'Do as you wish,' she said. Although it troubled me to oppose her, at the same time I felt alive again. After a year of toil and struggle to become what they expected me to be, it was heartening to discover that some of the real me had survived. My character and individuality had not been completely killed off. I lived to fight another day. The same night, while on the way out, deep in thought, I tripped and fell in the street and hurt myself. My friend's kindness in rushing to buy medicine and a bandage, and in helping me dress the wound, was a simple but moving reminder of the goodness that existed out there in the real world.

# 45

# The Final Divorce

I spent three full days at our 'rest base' recovering from exhaustion and injury. Every night more than fifty men went there to sleep; in the morning it was as dismal and empty as a junkyard. During those days I had nothing to do but think. My mind became a battleground in which my two halves – my Mojahed personality that I had struggled so long and hard to develop and maintain, and my own individuality, born and bred – slugged it out for dominance. On the one hand there was a hollow space inside me from which laughter, sorrow, joy, sadness and affection had been squeezed out. On the other hand, seeing Anna for a few seconds at Earls Court just long enough to say hello to each other, recognising the good-naturedness of friends and defending my friend against my *masoul* were experiences that seemed to show I was still capable of loving and caring. Once I swore an oath to God that I would never leave the Mojahedin as long as I lived. That was at a time when I saw them as the essence of the truth, the only existing means to fulfil our responsibility to humanity, history and country. For that cause, I had sacrificed everything I cared about personally. But now the organisation had lost its magnetism. I was going to have to prepare for a different kind of sacrifice. People I had worked with, the life I had led for almost twenty years: all this would be consigned to the past. I would feel defeated and humiliated, even at the hands of my nearest and dearest. I would have to face the unknown and accept new hardships I could not foresee.

The truth was, I reached the point when I could no longer accept, support or defend the organisation with my heart. I knew I could never be a 'full Mojahed, as Masoud and Maryam wanted. Maryam was right. The time for being half a Mojahed had passed. It was all or nothing.

On 28th June I called my old friend Shams and told him about my intentions. I also asked him to help me to the hospital as I was in acute pain, my legs partly numb. I telephoned my *masoul* before I left to tell her I was going to the hospital.

My final letter to the organisation was dated 6th July 1996 and sent via Shams. In it I expressed regret at having reached that point and expressed the wish to be useful again in the future. I wrote what I thought would make them happy, and the tone was conciliatory and somewhat contrite. The only lapse was when I accused them of wanting to change me into an ant in an ant colony; I had tried and failed, and as I couldn't bear to be useless I'd decided to leave. In a separate letter addressed to Rajavi as president of the NCR – which I did not date, so that they could insert any appropriate date they liked – I submitted my resignation as NCR member and representative in America. In this letter I gave my reason as partial disability caused by my back condition.

I didn't want to go to Shams's house, as his wife was a supporter. Nor I did tell my sister I had resigned. So I had no alternative but to become voluntarily homeless and ask for help. As a result I was moved temporarily to a hotel to allow me the opportunity for adjustment.

Most of the time I stayed in my room. I had no incentive to go anywhere or do anything. I was a stranger to the real world, like a character in a science-fiction film frozen in ice and reborn after thousands of years when the glacier melts. For almost twenty years I had lived and thought as a Mojahed, dependent on them and proud of denying myself any personal wants or wishes. I let them make all decisions for me – what to eat and drink, wear, feel.

Suddenly I had to think for myself. Myself? Who was that? I was neither the person I had been before joining the organisation, nor was I a Mojahed. It was no good looking for the 'me' I had known before: that was a person in his twenties. All my old principles had been discarded one by one, and the ones I had acquired in the Mojahedin were dead too. I was perhaps the poorest person on earth: not only did I have no money, but I also lacked ideas and a personality of my own. Later, I would learn from people around me how to want and desire, how to dress, how to enjoy life.

One day Shams brought me some old photographs of people who had escorted Anna and me to the airport when we left Iran for the first time. Among them were photographs of my parents. Suddenly it hit me how much I had missed them, how precious they were to me. Usually we take our parents for granted; they are like oxygen in the air, we hardly notice them. When they are gone we know their true value, but by then it is, unfortunately, too late. I studied the photographs in my hand for a long time. I sighed and grieved for my parents, not knowing how or when they died, nor where they were buried.

After a few days I called Sarvy and asked to see her. When I told her part of my story, she asked if I had left the organisation because of her. I said 'no', even though I knew she might have liked to hear an affirmative as proof of my love for her. Later she brought me some of my old belongings, which she had kept as souvenirs: our joint collection of photographs of Masoud and Maryam; pictures of them Sarvy and I had drawn and painted together; some of my books and magazines; even a towel. Apparently she had a collection of things that had belonged to her 'martyred father'. To protect herself from the pain of my absence and the thought that I didn't love them, she had martyred me in her mind.

Sarvy, Anna and her mother still supported the Mojahedin; a few days earlier, Sarvy and Anna had met Maryam, who had praised Sarvy. If the Mojahedin had succeeded in overthrowing the regime, Sarvy could perhaps have been proud of having a father like me, ready to sacrifice everything for freedom, his country and his people. But as things were, I was a fool, a loser, stupid or at least deceived, someone who had sacrificed everything for nothing. This image blotted out any good memory she may have had of me. The only things she could remember about me were bad things: how, once when she was a child, I forced her to eat food she didn't like; how I hadn't called her even once when she was at the Mojahedin school in France; how she had inherited some of my bad qualities. If I had been dead or in prison, she would have been able to love me as before, even be proud of me …

I realised that I had lost the love of my little daughter forever. Perhaps if I were lucky, she would love me as a friend – but not as a father. Then there was Hanif. According to Sarvy, 'he argues that this person who has done such wrong to our mother does not deserve to be seen, still less to be loved.' This may have been her way of expressing what she wanted to tell me herself, as her later actions did on many occasion. For the next three years, I could not see my son; those were his last three years of childhood, the time when perhaps I might have compensated for some of the things I had not given him earlier and left him with a good memory of a father. But it was not to be. Perhaps my family decided thus as a punishment.

These realisations underlined the fact that I had indeed lost everything: parents and children, sisters and brothers, relatives and old friends, my youth and health, my knowledge and experience of working and living in the ordinary world. I was a latter-day Hamlet, hesitating to see the truth and act upon it, and when I did it was too late; everything had been lost, perhaps for good. I became a prisoner again, this time a prisoner of life itself, atoning for the crime of wanting to be good but choosing the wrong direction.

When somebody asks me if I was wrong to follow the Mojahedin, my answer is 'yes', but if one asks if I was wrong to join them when I first did, it is 'no'. Not joining them would not have reflected my knowledge and understanding of them, but selfishness and cowardliness. Although I lost everything, I have no regrets because I kept my dignity and honour and because I sincerely did what I could in the service of liberty and justice, those pillars of morality that make us human.

One day, after a long spell of voluntary incarceration, I went to my sister's house. On my return to the hotel, was surprised to see two high-ranking sisters waiting for me in the manager's office. They had spent a lot of energy and time trying to track me down, and for the next three entire days they tried to persuade me to return with them to Paris. By way of inducement, they said they had a 'blank cheque' from Rajavi to give me whatever I wanted – any position within the organisation. I smiled, aware that they saw my reason for leaving as my personal *korsii* problem, which had nothing to do with the organisation. I told them I wanted one thing only: they should announce I was no longer a NCR representative, otherwise I could not be free in the outside world. Moreover, gossip about the absence of their representative in America might be damaging to the organisation. They even brought Maryam in, in the hope that my respect for her would bring a change of mind. They got me to answer a call on a mobile phone, but once I realised it was Maryam at the end of the line, I threw the phone down, ran from the room and locked myself in the toilet! I was being pulled in opposite directions. I was determined not to go back to the Mojahedin, but I simply could not bring myself to say 'no' to Maryam.

After that, thinking to escape, I went to stay at my sister's house for a day or two. No use. They followed her and watched the house, then called pretending to be agents of the regime. Perhaps they meant to show me what lay in store for me in the outside world if I had no protection. When I challenged them, they said it was the regime that was watching the house. 'In that case', I said, 'I am going to inform the police.' At that, the spies miraculously vanished.

They now tried a different tack. If I were to remain a 'private' citizen, could I not at least remain a member of the NCR? They would pay my expenses and provide other assistance. In fact, via Sarvy they sent me £400 and a computer so that I could maintain contact with them through the Internet. I spent some of the money on a mobile phone they asked me to have, again so that they could contact me, and used the rest to buy a printer and pay for repairs to the computer. I was also asked to make necessary amendments to the book I had written, so that it could be published. I declined to do so but told them I might write another book – and I wrote these memoirs using the same computer.

There were more sinister incidents. One day I was called to meet a sister, Fereshteh, and discuss an urgent matter. We agreed to rendezvous at the Baker Street Underground station. I was early, so to kill time I left the station by a different exit and was surprised to see a member of the organisation waiting there. 'So', he said, approaching me, 'you were told to be here too?'

I was almost certain he didn't know I had left the organisation, so I answered, 'Yes, that's right. I'm supposed to be meeting Sister Fereshteh by the other exit.'

He said, 'Exactly. I was told to wait here, and Bahman is waiting somewhere else.' I asked if he knew why we were there. 'I don't know,' he said, 'but I guess it is important. Apparently Sister Nasrin is here to take somebody back to Paris with her.'

'Who?' I asked.

'I don't know. Perhaps you can ask her, she's waiting in the car with another brother somewhere near here.' It suddenly struck me what they were up to. They intended to take me back to Paris at any price; if they could not persuade me, they would do so by other means. I excused myself, saying I had better go to my appointed meeting place, and instead rushed to the stairs and fled back to my flat. After that I received a few more phone calls requesting meetings, but did not let myself fall into the same trap again.

On 20th February I received a phone call from Rajavi himself. As I was in the habit of disconnecting the phone whenever they started harassing me, his first request was not to hang up. Then he asked me to come to Iraq, to an NCR meeting. This would give us an opportunity to talk, he said. 'What have I done wrong?' he continued. 'Why should I suffer because of the wrongs other people have done you? What are we to say to people who ask about you?' Perhaps with other words he might have persuaded me at least to hear his case. But here he was, presenting himself as pure and sinless and absolving himself of all blame. Perhaps in a sense he was right: according to his ideology, he had not done anything wrong. After all, he considered himself the representative of God on earth, and was merely exercising his divine right to play with the destinies of mere mortals, to decide for them what is right and wrong, praise them for doing right and punish them for doing wrong, deprive them of freedom of choice and reduce them to the status of animals or, worse, machines.

'If anyone asks about me, tell them that I am a *borida*,' I said. As *borida* was a word invented by the Mojahedin and defined as one who left the organisation, I wondered why defectors were so offended by the designation. It was something to be proud of, I thought. But Rajavi brushed the offer aside. (Later the official reason for my departure was variously given as my back condition – and loss of mental stability!)

'How can we say you are a *borida*?' he asked gruffly. 'Everybody knows you, and they are not going to accept that.' He asked me not to tell anybody I had left the organisation.

'I cannot lie about it,' I said. 'I try not to see any members of the NCR or Mojahedin. I know you are anxious that they should not learn about my situation, but if I see anyone, I will tell the truth.' I asked him again to announce that I was no longer their representative in America. He promised to do so and the announcement was duly made. At the same time, perhaps to make it seem unexceptional, they replaced all the NCR representatives in various countries who were male members of Mojahedin with female members – whether because of me or not, I don't know.

Rajavi's last words to me were that he did not want to see me '*khasara al donia an akharah*' – 'losing both life and afterlife'. This was too much for me to swallow. I took the antenna off the mobile in my palm, so that first his voice was mixed with static; then it died out altogether. I disconnected the phone.

That was the last contact I ever had with them. They sent me messages through the Internet referring to items in Iranian papers about my defection, but as they were in essence correct I had no comment and did not respond.

As my grandmother once said, revolutionaries live in a world of myths and legends. For me too, as a revolutionary, everything was a matter of life and death: black and white, with nothing in between. I paid a very heavy price to regain full-colour vision and see life as it really is. For the Mojahedin, I feel neither love nor hate. They, too, are part of life, not pure white as they believe themselves to be nor pitch black as their enemies believe. I use the terms 'black' and 'white' reluctantly: they are part of the language – 'black' is bad, 'white', good. But who can show me any more beautiful person than that elderly 'black' woman who came like an angel to my aid on the plane from Paris to Los Angeles?

# Postscript

This has been my life story, from 'zero' when I was born to 'zero' when I left the Mojahedin. Yes, I arrived at another zero, and perhaps I must congratulate them for that, as it was always their wish to reduce us to 'nobody' and 'nothing'. Zero: you are disconnected from any sense of belonging, your past, your memories, your friends and relatives and loved ones. Zero: you lose your identity, your individuality, your likes and dislikes, your principles and beliefs. Zero: you feel you know nothing; whatever you once knew is one big question mark. And again, zero: you have nothing; all your material possessions, plus your health and your youth, are lost. You start over, born again, but without the help given to a newborn child.

Such has been the fate of people like me, who thought they were doing right by following the right guru: the one whose word is prophecy, all-seeing, all-knowing. For them people like me denied themselves, burned their bridges to the past and future, ending broken lives by struggling for the survival of what remains of themselves.

We were and are ordinary mortals, fallible, without pretensions or delusions of grandeur – not like those whom we followed, who believe themselves infinitely superior, who see themselves as the signs and shadows of God on earth, the peak of human evolution; who believe it is their destiny to lead people towards glory at any price, even at the cost of millions of deaths and the misery of many more; who see their end or failure as the end of everything: hope and desire, happiness and fulfilment, evolution and civilisation. They are not prophets or philosophers. They are not people like Gandhi or Mossadegh – though there are similarities between those types and those to whom I refer, namely the belief in transcendence, of reaching beyond individual hopes and desires, recognising the human hope of becoming something more than a bag of soil at death. Both types believe life has a purpose, and advocate a utopian ideal. Both differ from ordinary political leaders, whose prime purpose is the struggle to gain and maintain power.

There the similarities end. These claimants to divinely inspired supremacy are after not only power but also eternity, and in the process they are prepared to sacrifice even their own lives. But the main difference between these leaders and the prophets is that the latter believe in the power of the people and the miraculous presence of a God while the former believe in the miracle of themselves. The leaders believe the ultimate end must be achieved in their own short life-spans. By contrast, prophets believe people must decide and fulfil their destinies; they see themselves as teachers or at most guides, mere humans trying to push their nations one step forward but never dreaming of attaining all their goals in their lifetimes. For these people any individual is as important as the whole nation; life is precious and should not be lost in vain.

Readers of this book may have a question in mind that persists to the last: why couldn't I see that I was wrong? Why didn't I leave the organisation sooner? It is a question I may never be able to answer satisfactorily. Let me try an analogy. As your white blood cells protect you against disease, so you have a degree of immunity that defends against any kind of invasion, physical or mental (or even ideological). Your individuality from birth, with its main objective of survival and later reproduction, is a kind of personal ideology that protects you against foreign ones that endanger your existence and goals. But if your defence system is paralysed for some reason, the protective shield crumbles and you are helpless against any minor incursion.

When your ideological immunity breaks down, your intellect and your education are no use to you. Gradually you are forced to deny your past and see it as wrong and corrupt. Submitting to the slogan 'the ugliness of selfishness', you reject the first objective of existence: survival of the individual. Step by step, you accept that your logic and principles, wants and desires, loves, likes and dislikes, relationships with everyone and ultimately not only your negative qualities but even your positive ones are all wrong and must be discarded. Then the foreign invader has triumphed.

This loss of immunity on account of a foreign ideology did not just apply to me personally. I believe it also afflicted Iran as a nation. No doubt many Iranians will totally disagree with me on this point. But that is the beauty of human thought in all its variety; where would we be if everyone always thought alike? But it seems to me that for a long time, owing to the losses and misfortunes of the Qajar era and then of World War Two, the nation at large and its intellectuals in particular lost faith in our culture and traditions, and our ability to deal with foreign invasions of any kind weakened.

After the 1953 American-British coup against Mossadegh's national government, most young Iranian intellectuals rejected out of hand our way of struggling for progress and welcomed foreign ideas. Turning away from Western culture and capitalism, they accepted instead the common antidote of 'imperialism', namely Marxism. Even if they were ashamed to accept the material part of Marxism, they could readily square with their consciences its claim to be a scientific interpretation of events. Lenin and then Mao's 'vanguard' theory, the notion of the organisation as absolute and on a plane above the individual and, finally, the acceptance of armed resistance as a rapid response solution for fundamentally changing society, were the legacy of revolutionary Marxists, especially in Latin America; our young intellectuals now began to call themselves revolutionaries as well. Mossadegh was one of the last Iranian politicians who believed in real democracy and trusted the Iranian way of politics. Instead of placing faith in an organisation he placed it in the people. He considered arms as the levy a democratic government might have to pay to defend the rights of the people. Finally, instead of believing in the vanguard or its traditional Shi'ite equivalent, the Imam, he championed the right of people to choose their representatives and leaders in free elections (or *bay'a*, the Islamic version).

After 1953 most Iranian intellectuals criticised Mossadegh for not using arms in the coup, or creating an organisation that could back him. After that, the creation of and reliance upon 'revolutionary organisations' on the one hand and 'armed struggle' in the form of guerrilla warfare on the other became the main objectives of the intellectuals and younger generation. Underpinning these active goals was an ideology of absolutist worship of the vanguard, under such names as 'heroic revolutionaries'. The immediate result of this new credo was to separate the people from the intellectuals, isolating the latter and confusing the former. Then, when the revolution came, the only group of people capable of leading the way were those who were still connected to the majority of ordinary people, namely the *mullahs*. They have pursued their path even until today.

I believe that as a nation and as individuals we still suffer because of that ideology. As an individual like many others, I didn't dare stand against our generation's new dogma of the 'organisation' and its heroic leaders and martyrs, nor question 'armed struggle' as it implied surrender to the dictatorship and betrayal of 'the people' and 'freedom'. After all, many organisations established after the 1953 coup – the Mojahedin above all – were based on the new revolutionary thinking. At the present time, the Mojahedin are the sole survivors of that path, which is why they have come to see themselves as defenders of extreme absolutism.

Another consequence of the pervasion of revolutionary ideology was that the younger generation lost its connection with its elders and could not benefit from their wisdom and problem-solving abilities. Hence they had to start from scratch, using a needle to bore into the mountain and finding their way by trial and error.

This book in its original manuscript form was bigger by two thirds; I had tried to impart the full weight of Iranian history, politics and philosophy in addition to my personal and organisational life down to the last detail, to show how one individual out of millions, a product of his entire culture, made a decision to change the course of his life. What has been realised here is a distillation of my experience against the backdrop of Iranian and world politics of the last century. I have done my best to be as accurate as possible. But I admit that my best may not be good enough; while writing I have had many flashbacks, and judged certain situations with the benefit of hindsight.

When I left the Mojahedin, I was still not able properly to see what had gone wrong. I knew only that I could not change myself anymore. I suppose that when struggling to keep your head above water, you cannot appreciate the strength or direction of the current. Only once on dry land again, looking from a distance, can you see the whole picture. With the passage of time I have been able to understand more, not only about the organisation and the events I experienced, but also about who I am and what I want. I am still at an early stage, trying to learn everything all over again, and perhaps I shall never stop doing so. So much has been lost that must be regained, a little at a time.

One thing did, at last, penetrate my mind soon after leaving the Mojahedin – something I could have learned it much earlier, when only a child: as my kind and ever-smiling grandmother told me, life is not black and white. I therefore paid a very heavy price to learn something originally given to me free. But I do not entirely regret having had to pay this price for such as priceless lesson. That is the message of this book: life is a rainbow, and 'black and white' is another world where people deal only in the extremes of love and hate, right and wrong, good and evil; it is a world to be repudiated and despised.

Am I again at zero? On second thought, perhaps not. Although I had lost everything, against all the organisation's efforts I retained my persona and my name. I couldn't very well call this book *My Persona*, so for a title I used the only other thing remaining to me. My name: Masoud.